Multicultural Education in a Pluralistic Society

FOURTH EDITION

Donna M. Gollnick
National Council for Accreditation of Teacher Education
Washington, DC

Philip C. Chinn
California State University, Los Angeles

Merrill, an imprint of
Macmillan College Publishing Company
New York
Maxwell Macmillan Canada
Toronto
Maxwell Macmillan International
New York Oxford Singapore Sydney

Cover photos: Mark Gibson
Editor: Linda A. Sullivan
Production Editor: Julie Anderson Tober
Photo Editor: Anne Vega
Cover Designer: Thomas Mack
Production Manager: Patricia A. Tonneman
Electronic Text Management: Marilyn Wilson Phelps, Matthew Williams, Jane Lopez, Karen L. Bretz

This book was set in Dutch by Macmillan College Publishing Company and was printed and bound by R.R. Donnelley & Sons Company. The cover was printed by Phoenix Color Corporation.

Printed in the United States of America

Macmillan College Publishing Company
866 Third Avenue
New York, NY 10022

Macmillan College Publishing Company is part of the
Maxwell Communication Group of Companies.

Maxwell Macmillan Canada, Inc.
1200 Eglinton Avenue East, Suite 200
Don Mills, Ontario M3C 3N1

Library of Congress Cataloging-in-Publication Data
Gollnick, Donna M.
Multicultural education in a pluralistic society / Donna M. Gollnick, Philip C. Chinn.—4th ed.
p. cm.
Includes bibliographical references and index.
ISBN 0-02-344491-6
1. Multicultural education—United States. 2. Social sciences—Study and teaching (Elementary)—United States. 3. Pluralism (Social scinces)—Study and teaching (Elementary)—United States. 4. Social sciences—Study and teaching (Secondary)—United States. 5. Pluralism (Social sciences)—Study and teaching Secondary)—United States. I. Chinn, Philip C. II. Title.
LC1099.3.G65 1994
370.19'341—dc20 93-37574
CIP

Printing: 2 3 4 5 6 7 8 9 Year: 4 5 6 7

Photo credits: Joe Di Dio/National Education Association, pp. 131, 218, 234, 322; District of Columbia Special Olympics, p. 173; Willard Loftis, pp. xvi, 19, 23, 36, 48, 69, 76, 102, 120, 127, 178, 197, 200, 252, 262; Barbara Schwartz/Macmillan, p. 30, 161; Susan Tucker, p. 283; Anne Vega/Macmillan, pp. 90, 112, 294, 315; Todd Yarrington/Macmillan, p. 150; Sheryl Zelhart, p. 236.

Dedication

To Maile C. Wilkerson
PCC

To Trisha Goldman, Carol Smith, and J. P. Taylor
DMG

Preface

The United States is a multicultural nation of persons of different ethnic backgrounds, classes, religions, and native languages. In addition, there are natural differences based on gender, age, and physical and mental abilities. Educators and their students are exposed to a social curriculum that makes positive and negative statements about these differences through radio, television, and newspapers, as well as through family attitudes. Often, distorted messages about people who are ethnically or religiously different from oneself are portrayed in the social curriculum. We learn that Italian Americans control organized crime, African Americans are on welfare, homeless are dangerous, females are weak, hard hats are racist, and individuals with disabilities are helpless. These stereotypes about groups of people are broad generalizations that totally neglect the majority of individuals within each of these groups. Decisions made by employers, educators, politicians, and neighbors are often based on such misconceptions. As educators, we must help students interpret and analyze the cultural cues that are forced on them daily.

More opportunities exist today for the career advancement of persons of color, women, and persons with disabilities than did twenty-five years ago. At the same time, the percentage of the population below the poverty level has increased and women, non-English speakers, children, Native Americans, and African Americans are disproportionately represented in this group. A number of college campuses and schools have experienced incidents of overt racism and sexism against students. Riots in Los Angeles pitted some Asian and European Americans against African Americans. Some of the nation's leaders led name-calling against persons from the Middle East during the Persian Gulf War. Some individuals declare that the Holocaust never occurred. Some individuals are nearly paralyzed by fear of persons from a different religious, ethnic, or language background. Many of us are still very parochial, having little or no experience with individuals from backgrounds different than our own. We continue to depend on the stereotypes, generally negative, that emerge from the social curriculum.

Education that is multicultural provides an environment that values cultural diversity and portrays it positively. Students' educational and vocational options are not limited by gender, age, ethnicity, native language, religion, class, or disability. Educators have the responsibility to help students contribute to and benefit from our democratic society. Diversity is used to develop effective instructional strategies for students in the classroom. In addition, multicultural education should help students and teachers think critically about institutionalized racism, classism, and sexism. Ideally, educators will begin to develop individual and group strategies for overcoming the debilitating effects of these societal scourges.

The greatest concern of students in too many parts of our country is of safety. For them, violence in their lives is a normal way of life; school may be one of the few havens of safety. Not only do these students suffer from hardships unknown to most of us, they are also often taught by teachers who are not qualified. Our best teachers work in suburban areas where safety is guaranteed, equipment is modern, pay is higher, and work conditions are better. Although there are some outstanding teachers in urban and rural schools, in many cases those schools are staffed by teachers who can not secure jobs in the suburbs, are new, or are not licensed to teach. There is fear of teaching in the communities where the need is the greatest and there is little reward for the effort. At the same time that educators implement multicultural education, they must be concerned with helping to change the conditions in society that lead to the vast differences among schools.

Our approach to multicultural education is based on a broad definition of the concept. By using culture as the basis for understanding multicultural education, we have presented descriptions of seven microcultures to which students and teachers belong. Of course, these are not the only microcultures to which individuals belong, but in our view these are the most critical in understanding pluralism and multicultural education at this time. Not limiting the approach to ethnicity, as many authors have, we focus on the complex nature of pluralism in this country. An individual's cultural identity is based not only on ethnicity, but also on such factors as class, religion, and gender. To further complicate matters, the degree of identification with one's ethnic origin, religion, and other microcultural memberships varies greatly from individual to individual. For example, we are not just men and women within the context of our ethnic, religious, and class background. The complexity of pluralism in the United States makes it difficult for the educator to develop expectations of students based on their group memberships. This text is designed to examine these group memberships and ways in which the educator can develop educational programs to meet the needs of those groups and the nation.

Multicultural Education in a Pluralistic Society provides an overview of the different microcultures to which students belong. The first chapter examines the pervasive influence of culture and the importance of understanding our own cultural background and experiences as well as those of our students. The following seven chapters examine the microcultures of class, ethnicity and race, gender, disability, religion, language, and age. The final chapter, Chapter 9, describes how the educator can portray and use pluralism in the implementation of multicultural education.

All of the chapters in this edition have been revised to reflect current thinking and research in the area. In particular,

- The chapter on age (Chapter 8) has been rewritten from a cultural perspective that addresses drug abuse, teen pregnancy, physical abuse, AIDS, and sexuality.

- As in the past, the first chapter provides the conceptual framework that supports our thinking about multicultural education.
- The final chapter integrates the most recent writing on critical pedagogy with research on teaching effectively.
- Each chapter opens with a scenario to place the topic in an educational setting.
- Throughout each chapter, highlighted and boxed exercises help the reader think about the issues.
- The brief case studies, "Critical Incidents," at the end of the book are real-life situations to which readers are challenged to figure out how they would react.

The reader should be aware of several caveats related to the language used in this text. Although we realize that the term American includes populations beyond the boundaries of the United States, we sometimes have used it to refer to the U.S. population. Although we tried to use the terms black and white sparingly, data about groups often have been categorized by racial identification rather than national origin such as African or European American. In many cases, we were not able to distinguish ethnic identity and have continued to use black, white, or men/women of color. We have limited our use of the term minority and have focused more on the poser relationships that exist between groups.

Students in undergraduate, graduate, and inservice courses should find this text helpful in examining social and cultural conditions that influence education. It is designed to assist them in understanding pluralism and how to use it effectively in the classroom and schools. Other professionals in the social services should find it helpful in understanding the complexity of cultural backgrounds and experiences as they work with their clients.

Acknowledgments

The preparation of any book involves the contributions of many individuals in addition to those whose names are found on the cover. We thank the following reviewers, whose recommendations were used to improve this edition: Theresa McCormick, Iowa State University; Virginia Pesqueira, Arizona State University; and James Uphoff, Wright State University. We are indebted to Willard Loftis for most of the pictures in the book. A special thanks is extended to Stephanie Evans and Charles Leyba for research and writing assistance on some of the chapters. The assistance, patience, and encouragement from our editors, Julie Tober and Linda Sullivan, are sincerely appreciated.

Donna M. Gollnick and Philip C. Chinn

Brief Contents

Contents

7 Language 219

8 Age 253

CHAPTER 1

Culture, Pluralism, and Equality

It was a long summer waiting to receive a job offer, but finally on August 5 Michelle Evans received an offer to teach at a school on the outskirts of the state capitol. It meant that she had only two weeks to find an apartment and move before reporting for new-teacher orientation. But she could hardly wait to begin her teaching career and to make a difference in the lives of children. She knew little about the city to which she was moving. Although she had been there before, she did not know much about the area in which her school was located.

Michelle found a nice, but very small apartment. It was outside the boundaries of the area served by the school, because her parents insisted that it would not be safe for her to live in that area.

Excited with the prospect of having her own class, but nervous about fitting in, she appeared at the teacher orientation. Early in the week, she learned that she would start with thirty-two students in her third-grade class. The school served a community in which many students have single parents—many who work two jobs to make ends meet. Over half of the students are eligible for free lunch. She learned that some of the students in her class had limited English proficiency, but the principal said they were quiet students and their English was getting better. She was disappointed in the condition of her classroom, but was assured that it would be repainted during one of the vacation periods. She decided to find some pictures and plants to brighten the room. After all, she and her students would be spending most of the next nine and a half months there; it should be as pleasant as she could make it.

Finally, the students arrived. Most were dressed in what appeared to be new school clothes and were very respectful. She knew that most of the students would be African American and Hispanic American, but she was surprised that she also had a student who had just moved from Bulgaria and spoke no English. She found that the native language of the families of two students was Farsi. She had had at least a couple of Spanish courses, but she knew little or nothing about the language or cultures of Bulgaria and Iran. She wondered about the white boy with the black eye, but guessed that he had been in a fight recently.

Will Michelle's own cultural background make her first year of teaching any easier? What else should Michelle know about the students' cultural backgrounds to help her teach effectively? If you were in Michelle's position, what would worry you? What kind of challenges would you face? What do you wish you had learned in college to help you be a better teacher in this school? Where could you go for help in working with students who speak little English? Would you have taken this job? Why or why not?

Diversity in Schools

In the 1980s, local, state, and national reports on education called on educators, parents, and students to push for excellence in the nation's schools. State legislators and local school boards responded by requiring more rigorous curricula and standards for student achievement. However, teachers have been provided with little direction or assistance to ensure that all students are able to realize that excellence or gain the rewards provided by such an educational opportunity. Thus, educators today are faced with an overwhelming challenge to prepare students from diverse cultural backgrounds to live in a rapidly changing society and a world in which some groups have greater societal benefits than others because of their race/ethnicity, gender, class, language, religion, disability, or age.

Schools of the future will become increasingly culturally diverse. Demographic data on birthrates and immigration indicate that children will be inexorably more Asian American, more Hispanic American (but not more Cuban

American), more African American, and less white. By the end of this century, one-third of the school population will be composed of students of color (American Council on Education [ACE], 1988). They already make up over 50 percent of the student population in two states, California and Texas. Minority students comprise at least half of the population in the largest twenty-five cities. In addition, nearly 25 percent of our children currently live below the poverty line. Although the national data are still sketchy, it appears that there is an increase in the number of children with physical and emotional disabilities.

To work effectively with the heterogeneous student populations found in our schools, educators need to understand and feel comfortable with their own cultural backgrounds. They also must understand the cultural setting in which the school is located to develop effective instructional strategies. They must help their students become aware of cultural diversity in the nation and in the world. A goal is to help students affirm cultural differences while realizing that individuals across cultures have many similarities.

Teachers who enter a classroom with thirty students will find that students have individual differences even though they may appear to be from the same cultural group. These differences extend far beyond intellectual and physical abilities. Students bring to class different historical backgrounds, religious beliefs, and day-to-day living experiences. These experiences direct the way the students behave in school. The cultural background of some students will be mirrored in the school culture. For others, the difference between home and school cultures will cause dissonance unless the teacher can use the cultural backgrounds of the students to develop a supportive environment. If the teacher fails to understand the cultural factors in addition to the intellectual and physical factors that affect student learning and behavior, it will be impossible to teach all thirty students effectively.

Multicultural education is the educational strategy in which students' cultural backgrounds are used to develop effective classroom instruction and school environments. It is designed to support and extend the concepts of culture, cultural pluralism, and equality into the formal school setting. An examination of the theoretical precepts of these concepts will lead to an understanding of the development and practice of multicultural education.

Culture

Everyone has culture. Unfortunately, many individuals believe that persons who are culturally different from them have an inferior culture. Until early in this century, the term *culture* was used to indicate groups of people who were more developed in the ways of the Western world and less primitive than tribal groups in many parts of the world. Individuals who were knowledgeable in the areas of history, literature, and the fine arts were said to possess culture.

No longer is culture viewed so narrowly. Anthropologists define culture as a way of perceiving, believing, evaluating, and behaving (Goodenough, 1987) or as "a shared organization of ideas that includes the intellectual, moral, and aesthetic standards prevalent in a community and the meanings of communicative actions" (LeVine, 1984, p. 67). Culture provides the blueprint that determines the way an individual thinks, feels, and behaves in society. At the same time, culture develops within "unequal and dialectical relations that different groups establish in a given society at a particular historical point" (Giroux, 1988, p. 116). These differing and unequal power relations have a great impact on "the ability of individuals and groups to define and achieve their goals" (Giroux, 1988, p. 117). The dynamics of those power relationships and the effect they have on the development of groups must also be an integral part of the study of culture.

Thus, in a classroom of thirty students, each student has culture. Parts of the culture are shared by all of the class members, whereas other aspects of the culture are shared only with family members or members of the same ethnic or religious community. All of the students belong to the same age cohort and so share membership in an age group. All live in the same country, state, and community and so are subject to the basic values, rules, and regulations that govern the dominant culture. Students with English as their first language may differ in the dialect spoken; other students will be learning English as a second or a third language. In most classes, there will be both boys and girls; within both groups, aspects of being either a male or a female are shared with others of the same sex. The class status of some students will be noticeable in their dress and access, or lack of access, to resources.

In one elementary classroom, a number of ethnic backgrounds may be identified. Even when the class is composed totally of white students, ethnic identities might include Swedish Americans, German Americans, Irish Americans, and Polish Americans. Students within each ethnic group may share the same religion, lifestyles, and values, and these may be somewhat different from those of classmates from a different ethnic background. Black students may identify themselves ethnically as Jamaican American, Puerto Rican, Panamanian American, Nigerian American, or African American.

Unless the school is parochial and limits attendance to children of a specific religion, a number of religious affiliations may be represented in the classroom. Many rural and small-town communities include students primarily of Protestant and Catholic families. Large urban schools may include students who identify themselves as Protestant, Roman Catholic, Greek Orthodox, Latter-Day Saint (Mormon), Jewish, Buddhist, or Islamic—in addition to those who claim no religious affiliation. Other cultural differences are based on the geographical areas from which the families may have recently moved.

To understand the different cultural experiences brought to the classroom by students, it is necessary first to examine culture itself. All people have the same psychological and biological needs for survival, but the ways in which they fulfill these needs vary greatly. These variations depend in part on the resources available and on the climatic conditions of the region. More importantly, they depend on the group's relationship to the dominant society.

All human groups undergo the same poignant life experiences of birth, marriage, helplessness, illness, old age, and death. We even share many of the same institutions, such as marriage ceremonies and incest taboos. However, the ways in which groups handle the same life experiences and create the same institutions are limitless. These differences are not innate, but are culturally determined. A traditional Greek American may show a great outpouring of emotion at the funeral of a family member. On the other hand, a third-generation Greek American who has been acculturated is likely to be more emotionally restrained at a public funeral. None of the events, reactions, or habits of a group of people can be understood without understanding the context of the culture of which they are a part.

Culture is so much a part of us that we do not realize that we might behave differently from others. Most of us do not think that sitting at a table to eat, eating three meals a day, having different foods for breakfast and dinner, brushing our teeth, or sleeping in a bed are culturally determined behaviors. We know these habits and customs as natural or the only way to act. These ways of doing things have become the accepted and patterned ways of behavior for people who live in the Western part of the world, particularly the United States. To be acceptable to other members of the culture, we must use these patterns. Culture gives us our identity through acceptable words; through our actions, postures, gestures, and tones of voice; through our facial expressions; through our handling of time, space, and materials; and through the way we work, play, express our emotions, and defend ourselves (Hall, 1977).

Generally accepted and patterned ways of behavior are necessary for a group of people to live together. Culture imposes order and meaning on all our experiences. It allows us to predict how others will behave in certain situations. On the other hand, it prevents us from predicting how people from a different culture will behave in the same situation. Misunderstanding cultural cues between teachers and students can inhibit learning in a classroom.

Culture gives us a certain lifestyle that is peculiarly our own. It becomes so peculiar to us that someone from a different culture can easily identify us as Americans. A traveler from our country who goes overseas will usually be identified as American by the people of the country being visited, regardless of whether the individual is an American with an African, Native, European, Hispanic, or Asian heritage.

Characteristics of Culture

We all have culture, but how did we get it? It is learned, and the learning starts at birth. Most individuals born in the United States first saw the world in a hospital delivery room, where attendants were dressed in uniforms. The first days of life were characterized by cleanliness—sterile sheets and gowns, sterile bottles and nipples, and a sterile environment behind glass, except during nursing hours. The way the baby was held, fed, bathed, and dressed was culturally determined. Parents and hospital personnel knew this procedure as the only way, or at least the best way, to care for a baby in the first days because it is the acceptable pattern in this country.

A person learns how to become a functioning adult within a specific society through culture. Two similar processes interact as one learns how to act in society: *enculturation* and *socialization*. Enculturation is the process of acquiring the characteristics of a given culture and generally becoming competent in its language. Socialization is the general process of learning the social norms of the culture (Abercrombie, Hill, & Turner, 1984). Through this process we internalize the social and cultural rules. We learn what is expected in roles such as mother, husband, student, or child, and in occupational roles such as teacher, banker, plumber, custodian, or politician.

Enculturation and socialization are processes initiated at birth by others, including parents, siblings, nurses, physicians, teachers, and neighbors. These varied instructors may not identify these processes as enculturation or socialization, but they demonstrate and reward children for acceptable behaviors. All people learn how to behave by observation of and participation in their society and culture. Thus, individuals are socialized and enculturated according to the patterns of the culture in which they are raised. The culture in which one is born becomes unimportant unless one is also socialized in that culture, as Kluckhohn (1949) illustrated:

> I met in New York City a young man who did not speak a word of English and was obviously bewildered by American ways. By "blood" he was as American as you or I, for his parents had gone from Indiana to China as missionaries. Orphaned in infancy, he was reared by a Chinese family in a remote village. All who met him found him more Chinese than American. The facts of his blue eyes and light hair were less impressive than a Chinese style of gait, Chinese arm and hand movements, Chinese facial expressions, and Chinese modes of thought. The biological heritage was American, but the cultural training had been Chinese. He returned to China. (p. 19)

Because culture is so much a part of us, we often tend to confuse biological and cultural heritage. Our cultural heritage is learned. It is not innately based on the culture in which we are born, as shown by Kluckhohn's example of the American man raised in China. Vietnamese infants adopted by Italian American, Catholic, middle-class parents will share a cultural heritage with middle-class Italian American Catholics, rather than with Vietnamese in Vietnam. Observers, however, may continue to identify these individuals as Vietnamese Americans because of physical characteristics and a lack of knowledge about their cultural experiences.

A second characteristic of culture is that it is shared. Shared cultural patterns and customs bind people together as an identifiable group and make it possible for them to live together and function with ease. An individual in the

PAUSE TO REFLECT

In your class, you have several students of mixed ethnic backgrounds: African European, Japanese Navajo, and Lebanese European. You must complete a form showing the cultural diversity in your class, using the five census categories of (1) white, non-Hispanic, (2) black, non-Hispanic, (3) Hispanic, (4) Asian American or Pacific Islanders, or (5) Native Americans or Eskimos. In what category will you place the three students with parents from different ethnic backgrounds? Why?

shared culture is provided the context for identifying with the group that shares that culture. Although there may be some disagreement about certain aspects of the culture, there is a common acceptance and agreement about most aspects. Actually, most points of agreement are outside our realm of awareness. We do not even realize their existence as culture—the way we communicate with each other and the foods we eat.

Third, culture is an adaptation. Cultures have developed to accommodate certain environmental conditions and available natural and technological resources. Thus, the Eskimo who lives with extreme cold, snow, ice, seals, and the sea has developed a culture different from the Pacific Islander, who has limited land, unlimited seas, and few mineral resources. The culture of urban residents differs from rural residents, in part because of the resources available in the different settings. The culture of oppressed groups differs from that of the dominant group because of power relationships within society.

Finally, culture is a dynamic system that changes continuously. Some cultures undergo constant and rapid change, while others are very slow to change. Some changes, such as a new word or new hairstyle, may be relatively small and have little impact on the culture as a whole. Other changes will have a dramatic impact. The introduction of technology into a culture has often produced changes far broader than the technology itself. For example, the replacement of industrial workers by robots is changing the culture of many working-class communities. Such changes may also alter traditional customs and beliefs.

Manifestations of Culture

The cultural patterns of a group of people are determined by how they organize and view the various components of culture. Culture itself is manifested in an infinite number of ways through social institutions, daily habits of living, and the individual's fulfillment of psychological and basic needs. To understand how extensively our lives are affected by culture, let's examine a few of these manifestations.

Our values are determined initially by our culture. Values are conceptions of what is desirable and important to us or to the group. Our values influence prestige, status, pride, family loyalty, love of country, religious belief, and honor. In many cultures, family loyalty is extremely important; it is so important that a relative is supported whenever possible. This support may include giving a relative a job regardless of his or her qualifications; it may also mean sharing all of one's money and resources with relatives if they need help. Such values are not reinforced in the dominant American culture. Status symbols differ across cultures. For many families in the United States, accumulation of material possessions is a respected status symbol. These factors, as well as what is decent or indecent, what is moral or immoral, and how punishment and reward are provided, are determined by the value system of the culture.

Culture also manifests itself in the nonverbal communication used by individuals. The meaning of an act or an expression must be viewed in its cultural context. Raising the eyebrow is an example: "To most Americans this means surprise; to a person from the Marshall Islands in the Pacific it signals an affirmative answer; for Greeks, it is a sign of disagreement. The difference is not so much in how the eyebrows are raised but in the cultural meaning of the act" (Spradley & Rynkiewich, 1975, p. 7). Culture also determines the manner of walking, sitting, standing, reclining, and gesturing. We must remind ourselves not to interpret acts and expressions of people from a different cultural background as having the same meaning as our own.

Language itself is a reflection of culture and provides a special way of looking at the world and organizing experiences that is often ignored in translating words from one language to another. There are many different sounds and combinations of sounds used in the languages of different cultures. Those of us who have tried to learn a second language probably have experienced difficulty in verbalizing the sounds that were not part of our first language.

Although we have discussed only a few of the daily patterns determined by culture, they are limitless. Among them are weaning children, toilet training, rites of passage, forming kinship bonds, choosing a spouse, sexual relations, and division of labor in the home. These patterns are shared by members of the culture and often seem strange and improper to nonmembers.

Ethnocentrism

Because culture helps determine the way we think, feel, and act, it becomes the lens through which we judge the world. As such, it can become an unconscious blinder to other ways of thinking, feeling, and acting. Our own culture is automatically treated as innate. It becomes the only natural way to function in the world. Even common sense in our own culture is naturally translated to common sense for the world. The rest of the world is viewed through our cultural lens; other cultures are compared with ours and evaluated by our cultural standards. It becomes difficult, if not impossible, to view another culture as separate from our own—a task that anthropologists attempt when studying another culture.

This inability to view other cultures as equally viable alternatives for organizing reality is known as *ethnocentrism*. It is a common characteristic of cultures, whereby one's own cultural traits are viewed as natural, correct, and superior to those of another culture, whose traits are perceived as odd, amusing, inferior, or immoral (Yetman, 1985).

Although it is appropriate to cherish one's culture, members sometimes see their culture as providing the *only* correct values and ways of behaving. They become closed to the possibilities of difference. They "even find it hard to learn new things which, placed alongside [their] personal history, can be meaningful" (Freire & Macedo, 1987, p. 126). Feelings of superiority over any other culture often develop.

The inability to view another culture through its cultural lens rather than through one's own cultural lens prevents an understanding of the second culture. This inability usually makes it impossible to function effectively in a second culture. By overcoming one's ethnocentric view of the world, one can begin to respect other cultures and even learn to function comfortably in more than one cultural group.

Cultural Relativism

"Never judge another man until you have walked a mile in his moccasins." This North American Indian proverb suggests the importance of understanding the cultural background and experiences of other persons rather than judging them by our own standards. The principle of cultural relativism is an attempt "to describe the practices of a society from the point of view of its members" (Abercrombie et al., 1984, p. 59). This ability becomes more essential than ever in the world today, where various countries and cultures are becoming more dependent on the resources of others. In an effort to maintain positive relationships with the numerous cultural groups in the world, the United States can no longer afford to ignore other cultures or to relegate them to an inferior status.

Within our own boundaries there are many cultural groups that have been historically viewed and treated as inferior to the dominant western European culture that has been the basis for most of our institutions. Hall (1977) found that intercultural misunderstandings occur even when there is no language barrier and large components of the major culture are shared by the people involved. These misunderstandings often occur because one cultural group is largely ignorant about the culture of another group. In addition, the members of one group are, for the most part, unable to describe their own cultural system (Hall, 1977). These misunderstandings are common among the various cultural groups in this country.

Cultural relativism would first have people learn more about their own culture than is commonly required. Then they would need to learn much more about other cultural groups. This intercultural process would involve learning and experiencing another culture so that one would know what it is like to be a member of the second culture and to view the world from that point of view. To function effectively and comfortably within a second culture, we must learn that culture.

Biculturalism and Multiculturalism

Individuals who have competencies in and can operate successfully in two or more different cultures are bicultural or multicultural, and are often multilingual as well. Having proficiencies in multiple cultures does not lead to rejection of the primary cultural identification. It does allow a broad range of abilities on which one can draw at any given occasion as determined by the particular situation (Gibson, 1988).

Goodenough (1987) defines multiculturalism as the normal human experience. All Americans participate in more than one cultural group or microculture. Thus, most persons have already become proficient in multiple systems for perceiving, evaluating, believing, and acting according to the patterns of the various microcultures in which they participate. "One's identity will be more flexible, autonomous, and stable to the degree that one recognizes one's self as a member of various different subcommunities simultaneously" (Burbules & Rice, 1991, p. 404). Individuals with competencies in several microcultures develop a fuller appreciation of the range of cultural competencies available to all individuals.

Many members of oppressed groups are forced to become bicultural to work or attend school and to participate effectively in their own ethnic community. Different behaviors are expected in the two settings. To be successful on the job usually requires proficiency in the ways of the dominant group. Because most schools reflect the dominant society, students are forced to adjust if they are going to be academically successful. On the other hand, many European Americans find almost total congruence between the culture of their family, schooling, and work. Most remain monocultural throughout their lives. They do not envision the value of becoming competent in a different culture.

In our expanding culturally diverse nation, it is critical that educators themselves become at least bicultural. Understanding the cultural cues of several different ethnic groups, especially oppressed groups, improves our ability to work with all students. It also helps us be sensitive to the importance of these differences in teaching effectively.

Culture in the United States

It is difficult to study our own culture because we are too close to it to identify traits that are characteristic of the culture (Spradley & Rynkiewich, 1975). Individuals who have lived in other countries for an extended period of time find it easier to identify American traits than those individuals who have never experienced a different culture. Although we may be able to identify differences among oppressed groups and between oppressed and dominant groups, it is difficult to recognize the cultural patterns that have become uniquely associated with the United States and are thus shared voluntarily or under protest by citizens.

A problem in studying the culture of the United States in particular is its complexity. Conflicting forces related to values, lifestyles, and societal impediments within and between cultural groups are integral to this complexity and the resulting cultural adaptations. The complexity and rapid change of culture from generation to generation make inevitable the lack of harmony between cultural elements. The U.S. culture, like all others, is constantly undergoing change. Nevertheless, some of its characteristics are described in the remainder of this chapter.

The U.S. macroculture is the dominant culture that is shared by many of the nation's citizens and impacts on all. In addition, numerous cultural groups exist with distinct cultural patterns that are not common to all Americans. These cultural groups are called microcultures and will be described briefly in this section and in greater detail in Chapters 2 through 8. Finally, there are also group cultures that have been studied by sociologists. These subcultures include occupational groups, gangs, drug cultures, peer groups, and other smaller, identifiable units of society.

The Dominant Culture

Historically, U.S. political and social institutions have evolved from a western European tradition. The English language is a polyglot of the languages spoken by the various conquerors and rulers of Great Britain throughout history. The legal system is derived from English common law. The political system of democratic elections comes from France and England. The middle-class value system has been modified from a European system (Arensberg & Niehoff, 1975). Even our way of thinking, at least the way that it is rewarded in school, is based on Socrates' linear system of logic (Hall, 1977).

Formal institutions, such as government, schools, social welfare, banks, and business, affect many aspects of our lives. Because of the strong Anglo-Saxon influence on these institutions, the dominant cultural influence on the United States also has been identified as Anglo-Saxon, or western European. More specifically, the major cultural influence on the United States, particularly on its institutions, has been white, Anglo-Saxon, and Protestant (WASP). But no longer is the dominant group composed only of WASPs. Instead, most members of the middle class have adopted these traditionally WASP institutions, which provide the framework for the traits and values that outsiders identify as U.S. culture. Although most of our institutions still function under the strong influence of their WASP roots, many other aspects of American life have been greatly influenced by the numerous cultural groups that make up the U.S. population.

Although we have an agrarian tradition, the population now is primarily located in metropolitan areas and small towns. The country has mineral and soil wealth, elaborate technology, and a wealth of manufactured goods. Mass education and mass communication are ways of life. We are regulated by clocks and calendars rather than by seas and the sun. Time is used to organize most activities of life. Most of us are employees whose salaries or wages are paid by large, complex, impersonal institutions. Work is done regularly, purposefully, and sometimes grimly. On the other hand, play is fun—an outlet from work. Money is the denominator of exchange. Necessities of life are purchased rather than produced. Achievement and success are measured by the quantity of material goods purchased. Religious beliefs are concerned with general morality.

The overpowering value of the dominant group is individualism, which is characterized by the belief that every individual is his or her own master, is in control of his or her own destiny, and will advance and regress in society only according to his or her own efforts (Bellah, Madsen, Sullivan, Swidler, & Tipton, 1985). Traits that emphasize this core value include industriousness, ambition, competitiveness, self-reliance, independence, appreciation of the good life, and the perception of humans as separate and superior to nature. The acquisition of possessions, such as televisions, cars, boats, and homes, measures success and achievement.

Another core value is freedom. However, freedom is defined by the dominant group as "being left alone by others, not having other people's values, ideas, or styles of life forced upon one, being free of arbitrary authority in work, family, and political life" (Bellah et al., 1985, p. 23). As a result, impersonality in relations with others is common. Communication is often direct or confrontive. Most members of the dominant group rely more on associations of common interest than on strong kinship ties. The nuclear family is the basic kinship unit. Values tend to be absolute (e.g., right or wrong, moral or immoral) rather than ranging along a continuum that includes degrees of right and wrong. Personal life and community affairs are based on principles of right and wrong rather than on shame, dishonor, or ridicule, and there is an emphasis on youthfulness (Arensberg & Niehoff, 1975).

Many Americans, especially middle-class Americans, share these traits and values to some degree. However, not all members of the dominant culture value these traits or accept them as the most desirable traits for the culture. Nevertheless, they are recognized patterns around which most of our lives are organized.

Most male members of the dominant group do not usually think about themselves as white, middle-class, Christian, English-speaking, or heterosexual. On the other hand, members of oppressed groups are constantly confronted with the difference of their race, language, class, religion, femaleness, and/or homosexuality. The degree of identification with the characteristics of the dominant culture depends in part on how much an individual must interact with our formal institutions for economic support and subsistence. The more dependence on formal institutions, the greater the degree of sharing, or being forced to adopt, the common traits and values of the macroculture.

ASK YOURSELF?

In elections most candidates stress the values of the dominant society to help them be elected. Think about the campaigns of Bill Clinton, George Bush, and Ross Perot—three candidates for the presidency in the last election. Using a scale of 1 = did not support, 2 = somewhat supported, and 3 = strongly supported, rate these candidates on their promotion of some of the characteristics associated with the dominant group.

	Clinton	Bush	Perot
Individualism	______	______	______
Freedom to be left alone	______	______	______
Competition over Cooperation	______	______	______
Nuclear family as only acceptable kinship unit	______	______	______
Values as absolute	______	______	______
Affirmation of cultural diversity	______	______	______

Why do you think the candidates promoted similar values? In what areas were they different? Why? Which values do you strongly support? Why may some families in your school have values that are different from yours?

Microcultures

Subsocieties within the United States contain cultural elements, institutions, and groups in which cultural patterns not common to the U.S. macroculture are shared. Traditionally, these groups have been called subsocieties or subcultures by sociologists and anthropologists because they exist within the context of a larger society and share political and social institutions as well as some of the traits and values of the macroculture. These cultural groups are also called microcultures to indicate that they have distinctive cultural patterns while sharing some cultural patterns with all members of the U.S. macroculture. People who belong to the same microcultures share traits and values that bind them together as a group.

Numerous microcultures exist in most nations, but the United States is exceptionally rich in the many distinct cultural groups that make up the population. Cultural identity is based on traits and values learned as part of our ethnic origin, religion, gender, age, socioeconomic level, primary language, geographical region, place of residence (e.g., rural or urban), and disabilities or exceptional conditions, as shown in Figure 1-1. Each of these groups has distinguishable cultural patterns shared with others who identify themselves as members of that particular group. Although sharing certain characteristics of the macroculture with most of the U.S. population, members of microcultures also have learned cultural traits, discourse patterns, ways of learning, values, and behaviors characteristic of the microcultures to which they belong. Unless a person is a member of the dominant group (i.e., a white, middle-class, non-disabled male), the cultural content of that person's learned experiences may be different from the cultural content of the schools. Critics of education argue that

> The dominant culture in the school is characterized by a selective ordering and legitimating of privileged language forms, modes of reasoning, social relations, and lived experiences. . . . School culture . . . functions not only to confirm and privilege students from the dominant classes, but also through exclusion and insult to disconfirm the histories, experiences, and dreams of subordinate groups. (Giroux, 1989, pp. xxx–xxxi)

Individuals sharing membership in one microculture may not share membership in other microcultures. For example, all men are members of the male microculture, but not all males belong to the same ethnic, religious, or class group. On the other hand, an ethnic group is composed of both males and females with different religious and socioeconomic backgrounds.

It is the interaction of these various microcultures and status within the macroculture that begin to determine an individual's cultural identity. "Forms of difference in human social life—gender, class, race, culture, history, etc.—are always experienced, constructed, and mediated in interrelation with each other" (Moore, 1988, p. 196). Membership in one microculture can greatly

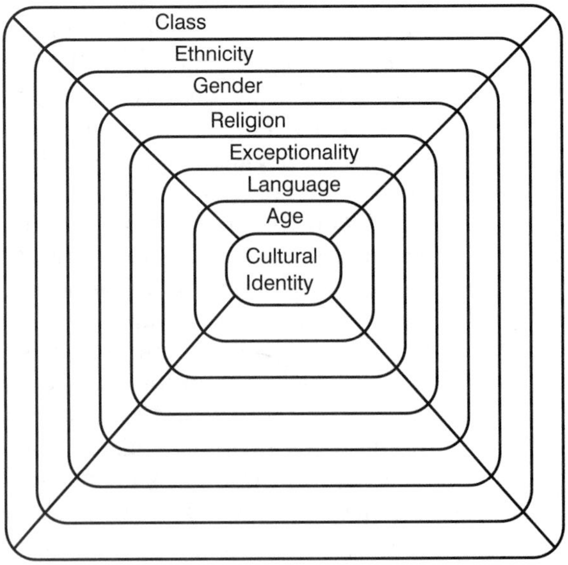

Figure 1-1. Cultural identity is based on membership in a number of microcultural groups that interact with each other. The importance of membership in each of these microcultures varies from one individual to another, but is impacted by discrimination in society.

influence the characteristics and values of membership in other microcultures. For instance, some fundamentalist religions have strictly defined expectations for women and men. Thus, membership in the religious group influences to a great extent the way a female behaves as a young girl, teenager, bride, and wife. One's class level will impact greatly on the quality of life for families, especially for children and the elderly in that group. The cultural patterns of an ethnic or religious group often influence one's behavior in the other microcultures of which one is a member.

This interaction is most dynamic across race/ethnicity, class, and gender relations. Hicks (1981) has found that "individuals (or groups) in their relation to their economic and political systems do not share similar consciousness or similar needs at the same point in time" (p. 221). The feminist movement, for example, traditionally has been influenced primarily by white, middle-class women. The labor movement had an early history of excluding minorities, women, and their causes; in some areas this antagonism continues. Membership in one microculture often conflicts with the interests of another.

One microculture may have a greater influence on identity than others. This influence may change over time and depends on life experiences. For example, a twenty-five-year-old, middle-class, Catholic, Polish American woman in Chicago may identify strongly with being Catholic and Polish American when she is married and living in a Polish American community. Other microcultural memberships may have a greater impact on her identity after she has divorced and becomes totally responsible for her financial well-being. Her femaleness and class status may become the most important representations in her identity. The degree to which individuals identify with their microcultural memberships and the related cultural characteristics determines to a great extent their individual cultural identities.

The interaction of these microcultures within the macroculture is also very important. Most political, business, educational, and social institutions (for example, the courts, the welfare system, and the city government) have been developed and controlled by the dominant group. The values and practices that have been internalized by the dominant group also are inherent within these institutions. Members of oppressed groups are usually beholden to the dominant group to share in that power. These groups "possess imperfect access to positions of equal power, prestige, and privilege in a society" (Yetman, 1985, p. 2).

Members of oppressed groups are affected by the status accorded them by the dominant group. "Different ways of thinking and behaving become differentially rewarded in the society at large, and membership in particular racial, ethnic, class, and gender groups has traditionally entailed the ascription of particular roles and statuses within a broader system of relations" (Lubeck, 1988, p. 55). African Americans, Hispanic Americans, Asian Americans, and other physically distinguishable groups generally experience institutional discrimination and are not allowed to share equally in societal benefits. Women, non-Protestants, the poor, non-English speakers, the disabled, children, and the elderly also are not able to share equally in power and societal benefits with the dominant group. This relationship with the dominant group can impact greatly on one's own cultural identity.

Thus, the interaction of these microcultures within the macroculture begins to answer the questions "Who am I?" and "Who are my students?" The various microcultures that educators are likely to confront in a classroom are examined in detail in Chapters 2 through 8.

Pluralism

There are a number of theories describing the culturally pluralistic nature of the United States. The most prevailing theory espoused by sociologists, politicians, and educators has been assimilation. A second popular theory is that of cultural pluralism, in which cultural groups, particularly ethnic groups, maintain separate and distinct identities from the dominant group. This section will describe these two theories and an ideology that bridges the two.

Assimilation

Assimilation is the process by which groups adopt or change the dominant culture. Either cultural patterns that distinguished the two groups disappear, or their distinctive cultural patterns become part of the dominant culture, or a combination of the two occurs. In the United States, the middle-class microculture reflects this process. In fact, the values and traits of this cultural group are often defined as the macroculture. However, many of the values and traits of the dominant middle-class microculture are not universally accepted by all members of the macroculture.

According to Gordon (1964), the assimilation process develops through stages in which the new cultural group: (1) changes its cultural patterns to those of the dominant group; (2) develops large-scale primary-group relationships with the dominant group; (3) intermarries fully with the dominant group; (4) loses its sense of peoplehood as separate from the dominant group; (5) encounters no discrimination; (6) encounters no prejudiced attitudes; and (7) does not raise any issues that would involve value and power conflict with the dominant group. Each of these stages also represents a degree of assimilation. The first stage is *acculturation,* in which cultural patterns of the dominant group are adopted by the new or oppressed group. This is the most common pattern for many groups that have immigrated during this century. Although some groups have tried to maintain the original culture, it is usually in vain as children go to school and participate in the larger society. Continuous and firsthand contacts with the dominant group usually result in subsequent changes in the original cultural patterns of either or both groups.

The rapidity and success of the acculturation process depends on several factors, including location and discrimination. If a minority group is spatially isolated and segregated (whether voluntarily or not) in a rural area, as is the case with many Native Americans on reservations, the acculturation process is very slow. Unusually marked discrimination, such as that faced by oppressed groups, especially African Americans, Native Americans, and Mexican Americans, deprives group members of educational and occupational opportunities and primary relationships with members of the dominant group. The acculturation process may be retarded indefinitely (Gordon, 1964).

Structural assimilation occurs when the two groups share primary group relationships, including membership in the same cliques and social clubs. Only limited structural assimilation has occurred for any of the groups except white Protestant immigrants from northern and western Europe. For most groups, success in becoming acculturated has not led to structural assimilation. It has neither eliminated prejudice and discrimination nor led to large-scale intermarriage with the dominant cultural group. If the assimilation process is effective, it leads to the disappearance of a cultural group that is distinct from the dominant group. Thirty years after Gordon's study, the amount of structural assimilation remains about the same.

It is important to note that acculturation is determined in part by the individual. That is, the individual can decide how much he or she wants to dress, speak, and behave like members of the dominant group. For members of many groups, there has been little choice if they wanted to share the American dream of success. They have had to give up native languages and behaviors or hide them at home. Even that did not guarantee acceptance by the dominant group since the extent of structural assimilation is determined by them. Therefore, most members of oppressed groups, even those who adopted the values and behaviors of the macroculture, have not been permitted to assimilate structurally.

A popular assimilation theory is what is called the *melting pot*, or *amalgamation*. It appealed to many immigrants, especially those with European backgrounds. It predicted the evolution of a new, unique American culture to which all ethnic groups contribute. This theory captured an egalitarian ideal, but in reality many groups were not allowed to melt because of the nation's racist policies and practices. Although some very light-skinned African Americans have passed into the white group and interracial marriages have occurred, the numbers have been, and remain, very small. Sociologists who have described the successful amalgamation of African Americans have focused on their intermarriages with mulattoes, and the projections have fallen far short of amalgamation (Williamson, 1980). Until 1967, African Americans, Hispanics, Asian Americans, and Native Americans were prevented by miscegenation laws in many states from intermarrying with persons of European descent. They were not expected to melt nor to be equal partners in the development of the nation.

Although many cultural groups have made tremendous contributions to American civilization, the cultural patterns from the various groups have not melted with the patterns of the native WASPs. Instead, the specific cultural contributions of other groups have been transformed into the macroculture. Assimilation into the macroculture has occurred to some degree for members of most cultural groups, with the help of images projected in public schools, television, and other mass media. Although some groups try to preserve their native culture, others have assimilation as their goal. Nevertheless, assimilation does not characterize the contemporary U.S. scene. We are a nation of many cultural groups distinguished by our ethnicity, gender, class, language, and religion. At the same time, theories of assimilation have impacted and continue to impact on our political, social, and educational policies and practices.

Cultural Pluralism

Refusing, or not being permitted, to assimilate into the dominant American culture, many immigrants and visible minority groups have maintained their own unique ethnic communities and enclaves. For most oppressed ethnic and religious groups, primary-group contacts have been maintained within the group, rather than across cultural groups as required in structural assimilation. Cross-cultural contacts occur only at the secondary level—in work settings and in interaction with political and civic institutions. Members develop within-group institutions, agencies, and power structures for services within their ethnic communities. These enclaves exist as Little Italy, Chinatown, Harlem, Korea Town, East Los Angeles, Amish and Hutterite communities, and a number of settlements in rural areas. In some places, the blind, the deaf, and gays have established communities in which they feel comfortable with other members of the microculture.

Societies organized according to a theory of cultural pluralism allow two or more distinct groups to function separately without requiring any assimilation of one into the other. Pratte (1979) identifies three stringent criteria for the application of cultural pluralism to a society:

1. Cultural diversity, in the form of a number of groups—be they political, racial, ethnic, religious, economic, or age—is exhibited in the society.
2. The coexisting groups approximate equal political, economic, and educational opportunity.
3. There is a behavioral commitment to the values of cultural pluralism as a basis for a viable system of social organization. (p. 141)

Most observers of U.S. society would agree that the condition of cultural diversity is met. Data on the income inequities that exist between men and women or between blacks and whites indicate that the condition for relative parity and equality between groups is not met. The commitment to the value of cultural pluralism is not supported broadly by individuals and groups in society. Native American nations within the United States probably come closest to a reflection of cultural pluralism in that some of them have their own political, economic, and educational systems. For cultural pluralism to be a reality,

Some students live in easily identified ethnic communities like Chinatown in which most primary-group contacts are with members of the same ethnic group.

the nation would recognize many ethnic and/or religious groups that could coexist with each other. It would require that power and resources be shared somewhat equitably across those groups.

The dominant power group is not going to willingly share its power and wealth with other groups. Some critics of the system believe that the dominant group uses a strategy of divide and conquer to keep ethnic groups segregated and fighting among themselves for the few resources available to them. Others believe that a societal goal should be integration of cultural groups and the promotion of more equality across groups through a united front. Still others believe that individuals should be able to maintain their ethnic identity while participating in the macroculture. These beliefs are not necessarily discrete from one another; for example, society could be integrated, but members not required to relinquish their ethnic identities. At the same time, an integrated society can lead to greater assimilation in that primary contacts across cultural groups are more likely.

Ideology of Voluntary Cultural Choice

Neither of the two preceding theories adequately addresses the cultural diversity that exists in this country or the ideal that might be desirable. While many of the advocates of cultural pluralism have treated pluralism and democracy as complements, critics have charged that it does not meet one of the key democratic values—that of calling for free choice for individuals as well as groups.

Within the concept of democracy and pluralism, diverse social-cultural groups should have the freedom to form and flourish free from the oppression of other groups (Appleton, 1983). Further, individuals should have the right to choose the importance of ascribed statuses such as gender, ethnicity, and age in determining who they are. At this time, however, a visible minority group member may become totally acculturated, but may not be allowed to structurally assimilate by the majority group, no matter how much he or she desires to assimilate. On the other hand, many minority group members, as well as some members of European ethnic groups, choose to preserve and maintain their cultural identity and to develop that identity for individual and group advantages.

As individual choice and mobility across cultural groups increase, social and cultural barriers are likely to decrease. We will move toward an open society in which cultural background may influence who an individual is, but become irrelevant in public interactions, especially as the reason for institutional discrimination. In this case, cultural differences will be valued, respected, and encouraged to flourish.

The single theory of cultural pluralism does not adequately support the goals of multicultural education. Too often it overlooks the social realities of race, gender, and class inequalities. When the emphasis of cultural pluralism is on culture rather than just ethnicity, it comes closer to recognizing the interaction of race, gender, class, age, geographical region, and physical and mental abilities on one's participation in society's benefits.

Equality in the United States

Traditionally, minority groups, women, and the poor have been recipients of institutional discrimination. As a result, they often exhibit anger at, dissatisfaction with, and alienation from the system. Racism, sexism, and class inequality characterize societies in which there are great disparities of income, wealth, and power. Competition over scarce resources increases conflicts between the various groups. Thus, fundamental changes in the structure of society must accompany changes in attitudes if voluntary cultural choice is to become a reality. Addressing the issue of equality is a key to such changes.

In Webster's dictionary (1983), *equity* is defined as "justice; impartiality; the giving or desiring to give to each man [woman] his [her] due" and *equality* is defined as "the state of being equal; likeness in magnitude or dimensions, values, qualities, degree, and the like; the state of being neither superior nor inferior." Equity is set in the context of jurisprudence and does not guarantee equality. The meaning of equality within our society varies according to one's assumptions about humankind and human existence. At least two sets of beliefs govern the ideologies of equality and inequality. The first accepts inequality as inevitable and promotes meritocracy. It stresses the right of access to society's resources as a necessary condition for equal rights to life, liberty, and happiness. The focus is on individualism and the individual's right to pursue happiness and obtain personal resources. The second set of beliefs is optimistic that a much greater degree of equality in society can be obtained and should be sought than exists today.

Even though egalitarianism is an often espoused goal of democracy in this country, the inequities that actually exist in society are continually overlooked. Thus, equality must be an essential tenet of multicultural education.

Individualism and Meritocracy

Schools and the mass media teach that the United States was founded by persons dedicated to building a nation and a society for the good of all its citizens. A constitution was fashioned with a coherent set of "checks and balances," making the systematic abuse of power virtually impossible. The principles of egalitarianism that are so widely praised suggest that while the United States is a nation of many different ethnic, regional, social, and economic groups, every group has a voice and no one group forever dominates the economic, political, social, and cultural life of the country. Finally, society and government, while not perfect, are promoted as allowing mass participation and steady advancement toward a more prosperous multicultural, egalitarian society.

It is generally accepted that different socioeconomic levels exist in society, and that, in fact, inequalities must exist. Proponents of this ideology accept the theories of sociobiology and/or functionalism, in which inequalities are viewed as natural outcomes of individual differences. Oppressed groups usually are seen as inferior, and their hardships are blamed on their personal characteristics.

A society based on meritocracy ensures that the ablest and most meritorious, ambitious, hardworking, and talented individuals will acquire the most, achieve the most, and become society's leaders (Ryan, 1981). The resulting inequalities are tolerable, fair, and just. They are viewed as a necessary consequence of equality of opportunity and roughly in proportion to inequalities of merit.

The belief system that undergirds meritocracy has at least three dimensions (Ryan, 1981). First, the individual is valued over the group. It is the individual who has the qualities, ambitions, and talent to achieve at the highest levels in society. Popular stories expound this ideology as they describe the poor immigrant who arrived on our shores with nothing, set up a vegetable stand to eke out a living, and became the millionaire owner of a chain grocery store.

The second dimension stresses differences rather than similarities between individuals. IQ and achievement tests are used throughout schooling to help measure differences. Students and adults are rewarded for outstanding grades, athletic ability, and artistic accomplishment. The third dimension emphasizes internal characteristics such as motivation, intuition, and character that have been internalized by the individual. External conditions, such as racism and poverty, are to be overcome by the individual; they are not accepted as the reason for an individual not to succeed.

Both individualism and equality have long been central themes of American demagogues. The problem, of course, is that the two are not complementary. Meritocracy places the individual as supreme. It stresses individuals' rights to pursue happiness and obtain as many resources as their abilities will allow. "In liberal societies people generally get what they deserve, or if they don't they should, and that's all they should get; and what they deserve is purely and simply a consequence of their own individual character and actions, nothing else" (Green, 1981, p. 167).

This dilemma forces supporters to promote, on the one hand, some equality while preventing any real equality from occurring. Affirmative action, for example, is viewed as evidence of group welfare gaining precedence over individual achievement. The outcry against reverse discrimination suggests that racism no longer exists and that decisions about employment, promotion, and so forth are no longer influenced by racism and sexism.

In a system of meritocracy, equality is to be achieved through equality of opportunity rather than through equality of results. "The ideology of the open or equal opportunity society holds that individuals may obtain social position and social rewards on the basis of merit: mental ability, ambition and motivation, diligent study, hard work, or loyal performance on the job" (Matras, 1984, p. 215).

Family background has been found to account for a large part of the variation in educational and occupational attainment; the opportunity to achieve equally is thwarted before one is born. Individuals born into a wealthy family are likely to achieve wealth; individuals born into a poor family will have difficulty in achieving wealth no matter how hard they work. Thus, families do all that is possible to protect their wealth to guarantee that their children can have the *good life*. This practice is even reflected in the system for funding schools in this country—one that is based on property taxes ensures that families with money will have the best schools. Poor children in a district with a poor tax base must fight unbelievable odds to achieve at the same level as students in an upper-middle-class community. Nevertheless, this ideology places the onus of responsibility on the individual alone, even though inequalities that exist in society most commonly lead to the perpetuation of inequalities in families.

Equal educational opportunity, or equal access to schooling, applies this principle to education. All students are to be provided equal educational opportunities that supposedly will give them similar chances for success or failure. Proponents of this approach believe that it is the individual's responsibility to use those opportunities to his or her advantage in obtaining life's resources and benefits. Critics find that "equal opportunity provides a rationale for discriminating against those who are poor risks. In the land of equal opportunity, poverty must be due to the deficient character and motivation of those who are poor. Thus, self-interest, social pressure, and ideology combine to perpetuate the victimization of those who are poor risks" (Deutsch, 1985, p. 60).

Students enter this competition with different advantages and disadvantages from birth. The opportunities available in schools differ greatly from school to school; thus, students receive neither equal resources nor equal treatment. In his study of the national reports on education released in 1983, Shor (1986) found that the themes for careerism, back-to-basics, and excellence justified inequality through testing and language regimes; disguised inequality as excellence; promoted standard English and a core curriculum

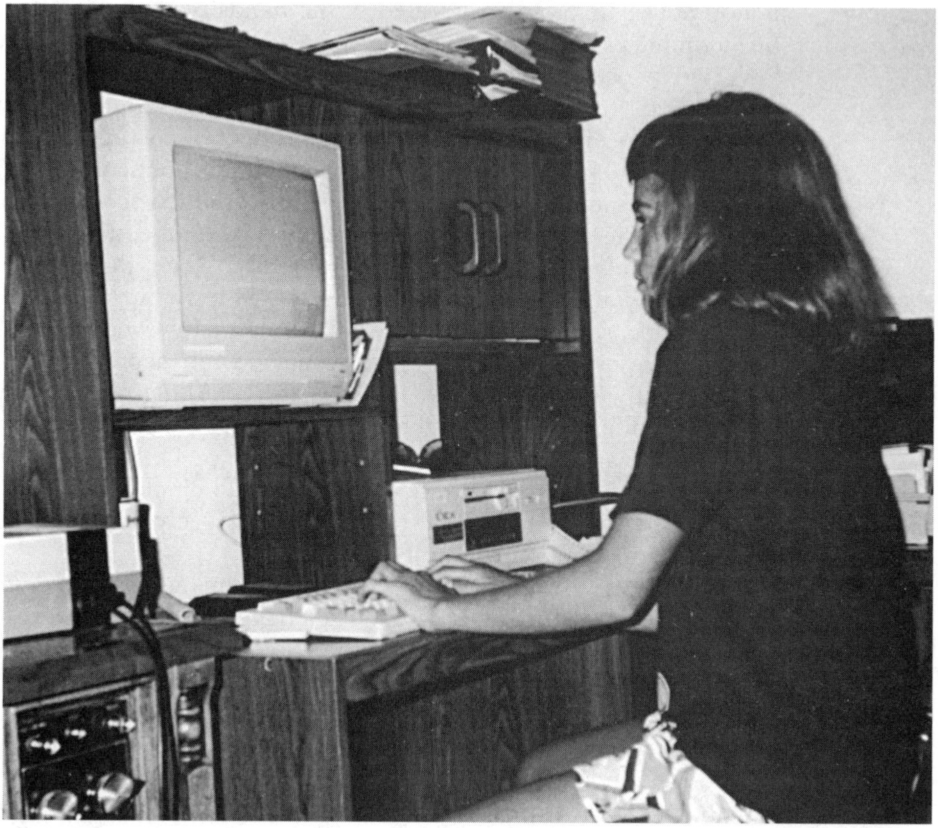

Students do not start life with an equal chance to succeed. Because of family income and wealth, some students have access to resources and experiences in their homes, communities, and often schools that are not available to most poor students.

based on the values of the dominant society (without providing an opportunity to critically analyze that society); discredited bilingual, bidialectical, interdisciplinary, women's, and minority studies; and used licensing exams to screen out minority candidates from the teaching force.

Equality

With the persistence of racism, poverty, unemployment, chronic crisis, and inequality in major social systems such as education and health, many persons have found it difficult to reconcile daily realities with the publicized egalitarianism that characterizes the public rhetoric. These persons view U.S. society as characterized by institutions and an economic system representing the interests of the privileged few rather than the pluralistic majority. Elections, the two-party system, freedom of speech and assembly, and the other democratic institutions are seldom effective measures against the dominant levers of the economic power that is concentrated in the hands of corporate control, which in turn dominates and controls the power of government. Even where institutions, laws, and processes have the appearance of equal access, benefit, and protection, they are almost always enforced in highly discriminatory ways. Finally, these patterns of inequality are not the product of corrupt individuals as such, but a reflection of how resources of economics, political power, and cultural and social dominance are built into the entire politico-economic system.

Even in the optimistic view that some degree of equality can be achieved, inequality is also expected. Not all resources can be redistributed so that every individual would have an equal amount, nor should all individuals expect equal compensation for the work that they do. However, the underlying belief is that there need not be the huge disparities of income, wealth, and power that currently exist (Ryan, 1981). Deutsch (1985) defines equality as distributive justice that "centers on the fairness of the distribution of the conditions and goods that affect individual well-being" (p. 1). Further, he believes that "we need economic policies that will foster full employment and substantially increase the share of the total income that is received by those in the bottom third of the income distribution" (p. 62).

Critics decry the proposed socialism as being against the democratic foundations that undergird the nation. They believe that equality of resources and societal benefits would undermine the capitalist system that allows a few individuals to acquire the great majority of those resources. They warn that equality of results would limit freedom and liberty for individuals. Ryan (1981) counters that "the only freedom threatened by economic equality is the freedom of one individual to oppress and exploit another by virtue of his or her specific talent for oppression or exploitation" (p. 92).

Deutsch (1985) has found that advocates of equality and egalitarianism primarily oppose:

> invidious distinctions among people but do not assume that all distinctions are invidious. Invidious distinctions are ones that promote (1) generalized or irrelevant feelings of superiority-inferiority (if I am a better tennis player or more good-looking than you, I am superior to you as a person); (2) generalized or irrelevant status differences (if I am a manager and you are a worker in a factory, I should have a higher standard of living than you); (3) generalized or irrelevant superordinate-subordinate relations (if I am a captain and you are a private, I can order you to shine my shoes); or (4) the view that the legitimate needs and interests of some people are not as important or do not warrant as much consideration as those of other people (this may be because of my sex, race, age, national or family origin, religion, political affiliation, occupation, or physical handicap, or because of special talents or lack of talent). (pp. 41-42)

Equality should mean more than just providing oppressed group members an equal chance. One proposal is the equal-results argument that is consistent with an optimistic projection of equality. Equal educational results are reflected in equal achievement by students of oppressed and dominant groups or in a similarity in the dropout rate, college attendance, and college completion of different ethnic/racial, gender, and class populations.

Shor (1986) proposes an agenda for educational equality that includes special funding for bilingual and bidialectical programs; support for students' rights to their own language; an end to tracking students out of the college-bound curriculum and into a nonacademic general curriculum; and students' and teachers' rights to free access to all books, materials, and ideas and unhindered discussions of all subjects. He also recommends open admission to colleges, free tuition for higher education, vigorous affirmative action in college admissions and faculty hiring, adequate financing of poor schools, raising teachers' salaries, and involvement of students and community in governance.

Traditionally, there has been a belief that education can overcome the inequalities that exist in society. However, the role of education in reducing the amount of occupation and income inequality appears to be limited. School reform cannot be expected to bring about significant social changes outside of the schools. Equalizing educational opportunity has very little to do with making adults more equal. Providing equal educational opportunity for all students will not guarantee equal results at the end of a specific number of years in school. Nevertheless, Gintis (1989) believes that "education can play an important role in attacking the roots of inequality" (p. 57). Education does help people "affirm their dignity as human beings and develop the skills and resources to control their lives in the larger society" (p. 57). It is also important that resources for providing quality instruction in environments that are conducive to learning be expended equally.

In her extensive work on the tracking of students, Oakes (1988) concluded that:

> Evidence of unequal participation and outcomes is, in itself, insufficient to establish schooling inequities as their cause. However, the existence of these discrepancies does document that schools have been considerably less successful with some groups of students than with others. Moreover, such substantially unequal participation and achievement among groups and the significant increases in outcome discrepancies over time in school provide noteworthy signals that schooling factors may contribute to them. (p. 108)

To establish equality, major changes in society must take place. This process is very difficult when power is held by those who believe in a meritocratic system. "Its proponents turn their principle into a defense of the status quo, that is, of unequal privileges already won in the past" (Green, 1981, p. 167). On the other hand, the advocates for equality support the dictum, "from each according to his [her] ability, to each according to his [her] needs."

PAUSE TO REFLECT

How do you view equality in society and schooling? Check the statements below that best describe your perceptions.

1. The ablest and most meritorious, ambitious, hardworking, and talented individuals should acquire the most, achieve the most, and become society's leaders.
2. The individual is more important than the group.
3. The U.S. economic system represents the interests of a privileged few rather than those of the pluralistic majority.
4. Huge disparities of income, wealth, and power should not exist in this country.
5. It is the student's responsibility to get the most out of school as possible.
6. Differences measured on standardized tests are more important than similarities.
7. External conditions, such as racism and poverty, should be overcome by the individual.
8. Students from all cultural groups can be academically successful.
9. Tracking of students promotes inequality.
10. Teachers can make a difference in the academic success of students.

Which of these statements are most related to a belief in meritocracy and which in a belief in equality?

Multicultural Education

Multicultural education is not a new concept. It is merely a relatively new name for concepts that have existed since the 1920s, when educators began writing about and training others in intercultural education and ethnic studies. The movement during the first two decades had an international emphasis with antecedents in the pacifist movement. Some textbooks were rewritten with an international point of view. Proponents encouraged teachers to make their disciplines more relevant to the modern world by being more issue oriented. The goal was to make the dominant majority populations more tolerant and accepting toward first- and second-generation immigrants in order to maintain national unity and social control (Montalto, 1978).

In the 1960s, desegregation was being enforced in the nation's schools. At the same time, students of color were being described as culturally deprived of the background required to attend schools based on the cultural content of the dominant society. Programs like Head Start and compensatory education and special education were developed to compensate for these shortcomings. Not surprisingly, those classes were filled with students of color, in poverty, or with disabilities. By the 1970s, these groups were described as culturally different to acknowledge that these students came from different cultural backgrounds but that those cultures were not deficient. The goal of the approach to teach the exceptional and culturally different was to develop the cultural patterns of the dominant society so that they could "fit into the mainstream of American society" (Sleeter & Grant, 1988, p. 37).

The civil rights movement brought a renewed interest in ethnic studies, discrimination, and intergroup relations. Racial and ethnic pride emerged from oppressed groups, creating a demand for African American and other ethnic studies programs in colleges and universities across the country. Later, similar programs were established in secondary schools.

Students and participants in ethnic studies programs of the 1960s and early 1970s were primarily members of the group being studied. Programs focused on the various ethnic histories and cultures, with the main objective of providing students with insight and instilling pride in their own racial/ethnic backgrounds. Most of these programs were ethnic-specific and only one ethnic group was studied. Sometimes the objectives included an understanding of the relationship and conflict between the ethnic group and the dominant or majority population, but seldom was a program's scope multiethnic.

Concurrent with the civil rights movement and growth of ethnic studies, emphasis on intergroup or human relations again emerged. Often these programs accompanied ethnic studies content for teachers. The objectives were again to promote intergroup, and especially interracial, understanding and to reduce or eliminate stereotypes. This approach emphasized the affective level—teachers' attitudes and feelings about themselves and others (Sleeter & Grant, 1988).

With the growth and development of ethnic studies came a realization that those programs alone would not guarantee support for the promotion of cultural diversity in this country. Students from the dominant culture also needed to learn about the history, culture, and contributions of oppressed groups. Thus, ethnic studies expanded into multiethnic studies. Teachers were encouraged to develop curricula that included the contributions of oppressed groups along with those of the dominant group. Textbooks were to be rewritten to represent more accurately the multiethnic nature of the United States. Students were to be exposed to perspectives of oppressed groups through literature, history, music, and other disciplines integrated throughout the regular school program.

As part of the civil rights movement, other groups that had suffered from institutional discrimination called their needs to the attention of the public. These groups included women, the poor, the disabled, the bilingual, and the aged. Educators responded by expanding multiethnic education to the more encompassing concept of multicultural education. This broader concept focused on the various microcultures to which individuals belong, with an emphasis on the interaction of membership in the microcultures, especially race/ethnicity, class, and gender.

Still, after six decades of concern for civil and human rights in education, educators struggle with the management of cultural diversity and provision of equality in schools. Many classrooms may be desegregated and mainstreamed, and both boys and girls may now participate in athletic activities, and yet African American, Hispanic American, and Native American students score below European American students on national standardized tests. Females and poor and minority students do not participate equally in science and mathematics classes. They often are offered no encouragement to enroll in advanced courses or to attend college. These groups "have less power to shape the terms of classroom interaction [which] means that their likelihood of school success is reduced and the prospects of alienation and lowered aspirations are increased" (O'Connor, 1988, p. 2).

In a country that champions equal rights and the opportunity for an individual to improve his or her conditions, we must be concerned with helping all students achieve academically, socially, and politically. After conducting a major study of the American high school, the president of the Carnegie Foundation stated that "Opportunity remains unequal. And this failure to educate every young person to his or her full potential threatens the nation's social and economic health" (Boyer, 1983, p. 5). It will no longer be possible to teach all students in the classroom equally, because they are not the same. They have different needs and skills that must be recognized in developing educational programs. Each student is different because of physical and mental abilities, gender, ethnicity/race, language, religion, class, and age. Students behave differently in school and toward authority because of cultural factors and their relationship to the dominant society. As educators, we behave in certain ways toward students because of our own cultural experiences within the power structure of the country.

When educators are given the responsibilities of a classroom, they need the knowledge and skills for working effectively in our culturally diverse society. An educational concept that addresses cultural diversity and equality in schools is multicultural education. This concept is based on the following fundamental beliefs and assumptions:

- There is strength and value in promoting cultural diversity.
- Schools should be models for the expression of human rights and respect for cultural differences.
- Social justice and equality for all people should be of paramount importance in the design and delivery of curricula.
- Attitudes and values necessary for the continuation of a democratic society can be promoted in schools.
- Schooling can provide the knowledge, dispositions, and skills for the redistribution of power and income among cultural groups.
- Educators working with families and communities can create an environment that is supportive of multiculturalism.

Many concepts undergird multicultural education. The relationships and interactions among individuals and groups are essential to understanding and working effectively with different cultural groups. Educators should understand racism, sexism, prejudice, discrimination, oppression, powerlessness, power, inequality, equality, and stereotyping. Multicultural education includes various components that often manifest themselves in courses, units of courses, and degree programs. These components include ethnic studies, global studies, bilingual education, women's studies, human relations, values clarification, special education, and urban education.

For multicultural education to become a reality in the formal school situation, the total environment must reflect a commitment to multicultural education. Sleeter and Grant (1988) refer to this commitment as "education that is multicultural." What would be the characteristics of a school that is multicultural? The composition of the faculty, administration, and staff would accurately reflect the pluralistic composition of the United States. Differences in academic achievement levels would disappear between males and females, dominant and oppressed group members, and upper-middle-class and poor students. The school curriculum would be unbiased and would incorporate the contributions of all cultural groups. Instructional materials would be free of biases, omissions, and stereotypes. Cultural differences would be treated as differences rather than deficiencies that must be addressed in compensatory programs. Students would be able to use their own cultural resources and voices to develop new skills and critically explore the subject matter. Students would learn "to take risks, to struggle with ongoing relations of power, to critically appropriate forms of knowledge that exist outside of their immediate experience, and to envisage versions of a world which is 'not yet'—in order to be able to alter the grounds upon which life is lived" (Simon, 1989, p. 140).

Schools can provide a multicultural environment that affirms diversity and helps students break out of stereotypical roles and activities that have limited their participation in society.

The faculty, administrators, and staff would see themselves as learners enhanced and changed by understanding, affirming, and reflecting cultural diversity. Teachers and administrators would be able to deal with questions of race and intergroup relations and controversial realities on an objective, frank, and professional basis.

Educators face a tremendous challenge in this decade to effectively teach all students. Each subject area should be taught from a multicultural perspective. Skills to function effectively in different cultural settings should be taught. For students to function effectively in a democratic society, they must learn about the inequities that currently exist. As teachers, counselors, and principals, we serve as the transmitters of our culture to children and youth. We should have the courage to try new methods and techniques, the courage to challenge ineffective and inequitable procedures and policies, and the strength to change schools to ensure learning and equity for all students.

Summary

Culture provides the blueprint that determines the way an individual thinks, feels, and behaves in society. We are not born with culture, but learn it through enculturation and socialization. It is manifested through societal institutions, daily habits of living, and the individual's fulfillment of psychological and basic needs.

The U.S. macroculture is the dominant culture that is shared by many of the nation's citizens. Historically, U.S. political and social institutions have developed from a western European tradition and still function under the strong influence of that tradition. Nevertheless, many other aspects of American life have been greatly influenced by the numerous cultural groups that make up the U.S. population.

In addition to participating in the macroculture, individuals belong to a number of microcultures with cultural patterns that may not be common to the macroculture. Cultural identity comes from traits and values learned through membership in microcultures based on ethnic origin, religion, gender, age, class, native language, geographical region, and disabling or exceptional conditions. The interaction of these various microcultures within the macroculture begins to determine an individual's cultural identity. Membership in one microculture often greatly influences characteristics and values of other microcultures, especially of race, gender, and class.

Assimilation, the process by which microcultures adopt the macroculture, has been the most prevailing theory used to describe the nature of cultural diversity in the United States. The theory of cultural pluralism promotes the maintenance of the distinct differences among cultural groups. However, the ideology of voluntary cultural choice may better describe the direction in which we would like to move. This ideal allows individuals to maintain their family's cultural identity or develop new ones.

Multicultural education is a concept that incorporates cultural diversity and provides equality in schools. For it to become a reality in the formal school situation, the total environment must reflect a commitment to multicultural education. The diverse cultural backgrounds and microcultural membership of students and families are as important in developing effective instructional strategies as are their physical and mental capabilities. Further, educators must understand the influence of racism, sexism, and classism on the lives of their students and ensure that they are not perpetuated in the classroom.

Questions for Review

1. What is culture? How is culture determined?
2. What are the differences between the U.S. macroculture and microcultures? Give examples of microcultural memberships that have greatly influenced your life and explain why.
3. Why do the authors believe that the ideology of voluntary cultural choice should be supported in educational policies and practices?
4. What are the differences between dominant and oppressed cultural groups?
5. How are meritocracy and individualism in conflict with the ideal of equality?
6. How is multicultural education more than an addition to the curriculum used in schools? How does it differ from multiethnic studies and intercultural education?
7. What is the danger of stereotyping students based on their membership in only one microculture?
8. Why is multicultural education essential to "good" education for all students?

References

Abercrombie, N., Hill, S., & Turner, B. S. (1984). *Dictionary of sociology.* New York: Penguin Books.

American Council on Education and Education Commission of the States. (1988). *One-third of a nation.* Washington, DC: American Council on Education.

Appleton, N. (1983). *Cultural pluralism in education: Theoretical foundations.* New York: Longman.

Arensberg, C. M., & Niehoff, A. H. (1975). American cultural values. In J. P. Spradley & M. A. Rynkiewich (Eds.), *The nacirema: Readings on American culture* (pp. 363–378). Boston: Little, Brown.

Bellah, R. N., Madsen, R., Sullivan, W. M., Swidler, A., Tipton, S. M. (1985). *Habits of the heart: Individualism and commitment in American life.* New York: Harper & Row.

Boyer, E. L. (1983). *High school: A report on secondary education in America.* New York: Harper & Row.

Burbules, N. C., & Rice, S. (1991). Dialogue across differences: Continuing the conversation. *Harvard Educational Review,* 61(4), 393–416.

Deutsch, M. (1985). *Distributive justice: A social-psychological perspective.* New Haven, CT: Yale University Press.

Freire, P., & Macedo, D. (1987). *Literacy: Reading the word and the world.* South Hadley, MA: Bergin & Garvey.

Gibson, M. A. (1988). *Accommodation without assimilation: Sikh immigrants in an American high school.* Ithaca, NY: Cornell University Press.

Gintis, H. (1989). Education, personal development, and human dignity. In H. Holtz, I. Marcus, J. Dougherty, J. Michaels, & R. Peduzzi, *Education and the American dream: Conservatives, liberals and radicals debate the future of education* (pp. 50–60). Granby, MA: Bergin & Garvey.

Giroux, H. A. (1988). *Teachers as intellectuals: Toward a critical pedagogy of learning.* Granby, MA: Bergin & Garvey.

Giroux, H. A. (1989). Introduction: Education, politics, and ideology. In H. Holtz, I. Marcus, J. Dougherty, J. Michaels, & R. Peduzzi (Eds.), *Education and the American dream: Conservatives, liberals and radicals debate the future of education* (pp. 1–7). Granby, MA: Bergin & Garvey.

Goodenough, W. (1987). Multi-culturalism as the normal human experience. In E. M. Eddy & W. L. Partridge (Eds.), *Applied anthropology in America* (2nd ed.). New York: Columbia University Press.

Gordon, M. M. (1964). *Assimilation in American life: The role of race, religion, and national origins.* New York: Oxford University Press.

Green, P. (1981). *The pursuit of inequality.* New York: Pantheon Books.

Hall, E. T. (1977). *Beyond culture.* Garden City, NY: Anchor Press.

Hicks, E. (1981). Cultural Marxism: Nonsynchrony and feminist practice. In L. Sargent (Ed.), *Women and revolution.* Boston: South End Press.

Kluckhohn, C. (1949). *Mirror for man: The relation of anthropology to modern life.* New York: McGraw-Hill.

LeVine, R. A. (1984). Properties of culture: An ethnographic view. In R. A. Shweder and R. A. LeVine, *Culture theory: Essays on mind, self, and emotion* (pp. 67–87). New York: Cambridge University Press.

Lubeck, S. (1988). Nested contexts. In L. Weis (Ed.), *Class, race, and gender in American education.* Albany, NY: State University of New York Press.

Matras, J. (1984). *Social inequality, stratification, and mobility.* Englewood Cliffs, NJ: Prentice-Hall.

Montalto, N. V. (1978). The forgotten dream: A history of the intercultural education movement, 1924-1941. *Dissertation Abstracts International, 39A,* 1061. (University Microfilms No. 78-13436)

Moore, H. L. (1988). *Feminism and anthropology.* Minneapolis: University of Minnesota Press.

Oakes, J. (1988). Tracking in mathematics and science education: A structural contribution to unequal schooling. In L. Weis (Ed.), *Class, race, and gender in American education* (pp. 106–125). Albany, NY: State University of New York Press.

O'Connor, T. (1988, November). *Cultural voice and strategies for multicultural education.* Paper presented at the annual meeting of the American Educational Studies Association, Montreal, Canada.

Pratte, R. (1979). *Pluralism in education: Conflict, clarity, and commitment.* Springfield, IL: Thomas.

Ryan, W. (1981). *Equality.* New York: Vintage Books.

Shor, I. (1986). *Culture wars: School and society in the conservative restoration 1969–1984.* Boston: Routledge & Kegan Paul.

Simon, R. I. (1989). Empowerment as a pedagogy of possibility. In H. Holtz, I. Marcus, J. Dougherty, J. Michaels, & R. Peduzzi, *Education and the American dream: Conservatives, liberals and radicals debate the future of education* (pp. 134–146). Granby, MA: Bergin & Garvey.

Sleeter, C. E., & Grant, C. A. (1988). *Making choices for multicultural education: Five approaches to race, class, and gender.* New York: Merrill/Macmillan.

Spradley, J. P., & Rynkiewich, M. A. (Eds.). (1975). *The nacirema: Readings on American culture.* Boston: Little, Brown.

Webster's new twentieth century dictionary (2nd ed.) (1983). New York: Simon & Schuster.

Williamson, J. (1980). *New people: Miscegenation and mulattoes in the United States.* New York: New York University Press.

Yetman, N. R. (Ed.) (1985). *Majority and minority: The dynamics of race and ethnicity in American life* (4th ed.). Boston: Allyn and Bacon.

Suggested Readings

Appleton, N. (1983). *Cultural pluralism in education: Theoretical foundations.* New York: Longman.

This analysis of theories and ideologies of cultural pluralism includes the presentation of related court cases and cultural conflict. Suggestions are presented for incorporating cultural pluralism in the schools.

Hall, E. T. (1977). *Beyond culture.* Garden City, NY: Anchor Press.

This book describes those aspects of culture that are so innate that they are not easily recognized as culturally determined. The need for understanding culture is clearly outlined.

Holtz, H., Marcus, I., Dougherty, J., Michaels, J., & Peduzzi, R. (1989). *Education and the American dream: Conservatives, liberals and radicals debate the future of education.* Granby, MA: Bergin & Garvey.

This collection of papers presented at a symposium addresses values, society, inequality, computers, gender, race, class, excellence, and reform. It provides an excellent overview of conservative, liberal, and radical perspectives on education.

Pratte, R. (1979). *Pluralism in education: Conflict, clarity, and commitment.* Springfield, IL: Thomas.

This theoretical examination of the concept of cultural pluralism and its application to education provides a careful analysis of theories and ideologies.

Spradley, J. P., & Rynkiewich, M. A. (Eds.) (1975). *The nacirema: Readings on American culture.* Boston: Little, Brown.

Aspects of American culture that are often overlooked as traits and institutions unique to U.S. culture are presented from an anthropological perspective. The informative discussion of the Nacirema provides an amusing critique of the culture.

Weis, L. (Ed.). *Class, race, and gender in American education.* Albany, NY: State University of New York Press.

These articles examine class, race, and gender issues in U.S. schools. The overview discusses the distinctions between cultural and structural approaches to the study of schooling. The first section of the book focuses on different knowledge, unequal structures, and unequal outcomes; the second section examines cultural forms in schools.

CHAPTER 2

Class

Tomas Juarez long ago decided that he wanted to work with low-income children. After teaching for a couple of years in a culturally diverse suburban school around Denver, he decided that he was ready to take on the challenge of an inner-city school where all of the students were members of oppressed groups. As soon as he stepped into his new school, he realized that he had been spoiled in the suburbs.

First, the smell wasn't right and the halls were dirty even though it was the beginning of the school year. The room that was to be his classroom did not have enough chairs for all of the students who had been assigned to the class. Not only did the room look as if it had not been repainted for twenty years, several window panes were covered with a cardboard-looking substance, and numerous ceiling tiles were missing. His first thought was that both he and the students would be exposed to asbestos and lead poisoning throughout the year. Going outside into the playground was almost worse. There was no grass, the stench from local factories was overbearing, and the football field did not even have goalposts.

During Mr. Juarez's first few weeks, he found that the students were terrific. They were enthusiastic about being back in school and seemed to like him. However, there were enough textbooks for only half of the class and there was no money to purchase more. Chalk was limited and most of the audiovisual equipment had been stolen last year and never replaced.

Why were conditions at Mr. Juarez's new school so much different from those in the suburbs? How can a teacher overcome environmental conditions that are not supportive of effective learning? What are the chances of the new students being academically successful in the same way as the students in the suburban school? Why are the new students more likely to drop out, become pregnant, and not attend college? Why has society allowed some students to go to school under such appallingly poor conditions?

Class Structure

The two views of equality in U.S. society that were outlined in Chapter 1 suggest different class structures in the country. One view accepts the objective existence of different socioeconomic levels or classes in society. It also strongly supports the notion that one can be socially mobile and move to a higher class if one works hard enough. These dichotomous groups—those who control most of the resources and those who are oppressed—struggle for control of society. Thus, conflict between the two is inherent in this explanation. Oppressed groups in this view are usually seen as inferior, and their hardships are blamed on their lack of middle-class values and behaviors.

In the second view of U.S. society, distinct class divisions are recognized. Those individuals and families who own and control corporations, banks, and other means of production compose the privileged upper class. Persons who earn a living primarily by selling their labor power make up other classes. Although inequality is acknowledged, it is not explained in terms of class differences and conflict between classes. Instead, it is explained in terms of lack of motivation and ability. Thus, it is the individual's fault for not moving up the class ladder—a phenomenon called blaming the victim. Another class includes those persons who are unable to work or who can find work only sporadically. Although some individuals are able to move from one class to another, such cases are rare. Most people are caught in the socioeconomic strata into which they were born, and the politico-economic system ensures that they remain there.

"While having to recognize the existence of unequal outcomes—inequalities in the possession of wealth, power, and prestige—Americans have characteristically emphasized the equal chance: in reality, the equal chance for individuals to wind up unequal" (M. Lewis, 1978, p. 4). Many Americans believe that the United States is a model of egalitarianism, a value that is highly regarded and viewed as uniquely American. However, this idea is misleading. There are "real limitations on what most of us can achieve—limitations which have very little to do with our willingness to work or the quality of our effort" (M. Lewis, 1978, p. 17). This chapter will explore inequalities related to the class structure in this country and some of the limitations or advantages that may result.

Social Stratification

Social stratification is possible because consistent and recurring relationships exist between people who occupy different levels of the social structure. Many individuals accept and follow socially defined positions based on occupation, race, gender, and class, for which patterns of behavior have been institutionalized. Civil rights and women's organizations are trying to combat that institutionalized acceptance and expectation of behavior for a group of people.

Inequality results, in part, from differential rankings within the division of labor. Different occupations are evaluated and rewarded unequally. Some jobs are viewed as more worthy, more important, more popular, and more preferable than others. Finally, the rewards and evaluations of higher-ranking positions produce common interests among those who hold those positions. They then restrict the chances of others to obtain the same status—and that is the key to establishing and maintaining a system of stratification.

Many persons in the United States receive high or low rankings in the social stratification system based on characteristics over which they have no control. Women, disabled persons, elderly persons, children, and persons whose skin color is not white often receive a low prestige ranking. Ascribed status affects who is allowed entrance into the higher-ranking socioeconomic positions. On the other hand, ascribed status does not ensure that all white, nondisabled men will achieve a high-ranking position. They are found at all levels of the continuum, from a very low socioeconomic status to the highest socioeconomic status, but they and their families are overrepresented at the highest level. People of color, women, the young, the elderly, and disabled persons have a disproportionately high representation at the low end of the continuum. At the same time, members of these groups can be found at all levels of the continuum, with a few at the top of the socioeconomic status scale.

Such inequities are in large part a result of historical discrimination against some groups of people, as described in other chapters of this book. One's ascribed status affects one's socioeconomic status from birth. It influences one's ability to choose alternative courses of action, to control one's own behavior, and to achieve one's goals (Rothman, 1978). How socioeconomic status is affected by ascribed statuses for which individuals suffer the most, namely ethnicity, gender, and age, will be examined later in this chapter.

Socioeconomic Status

Socioeconomic level influences many aspects of the lives of students and their parents. Historically, the American way has emphasized the necessity for the individual and the family to want and to achieve the "good life." The first immigrants subscribed to the belief that everyone had the opportunity to be successful by utilizing the fullest extent of his or her talents. As a matter of fact, many people today believe that it is an individual's birthright to desire and aspire to reach that potential.

How is the economic success or achievement of Americans measured? The U.S. Bureau of the Census measures the economic condition of individuals with a criterion called socioeconomic status (SES). It serves as a composite of the economic status of a family or unrelated individuals based on *occupation, educational attainment,* and *income.* Related to the three factors used by the Census Bureau are *wealth* and *power,* which also help determine an individual's socioeconomic status but are more difficult to measure through census data.

These five determinants of socioeconomic status are interrelated. Although there are many forms of inequality, these factors are probably the most salient for the individual because they affect how one lives. A family's socioeconomic status usually is observable—in the size of their house and the part of town in which they live, the schools the children attend, or the clubs to which the parents belong. Many educators place their students at specific socioeconomic status levels based on similar observations.

Income

Income is the amount of money earned in wages or salaries throughout a year. Economists look at income distribution by dividing the population into fifths; the lowest fifth earns the least income, and the highest fifth earns the highest income. Figure 2-1 shows what percentage of the total income earned in 1990 was earned by each fifth of the population and the total wealth held by each fifth. The top 20 percent of the population earned 44.3 percent of the total income, while the bottom 20 percent earned 4.6 percent of the total income (Bureau of the Census, 1992). "The top 4 percent of American's workforce earned as much as the bottom 51 percent" (Barlett & Steele, 1992).

Many Americans view this income inequity as a natural outcome of the American way. Because some individuals have achieved at a much higher level than most of the population, many people believe that they deserve to be paid more for their effort. Persons at the lower end of the continuum are either unemployed or work in unskilled jobs and thus are not expected to receive the same economic rewards. However, the degree of difference is quite large. The president of a large corporation can earn millions of dollars annually, whereas persons earning minimum wage receive less than $10,000 annually.

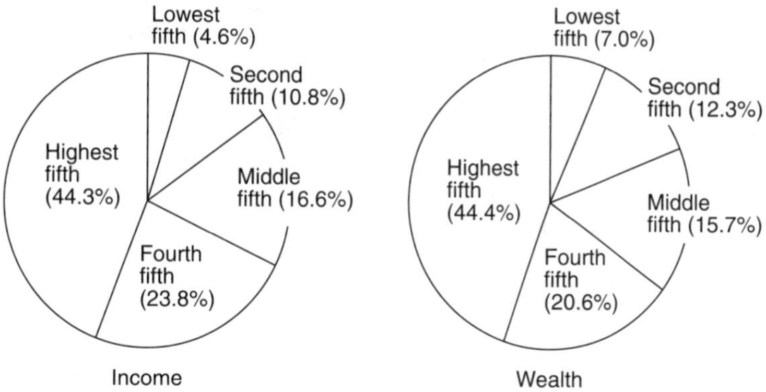

Figure 2-1. The figure on the left shows the distribution of total income in fifths of the population. The figure on the right shows the distribution of wealth in this country.

Between World War II and 1973, the growth of the American economy allowed incomes of workers at all levels to increase at a faster rate than expenditures. Many middle-income families were able to purchase homes, cars, boats, and luxuries for the home; often there was money left over for savings. Between 1947 and 1973, the annual median income of all persons fourteen years old and older nearly tripled, from $1,787 to $5,004. The standard of living for most of the population was markedly better in 1973 than in 1940. Beginning in 1973, however, the cost of living (the cost of housing, utilities, food, and other essentials) began to increase faster than income. Except for the rich, all families felt the financial pressure. No longer did they have extra income to purchase nonessentials. No longer was one full-time worker in a family enough to maintain the same standard of living. In 1990, the median annual income of a family was $35,353. In constant dollars, the median income in 1986 was less than that in 1973 (Bureau of the Census, 1992). Of those families with incomes above $25,000, nearly 60 percent had paychecks from two full-time workers.

Income sets limits on the general lifestyle of a family, as well as on its general welfare. It controls the consumption patterns of a family—the amount and quality of material possessions, housing, consumer goods, luxuries, savings, and diet. The house, the new car, the furnishings, the food, the clothes, and the entertainment portrayed in many television advertisements reflect an accepted pattern of living well. According to our American mythology, almost every American lives this way; the few who have not attained such a lifestyle expect to do so as soon as they "get on their feet." But according to statistics, only about one-fourth of our families come close to the ideal.

Wealth

Although the difference in income between families is great, an examination of income alone does not indicate the vast differences in the way families live. Income figures show the amount of money earned by a family for their labors

PAUSE TO REFLECT

Did you know how great the disparities in income and wealth are in this country? What surprised you the most about these data? What factors cause such great disparities? How do these differences affect families and schools?

during a year, but do not include the amount of money earned from investments, land, and other holdings. They do not present the net worth of a family. (Net worth is the amount of money remaining if all owned property were converted to cash and all debts paid.) The wealth of a family includes savings accounts, insurance, corporate stock ownership, and property. Wealth provides a partial guarantee of future income and has the potential of producing additional income and wealth. However, "for most Americans, the majority of their wealth comes from the equity value of their homes and the residual value of their consumer durables. Fewer than one-third have any significant financial holdings" (Rose, 1992, p. 21).

Whereas income can be determined from data gathered on federal income tax forms by the Internal Revenue Service, wealth is difficult to determine from these or any other standard forms. It is known, however, that the distribution of wealth is concentrated in a small percentage of the population. "The 9 percent of the population worth more than $250,000 holds almost one-half of all net worth . . . fully 55 percent of all American households had *no* net financial assets. By contrast, 54 percent of financial assets were held by the top 2 percent of wealth holders; 86 percent were held by the top 10 percent" (Rose, 1992, pp. 21–22). Figure 2-1 shows how wealth is distributed across fifths of the population.

Wealth ensures some economic security for its holders, even though the amount of security depends on the amount of wealth accumulated. It also enhances the power and prestige of those who own it. Great wealth accrues power, provides an income that allows luxury, and creates values and lifestyles that are very different from those of persons without great wealth.

Occupation

For most Americans, income is determined by their occupation. Generally speaking, Americans believe that income is a fair measure of occupational success—both of the importance of the occupation to the society and of one's individual skill at the job. In addition to providing an income, a person's occupation is an activity that Americans consider important. Those individuals who are unemployed often are characterized as noncontributing members of society who cannot take care of themselves. Even individuals with great wealth usually work, although additional income is unnecessary.

Just over half of today's workforce is composed of white-collar workers, that is, individuals who do mental rather than manual work. The percentage of service workers is growing, although the percentage who are private household workers continues to decline. Between now and 2005, the fastest growing occupations will include home health aides, systems analysts and computer scientists, personal and home care aides, medical assistants, human service workers, radiological technologists and technicians, medical secretaries, psychologists, travel agents, and corrections officers (Bureau of the Census, 1992).

Within the working classes, the type of job one holds is the primary determinant of the income received. The job provides a relatively objective indicator of an individual's socioeconomic status. It often indicates one's education, suggests the types of associates with whom one will interact, and determines the degree of authority and responsibility one has over others. It gives individuals both differing amounts of compensation in income and differing degrees of prestige in the society.

Occupational prestige is often determined by the requirements for the job and by the characteristics of the job. The requirements for an occupation with prestige may include more education and training. Job characteristics that add to the prestige of an occupation are rooted in the division between mental and manual labor. When the prestige of an occupation is high, fewer people gain entry into that occupation. When the prestige of an occupation is low, employees are allotted less security, income, and prestige, and there is greater accessibility to that occupation. Those occupations with the highest prestige generally receive the highest salary. In most cases, an individual's occupation will determine his or her socioeconomic status.

Education

The best predictor of occupational prestige is the amount of education that one acquires, and the amount and quality of education one acquires is generally determined by one's "place" within society. In general, occupations require more education and more training as their prestige increases.

Financial compensation is usually greater for occupations that require more years of education. For example, medical doctors and lawyers remain in school for several years beyond the bachelor's degree program. Many professionals and other white-collar workers have completed at least an undergraduate program at a college or university. Craft workers are an exception in that they often earn more money than many white-collar workers. At the same time, their positions require specialized training that often takes as long to complete as a college degree. There continues to be a great discrepancy in the income of persons who have less than a high school education and those who have completed professional training after college.

The job one has and the income received is related to the amount of education obtained. For example, in 1990 the mean income of a male who had not completed the ninth grade was $19,188; it was $44,554 if he had completed four years of college. The differential for a female was $13,322 and $28,911 (Bureau of the Census, 1992).

Many Americans still view education as a way to enhance economic status. The sale of one's labor power in the U.S. labor market usually is enhanced by years of education. The credentials obtained through education are important in determining one's socioeconomic status. However, some people end up with more impressive educational credentials than others, and there are reasons for this. The most important determinant of educational attainment is family background, which is accounted for partly by economic differences between families and partly by more elusive noneconomic differences.

The higher the socioeconomic status of students' families, the greater their chances of finishing high school and college. The conditions under which poor students live often make it difficult for them to go to school instead of work. The greater the income of families, the greater are the chances that students will have available books, magazines, and newspapers in the home; will have attended plays or concerts; and will have traveled beyond the region in which they live. Even the colleges that students attend are influenced more by the socioeconomic status of the family than by the academic ability of the student. Many students simply cannot afford to attend private colleges and choose instead state colleges or universities or community colleges. Thus, a student's socioeconomic origins have a substantial influence on the amount and type of schooling received and the type of job obtained.

Education is one of the main ways in which families pass on class position to their children. One's class position determines, in great part, the material conditions that affect one's lifestyle. Thus, educational level is a strong determinant of the future occupation and income of a family's children.

Power

Individuals and families who are at the upper socioeconomic status levels exert more power than those at any other level. These individuals are more likely to sit on boards that determine state and local policies, on boards of colleges and universities, and on boards of corporations. They determine who receives benefits and rewards in governmental, occupational, and community affairs. Parenti (1988) describes this control:

> The owning class has the power to influence policy decisions through the control of jobs and the withholding of investments. In addition, since no system automatically maintains and reproduces itself, the capitalists use some portion of their vast wealth to finance or exercise trusteeship over social and educational institutions, foundations, think tanks, publications, and mass media, thereby greatly influencing society's ideological output, its values and information flow. (p. 196)

Groups and individuals with power control resources that influence their lives and the lives of others. Groups or individuals with little power do not have the means to get what they need or want or the access to others who could influence their interests. Powerless groups continually obtain fewer of the good things in life because they lack accessibility to power sources. The sphere of education is not exempt from these relationships.

Class Differences

Many Americans identify themselves as middle class. It is an amorphous category that often includes everyone who works steadily and who is not accepted as a member of the upper class. It ranges from well-paid professionals to service workers. Most white-collar workers, no matter what their salary, see themselves as middle class. Manual workers, on the other hand, often view themselves as working class rather than middle class; however, for the most part their incomes and cultural values are similar to those of most white-collar workers.

Despite the popular myth, most people in America are not affluent. Rose (1992) figured a medium budget that represented what might be a reasonably comfortable life in America today. In 1992, that budget, which was for $35,617, was far above the poverty level. While only 13.5 percent of the population is considered poor by federal poverty standards, 42.1 percent of households earned less than $25,000 in 1990 (Bureau of the Census, 1992). Many of these persons identify themselves as middle class, but are unable to obtain the material goods and necessities to live comfortably. The so-called middle class is certainly not homogeneous. The differences in education, occupation, prestige, income, and the ability to accumulate wealth vary widely among persons who identify themselves in this group.

This section will provide a broad sketch of classes often categorized in describing Americans: the underclass, the working class, the middle class, and the upper class.

The Underclass

The term *underclass* is sometimes viewed as negative and as an inappropriate label for the portion of the population who suffer the most from the lack of a stable income or other economic resources. It usually does not include those individuals who are temporarily poor because of a job loss or family illness; it does include the long-term poor. Of the individuals classified as in poverty, "only 2.2 percent were persistently poor (lived in poverty for at least eight out of the last ten years)" (Rose, 1992, p. 23).

Auletta (1982) grouped the underclass into the following four distinct groups:

> 1. The passive poor, usually long-term welfare recipients
> 2. The hostile street criminals who terrorize most cities, and who are often school dropouts and drug addicts
> 3. The hustlers, who, like street criminals, may not be poor and who earn their livelihood in an underground economy, but rarely commit violent crimes
> 4. The traumatized drunks, drifters, homeless shopping-bag ladies and released mental patients who frequently roam or collapse on city streets. (p. xvi)

The underclass includes the hard-core unemployed—those who have seldom, if ever, worked and who lack the skills to find and maintain a job. It also includes many discouraged workers who have given up looking for work and who are no longer included in the federal government's report of the unemployed. Disproportionately, these families are headed by single mothers, often teenagers who have had to drop out of school. The number of persons included in this group is not found in the census data. Researchers suggest that it varies from two to fifteen million (Auletta, 1982).

Members of the underclass have become socially isolated from the dominant society. They usually are not integrated into, nor wanted in, the communities of the other classes. Recommendations to build low-income housing, homeless shelters, or halfway houses in middle- or working-class communities often result in vocal outrage from the residents of these communities. Some analysts think that the lack of integration has exacerbated the differences in behavior between members of the underclass and those of other classes. In a study of the inner city, Wilson (1987) concluded that

> The exodus of middle- and working-class families from many ghetto neighborhoods removes an important "social buffer" that could deflect the full impact of the kind of prolonged and increasing joblessness that plagued inner-city neighborhoods in the 1970s and early 1980s, joblessness created by uneven economic growth and periodic recessions. This argument is based on the assumption that even if the truly disadvantaged segments of an inner-city area experience a significant increase in long-term spells of joblessness, the basic institutions in that area (churches, schools, stores, recreational facilities, etc.) would remain viable if much of the base of their support comes from the more economically stable and secure families. Moreover, the very presence of these families during such periods provides mainstream role models that help keep alive the perception that education is meaningful, that steady employment is a viable alternative to welfare, and that family stability is the norm, not the exception. (p. 56)

Over the past decade, the number of homeless persons and families has increased dramatically. For the first time since the Great Depression, children and families beg on the streets of our major cities. The estimates of the number of homeless differ, depending on who reports the figures, from 250,000 to three million—at least one percent of the population. "Estimates of the number of children who are homeless on any given night range from 68,000 to half a million. . . . [In addition,] there are nearly 14 million 'hidden homeless' . . . [that is,] families living doubled up with friends or relatives as a temporary placement" (Linehan, 1992, p.62). Half of the homeless are now families and one-third of the residents of homeless shelters are children. Other homeless include persons who have been released from mental institutions, runaway teenagers, and other single persons. Many work, but at such low wages they are unable to afford housing. Half of the homeless have graduated from high school; 20 percent have attended college; and 5 percent have college degrees (Gorder, 1988).

"Contrary to popular belief, most of the people who are homeless actually do not choose to be homeless" (Gorder, 1988, p. 23). In many communities now, the homeless can be observed sleeping in parks or on grates. However, only 5 percent choose to live on the streets; most use shelters when available. In some areas, tent cities have been established by homeless persons and families (Gorder, 1988).

Who are the homeless families? Gorder (1988) reports the following characteristics of homeless families in Atlanta:

- Eighty-three percent are headed by single females.
- Forty-three percent are employed but not able to make it on their salaries.
- Sixty percent of the children are under the age of five.
- The average number of children is two.
- The parents' average age is twenty-nine.
- Only 36 percent have been on welfare programs previously. (p. 68)

What happens to the children in these families? In a number of school districts, they cannot be registered for school because they do not have an address. Therefore, many do not attend school for extended periods of time. "Many of these kids grow up surrounded by diseases no longer seen in most developed nations. Whooping cough and tuberculosis, once regarded as archaic illnesses, are now familiar in the shelters. Shocking numbers of these children have not been inoculated and for this reason cannot go to school. Those who do attend school may be two years behind grade level" (Kozol, 1991a, p. 7). They suffer from hypothermia and are often hungry. Further, they are more likely to be abused or neglected by parents and other adults.

The underclass suffer from economic insecurity and social, political, and economic deprivation. When they hold full-time jobs, the jobs are of the lowest prestige and income and are often eliminated as economic conditions tighten, resulting in their being unemployed again. The work for which they are hired is often the dirty work—not only physically dirty, but also often dangerous, menial, undignified, and degrading. The jobs are the least desirable ones in society, and they are performed by persons with no other options if they are going to work.

Too often, the underclass is blamed for its own condition. The members are generally unnoticed when they remain isolated from the majority and work

An increasing number of homeless adults, families, and children are found in communities around the country.

sporadically. However, those who are on welfare are subjected to the pejorative and inaccurate opinions of many Americans. "To be poor in America is to be stigmatized" (Beeghley, 1978, p. 139). The poor are often attributed personal qualities of dishonesty and loose morals. They are stereotyped as lazy and unwilling to work. The implication of such stereotypes is that they as individuals must not be working hard enough; otherwise, they would not be poor.

Many stereotypical notions about the underclass need to be overcome for teachers to effectively serve students who come from this background. Such students should not be blamed if they show acceptance, resignation, and even accommodation to their poverty as they learn to live with their economic disabilities. Should they be blamed for lethargy when their diets are inadequate to sustain vigor, or for family instability when they are under torturing financial stress, or for low standardized-test scores when their education has been poor, or for loose workforce attachments when they are in dead-end jobs that cannot lift them out of poverty anyway (Perlman, 1976)?

Anthropologists and sociologists have studied the relationship between cultural values and poverty status. Some have proposed a thesis called culture of poverty that asserts that the poor have a unique way of life that developed as a reaction to their impoverished environment (0. Lewis, 1969). This thesis suggests that those people who are poor have a different value system and lifestyle that are perpetuated as a microculture in American society.

Critics of the culture of poverty thesis believe that the cultural values of the poor are much like those of the rest of the population but have been modified in practice because of situational stresses (Valentine, 1968). In a classic study of street-corner men, Liebow (1967) suggested the following about a poor person's behavior: "Behavior appears not so much as a way of realizing the distinctive goals and values of his own microculture, or of conforming to its models, but rather as his way of trying to achieve many of the goals and values of the larger society, of failing to do this, and of concealing his failure from others and from himself as best he can" (p. 222).

This explanation suggests that the differences in values and lifestyles of the poor are not passed from one generation to the next, but are the adaptations by the poor to the experience of living in poverty.

The Working Class

The occupations pursued by the working class are those that require manual work for which income varies widely, depending on the skill required in the specific job. The factor that is most important in the description of the working class is the subordination of members to the capitalist control of production. These workers do not have control of their work. They do not give orders; they take orders from others, usually members of the middle class. Included in the working class are craft and precision workers, operators, fabricators, and laborers. When farm laborers and service workers are added to this group, the working class comprises 42.6 percent of the employed population (Bureau of the Census, 1992).

In 1991, the median income of these workers, sometimes called blue-collar workers, varied from $8,476 for private household workers to $26,624 for some craft and precision workers (Bureau of the Census, 1992). Although the income of many blue-collar workers is equal to and sometimes higher than that of nonprofessional white-collar workers, there is less job security. Work is more sporadic and unemployment is unpredictably affected by the economy. Jobs are uncertain because of displacement as a result of technology and more stringent educational requirements. Fringe benefits available to these workers are often not as good as those offered other workers. Vacation time is usually shorter, health insurance is available less often, and working conditions are more dangerous.

The education required for most blue-collar jobs is not as high as for white-collar jobs. However, the better-paying, skilled jobs require specialized training and apprenticeships. Without additional training, it becomes difficult to move into a higher-level position. Many factory workers earn little more after twenty years on the job than a beginner, and within a few years the new worker is earning the same pay as the worker with seniority.

Except for the skilled jobs and some of the service and farm jobs that allow autonomy to the worker, most jobs at this level are routine and are often perceived as not very meaningful nor satisfying to the worker. Some studies report that blue-collar workers are more likely to separate work and social activities than workers at other levels. They tend not to socialize with coworkers to the same degree as other workers, but maintain strong kinship ties with parents and siblings for social life.

The blue-collar workers perceive themselves as hardworking, honest, and performing decent and important work for society. They want to be successful, and often they hope that their children will not have to spend their lives in a factory. Mistakenly, they are often perceived by others as authoritarian and intolerant of civil rights—an image portrayed by the term *hard hat* during the 1960s. This image, however, has not proved accurate. Blue-collar workers are no more intolerant or prejudiced than members of other classes.

The Middle Class

In the past, the image of middle-class Americans was a married couple with two or three children in a suburban house with a double garage, a color television set, and the latest household gadgets; the father was almost always the primary breadwinner. In reality, only 4 percent of all American families fit the middle-class myth (Hodgkinson, 1986).

The incomes of those Americans who are popularly considered middle class vary greatly. Contrary to myths about affluent workers, the average annual pay for full-time employees in all domestic industries was $25,889 in 1990 (Bureau of the Census, 1992). Families generally are classified as middle class if their incomes fall between $20,000 and $50,000—about 35 percent of those submitting tax returns (Barlett & Steele, 1992). While some members of this supposed middle class have comfortable incomes, they have virtually no wealth. Many live from paycheck to paycheck with little cushion against the loss of earning power through catastrophe, recession, layoffs, wage cuts, or old age. At various periods in the life cycle, many members of this middle class fall into poverty for brief periods of time. Many families have found it necessary for both the husband and the wife to work to make ends meet. For discussion, the middle class will be divided into two distinct groups: white-collar workers and professionals/managers.

The jobs held by the middle class differ greatly, especially in income compensation (see Figure 2-2). Although white-collar workers perform nonmanual labor, professionals, managers, and administrators are accorded higher pres-

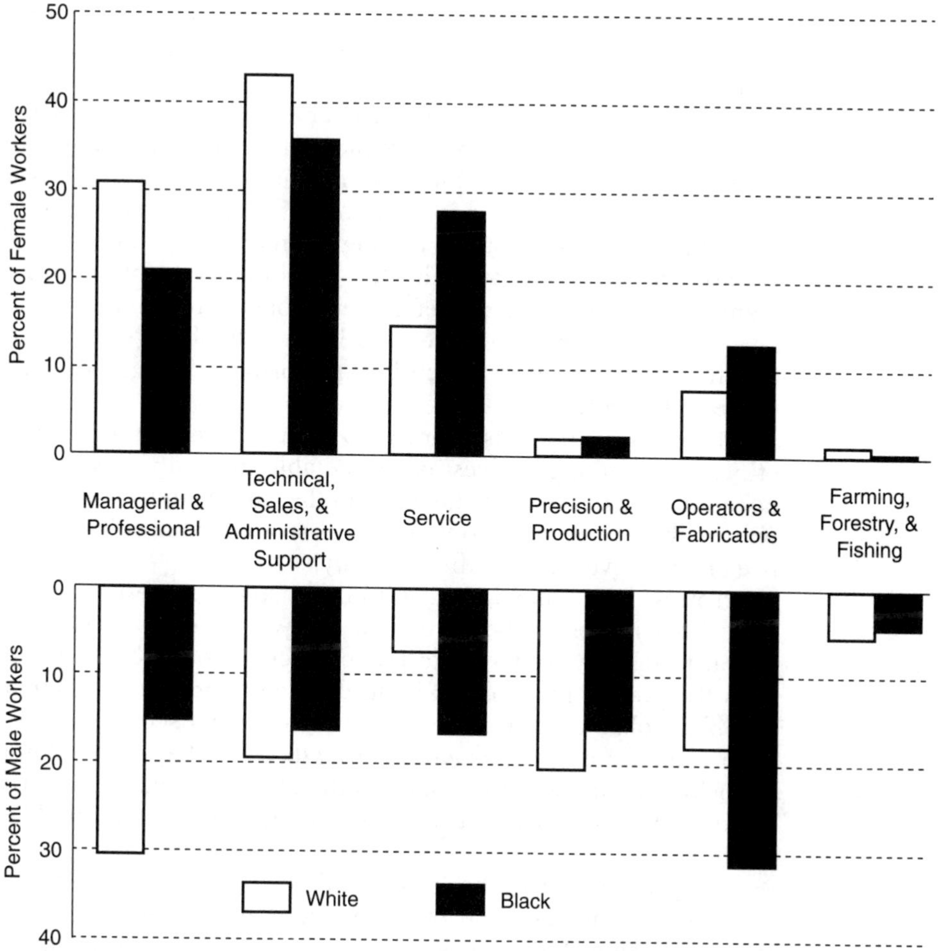

Figure 2-2. Percent of white and black male and female workers employed in different occupations in 1991.

tige in society. A major difference between these two groups is the amount of control they have over their work and the work of others. White-collar clerical workers, technicians, and salespersons are usually supervised by the professionals, managers, or administrators.

Overall, middle-class workers earn a median income above that of most blue-collar workers except for skilled workers and many operatives. The median income of sales workers was $22,335 in 1991; persons who provide administrative support, including clerical work, earned less, with a median income of $19,360. The median income for the professional category was $33,947, with administrators earning more than the professionals (Bureau of the Census, 1992). As a group, these workers have greater job security and better fringe benefits than many blue-collar workers. Whereas the formal education required for these jobs varies, more formal education is usually expected than for blue-collar jobs.

As white-collar jobs expanded over the past four decades, many people believed that such jobs were more meaningful and satisfying than jobs in blue-collar occupations. How meaningful and satisfying the jobs are, however, depends on the particular job. Certainly, many are as routine and boring as many blue-collar jobs; others are highly interesting and challenging. Still others are extremely alienating in that employees cannot control their environment. Some employees perceive their work as meaningless, are socially isolated from coworkers, and develop low levels of self-esteem. The type of job and the environment in which it is performed vary greatly for workers with white-collar jobs.

Members of this class appear to believe strongly in the Protestant work ethic. They see themselves as respectable and adhering to a specific set of beliefs and values that are inherent in the American way of life. While they are only slightly better off economically than their blue-collar counterparts, they live or try to live a more affluent lifestyle.

Professionals, managers, and administrators are the elite of the middle class. They represent the status that many Americans who are concerned with upward mobility are trying to reach. Their income level allows them to lead lives that are in many cases quite different from those of other white-collar and blue-collar workers. They are the group that seems to have benefited the most from the nation's economic growth since the 1940s. Although at a level far below the upper class, they are the affluent middle class. They reflect the middle-class myth more accurately than any of the other middle-class groups described.

The professionals who best fit this category include those persons who must receive professional or advanced degrees and credentials to practice their profession. Judges, lawyers, physicians, college professors, teachers, and scientists are the professionals. Excluding teachers, most professionals earn far above the median income of $26,260 reported for this category. They may be classified as members of the upper middle class, earning over $50,000 annually. They usually own a home and a new car and are able to take vacations to other parts of the country and abroad (Rose, 1992).

This group also includes managers and administrators, who make up 12.8 percent of the employed population. They are the successful executives and businesspeople. They range from the chief executive officers of a major corporation to the president of a college to the owner and administrator of a local nursing home. Those who are the most affluent make up the middle and upper management in financing, marketing, and production. Although the median salary of this census category is $33,678, the administrators of large corporations earn salaries far above this level; their salaries and fringe benefits place them in the upper class instead of the middle class.

PAUSE TO REFLECT

What images do you conjure up when you think of the underclass, the working class, and the middle class? Which characteristics are positive and which ones are negative? Why are your perceptions value laden? What will you have to watch for in your own perceptions to ensure that you do not discriminate against students from one of these groups?

Educational credentials are more important for the professionals and managers at this level than at any other class level. For most of these occupations, knowledge is gained through formal education; a college degree, often an advanced degree, is a prerequisite. The prospect of gaining the necessary qualifications to enter this level is severely restricted in that children of parents with college degrees are much more likely to attend and graduate from college than are children of parents who did not attend college. Thus, position in this status level most often becomes a part of one's inheritance as a result of the advantages that prestige and income bring to members of the upper middle class.

The incomes and opportunities to accumulate wealth are high for this group in comparison with the bulk of the population. Members of this class play an active role in civic and voluntary organizations. Their occupations and incomes give them access to policy-making roles within these organizations. They are active participants in political processes and thus are major recipients of public benefits. Of all the groups studied so far, this one holds the greatest power.

Their occupations play a central role in their lives, often determining their friends as well as their business and professional associates. Their jobs allow more autonomy than jobs at any of the levels previously discussed. For the most part, they are allowed a high amount of self-direction. Members of this group tend to view their affluence, advantages, and comforts as universal rather than unique. They believe that their class includes almost everyone (Rose, 1992). They believe in the American dream of success because they have been successful.

The Upper Class

Whereas there is an abundance of studies about the working and middle classes in the United States, there is a dearth of information about the upper class. High income and wealth are necessary characteristics for entering the upper class as well as for acceptance by those persons who are already members. However, within the upper class there are great variations in the amount of wealth held by a family.

The upper class includes two groups. One group includes the individuals and families who control great inherited wealth; the other includes top-level administrators and professionals. Prestige positions, rather than great wealth, allow some families to enter or to maintain their status at this level. The upper class includes persons with top-level and highly paid positions in large banks, entertainment corporations, trade unions, state and large city governments, Congress and the executive branch, the military, and industrial corporations. It also includes those who serve as primary advisors to these leaders, for example, corporate lawyers.

The disparity between the income and wealth of members of this class as compared to members of other classes is astounding. "In 1979 the difference between the salary of corporate chief executive officers and their manufacturing employees was a multiple of 29. By 1985, the multiple stood at 40, and by 1988 *Business Week* reported that it had reached 93" (Phillips, 1990, pp. 179–180). During the 1980s, "the number of people reporting incomes of more than a half-million dollars rocketed from 16,881 to 183,240—an increase of 985 percent" (Barlett & Steele, 1992, p. 4). This increase in the size of the upper class has been due, in part, to the income received from increased rent, dividend, and interest payments available to the holders of financial assets, including property and stock.

A study of elite boarding schools attended by the upper class identified some characteristics that confirm the differences between this and the other classes. In 1985, nearly half of the students were from families with an annual income of over $100,000 (this figure is income only and does not include earnings from wealth). The wealthiest students are from Jewish, Presbyterian, Episcopalian, and Catholic backgrounds. Fifty percent of the fathers were professionals, and 40 percent were managers. Over three-fourths of the parents had finished college. "Nearly two-thirds of the fathers have attended graduate or professional school, compared to less than one-tenth of the fathers of high school seniors nationally. One-third of boarding school mothers have attended graduate or professional schools, while nationally less than one in twenty mothers of high school students have attended graduate school" (Cookson & Persell, 1985, p. 59). Families travel with their children; 69 percent of the students had traveled abroad. Books abound in the home; 51 percent had over five hundred books at home. Graduates of these schools attend elite colleges and universities at a higher rate than other students (Cookson & Persell, 1985).

Wealth and income ensure power. The extremely small proportion of the population that holds a vastly disproportionate share of the wealth also benefits disproportionately when resources are distributed. Their power allows them to protect their wealth. The only progressive tax in this country is the federal income tax, in which a greater percentage of the income is taxed as the income increases. Loopholes in the tax laws provide benefits to those whose unearned income is based on assets. What does this mean in terms of advantage to the rich? Although the 1986 tax reform law was supposedly written to eliminate many tax shelters for the rich, Parenti (1988) reported that it "channels at least 16 percent of the total tax relief to half of 1 percent of the upper-income bracket, those making $200,000 or more" (p. 101). In 1989 the average tax savings ranged from $37 for families earning under $10,000 to $281,033 for families earning over a million dollars (Barlett & Steele, 1992). Thus, while tax relief for the poorest families was less than 0.4 percent of their income, relief to the wealthy was at a rate of 28 percent, providing them more extra spending money than the other 99 percent of families earned for the year.

Power is also an important element in terms of civic and voluntary organizational involvement of the rich. They serve primarily in policy-making roles as members of boards for various organizations, colleges and universities, and corporations. "Nearly 90 percent of all U.S. cabinet officers between 1897 and 1973 were members of either the business or social elite" (Cookson & Persell, 1985, p. 200).

While the families with inherited wealth do not represent a completely closed status group, the group has an overrepresentation of Anglo, native-born, and Protestant members. They tend to intermarry with other members of the upper class. They are well educated, although a college degree is not essential. The educational mark of prestige is attendance at the elite private prep schools. For example, less than 10 percent of U.S. high school students attend private schools. Less than 1 percent of the high school population attends the elite prep schools, and these students are overwhelmingly the children of the upper class. In a study of America's elite boarding schools, Cookson and Persell (1985) found that "where a person goes to school may have little to do with his and her technical abilities, but it may have a lot to do with social abilities. . . . Where individuals go to school determines with whom they associate" (p. 16). Former President George Bush attended Phillips Andover, former Secretary of State James Baker attended Hill School, and former President John F. Kennedy attended Choate.

The upper class probably represents the most distinct and closed microcultural group of all of those studied. Cookson and Persell (1985) report that

> The founding of boarding schools in the United States was part of an upper-class "enclosure movement" that took place in the late nineteenth century. In order to insulate themselves from the rest of society, the American upper class established their own neighborhoods, churches, suburban and rural recreational retreats, and a number of social and sporting clubs. It was during this period that the Social Register was first published and, in lavish displays of conspicuous consumption, the social season was highlighted by debutante balls and charity benefits. (p. 23)

Greater assimilation of lifestyles and values has occurred within this class than any other. Although diversity exists within the group, members of the upper class may be the most homogeneous group, and they are likely to remain so as long as their cross-cultural and cross-class interactions are limited.

The Interaction of Class with Other Microcultures

Poverty is most likely to be a condition of the young, the old, minorities, women, full-time workers in the lowest-paying jobs, and the illiterate. In 1990, the federal government's poverty level was $6,652 for a one-person family and $13,359 for a four-person family. Based on this poverty threshold, there were 33.6 million poor persons in the United States, or 13.5 percent of the total population; many of these individuals were members of poor families, of which there were 7.1 million, or 10.7 percent of all families (Bureau of the Census, 1992). The poor include members of the following groups:

Group	Number	Percentage
White poor	22.3 million	10.7% of all whites
Black poor	9.8 million	31.9% of all blacks
Hispanic poor	6.0 million	28.1% of all Hispanics
Older than 65 years	3.7 million	12.2% of all such persons
Younger than 16 years	12.3 million	21.1% of all such persons
Children under 6 years	5.2 million	23.0% of all such persons
Female-headed households	17.2 million	32.4% of all such families
All other families	15.0 million	7.8% of all such families

Many poor persons do have full-time, year-round jobs but are not paid wages high enough to move their families out of poverty. "Some two million people work full time year round but live in poverty and another seven million poor individuals work full time for part of the year or in part-time jobs" (Levitan & Shapiro, 1987, p. vii). The working poor can be found in all occupational groups, but they are disproportionately located in service and agricultural occupations. "Sixteen percent of food service workers and 31 percent of farm operators and managers worked full time year round but lived in poverty" (Levitan & Shapiro, 1987, p. 29).

Although the ceiling for poverty level is supposed to indicate an income level necessary to maintain an adequate, not comfortable, living, it is misleading to assume that any family above this level can live adequately or comfortably. Many families who have incomes above this level find it difficult to pay even for essential food, housing, and clothing, let alone live comfortably by the American standard. Thus, there are probably more than fifty million persons in this country who are economically poor in the sense that they do not have enough money to purchase the necessary essentials for their families to live adequately (Harrington, 1984).

The poor are a very heterogeneous group. They do not all have the same values or lifestyles. They cannot be expected to react alike to the conditions of poverty. To many, their ethnicity or religion is the more important determinant of the way that they live within the economic constraints of poverty. To others, the effect of poverty is the greatest influence in determining their values and lifestyles. No matter what aspects of the various microcultures have the greatest impact on the lives of individuals or families, their lifestyles are limited severely by the economic constraints that keep them poor. Individual choice is more limited for persons who are poor than for any other microcultural group studied in this book.

Ethnic Inequality

African Americans, Hispanic Americans, and Native Americans experience the most severe economic deprivation of all ethnic groups in this country. Although the census data on consumer income are not broken down for American Indians, Eskimos, and Aleuts, they probably suffer more from economic inequity than any other group. Harrington (1984) describes the plight of American Indians: "Their poverty is extreme. Life expectancy is roughly twenty years less than whites; unemployment rates are stratospheric, and the 1970 census found that, on the twenty-four largest Indian reservations, 55.1 percent of the people were below the poverty line" (p. 221).

The median income of most European groups who immigrated early in this century now nearly equals or has surpassed that of the dominant group. In 1990, the median income of white families was $36,915; of black families, $21,423; and of Hispanic families, $23,431. Thus, black families have a median income that is 58 percent that of whites; Hispanics earn 63 percent of the median income of whites (Bureau of the Census, 1992). A study released in 1993 by UNESCO, which compared the standard of living of different nations, clearly showed the difference in the way most whites live as compared to blacks and Hispanics in this country. The United States was ranked sixth of the nations in the study. If the data had included only whites, we would have ranked first. Blacks would have ranked thirty-first—at the same level as an underdeveloped country (Spencer, 1993).

In 1990, when husband-wife families were compared, blacks earned 84 percent and Hispanics earned 69 percent of the median income of whites. When both wife and husband worked, the gap narrowed even more to 85 percent for blacks and 74 percent for Hispanics (Bureau of the Census, 1992). Thus, when age, education, experience, and other factors are equal to those of white men, the earnings of minorities and whites become more similar, but the income ratios between the groups still favor whites.

People of color make up a disproportionately high percentage of persons in poverty. Of the white population, 11 percent fall below the poverty level compared with 32 percent of the black population and 38 percent of the Hispanic population (Bureau of the Census, 1992). Within the Hispanic population, Puerto Ricans suffer the most (41 percent) from poverty and Cuban Americans the least (17 percent). "For whites, poverty tends to be viewed as atypical or accidental. Among blacks, it comes close to being seen as a natural outgrowth of their history and culture" (Hacker, 1992, p. 100). One reason for this may be that urban black families are more visibly segregated than white families. Seventy percent of black households are located in low-income areas. Poor white families are not as segregated in urban areas. Two-thirds of them live in the suburbs or rural areas (Hacker, 1992).

Persons of color are more likely to be unemployed and more likely to be concentrated in lower-paying jobs. Figure 2-3 shows the occupational levels of blacks and whites in 1990. The percentage of blacks in the higher-paying and higher-status jobs is much lower than that of whites, especially for men. While both absolute and relative gains in the occupational status of blacks have been made over the past thirty years, blacks are still heavily overrepresented in the semiskilled and unskilled positions.

This inequitable condition is perpetuated by a number of factors. Students of color drop out of school in greater proportions. This situation is even more dire in central-city poverty areas, where more than half of all black household heads have not finished high school (Levy, 1986). Less education results in lower-paying jobs in lower-status occupations. It often means unemployment, because such jobs offer less security than higher-status positions. Unemployment for people of color is higher than for whites; at the end of 1991, 6 percent of the white population was unemployed, compared with 12.4 percent of

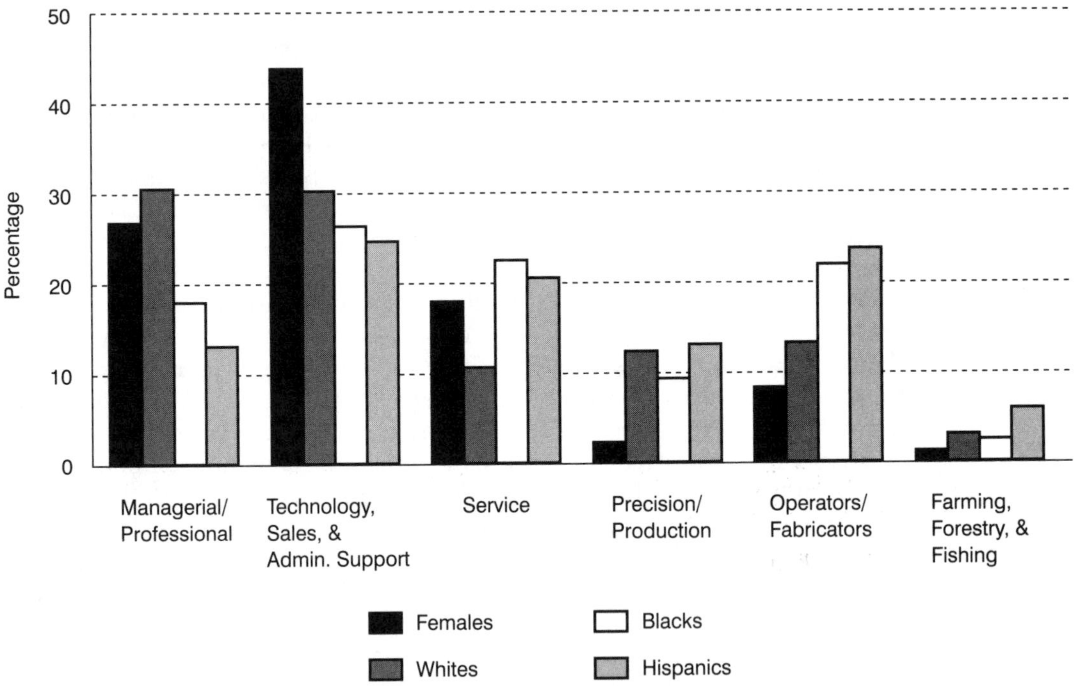

Figure 2-3. Percentage of working females, blacks, whites, and Hispanics who were employed in different occupations in 1990.

the black population and 9.9 percent of the Hispanic population. For sixteen- to nineteen-year-olds, the differences were even greater, with 16.4 percent of white, 36.3 percent of black, and 22.9 percent of Hispanic unemployed (Bureau of the Census, 1992).

The historical experiences of ethnic groups have had a great impact on a group's gains in socioeconomic status. For example, the absolute class position (income, occupation, rate of employment) of African Americans improved as a result of their migration to America's large cities during the first half of this century, and especially during the 1940s. Since then, educational attainments have narrowed the formerly enormous gap between blacks and whites with regard to completion of high school, median number of school years completed, and, to a lesser degree, prevalence of college education.

Since the 1960s, the number of African American families who have entered the middle class has increased significantly. However, the gap between the middle class and the poor has also grown. Levy (1986) found that black "men at the top of the distribution [i.e., above $25,000] were doing progressively better while blacks at the bottom [i.e., under $5,000]—between a fifth and a quarter of all black men ages twenty-five to sixty-six—were doing progressively worse" (p. 19). As a part of the move into the middle class, African Americans have increasingly moved from the inner city. "Accompanying the black middle-class exodus has been a growing movement of stable working-class blacks from ghetto neighborhoods to higher-income neighborhoods in other parts of the city and to the suburbs." These moves have left the inner city "populated almost exclusively by the most disadvantaged segments of the black urban community" (Wilson, 1987, p. 7–8).

The other oppressed groups with a disproportionately low socioeconomic status have different historical experiences from those of blacks, but suffer similarly from discrimination. Mexican Americans are highly overrepresented as farm laborers, one of the lowest-status occupations. Many Native Americans have been isolated on reservations away from all occupations except those lowest in prestige, and the numbers of such positions are limited. Thus, a highly disproportionate number of persons of color remain with a low socioeconomic status. Asian Americans, who as a group have a high educational level and a relatively high socioeconomic status, often reach middle-management positions but are seldom allowed to move into upper management. Although the most powerful class in the United States contains all ages and both genders, it does not include all ethnic, religious, and racial groups at a level equal to their representation in the population.

Gender Inequality

As a group, women earn less and are more likely to suffer from poverty than any other group, with women of color suffering the greatest oppression. The reasons for such inequality, however, have very different origins from inequality based on ethnicity. Institutional discrimination based on gender has origins in women's traditional roles as mother and wife and the assignment to jobs in which subordination has been expected. This status has limited their job opportunities and kept their wages low. Overt discrimination against women has resulted in the use of gender to determine wages, hiring, and promotion of individuals. Similar mechanisms that promote this inequality operate in regard to members of other oppressed groups.

The median income of men and women who have year-round and full-time jobs differs substantially. In 1990, the median income was $29,172 for men and $20,586 for women (Bureau of the Census, 1992). Thus, women who worked full time earned 71 cents for every $1 that a man earned—a ratio that has risen from 59 cents, where it had been for most of three decades.

Women, especially those who are the heads of households, are more likely to fall below the poverty level than men. Families maintained by women with no husband present are the most likely group to be in poverty; 32.4 percent of all persons in such families are below the official poverty level. The total number of poor families maintained by women has increased from 10.4 million in 1969 to 17.2 million in 1990 (Bureau of the Census, 1992). In 1984, 20 percent of all poor white families were headed by women; 70 percent of poor black families had a female head, as did almost 50 percent of the Hispanic households. This increase is primarily a result of an increase in divorces, separations, and out-of-wedlock births, all leading to the formation of more female-headed households.

The number of women in the workforce has increased dramatically over the past two decades. By the end of this century, it is projected that 62 percent of all women will be working in the civilian workforce as compared with 76 percent of all men. Sixty-one percent of all black women, 62 percent of white women, and 57 percent of Hispanic women will be in the workforce (Bureau of the Census, 1992). To maintain an adequate or desirable standard of living today, both the husband and wife in many families must work. The difference that two incomes makes on the family income is obvious. Although the percentages in the workforce of women who are single, widowed, divorced, or separated have increased over the past twenty years, the percentages of married women and white women in the workforce have increased dramatically since 1940. In 1940, only 16.7 percent of all married women worked outside the home; by 1991, 58.5 percent of them did. Over half of the married women with children under eighteen years old worked outside the home. Only 31 percent of all white women worked outside the home in 1947, but 57 percent of them did by 1991. These figures reveal the stagnation of groups most likely to suffer poverty (i.e., unmarried persons and persons of color), with the increases concentrated in those groups least susceptible to poverty (i.e., married white women).

Below graduate and professional school levels, the percentages of graduates at the various levels of education are similar for men and women, matching closely their percentage of the population (that is, 52 percent female and 48 percent male). In 1991, 52.4 percent of all high school graduates and 52.6 percent of all college graduates were women. In 1989, women received 40.8 percent of all law degrees, 33.2 percent of all medical degrees, and 13.6 percent of all engineering degrees (Bureau of the Census, 1992). However, compared with the earnings of men with the same education, women still earn less.

Historically, there has been a fairly rigid sexual division of labor. The roles of women were limited to reproduction, child rearing, and homemaking. When they did work outside the home, the jobs often were similar to roles in the home, that is, caring for children or the sick. Jobs were stereotyped by gender. As recently as 1991, women composed over 85 percent of the workforce in the following occupations (Bureau of the Census, 1992):

Dental hygienists	99.8%
Secretaries	99.0%
Prekindergarten/kindergarten teachers	98.7%
Dental assistants	98.2%
Child care workers	96.0%
Licensed practical nurses	95.0%
Receptionists	97.1%
Cleaners and servants	95.8%
Typists	95.1%
Registered nurses	94.8%
Welfare service aides	94.7%
Health record technologists	93.9%
Dieticians	93.7%
Teachers' aides	93.1%
Bookkeepers, accounting, audit clerks	91.5%
Bank tellers	90.3%
Hairdressers and cosmetologists	90.2%
Sewing and stitching workers	89.2%
Telephone operators	89.2%
Data entry keyers	86.0%
Elementary school teachers	85.9%

These jobs are accompanied by neither high prestige nor high income. Those that fall in the category of professional (that is, teachers and nurses) do not compete in income or prestige with architects and engineers. Figure 2-3 outlined the job categories in which women participate. Note that women continue to be overrepresented as clerical and service workers and underrepresented as managers and skilled workers.

Women as individuals are assigned a lower status than men in the stratification system of this country. The occupations most open to women are the low-status and low-paying ones. One-third of the women who maintain their own households without a husband are below the official poverty level. Many women, particularly nonworking married women, are economically dependent on men. They are powerless in that they do not hold direct power over their own lives. Even with the same education and occupation as men, women typically do not receive the same income or prestige as their male counterparts.

Age Inequality

The highest incidence of poverty occurs at both ends of the life span. Children and persons over sixty-five years old are at ages that society has determined to be nonworking periods. The poverty rate for persons at both ends of the life span is much greater than for all other ages and is shown in Figure 2-4.

Men between the ages of forty-five and fifty-four earn more than at any other period in their lives; women earn their maximum between the ages of thirty-five and forty-four. The median income of persons who are fourteen to nineteen years old is lower than for any other group, primarily because most of these persons are just beginning to enter the workforce at the end of this period and may not enter for several more years, especially if they attend college. Income then increases steadily for most persons until after they reach fifty-five years of age. The income of women remains fairly constant throughout much of their working life, whereas the income for a large percentage of men increases dramatically during their lifetime.

"Although 20 percent of American children live in poverty this year, it is estimated that 45 percent of white children and 85 percent of black children will experience poverty while growing up" (Rose, 1992, p. 23). Children's class status depends on their family, and they have little or no control over their destiny during their early years. Weissbourd (1992) reports that:

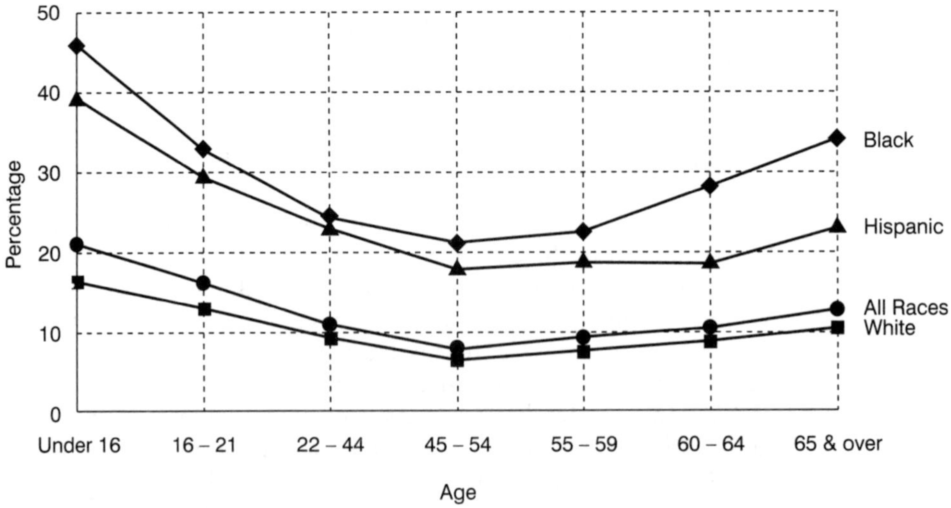

Figure 2-4. Percentage of persons in poverty by age and ethnicity in 1986.

> The number of these children who are unhealthy, malnourished, uneducated, and homeless runs startlingly high. Family disintegration, abuse and neglect, and transience—problems that damage children in every economic class—also beset these children disproportionately. Although many poor children will overcome these assaults, high numbers will bail out of school or abuse drugs. Smaller but still large numbers will become parents too early or commit crimes. Millions, suffering severe vulnerabilities and lacking rudimentary skills, will fail to obtain jobs or to create stable families of their own. We now commonly speak of "losing" a wide band of poor children—to early death, to lengthy incarceration, to joblessness, to one form of misery or another. (p. 6)

Children born in poor families will be disadvantaged in developing their adult earning power by inferior schooling, an oppressive financial environment, and poor health. Once they enter the adult world, they may be able to earn an adequate income to keep themselves and their children out of poverty.

The presence of children in families headed by women is the basis of high poverty rates among women and children in such families. The poverty rate rises as the number of children in a low-income family increases. Contrary to popular belief, however, there is no tendency for low-income families to have more children than those families higher on the income scale.

To prevent poverty after sixty-five years of age, individuals must plan throughout their working life to defer or save income that can be used for support once they stop earning a regular income. Social Security benefits provide some support to the elderly, and often these may be the only support available. Some workers participate in pension plans that provide an income after a lifetime of work, but many employees, especially blue-collar and low-level white-collar workers, still do not have the opportunity to participate in such programs. Therefore, over 12 percent of all persons older than sixty-five have an income under the poverty level (Bureau of the Census, 1992).

In a society in which high ranking is given individuals who either control wealth or are productive in the labor force, persons who do not contribute to this production are assigned a low status. Many elderly persons receive financial and medical support from the government, making them nonproductive drawers of the nation's wealth. Often they are accorded little deference and instead face impatience, patronization, and neglect by persons still in the workforce.

Class Identification

Most Americans, if asked, could identify themselves by class. Whereas they do not strongly vocalize their identity with a specific class, they participate socially and occupationally within a class structure. Their behavior and value system may be based on a strong ethnic or religious identification, but that specific identification is greatly influenced by class as well. For example, although the professional Italian American family may share the ethnic ethos of the blue-collar Italian American family, the professional family will be more likely to interact primarily with other professional families of Italian American descent and of other ethnic origins instead of interacting with Italian Americans at a different class level. Many of their primary relationships may be with other Italian Americans, but these will be developed at the same socioeconomic level. The first generation of a group that has moved to the middle class may continue to interact at a primary level with friends and relatives who are in the working class and underclass. However, time and differences in circumstances often lead to the reduction of those cross-class ties.

Most Americans exhibit and articulate less concern about class consciousness than many of their European counterparts. Nevertheless, many have participated in class actions like strikes or work stoppages to further the interests of the class to which they belong (Vanneman & Cannon, 1987). Class consciousness, or solidarity with others at the same socioeconomic level, may not be so pronounced here because there has been overall improvement in the standard of living at all levels, especially during the period from 1940 to the early 1970s. In addition, American cultural values and belief systems emphasize the individual's personal responsibility for his or her class position.

Class consciousness is probably strongest and most developed among the upper class, perhaps the only group that sees the value of solidarity in the protection and maintenance of their power and privilege. Fissures within all other classes in terms of income, occupation, ethnicity, race, and gender prevent coalition around socioeconomic concerns.

In the classroom, teachers are likely to find students from diverse socioeconomic backgrounds. Unless one teaches in a private preparatory school, the teacher is unlikely to find children of the upper class in the classroom. Students may not identify themselves as members of a specific class, but they can identify the factors that determine their socioeconomic status. They usually know the occupation of their parents, the area of the city in which they live, the amount of education of their parents, the amount of education that they plan to seek, and their parents' involvement or noninvolvement in civic and other organizations. Even more important in determining class status are ethnicity, age, and sex. These factors will continue to influence unequal socioeconomic outcomes until institutional discrimination is overcome.

Students, like everyone else, tend to interact most with other students with whom they feel most comfortable. In most instances, the significant peer group will include students from the same socioeconomic level and the same or similar ethnic background. They share the same cultural values and patterns and have been influenced similarly by socioeconomic conditions and environments beyond their control. They have learned to react to the environment in a similar way.

Educational Implications

Many social reformers, educators, and parents view education as a powerful device for achieving social change and the reduction of poverty. From the beginning of the public school movement in the early nineteenth century, low incomes of the poor were believed to result from inadequate education. Discrimination in employment and housing was blamed on the lack of education in other segments of the population. This view was still pervasive in the 1960s as the federal government attempted to eliminate poverty through the establishment and funding of Head Start, Title I (compensatory education), Upward Bound, Job Corps, Neighborhood Youth Corps, and other educational programs. However, test scores of students from oppressed groups have not appeared to improve and racial/ethnic segregation between and within schools has increased.

This lack of progress in overcoming the effects of poverty on students should not suggest that educational reforms are not worthwhile. Some changes make schooling more attractive to students and even increase the achievement of many individual students; educational resources also become more equitably distributed. Nevertheless, the intended goal of increasing income equity and eliminating poverty has not been realized. Different sociohistorical interpretations of education explain the role of schools in society and the degree to which this goal and others are met. Two views are prevalent. One assumes that the schools can be an agent of social reform and improve the chances of economic success for its graduates. The second view assumes that schools exist as an agent of the larger social, economic, and political context, with the goal of inculcating the values necessary to maintain the current socioeconomic and political systems.

Supporters of the first view are much more benign in their description of the role of schools in helping students become socially mobile. They are optimistic that social reform can be achieved by providing poor students with more effective schools. Others see schools as preparing students to work efficiently at appropriate levels in corporate organizations. The needs of business and industry are met "by developing lower-class children to be better workers and middle-class ones to be better managers in the corporate economy and by reproducing the social relations of production in the schools to inculcate children with values and norms supportive of capitalist work organizations" (Carnoy & Levin, 1976, p. 10). Students are tracked in courses for either college or vocational preparation. The curriculum sorts and selects children so that children of blue-collar or unemployed workers and children of the elite will be socialized for jobs that they later will hold. Thus, rather than providing equal educational opportunity, schools perpetuate existing social and economic inequities in society.

This condition is further exacerbated by the fact that the current system for funding schools mirrors these inequities. Students in rich and poor schools experience very different kinds of education and environments in which learning is to occur. It is little wonder that the gap in academic achievement in such different schools is so great. Kozol observes that "to use the local property tax as even a portion of school funding is unjust because it will always benefit the children of the most privileged people" (Scherer, 1993, p. 6). Through the schools, wealthy and upper-middle-class parents are able to pass on their economic advantages.

Teacher Expectations and Tracking

Students in most classrooms will be heterogeneous in terms of ethnicity, gender, religion, and conditions of disability. The teacher may not be able to easily identify a student's class or socioeconomic level. Too often, however, teachers do classify their students by class and assign certain expectations to them based on perceived class status. Students who are not easily recognized as from the middle class often are viewed as academically inferior and expected to exhibit disruptive classroom behavior. Most of these students are harmed by such expectations. In contrast, students from the upper middle class usually benefit from a teacher's judgments because they are expected to perform better in school, are treated more favorably, and do perform at a higher level in most cases.

"Patterns of lower achievement and underparticipation for minorities and poor children begin early in the educational process. And perhaps most troublesome is that the discrepancies among groups grow larger the longer children remain in school" (Oakes, 1987, p. 3). Differences in mathematics and science achievement based on class and race are found by age nine, but are clearly in place by age thirteen. In junior high school, students from oppressed groups typically take fewer courses in mathematics and science, which contributes to later differences in college enrollments and vocational choices. In many schools with large minority and poor populations, advanced courses in these subjects are often not even offered. Thus, even those students who are achieving at a level equal to students from the dominant group are further stifled in their attempts to achieve equitably. "The existence of these discrepancies does document that schools have been considerably less successful with some groups of students than with others" (Oakes, 1987, p. 3).

In an early ethnographic study of an inner-city school, Rist (1970) documented how students are classified, segregated, and taught differently starting with their first days in school. Most teachers can identify those personal characteristics of students that will lead to academic success. They then develop instruction and interaction with their students that ensure that the students will, in fact, behave as the teachers expect—a phenomenon called the *self-fulfilling prophecy*. Rist found that a kindergarten teacher was able to divide students into three reading and mathematics groups as early as the eighth day of school. While such groupings may be helpful in providing the most effective instruction to students who enter the classroom with different skills, the researcher found that the groups were organized by nonacademic factors. Students in the highest group were all dressed in clean clothes that were relatively new and well pressed; they interacted well with the teacher and other students; they were quite verbal and used standard English; and they came from "better families." Students in the lower two groupings were poorly dressed and often in dirty clothes; they frequently carried the odor of urine; they used black dialect; and their families were less stable than those of students in the highest group. Throughout the year, the teacher interacted more with the students in the highest group than with either of the other groups. This division of students and the teacher's differing degrees of involvement with the three groups continued through the second grade, at which time the study ended. Students in the highest group continually performed better academically and behaved in a more acceptable manner than students in the other two groups. As the kindergarten teacher had projected, these students were more successful in school than the students from lower socioeconomic levels.

When teachers make such judgments about students, they are taking the first step in preventing students from having an equal opportunity for academic achievement. Rather than ensuring that students have access to an egalitarian system, such classification and subsequent treatment of students ensure the maintenance of an inequitable system. This action is not congruent with the democratic belief that all students should have equal educational opportunities.

Educational researchers continue to find that simply being in the low-ability group diminishes students' achievement. Such students are provided fewer and less effective opportunities to learn than other students. Critical thinking tasks are reserved for the high-ability groups. Oral recitation and structured written work are common in low-ability groups. Students are exposed to low-status knowledge at a slower pace than their peers in higher-ability groups, helping them fall further behind in subjects like mathematics, foreign languages, and sciences (Gamoran & Berends, 1987).

Teachers in low-ability classrooms spend more time on administration and discipline and less time actually teaching. As one might expect, student behavior in low tracks is more disruptive than in higher-level groups, but this probably happens in part because students and teachers have developed behavioral standards more tolerant of inattention rather than because of the students' individual abilities (Peterson, Wilkinson, & Hallinan, 1984). To compound the problem, the more experienced and more successful teachers are disproportionately assigned to the higher-ability groups. Unfortunately, teachers generally view high-track students positively and low-track students negatively (Gamoran & Berends, 1987).

Disproportionately large numbers of students from lower socioeconomic levels are assigned to low-ability groups beginning very early in their school careers. The long-term effects are similar to those that Rist found in the 1960s. These students are seen by teachers as less able academically, assigned to a low-ability track, and perhaps condemned to that level for the rest of their academic lives (Peterson et al., 1984). Even more tragic is the fact that the number of students from low socioeconomic levels classified as mentally retarded is disproportionately high. This type of classification causes double jeopardy for students of color because they also disproportionately suffer from poverty. After an extensive review of the literature on tracking and conducting his own research, Gamoran (1992) concluded that "grouping and tracking rarely add to overall achievement in a school, but they often contribute to inequality. . . . Typically, it means that high-track students are gaining and low-track students are falling further behind" (p. 13).

How can we prevent the development of negative and harmful expectations for students? Teachers, counselors, and administrators must be aware that they can consciously fall into such behavior because they have learned that poverty is the fault of the individual. As a result, students are blamed for circumstances beyond their control. Instead, we should see as a challenge the opportunity to provide these students with the knowledge and skills to overcome poverty. Educators should select approaches that they would use for the most gifted students (Wheelock, 1992). The goal should be to *level up* the educational experiences for the students who previously would have been tracked into the low-ability classes.

It is helpful to systematically evaluate interactions with students. Such evaluations should indicate whether certain students are receiving more of the teacher's attention or are being encouraged to participate in the learning process to a greater degree. Necessary corrections in instructional methods and student-teacher interactions can then be made to ensure that all students in the classroom have access to one's best teaching skills.

In overcoming the stigma of being poor, educators must consciously review their expectations for students. Homeless students often do not go to school because they are so embarrassed by their inability to shower daily or dress appropriately. Teachers must figure out strategies to ensure that they do not further exacerbate the students' feelings of low esteem. Seeing students as individuals rather than members of a specific socioeconomic group also may assist the educator in overcoming class biases that may exist in the school and the community. Information about a student's family background can be used to understand the power of environment on a student's expression of self; it must not be used to rationalize stereotypes and label students (Lightfoot, 1983). Educators must be aware of any prejudices that they themselves hold against members of lower socioeconomic groups. Otherwise, discriminatory practices will surface in the classroom in the form of self-fulfilling prophecies that harm students and perpetuate societal inequities.

Finally, in inner-city schools, the educator will face large numbers of poor and working-class students whose environment outside the school is very dissimilar from that of students in most suburban schools. Isolated rural areas require families to respond to their nonschool environment much differently than families in other areas. Educators should not expect to be able to teach every student effectively in the same way. Equal education does not mean that

Some inner-city schools are squeezed between office buildings and housing units, leaving small playgrounds that differ greatly from those in suburban and rural areas.

the same instructional strategies must be used to teach all students. While it is essential to ensure that all students learn the basic skills, how the educator teaches these skills may vary, depending on the environment in which students live—a factor greatly dependent on the family's socioeconomic status.

Curriculum for Equality

The discussion so far has focused on teachers' expectations for students based on socioeconomic status. However, the curriculum should also reflect accurately the class structure and inequities that exist in the United States. Too often, "the voice of democracy, participation, and equality is being muted" (Apple, 1988, p. 27).

The curriculum and the textbooks focus on the values and experiences of a middle-class society. They highlight the heroes of our capitalist system and emphasize the importance of developing the skills to earn an income to enable students to soon own the home, the car, and the furniture and appliances that have become the symbols of middle-class living. They often ignore the history and heroes of the labor struggle in this country. The inequities based on the income and wealth of one's family are usually neither described nor discussed. In classrooms, students should learn of the existence of these discrepancies.

They should understand that the majority of the population does not live the American dream.

Often overlooked are the experiences brought to the classroom by students. School is definitely not the only place in which students learn about life. Differences in school behavior and knowledge among students from dissimilar socioeconomic levels are strongly dependent on the knowledge and skills needed to survive appropriately in their community environments. Most poor students, especially those in urban areas, have learned how to live in a world that is not imaginable to most middle-class students or teachers. Yet the knowledge and skills that they bring to school are not valued by teachers and a system with a middle-class orientation. Educators must recognize the value of the community's informal education in sustaining its own culture and realize that formal education is often viewed as undermining that culture (Lightfoot, 1983).

The curriculum does not serve students well if it reflects only the perspective of middle-class America. Students need to see some of their own cultural experiences reflected in the curriculum. They need to be helped to see themselves as desirable and integral members of the school community rather than as second-class citizens who must learn the ways of the more economically advantaged to succeed even in school.

Educators should become cognizant of the materials, films, and books used in class. If students never see their communities in these instructional materials, their motivation and acceptance are likely to be limited. All students should be encouraged to read novels and short stories about people from different socioeconomic levels. When studying historical or current events, they should examine the event from the perspective of those in poverty as well as from the perspective of our country's leaders. Teaching can be enhanced by drawing examples from experiences with which students are familiar, even if they are different from the teacher's own experiences.

Instruction should show that not all persons share equally in material things in this country, but that all persons have potential to be developed. All students, no matter what their socioeconomic status, must be helped to develop strong and positive self-concepts. Many students do not realize the diversity that exists in this country, let alone understand the reasons for the diversity. Most middle-class children, especially those of white-collar and professional levels, believe that most persons are as well off as they are. As educators, we are expected to expand our students' knowledge of the world, not to hide from them the realities that exist because of class differences.

In a classroom in which democracy and equity are important, social justice should inform the curriculum. The curriculum should affirm the validity of points of view of oppressed groups, even though they may differ from those of the teacher. The interests of the poorest students should be the most privileged. These students should receive priority time from teachers and have access to the necessary resources to become academically competitive with middle-class students (McCarthy, 1990). "According to our textbook rhetoric,

Americans abhor the notion of a social order in which economic privilege and political power are determined by hereditary class. . . . By this standard, education offered to poor children should be at least as good as that which is provided to the children of the upper-middle class" (Kozol, 1991b, p. 207).

Finally, students should be encouraged to be critical of what they read, see, and hear in textbooks, through the mass media, and from their parents and friends. The curriculum should encourage the development of critical thinking and problem-solving skills. Unfortunately, schools traditionally have talked about our democratic vision, but have been unwilling to model it. Students and teachers who become involved through the curriculum in asking why the inequities in society exist are beginning to practice democracy.

Compensatory Education

The most common strategy for working with economically disadvantaged students has been compensatory education. In this program, extra resources are made available to schools to help overcome the educational deficiencies of poor students and increase their academic achievement. It is based, in part, on the belief that students from the lower socioeconomic levels do not learn as quickly or as well as other students and that their families have been unable to provide an intellectually stimulating environment that will assist them in school. It focuses on school readiness and academic performance. The underlying belief is that "if only practitioners could help boost the academic performance of subordinated minority youth, black students could pull even with their white counterparts. The future of the former would be secure. The problems associated with racial inequality would go away" (McCarthy, 1990, p. 33).

Compensatory programs are most often remedial in nature to help students catch up with their middle-class counterparts. Carnoy and Levin (1976) recommend a positive alternative to current compensatory education programs. Their strategy contradicts the theory of poor and good learners and instead assumes that learning is conditional:

> All groups of children can learn equally well but under different conditions. We may find that children's motivation is affected much more by the structure of the learning environment than by the number of years of teacher's academic preparation. The low probability of success of compensatory programs within the existing framework points to the need for new educational strategies for ethnic and racial minorities if equality is to be achieved. The solution may be to change schooling for all children and to create an educational process that does not preconceive social roles or even clearly define what or how a child must learn. This process would require new kinds of tests to measure results and a different kind of teacher to produce them. Education of this type could allow a child's own stereotypes of himself [herself] and others to be destroyed and be replaced by personal relationships. The alternative strategy, then, creates equality among groups of children, by building an educational structure that allows children to express themselves in various ways, all equally acceptable. (pp. 215-216)

Summary

Socioeconomic status (SES) is a composite of the economic status of a family or unrelated individuals based on income, wealth, occupation, educational attainment, and power. It is a means of measuring inequalities based on economic differences and the manner in which families live as a result of their economic well-being. Families' socioeconomic statuses range from the indigent poor to the very rich. Where a family falls along this continuum affects the manner in which its members live, how they think and act, and the way in which others react to them. Persons who share the same class form a microculture. Although a family may participate actively in other microcultural groups centered around ethnicity, religion, gender, exceptionality, language, or age, the class to which the family belongs is probably the strongest factor in determining differences among groups.

Social stratification is possible because consistent and recurring relationships exist between people who occupy different levels of the social structure. Minorities, women, young and old people, and disabled individuals are disproportionately represented at the low end of our social stratification system.

The United States can be divided into a number of classes based on their income and occupation. In this chapter, the following classes were described: underclass, working class, middle class, and upper class. The income and wealth that keeps families at one of these levels varies greatly. Individual choice is most limited for those persons who are poor and who often can barely meet essential needs. Whereas ethnic and religious diversity exists at all levels, the upper class is the most homogeneous. Minorities and women who head families are overly represented in the underclass, working class, and lower middle class.

One's socioeconomic level has a dramatic influence on how one is able to live, but U.S. citizens exhibit and articulate less concern about class consciousness than their European counterparts. Although they may not verbalize their class identification, most of their primary relations are conducted within the same class. Class consciousness is strongest among the upper classes, whose members know the value of solidarity in the protection and maintenance of their power and privilege.

Disproportionately large numbers of students from lower levels of socioeconomic status are assigned to low-ability groups in their early school years. Educators must consciously review their expectations for students and their behavior toward students from different levels of socioeconomic status to ensure that they are not discriminating. Instructional methods and teaching strategies may vary greatly, depending on the environment in which students live. What is essential is that all students be provided a quality education.

Educators also need to pay attention to the curriculum. Too often, poor students are placed in remedial programs because of discriminatory testing and placement. In addition, the curriculum does not serve students well if it reflects only the perspective of middle-class America. Students need to see some of their own cultural values reflected in the curriculum in addition to learning about the cultural values of others.

Questions for Review

1. What factors promote social stratification, and how do they do it?
2. Describe the different social stratification and class theories discussed in this chapter, indicating how they differ from each other.
3. Explain why the United States is not the model of egalitarianism that many believe it to be.
4. Develop an argument against the statement, "Social mobility is possible for anyone who works hard enough."
5. Describe the mythical middle class, and explain why it does not match reality.
6. Why are blue-collar workers often called the working class?
7. What socioeconomic factors make it difficult for members of the underclass to improve their conditions?
8. Why did the authors separate the middle class into two distinct categories?
9. Contrast the two perspectives on why the schools have not been able to eliminate poverty.
10. Define the self-fulfilling prophecy, and explain why it is appropriately addressed in a chapter on class.

References

Apple, M. W. (1988). *Teachers and texts: A political economy of class and gender relations in education.* New York: Routledge.

Auletta, K. (1982). *The underclass.* New York: Random House.

Barlett, D. L., & Steele, J. B. (1992). *America: What went wrong?* Kansas City: Andrews and McMeel.

Beeghley, L. (1978). *Social stratification in America: A critical analysis of theory and research.* Santa Monica, CA: Goodyear.

Bureau of the Census. (1992). *Statistical Abstract of the United States, 1992* (108th ed.). Washington, DC: Government Printing Office.

Carnoy, M., & Levin, H. M. (1976). *The limits of educational reform.* New York: McKay.

Cookson, P. W., & Persell, C. H. (1985). *Preparing for power: America's elite boarding schools.* New York: Basic Books.

Gamoran, A. (1992). Is ability grouping equitable? *Educational Leadership, 50*(2), 11–17.

Gamoran, A., & Berends, M. (1987, Winter). The effects of stratification in secondary schools: Synthesis of survey and ethnographic research. *Review of Educational Research, 57*(4), 415–435.

Gorder, C. (1988). *Homeless!: Without addresses in America: The social crisis of the decade.* Tempe, AZ: Blue Bird.

Hacker, A. (1992). *Two nations: Black and white, separate, hostile, unequal.* New York: Ballantine.

Harrington, M. (1984). *The new American poverty.* New York: Holt, Rinehart & Winston.

Hodgkinson, H. (1986). *The schools we need for the kids we've got.* Paper presented at the 1987 annual meeting of the American Association of Colleges for Teacher Education.

Kozol, J. (1991). Introduction. In *Outside the dream: Child poverty in America.* (1991). New York: Aperture Foundation.

Kozol, J. (1991). *Savage inequalities: Children in America's schools.* New York: Crown.

Levitan, S. A., & Shapiro, I. (1987). *Working but poor.* Baltimore: The Johns Hopkins University Press.

Levy, F. (1986). *Poverty and economic growth.* Unpublished manuscript, University of Maryland, School of Public Affairs, College Park, MD.

Lewis, M. (1978). *The culture of inequality.* Amherst, MA: University of Massachusetts Press.

Lewis, O. (1969). *A death in the Sanchez family.* New York: Random House.

Liebow, E. (1967). *Tally's corner: A study of Negro street corner men.* Boston: Little, Brown.

Lightfoot, S. L. (1983). *The good high school: Portraits of character and culture.* New York: Basic Books.

Linehan, M. F. (1992). Children who are homeless: Educational strategies for school personnel. *Phi Delta Kappan, 74*(1), 61–66.

McCarthy, C. (1990). *Race and curriculum: Social inequality and the theories and politics of difference in contemporary research on schooling.* New York: Falmer Press.

Oakes, J. (1987, April). *Race, class, and school responses to "ability": Interactive influences on math and science outcomes.* Paper presented at the annual meeting of the American Educational Research Association, Washington, DC.

Parenti, M. (1988). *Democracy for the few* (5th ed.). New York: St. Martin's Press.

Perlman, R. (1976). *The economics of poverty.* New York: McGraw-Hill.

Peterson, P., Wilkinson, L. C., & Hallinan, M. (Eds.). (1984). *The social context of instruction: Group organization and group processes.* New York: Academic Press.

Phillips, K. P. (1990). *The politics of rich and poor.* New York: Random House.

Rist, R. C. (1970). Student social class and teacher expectations: The self-fulfilling prophecy in ghetto education. *Harvard Educational Review, 40*(3), 70–110.

Rose, S. J. (1992). *Social stratification in the United States.* New York: New Press.

Rothman, R. A. (1978). *Inequality and stratification in the United States.* Englewood Cliffs, NJ: Prentice-Hall.

Scherer, M. (1993). On savage inequalities: A conversation with Jonathan Kozol. *Educational Leadership, 50*(4), 4–9.

Spencer, R. (May 18, 1993). U.S. ranks 6th in quality of life; Japan is 1st. *The Washington Post,* A7.

Valentine, C. A. (1968). *Culture and poverty: Critique and counter-proposals.* Chicago: The University of Chicago Press.

Vanneman, R., & Cannon, L. W. (1987). *The American perception of class.* Philadelphia: Temple University Press.

Weissbourd, R. (1992). Making the system work for poor children. *Equity and Choice, 8*(2), 5–15.

Wheelock, A. (1992). The case for untracking. *Educational Leadership, 50*(2), 6–10.

Wilson, W. J. (1987). *The truly disadvantaged: The inner city, the underclass, and public policy.* Chicago: The University of Chicago Press.

Suggested Readings

Knapp, M. S., & Turnbull, B. J. (January 1990). *Better schooling for the children of poverty: Alternatives to conventional wisdom.* Washington, DC: U. S. Department of Education.

This report summarizes the findings of a study of teaching and learning in the elementary grades in high poverty schools. It examines the effective academic instruction found in high-performing classrooms in schools serving high concentrations of poor children and identifies school and district conditions that facilitate effective instruction.

Kozol, J. (1988). *Rachel and her children: Homeless families in America.* New York: Crown.

This chronicle of the lives of homeless families headed by women provides descriptions of life in emergency shelters and welfare hotels and the humiliation felt by these women and their children.

Kozol, J. (1991). *Savage inequalities: Children in America's schools.* New York: Crown.

These descriptions of rich and poor schools are a powerful statement on the class and racial inequities that exist in this country. Interwoven with the stories of students and educators is an analysis of the inadequacy of the current funding of schools.

Lightfoot, S. L. (1983). *The good high school: Portraits of character and culture.* New York: Basic Books.

This book includes the portraits of six exemplary U.S. high schools, including two inner-city schools, two upper-middle-class suburban schools, and two elite prep schools. The personalities of principals, teachers, and students, teaching styles, curricula and school climate are described.

Linehan, M. F. (1992). Children who are homeless: Educational strategies for school personnel. *Phi Delta Kappan, 74*(1), 61–66.

The conditions and effects of homelessness on children are described along with useful intervention strategies that can be used by educators.

Outside the dream: Child poverty in America. (1991). New York: Aperture Foundation.

This collection of photographs captures the meaning of poverty for children, men, and women who are caught in its web. The foreword by Jonathan Kozol, afterword by Marian Wright Edelman, and accompanying notes describe the plight of being poor in this country.

Parenti, M. (1988). *Democracy for the few* (5th ed.). New York: St. Martin's Press.

This analysis of class inequality in the United States examines the role of politics and government in maintaining inequalities.

Peterson, P., Wilkinson, L. C., & Hallinan, M. (Eds.). (1984). *The social context of instruction: Group organization and group processes.* New York: Academic Press.

This collection of research papers addresses ability grouping, tracking of students, influence of group culture on student behavior, independent and group learning, peer interaction in the learning process, and teacher expectations. Questions about the value of tracking and ability groups for so-called low-ability students are raised.

Rose, S. J. (1992). *Social stratification in the United States.* New York: New Press.

This booklet, and accompanying poster, compiles and analyzes data on income, wealth, race, and marital and occupational status. The poster and its discussion provide a vivid description of the U.S. social structure.

Vanneman, R., & Cannon, L. W. (1987). *The American perception of class.* Philadelphia: Temple University Press.

This analysis of class consciousness in the United States empirically refutes the myth that Americans are not class- conscious. It examines class theory, the social psychology of stratification, and the interaction of class with gender and race.

CHAPTER 3

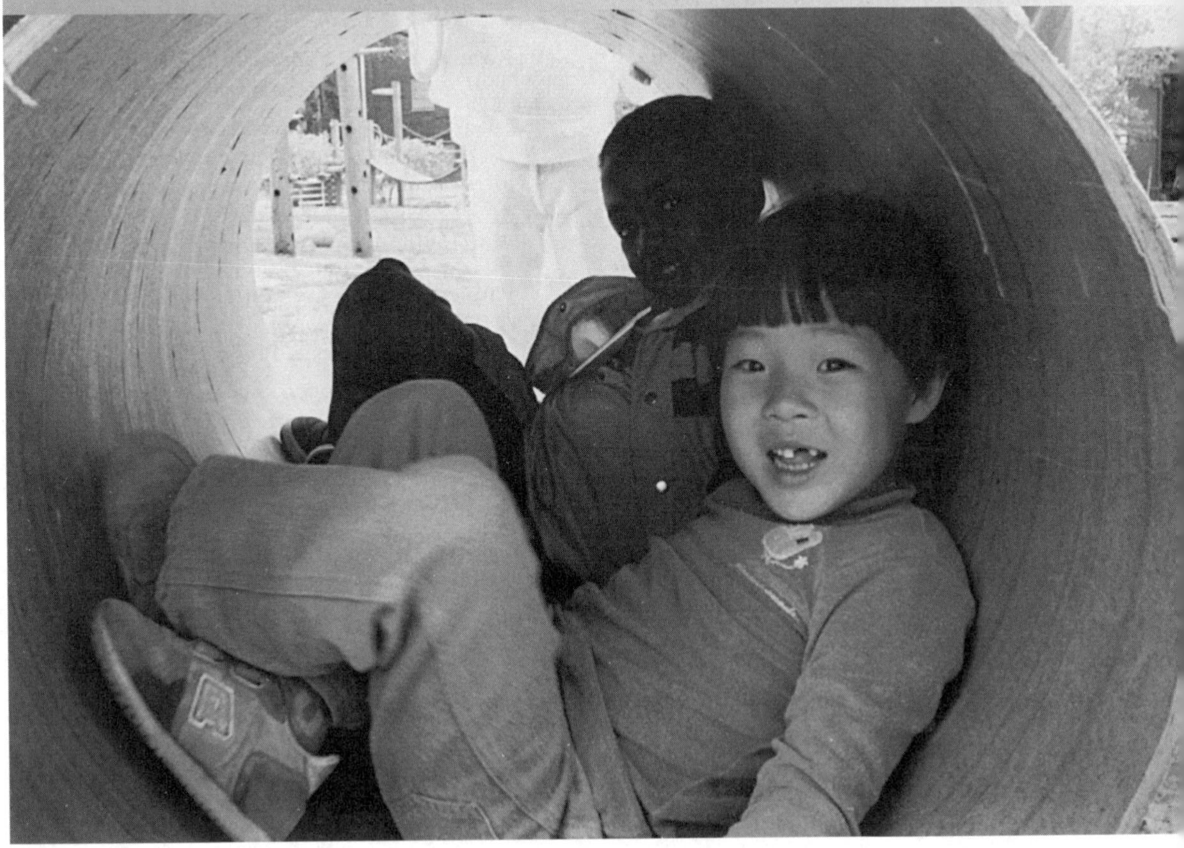

Ethnicity and Race

Ellen Kuhn has become increasingly aware of the racial tension in the high school in which she teaches, but she was not ready for the hostility that erupted between some black and white students that Friday. In the week that followed, the faculty decided that they had to do more to help students develop positive interethnic and interracial relations. They established a committee to identify consultants and other resources to guide them in this effort.

However, Ms. Kuhn felt that neither she nor her students could wait for months to receive a report from the committee. She was about ready to introduce the civil rights movement in her eleventh-grade social studies class. It seemed a perfect time to promote better cross-cultural communications. She decided that she would let students talk about their feelings.

She soon learned that this topic was not an easy one to handle. African American students expressed their anger at the discriminatory practices in the school and the community. Most European American students did not believe that there was any discrimination. They believed that there were no valid reasons for the anger and that if they just followed the rules and worked harder, they would not have these problems. She felt that the class was getting nowhere. In fact, some-

times the anger on both sides was so intense that she worried that a physical fight would erupt. She was frustrated that the class discussions and activities were not helping students correct their stereotypes and prejudices. At times, she thought that the students were just becoming more entrenched in them. She wondered if there was anything that she could do in her class to improve understanding, empathy, and communications across groups.

What may be happening in a school to contribute to racial or ethnic disruptions? Why does so much misunderstanding between students from different ethnic backgrounds develop in some schools? What ethnic group has the greatest impact on the school curriculum and activities? How can a classroom reflect the ethnic diversity of its students? What were the positive and negative outcomes of the steps taken by Ms. Kuhn? What would you have done to improve cross-cultural relations among class members?

The Expansion of Ethnic Diversity

All of us could trace our ancestry to one or more nations that existed at one time in history. In the United States, the indigenous Native American people make up less than one percent of the total population. The majority of Americans are recent immigrants or have ancestors who were immigrants. According to the Harvard Encyclopedia of American Ethnic Groups, this nation is composed of at least 276 different ethnic groups, including 170 different Native American groups.

For those of us whose families emigrated here over the past four hundred years, the reasons for coming have varied greatly. Most Africans originally were imported involuntarily to this country to provide labor for an expanding southern agricultural economy. Many immigrants in the nineteenth and twentieth centuries voluntarily came to the United States to escape oppressive political, religious, or economic conditions. At the same time, they were often recruited to meet the expanding labor needs of a developing industrial nation. Some of today's immigrants come to join family members who have already settled here. Others are fleeing oppressive conditions in their native countries, and still others are seeking the perceived advantages of U.S. citizenship.

Many of us forget that the United States was already populated by the time Europeans arrived on its shores. As more and more foreigners arrived, Native Americans were not treated as equal citizens in the formation of the new nation. Eventually, most Native Americans were forced into segregation from the dominant group and, in many cases, moved from their geographical homeland to reservations in other parts of the country, leading to a pattern of isolation that still exists today.

Although most of the first European settlers were English, the French, the Dutch, and the Spanish also established early settlements. After the consolidation and development of the United States as an independent state, successive waves of western Europeans joined the earlier settlers. Irish, Swedish, and German immigrants often came to escape economic impoverishment or political repression in the countries of origin. These early European settlers brought with them the political institutions that provided the framework for our government. The melding of their cultures over time became the dominant culture to which other immigrant groups strived or were forced to assimilate later.

People of African descent have been a part of the American experience from the early days of colonization. The thousands of Africans who were kidnapped and sold into bondage underwent a process that was quite different from that of the Asian and European immigrants who voluntarily emigrated. Separated from their families and homelands, robbed of their freedom and culture, they developed a new culture out of their different African heritages and unique experiences in this country.

Initially, the majority of African Americans lived in the South. Even after the Civil War, they remained the majority population in many counties across the southern states. However, in this century, large numbers of African Americans migrated to northern, eastern, and western cities. This migration was generally fueled by the same factors that brought eastern and southern Europeans to the United States—the need for labor in industrial jobs.

Another factor that contributed to this migration was the racism and political terror that existed in much of the South at that time. Even today a racial ideology is implicit in the policies and practices of our institutions. It also continues to block significant assimilation of many African Americans into the dominant society. Although the civil rights movement of the 1960s reduced the political barriers that prevented most African Americans from enjoying the advantages of the middle class, the number of African Americans who remain in poverty is disproportionately high. At the same time, the number of families and individuals who have been able to join the ranks of the middle class has increased dramatically over the past twenty-five years.

Mexican Americans also occupy a unique role in the formation of the United States. Spain was the first European country to colonize Mexico and the western and southwestern parts of the United States. In 1848, the U.S. government annexed the northern sections of Mexican Territory, including Texas, Arizona, New Mexico, and southern California. The Mexican population and Native American peoples living within that territory became an oppressed minority—in the area in which they had previously been the dominant population. Dominant supremacy theories based on color and language also were used against these ethnic groups in a way that prevents many of them even today from assimilating fully into the dominant culture.

The industrial opening of the West in the nineteenth century signaled the need for labor that could be met through immigration from Asia. Thus, Chinese, Japanese, and Filipino workers were recruited to provide the labor needed on the West Coast. Later immigrants came from the relatively more impoverished eastern and southern European countries to work primarily in midwestern and eastern cities. At the end of the nineteenth and the beginning of the twentieth centuries, large numbers of immigrants arrived from nations such as Poland, Hungary, Italy, Russia, and Greece. The reasons for immigration were the same as for earlier immigrants—devastating economic and political hardship in the homeland and demand for labor in the United States. Many immigrants came to the United States with the hope of sharing the better wages and living conditions that they thought existed here. Many found conditions much worse than they had expected. Most were forced to live in poor housing near the business and manufacturing districts where they worked, in urban ghettos that grew into ethnic enclaves in which others from the same country continued to use the native language. To support their social and welfare needs, ethnic institutions often were developed.

Just as dominant racist policies had been used against African Americans, Mexican Americans, and Native Americans earlier, they came to be used against the new immigrants. At various times, Congress prohibited the immigration of different national or ethnic groups on the basis of the racial superiority of the older, established immigrant groups that had colonized the nation. As early as 1729, immigration was being discouraged. In that year, Pennsylvania passed a statute that increased the head tax on foreigners in that colony. Later that century, Congress passed the Alien and Sedition Acts, which lengthened the time required to become a citizen from five years to fourteen years. In the nineteenth century, native-born Americans began to worry about their majority and superiority status over entering immigrant groups. This movement, nativism, was designed to restrict immigration and protect the interests of native-born Americans. It was an extreme form of nationalism and ethnocentrism.

In 1881, Congress passed the Chinese Exclusion Act, which halted all immigration from China. The Dillingham Commission reported in 1917 that all immigrants should be able to pass a literacy test. The nativists received further support for their views when Congress passed the Johnson-Reed Act in 1924, which discriminated against southern and eastern Europeans and nonwhite nations; the act also stopped all immigration from Japan. The act was so written that the annual immigrant quotas were disproportionately large for citizens from western European countries.

The Johnson-Reed Act was not abolished until 1965, when a new quota system was established that allowed 170,000 persons from the eastern hemisphere and 120,000 from the western hemisphere to immigrate annually. As shown in Figure 3-1, the change in the immigration law has allowed the influx of immigrants from nations that formerly were restricted or excluded. Thus,

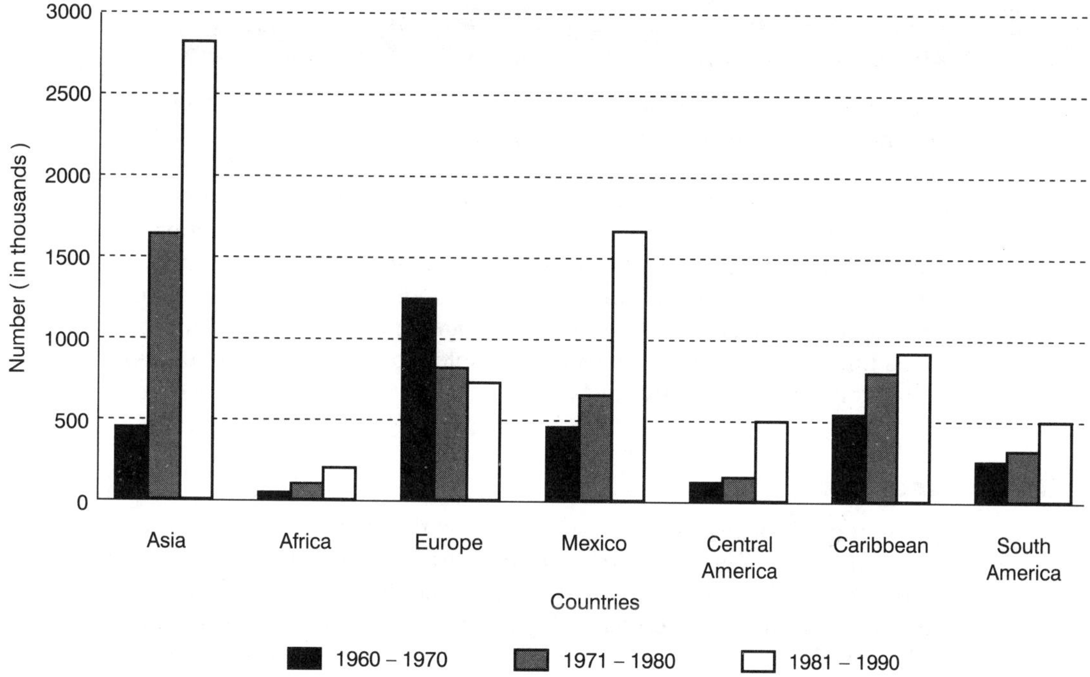

Figure 3-1. Immigration patterns to the United States from selected countries and continents have changed over the past three decades as shown above. (Numbers are in the thousands; 500 equals 500,000.)

the nation continues to become even more multiethnic with the larger number of immigrants now from non-European nations.

Refugees are also sometimes admitted under special acts of Congress. Favoritism is granted to refugees who are fleeing Communist regimes or other countries not supported by the U.S. government. In the 1980s, the largest number of refugees came from Vietnam; in addition, over 100,000 refugees from Laos, Cambodia, and Cuba were admitted. Most refugees from some countries, like Haiti, are refused entry, no matter how oppressive the government may be. As a result of government immigration and refugee policies, the composition of the U.S. population from various national and ethnic groups has been controlled.

Thus, persons from all over the globe joined Native Americans in populating this nation. They brought with them cultural experiences from their native country. The conditions they encountered, the reasons they came, and their expectations about life here differed greatly, causing each ethnic group to view itself as distinct from other ethnic groups. Although we all share a common history, our experiences in that history have varied greatly from group to group.

Ethnic and Racial Groups

There is a uniqueness about an individual, a family, and sometimes a neighborhood that can be identified as ethnic by an outsider. Children become aware of gender, race, ethnicity, and disabilities between the ages of two and five. At the same time, they become sensitive to the positive and negative biases associated with those groups (Derman-Sparks, 1989). Often this distinction is made because of the physical characteristics of individuals or the distinct language and shops in a neighborhood. Other times the distinction may be based on observed behaviors that suggest a particular ethnic background. This uniqueness is often based almost solely on the color of one's skin or other distinctive physical characteristics.

Ethnic Groups

Many definitions have been proposed for the term *ethnic group* over the past three decades. Gordon (1964) wrote that the ethnic identity of an American is based on national origin, religion, and race. Some writers have expanded the definition to include gender, religion, class, and lifestyle. Many authors identify Jewish Americans as an ethnic group, in part because many members of the Jewish faith emphasize their Jewishness, rather than their national origin, as the most meaningful basis of their identity. Jews from Germany, Spain, and India may share more commonalities because of religion than they share with non-Jewish Germans, Spaniards, or Indians. In this text, religious differences are examined separately from ethnicity and *ethnic group* is defined only as an individual's national origin or origins.

A nation is a historically constituted stable community of people formed on the basis of a common language, territory, economic life, and psychological makeup or culture. Ethnic identity is determined by living in a nation or maintaining ancestral ties even after having emigrated from a country. The strongest support for the country of origin is usually based on continuing family ties in that country. However, family ties in the country of origin usually weaken after several generations. Without extensive tracing of the family lineage, most members of ethnic groups who have been in this country for a century could not identify relatives in their country of origin. Yet, support for the country of origin often continues. For example, in the aftermath of the 1980 earthquake in Italy, Italian Americans across the United States organized benefits to collect money for relief. When cuts are being made in foreign aid, ethnic groups sometimes lobby on behalf of their country of origin.

Many members of ethnic groups in the United States maintain some of the cultural uniqueness of their national origin. A common bond is developed through family, friends, and neighbors with whom the same intimate characteristics of living are shared. These are the people invited to baptisms, marriages, funerals, and family reunions. They are the people with whom we feel the most comfortable. They know the meaning of our behavior; they perform the same rituals and patterns regarding such things as eating, grooming, marrying, and raising children. Endogamy, segregated residential areas, and restriction of activities with the dominant group help to preserve ethnic cohesiveness across generations.

The ethnic group allows for the maintenance of group cohesiveness. It helps sustain and enhance the ethnic identity of its members. It establishes the social networks and communicative patterns that are important for the group's optimization of its position in society. As a result, members are inherently ethnocentric.

The character of an ethnic group changes in differing degrees from its existence in the country of origin as a result of the group's experiences in the United States. Members within ethnic groups have different attitudes and behaviors based on their experiences in the United States and the conditions in the country of origin at the time of emigration. Recent immigrants may have little in common with other ethnic group members whose ancestors immigrated a century or even twenty years before. Ethnic communities undergo constant change in population characteristics, locations, occupations, educational levels, and political and economic struggles. All of these aspects affect the nature of the group and its members.

A person does not have to live in the same community with other members of the ethnic group to continue to identify with the group. The boundaries are maintained by ascription from within the group as well as from external sources that place persons in a specific group because of the way they look, the color of their skin, the location of their home, or their name. Although many individuals are several generations removed from an immigrant status, some continue to choose consciously to emphasize their ethnicity as a meaningful basis of their identity. In this case, whether to maintain one's identity with an ethnic group becomes a choice and is no longer ascriptive. Gans (1985) labels this identification as symbolic ethnicity that is "characterized by a nostalgic allegiance to the culture of the immigrant generation, or that of the old country; a love for and a pride in a tradition that can be felt without having to be incorporated into everyday behavior" (p. 435). As the dominant society allows members of an ethnic group to assimilate, it views that particular ethnic group as less distinct. Ethnicity then becomes more voluntary for group members—a process much more likely to occur for those with European backgrounds and others who look white.

Group identity is reinforced by the political and economic barriers established by the dominant society to prevent the assimilation of oppressed groups. Ethnicity is strongest within groups that develop group solidarity through similar lifestyles, common social and economic interests, a high degree of interpersonal associations developed through working relationships, and common residential areas (Yancey, Ericksen, & Juliani, 1985). Historically, oppressed groups have often been segregated from the dominant group and have developed enclaves in cities and suburbs that help members maintain a strong ethnic identity.

The upper strata of oppressed ethnic groups naturally respond to existing injustices. They appeal to their "brothers and sisters" and begin to agitate about their lack of rights and power, claiming that their cause is the cause of the ethnic community as a whole. The broad masses within these ethnic groups do not always remain passive and unresponsive to these appeals. Sometimes they rally around the banner of these spokespersons because the harsh economic and political realities imposed on them by the dominant group affect them even more than they do the upper strata of intellectuals and leaders. Thus, at different junctures, movements for democratic rights and economic justice are initiated among the different ethnic groups. These movements invariably entail a rise in the concern of the community with its original or indigenous culture, as this aspect of their lives also has been suppressed and excluded by the dominant majority.

This reaction was seen in the United States in the civil rights movement of the 1960s as a result of African Americans' recognition of their oppressed status in society. The call for black power followed years of civil rights struggle that led to the passage of the 1964 Civil Rights Act and the 1965 Voting Rights Act. Yet, changes did not follow. Although legislation guaranteed equality, many European Americans continued to fight against desegregation of schools and other public facilities. Frustrations with the majority group led members of oppressed groups to identify strongly with other members of their ethnic group and to fight the discrimination and inequality with a unified voice.

Racial Groups

Are racial groups also ethnic groups? In the United States, many people use the two terms interchangeably. Race is a concept that was developed by physical anthropologists to assist them in describing the physical characteristics of people in the world. Racial groups include many ethnic groups, but ethnic groups may include members of one or more racial groups. How has such mixed usage of the terms developed in this country?

Throughout U.S. history, racial identification has been used by policymakers and much of the population to classify groups of people as inferior or superior to another racial group. Some theorists (e.g., Ogbu, 1988, and Berreman, 1985) suggest that race as used in the United States is equivalent to caste in other countries. Both are "invidious distinctions imposed unalterably at birth upon whole categories of people to justify the unequal social distribution of power, livelihood, security, privilege, esteem, freedom—in short, life chances" (Berreman, 1985, p. 37).

Because the institutions of government in the United States were established by northern and western Europeans, many members of that group view themselves as the superior racial and ethnic group. At one time, slaves and Native Americans were perceived as so inferior to the dominant group that they were counted by the government as only a fraction of a person. This phenomenon of racial consciousness in the United States was repeated on the

West Coast in the late nineteenth century when Chinese immigrants were charged an additional tax for their braids. Even the large influx of southern and eastern Europeans in the late nineteenth and early twentieth centuries led to their being labeled as inferior because they came from a different race. This feeling of the superiority of one race over all others became a popular and emotional issue of the American people during this period. It later fueled the deadly Holocaust under German Nazism in World War II.

This American racist ideology was detailed in 1916 in *The Passing of the Great Race* by Madison Grant. Northern and western Europeans of the Nordic race were described as "the political and military genius of the world" (Higham, 1975, p. 221). Protecting the purity of the Nordic race became such an emotional and popular issue for the majority of U.S. citizens that laws were passed to severely limit immigration into this country from any region except northern European countries. Miscegenation laws legally prevented the marriage of whites to members of other races in many states until the Supreme Court declared the laws unconstitutional in 1967. The immigration quota system passed by Congress in 1921 remained in effect until it was repealed in 1965. The fact that race became a supreme value in state and federal law set the stage for the continued emphasis on racial, rather than ethnic, identity.

Once race identification was codified, it was acceptable, even necessary, to identify oneself by race. Federal forms and reports classify the population based on a mixture of racial, ethnic, and language identification: white, black, Hispanic, Asian or Pacific Islander, and American Indian or Eskimo. Figure 3-2 indicates how individuals identified themselves in the 1990 census.

The problem with identifying the U.S. population by such characteristics is that it tells little about the people in these groups. Although whites are numerically dominant, this classification includes many different ethnic groups. Moreover, neither the ethnic identification nor actual racial heritage of African

Figure 3-2. In the 1990 census, people in the United States identified themselves according to these ethnic and racial categories.

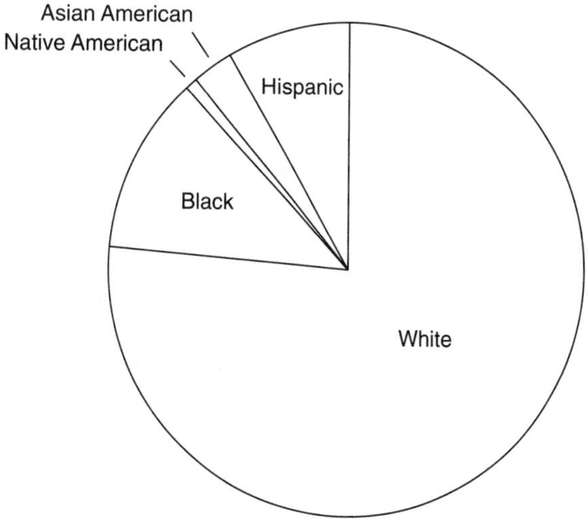

Americans is recognized. Further, the Hispanic grouping includes different racial groups and mixtures of racial groups as well as at least four distinct ethnic groups in this country: Mexican Americans, Puerto Ricans, Spanish Americans, and Cuban Americans. In addition, the category includes persons with Central and South American roots.

Although ideas about racial superiority have found no support within the scientific community, many people continue to believe in the inferiority of races other than white. This belief can be observed in cases of mixed racial heritage. Individuals of black and white parentage are usually classified as black, not white; those of Japanese American and white heritage usually are classified as nonwhite. In some areas of the country, state laws specify that a small percentage of nonwhite heritage requires that one be classified as a minority group member, regardless of physical or cultural characteristics.

Race is no longer a function of biological or genetic differences among groups. It is a social historical concept (Omi & Winant, 1986) that is dependent on society's perception that differences exist and that these differences are important. The cultural distinctions between racial groups become the rationale for an inferior status, discrimination, and inequality (Cashmore & Troyna, 1990). In their study of racial formation in the United States, Omi and Winant (1986) discovered that

> Historically, a variety of previously racially undefined groups have required categorization to situate them within the prevailing racial order. Throughout the nineteenth century, many state and federal legal arrangements recognized only three racial categories: "white," Negro," and "Indian." In California, the influx of Chinese and the debates surrounding the legal status of Mexicans provoked a brief judicial crisis of racial definition. California attempted to resolve this dilemma by assigning Mexicans and Chinese to categories within the already existing framework of "legally defined" racial groups. In the wake of the Treaty of Guadalupe Hidalgo (1848), Mexicans were defined as a "white" population and accorded the political-legal status of "free white persons." By contrast, the California Supreme Court ruled in People v. Hall (1854) that Chinese should be considered "Indian" and denied the political rights accorded to whites. (p. 75)

African Americans range in skin color along a continuum from very light to very dark skin. Thus, it is not the color of their skin that defines them. Their identification is based, in part, on sharing a common national origin that can be traced to numerous African tribes and European and Native American nations. They have become a single ethnic group because they share a common history, language, economic life, and culture that have developed over four centuries of living in the United States. Nevertheless, race remains a central factor in their identity. Appiah (1990) reports that "what blacks in the West . . . have mostly in common is that they are perceived—both by themselves and by others—as belonging to the same race, and that this common race is used by others as the basis for discriminating against them" (p. 11).

Because individuals appear to be African American is not an indication that they identify themselves as African Americans. Some members identify themselves as blacks; others identify themselves with another specific ethnic group, for example, Puerto Rican or Nigerian American or West Indian. Africans who are recent immigrants generally identify themselves ethnically by the nation or tribe of origin. In the same way, Polish Americans may be classified as white, but many will identify themselves as Polish Americans rather than white.

To understand the cultural underpinnings of groups of people in the United States, ethnic and racial identity remains important. However, race has historically been important in this country only because racial identity singled out certain people as inferior to whites of northern and western Europe. Thus, they were eligible for discriminatory treatment. "Particular meanings, stereotypes and myths can change, but the presence of a system of racial meanings and stereotypes, of racial ideology, seems to be a permanent feature of U.S. culture" (Omi & Winant, 1986, p. 63).

Minority Groups

Minorities and *minority groups* are terms often used in discussions about ethnic/racial groups and their relationships to the dominant group in the United States and other countries. What determines whether an ethnic group is a minority group in a country? Although the term *minority* usually refers to a numerical minority, it is used in the ethnic context to connote a subordinate power position in society. Minority groups do not share in the benefits available to members of the dominant group. Those minority groups without social, economic, or political power are sometimes referred to as oppressed groups. Numerical superiority does not guarantee majority status, as exemplified by the situation in South Africa, where thirteen million blacks are in a subordinate position to three million ruling whites.

Members of minority groups experience a wide range of discriminatory treatment and frequently are relegated to positions relatively low in the status structure of a society. Any ethnic group that does not have sufficient power to fulfill its political, economic, social, or cultural needs is in a subordinate position and can be regarded as an oppressed minority group (Teper, 1977). Minority status is also evident when an ethnic group must be constantly vigilant to see that its needs are met by society. Members of an oppressed group cannot be assured of receiving the same societal benefits as members of the majority group.

Ogbu (1988) has found that "subordinate minorities usually react to their subordination and exploitation by forming ambivalent or oppositional identities as well as oppositional cultural frames of reference" (p. 176). They do not view the attitudes and behaviors of the dominant group as appropriate for them. Many members of the minority group develop attitudes and behaviors that are clearly opposed to those of the dominant group. Minority group members who cross the boundaries into the dominant group "may experience both internal opposition or identity crisis and external opposition or peer and community pressures" (Ogbu, 1988, p. 176).

This opposition becomes very important in schooling because members of many oppressed groups (especially African Americans, Mexican Americans, and Native Americans) equate schooling with accepting the culture of the dominant group and giving up their own cultural identity. They believe "that in order for a minority person to succeed, academically, in school, he or she must learn to think and act white" (Ogbu, 1988, p. 177). In many cases, minority students resist assimilation by developing strategies of resistance, including poor academic achievement (Fordham, 1988; Gibson, 1988; Ogbu, 1988).

In the United States, minority status more often than ethnic identity has come to be identified with races other than white. Because members of the dominant group are white, it is easy to identify those persons who are not members. Minority members usually have unique physical or cultural characteristics that make them easily identifiable. They have been, and in most cases continue to be, victims of racism and negative stereotypes, and they are disproportionately poor or near-poor.

Native Americans, African Americans, and Mexican Americans have long histories of oppression in the United States. Asian American, Puerto Rican, and southern and eastern European ethnic groups have more recent histories of subordination, but most of the European groups have now become accepted as part of the dominant group. Immigrants from the Middle East, Central America, and Southeast Asia are the latest ethnic group members who suffer from an oppressed minority status.

Ethnic Identity

Students in a classroom are likely to come from several different ethnic groups, although physical differences are not always identifiable. Two white students who appear to be from similar backgrounds may actually identify strongly with their German or Polish background. The two families may live next door to each other in similar houses, but the insides of the houses may be furnished or decorated differently. The churches that they attend may differ, as well as their ideas about raising children and maintaining the family. Their political ideologies are likely to differ markedly. Yet students often are viewed as coming from the same cultural background if they have similar racial characteristics, even though their families may be African American, Nigerian American, Puerto Rican, or Jamaican American. The educator must beware of assuming that all students who look alike come from the same ethnic background. Factors other than physical characteristics must be used to determine a student's ethnicity.

The degree of ethnic identity differs greatly from student to student, family to family, and community to community. Some Americans grow up in ethnic enclaves and not in multiethnic communities. Chinatown, Little Italy, Harlem, and Little Saigon are examples of ethnic enclaves in the nation's cities. The suburbs also include pockets of families from the same ethnic background. Throughout the country, there are small towns and surrounding farmland where the population comes from the same ethnic background, all the residents being African American, German American, Danish American, Anglo American, or Mexican American. These individuals may be culturally encapsulated, so that most of their primary relationships and many of their secondary relationships are with members of their own ethnic group. They may not have the opportunity to interact with members of other ethnic groups nor to recognize or share the richness of a second culture that exists in another setting. They may never learn how to live with people who speak a different language or dialect, eat different types of foods, and value things that their own ethnic group does not value. They often learn to fear or denigrate individuals from different ethnic groups primarily because their ways are seemingly strange and thus perceived as wrong or bad.

With few exceptions, however, the ethnic enclave itself does not increase in size. Families move away because of job opportunities and economic rewards available outside of the community itself. Children who move away to attend college often do not return. Yet some families continue to maintain a strong identity with the ethnic group even after they have moved away. Nevertheless, children are less likely to maintain such strong identity with the ethnic group because many of the primary relationships are with members of other ethnic groups. Many whites become assimilated into the majority group. Others participate in some ethnic activities, although their acceptance and practice of the ethnic ethos may decrease significantly as they move geographically and emotionally away from the community. Second- and third-generation ethnics living in the suburbs often rediscover their ethnic ties and identity. Although their primary relationships may not be restricted totally to other members of the ethnic group, they tend to organize or join ethnic social clubs and organizations or revitalize their identification with their national origin.

Other students may have mixed ancestry, allowing them to identify with two or more national origins. Identification with one ethnic group more than others may occur, or students may view their ethnicity as just American. Although some students may not see their ethnic identity as very important in understanding who they are, others may continue to respond to them based on their identifiable ethnicity. Sometimes the ethnic group itself makes it very difficult for an individual to withdraw from the ethnic group and assimilate into the majority group.

Unlike their white counterparts, most people of color usually are forced out of their ethnic encapsulation to achieve social and economic mobility. Many secondary relationships are with members of other ethnic groups because they often work with or for members of the dominant group. However, members of the dominant group rarely take the opportunity to develop even secondary relationships with members of other ethnic groups, particularly minority

Many individuals and families in this country maintain ties with their national origin or ethnic group. They often participate in traditional ethnic events, such as this one.

members. Dominant group members could spend their lives not knowing or participating in the culture of another ethnic group.

An individual's degree of ethnic identity is influenced early in that person's life by whether or not the family members recognize or promote ethnicity as an important force in determining who they are. Sometimes, the choice about how ethnic one should be is imposed; this is particularly true for members of oppressed ethnic minority groups. When the ethnic group believes that strong and loyal ethnic identity is necessary to maintain the group solidarity, the pressure of other members of the group may make it difficult not to have a strong ethnic identity. For many members of the group, this ethnic identity provides them with the security of belonging and knowing who they are. The ethnic identity becomes the primary source of identification, and they feel no need to identify themselves differently. In fact, they may find it emotionally very difficult to sever their primary identification with that group. These families fight the assimilative aspects of schooling that draw children into adopting the dress, language, music, and values of their peers from the dominant culture.

Because of prejudice and discrimination against members of oppressed groups, an individual usually faces the discriminatory practices used against all other members of that same group. Many individuals from oppressed groups have been acculturated and share the same cultural characteristics with dominant group individuals. However, denied full access into the economic, political, and social spheres of the dominant group, they cannot assimilate. In the process of acculturation, some individuals reject the traditional culture of the ethnic group and are in a transitional stage between the ethnic minority group and the assimilated majority. The majority of these individuals probably function biculturally, participating as appropriate in either the oppressed group or the dominant group. Others reject the culture of the ethnic group to assimilate into the culture of the dominant group. If the dominant group denies assimilation, some of these individuals become suspended between two cultural groups, belonging to neither and developing problems with self-identity.

Educators must be aware of intragroup differences. The degree of ethnic identity varies greatly among individuals whom we classify as members of an ethnic group. Members of the same ethnic group differ in their own historical experiences gathered from the old country as well as from this country. For example, families who emigrated from Vietnam in the early 1970s were predominantly from the wealthy and professional middle classes. They differ greatly in their social and economic backgrounds from Vietnamese who emigrated from peasant and rural backgrounds in the late 1970s. To expect the same cultural patterns for individuals from both groups might lead to ineffective instructional planning for them. Knowing what students and their families expect within an ethnic context can be very helpful in preparing effective instructional strategies.

Identifying the degree of students' assimilation into the majority culture may be helpful in developing instructional strategies. Such information may help the educator understand the students' values, particularly what the students' expectations for school may be. It also allows the teacher to more accurately determine the learning styles of the students so that the teaching style can be effectively adapted to individual differences. The only way to know the importance of ethnicity in the lives of students is to objectively listen and observe them. Familiarity and participation with the community from which students come will also help the educator know the importance of microculture membership to students and their families.

Finally, the educator must remember that students from oppressed groups face societal constraints and restrictions that seldom affect dominant students. Such recognition is essential in the development of instructional programs and schools that effectively serve diverse populations that as yet do not share equally in the benefits that education offers.

Interethnic Relations

An area that has received much media coverage is interethnic relations in the United States. This attention extends into the schools. Fights between students from different ethnic backgrounds are often described as ethnic or racial in origin, rather than personal. Such violence in schools appears to be increasing. The Southern Poverty Law Center reports that there were hundreds of incidents in the 1991–92 academic year. The occurrences ranged "from swastikas on lockers and anti-Semitic slurs on the playground, to violent clashes between blacks and whites" (Violence, 1992). In response, educators express concern about developing and maintaining positive interethnic relations among students, teachers, and the communities. An examination of factors that affect interethnic relations may help the professional educator understand the reasons for conflict between groups and the different perceptions of contact and conflict held by participants in interethnic communication.

Prejudice and Discrimination

Two causes of ineffective interethnic relations are *prejudice* and *discrimination*. Both stem from a combination of several factors: (1) a lack of understanding of the history, experiences, values, and perceptions of ethnic groups other than one's own; (2) stereotyping the members of an ethnic group without consideration of individual differences within the group; (3) judging other ethnic groups according to the standards and values of one's own group; (4) assigning negative attributes to members of other ethnic groups; and (5) evaluating the qualities and experiences of other groups as inferior to one's own. In other words, prejudice and discrimination are extreme forms of ethnocentrism.

"Prejudice is a negative attitude toward an entire category of people" (Schaefer, 1988, p. 55). This aversion to members of certain ethnic groups manifests itself in feelings of anger, fear, hatred, and distrust about members of the out-group. These attitudes are often translated into fear of walking in the neighborhood of the out-group, fear of being mugged by members of the out-group, distrust of any merchant from the out-group, anger at any advantages that members of the out-group may be perceived as receiving, and fear of a member of the out-group moving next door. "The forms of prejudice may range from a relatively unconscious aversion to members of the out-group to a comprehensive, well-articulated, and coherent ideology, such as the ideology of racism" (Yetman, 1985, p. 11). Such an ideology undergirds the activities of the Nazis, Ku Klux Klan, and other white racist groups that currently exist in our society.

Since World War II, overt individual prejudice and discrimination have decreased dramatically. In the early 1940s, segregation of and discrimination against blacks were supported by the majority of whites. Today, most whites support policies against racial discrimination and prejudice. However, their support of government intervention to guarantee equality for minorities is not nearly as strong (Schuman, Steech, & Bobo, 1985). Moreover, during the 1980s, it became more acceptable to openly express one's prejudice, as evidenced by cross burnings and racist themes at fraternity parties on a number of college campuses. One wonders whether racial attitudes have really changed in the past fifty years or whether the prejudice against ethnic and racial groups other than one's own has just been less public.

Whereas prejudice focuses on attitudes, discrimination focuses on behavior. Discrimination "involves behavior that excludes all members of a group from certain rights, opportunities, or privileges" (Schaefer, 1988, p. 55). Prejudice is the arbitrary denial of the privileges and rewards of society to those whose qualifications are equal to the dominant group. Although prejudice may not directly hurt members of the out-group, it can be easily translated into discriminating behavior that does harm members of that group.

Discrimination occurs at two levels: individual and institutional. Individual discrimination is attributed to or influenced by prejudice. Individuals discriminate against a member of the out-group for at least two reasons: either they have strong prejudicial, or bigoted, feelings about the ethnic group, or they feel that societal pressures demand that they discriminate even though they may not be prejudiced. Realtors, personnel managers, receptionists, and membership chairpersons all work directly with individuals. Their own personal attitudes about members of certain ethnic groups can influence whether a house is sold, a job is offered, an appointment is made, a meal is served, or a membership is extended to a member of the out-group. The action of these individuals can prevent the member of the out-group from gaining the experiences and economic advantage that these activities offer.

An individual has less control in the other form of discrimination. Institutional discrimination cannot be attributed to prejudicial attitudes. It "refers to the effects of inequalities that are rooted in the system-wide operation of a society and have little relation to racially related attitudinal factors or the majority group's racial or ethnic prejudices" (Yetman, 1985, p. 17–18).

We face a dilemma because we have grown up in a society that has inherently discriminated against minority groups since the first explorers arrived. Throughout our lives, we have participated in a number of societal institutions, including schools, Social Security, transportation, welfare, and housing patterns. Not all people benefit equally from these institutions. However, we often do not realize the extent that members of other ethnic groups receive the benefits and privileges of these institutions. Because we feel that we have never been discriminated against, we should not assume that others do not suffer from discrimination.

Many individuals might argue that institutional discrimination no longer exists because today's laws require equal access to the benefits of society. Omi and Winant (1986) suggest that

> With the exception of some on the far right, the racial reaction which has developed in the last two decades claims to favor racial equality. Its vision is that of a "colorblind" society where racial considerations are never entertained in the selection of leaders, in hiring decisions, and the distribution of goods and services in general. As the right sees it, racial problems today center on the new forms of racial "injustice" which originated in the "great transformation." This new injustice confers group rights on racial minority groups, thus granting a new form of privilege—that of preferential treatment.
>
> The culprit behind this new form of "racism" is seen as the state itself. Advocates of this view believe that the state went too far in attempting to eliminate racial discrimination. It legitimated group rights, established affirmative action mandates, and spent money on a range of social programs, which, according to the right, debilitated, rather than uplifted, its target populations. In this scenario, the victims of racial discrimination have dramatically shifted from racial minorities to whites, particularly white males. (p. 114)

PAUSE TO REFLECT

Affirmative action was designed to ensure that members of groups that have traditionally been discriminated against in employment have a fair chance to compete with members of dominant groups in being admitted to colleges and professional schools and in finding jobs. How do you react to affirmative action? Does it discriminate against members of the dominant group? Why or why not? Under what circumstances do you think affirmative action programs are appropriate and/or helpful? Why do some members of the dominant group believe that such practices are discriminatory?

The problem is that the criteria for access are often applied arbitrarily and unfairly. A disproportionately high number of minorities do not possess the qualifications for skilled jobs or college entrance or have the economic resources to purchase a home in the suburbs. As businesses and industries move from the city to the suburbs, access to employment by minorities who live in the inner city is limited. The crucial issue is not the equal treatment of those with equal qualifications, but the accessibility of minority group members to the qualifications and jobs themselves.

The consequences are the same in individual and institutional discrimination. Members of certain ethnic groups do not receive the same benefits from society as the dominant group. Individuals are harmed by circumstances beyond their control because of their membership in a specific ethnic group. The role of teachers and other professional educators requires that they not discriminate against any student because of the student's ethnic background. This consideration must be paramount in assigning students to special education classes and in giving and interpreting standardized tests. Classroom interactions, classroom resources, extracurricular activities, and counseling practices must be evaluated to ensure that discrimination against students from various ethnic groups is not occurring.

Racism

Racism is a mixed form of discrimination and prejudice directed at ethnic groups that are racially different from the dominant group members. Traditionally, racism referred to the conscious or unconscious belief that members of racial groups other than one's own were innately inferior. In this sense, racism is a form of prejudice. Often this prejudice is transferred by individuals and government policy into discrimination against groups in immigration policies, the availability of housing and jobs, etc.

Since the 1950s, the term *racism* has described prejudice and discrimination against people of color. Although many whites may no longer believe that African Americans are genetically inferior to European Americans, they do believe in another ideology. This "dominant white ideology is that of free will; anyone can 'better himself [herself]' if he [she] is not too lazy to make the effort" (Yetman, 1985, p. 15). Such an ideology refuses to acknowledge the impact of the oppressive social and economic conditions on oppressed group members. It places the responsibility for the disadvantage on the group itself. This emphasis implies that members of the minority group must certainly be inferior to whites, or they would be doing as well as whites. European Americans often describe their own ancestors as poor when they immigrated to this country, but they point out how hard they worked to accumulate the resources to move them into the middle class, where they can enjoy the privileges and rewards of society. Some believe that if oppressed group members would work just as hard, they would also receive the same benefits. These individuals reject the existence of external impingements and disabilities that make it much more difficult for people of color to shed their minority status than it was for their own European ancestors. They ignore the fact that some people of color have adapted the cultural values and standards of the dominant group to a greater degree than many white ethnic groups. Yet discriminatory policies and practices prevent them from sharing equally in society's benefits with whites. In addition, the opportunities to gain qualifications with which people of color could compete equally with whites have been severely restricted throughout most of our history.

The most crucial factor in understanding racism is that the dominant group has power over an oppressed group. This power has been used to prevent people of color from securing the prestige, power, and privilege held by whites. Professional educators must prevent such practices from occurring in their classrooms and schools.

A first step for educators is the recognition that racism exists and that if they are white, they have benefited from it. This is not an easy process. In describing her experiences in teaching a course on the psychology of racism to college students, Tatum (1992) reported that "the introduction of these issues of oppression often generates powerful emotional responses in students that range from guilt and shame to anger and despair" (pp. 1–2). We often resist discussion of these issues because we must eventually confront our own feelings. In predominantly white college classrooms, Tatum found three sources of resistance:

1. Race is considered a taboo topic for discussion, especially in racially mixed settings.
2. Many students, regardless of racial-group membership, have been socialized to think of the United States as a just society.
3. Many students, particularly white students, initially deny any personal prejudice, recognizing the impact of racism on other people's lives, but failing to acknowledge its impact on their own.

The challenge is to confront these issues seriously before entering a classroom. There are stages of racial identity that are experienced as we learn to accept the existence of racism and to feel comfortable with our own racial identity. The developmental stages differ for members of oppressed and dominant groups due to their own lived encounters with racism and oppression (Cross, 1991). It is important that educators seek opportunities to confront these issues in their own lives. Once in the classroom they will be in the position to help students grapple with these topics and their own feelings. The goal should be to attack racism and oppression in daily life, rather than reinforcing it in the classroom.

Intergroup Conflicts

The reader should begin to realize why intergroup conflicts are likely to occur in the nation's schools. The fact that some groups receive more rewards from society than other groups is experienced by the members of oppressed groups. This resentment often causes tension between ethnic groups that can lead to conflict. Accepting an oppressed status has not become any easier, even with the knowledge that most members of the dominant group are not prejudiced or do not discriminate. Whites often find this attitude frustrating because individually they may not deserve the criticism and blame laid on them by the oppressed groups. However, it is essential to understand the cause of the criticism, namely, the overt prejudice and discrimination faced by these groups. Historically, the oppressed groups have had to adjust to the dominant standards. Many minority members adopt the cultural patterns of the dominant group—a process called acculturation. However, no matter how much of the dominant culture has been adopted by minority groups, members of those groups assimilate into the dominant group only to the extent that the dominant group allows. African Americans provide a classic example of this phenomenon.

Interethnic conflict is certainly not new in the United States, although the intensity of such conflicts has been mild compared to that in many other nations. Revolts were organized by slaves to overcome their oppressed role in society. Native American and European conflicts were common in the attempt to subjugate the native peoples.

What are the reasons for continued interethnic conflict as we enter the twenty-first century? Discriminatory practices have protected the superior status of the dominant group for centuries. When other ethnic groups try to share more equitably in the rewards and privileges of society, the dominant group must concede some of its advantages. Most recently, this concern about giving up some of the advantages of the oppressor has been reflected in reactions to affirmative action programs. As long as one ethnic group has an institutional advantage over other ethnic groups, some interethnic conflict is likely to occur.

Another reason for interethnic conflict is competition for economic resources. As economic conditions become tighter, fewer jobs are available. Discriminatory practices in the past have forced people of color into positions with the least seniority; as jobs are cut back, disproportionately high numbers are laid off. As evident in the 1992 riots in Los Angeles, the tension between ethnic groups increases as members of specific groups determine that they disproportionately suffer the hardships resulting from economic depression. Conflict sometimes occurs between oppressed groups when they are forced to share limited societal resources, such as low-income housing and access to bilingual education programs. Conflict as a result of inequitable distribution of economic rewards is likely to continue as long as members of ethnic groups can observe and feel those inequities (Appleton, 1983).

During the past fifty years, a number of educational strategies have been developed to reduce and overcome interethnic conflicts. These strategies have focused on training teachers to be effective in intergroup or human relations; attempting to change the prejudicial attitudes of teachers; fighting institutional discrimination through affirmative action and civil rights legislation; encouraging changes in textbooks and other resources to more accurately reflect the multiethnic nature of society; and attempting to remove discriminatory behavior from classroom interactions and classroom practices. All these strategies are important to combat prejudice and discrimination in the educational setting. Alone or in combination, however, the strategies do not appear to be enough. This fact is not to diminish the need for professional educators to further develop the strategies. It is not a sign of failure, but a recognition that prejudice, discrimination, and racism are diseases that infect all of society, not only the schools and professional educators.

Educational Implications

Educators must understand the importance of the role ethnicity plays in the lives of many students and communities. Membership in oppressed ethnic and racial groups has a very significant impact on students' perceptions of themselves. It is also very significant for educators because the environment of schools is usually incongruent with the cultural experiences of the students. This incongruence may lead to students dropping out of school at different rates based on ethnicity and race. In 1990, for instance, 12 percent of white youth who were between sixteen and twenty-four years old had dropped out of school; 13 percent of the black and 32 percent of the Hispanic young people had dropped out (National Center, 1992).

Although 80 percent of the U.S. population was white in 1990, the percentage is decreasing. This change is particularly evident in the school-age population. It is projected that by the beginning of the twenty-first century 33 percent of the students will be members of minority groups (American Council on Education [ACE], 1988). At the same time, the number of Hispanics will have surpassed African Americans as the largest minority group. By 2020, the percentage of minority students will have risen to 39 percent (ACE).

In responding equitably to ethnic differences, the educator should be able to

1. encourage students to build and maintain a positive self-concept
2. use the ethnic backgrounds of students to teach effectively
3. help students overcome their ethnic prejudices
4. expand the knowledge and appreciation of the historical, economic, political, and social experiences of ethnic and national groups
5. assist students in understanding that the world's knowledge and culture have been and continue to be created from the contributions of all ethnic groups and nations.

Schools need to provide environments in which students can learn to participate in the dominant society while maintaining distinct ethnic identities if they choose. In the scenario at the beginning of this chapter, which of the areas above was Ms. Kuhn attempting to address?

Respect for and support of ethnic differences will be essential in this effort. Students know when a teacher or counselor does not respect or value the students' ethnic background. As educators, we cannot afford to reject or neglect students because their ethnic backgrounds are different from our own. We are responsible for making sure all students learn to think, read, write, and compute so that they can function effectively in society. We can help accomplish this goal by accurately reflecting ethnicity in the curriculum and positively using it to teach and interact with students.

There are at least two theories to consider in developing strategies to better serve minority students. The cultural discontinuity theory attributes the differences in outcomes between students of oppressed groups and students of dominant groups to the differences between the culture and language of the school and those of the students. The school reflects the culture and values of the dominant society and usually ignores or denigrates the culture and values of the ethnic groups from which students come. For example, many schools have set aside the month of February to celebrate black history. This in itself may be a helpful strategy for learning about a specific ethnic group. However, it often substitutes for integrating the contributions and experiences of African Americans throughout the curriculum during the whole school year. Often other groups are studied only by students' participating in a traditional ethnic event or in tasting ethnic foods. The advantage in these cases goes to the students of the dominant group. The curriculum almost always reflects their culture, and their behavior requires little or no adjusting.

The structural inequalities theory "emphasizes the status of a particular minority or social class group within the socioeconomic structure of the host society and the group's relationship with the dominant majority" (Gibson, 1988, p. 30). The low achievement of minority students in schools reflects the social stratification system that operates in society, and most schools are designed to maintain that status quo. Thus, students from oppressed groups are tracked into low-ability groups and vocational programs in which low achievement is expected. Upon entry into junior and senior high school, disproportionately few are placed in advanced, more rigorous academic classes. Participation in mathematics and science courses varies considerably by race, class, and gender, leading to unequal outcomes in achievement (Oakes, 1988).

Students are not always inactive participants in the stratification that occurs in schools. Researchers are finding that many working-class boys and minority students develop resistance or oppositional patterns to handle their subordination within schools (Ogbu, 1988; Solomon, 1988; Willis, 1977). This opposition often takes the form of breaking school rules and norms, belittling academic achievement, and valuing manual over mental work. These students equate schooling with accepting the culture of the dominant group and thinking and acting white or middle class—characteristics that could have them expelled from the minority or class peer group. In many cases, especially for African Americans, "students embrace education, the achievement ideology, and develop high educational aspirations. In the meantime, however, their counter-school activities do not allow them to achieve these ends" (Solomon, 1988, p. 260). While middle-class African American students perform academically better than their working-class peers, they do not do as well as white students, in part because of this oppositional process.

Not all minority students adopt an oppositional form, and not all minority groups are equally affected. Asian American students have high achievement records in mathematics and science and attend college at rates disproportionately higher than other groups. One explanation might be that Asian American adults are overrepresented in professional occupations, which should indicate an income above that of most other minority groups. Oakes (1988) attributes their high levels of achievement and participation in mathematics and science to the economic advantages in the home backgrounds of many of these students. Generally, the cultural group values math and science skills, and families provide experiences that encourage their development.

At the same time, it is unfair to expect that all Asian American students have the characteristics that are congruent with the school culture. Many families do believe in the folk theory of the white middle class and trust white institutions. Thus, most students may assimilate well in the school setting. However, "while this image has led many teachers and employers to view Asians as intelligent and hard-working and has opened some opportunities, it has also been harmful. Asian Americans can find their diversity as individuals denied: many feel forced into the "model minority" mold and want more freedom to be their individual selves, to be 'extravagant'" (Takaki, 1989, p. 477).

Whether the high academic achievement levels will be maintained by the more recent refugees from Southeast Asia is yet to be determined.

Recent immigrants also appear not to develop the oppositional forms of the long-established minority groups. Gibson (1988) found that they are more willing to accept school norms and succeed academically, in part because they compare the conditions of living in the United States with those in the country that they have just left. At the same time, many families are not willing to surrender their ethnic culture totally to become assimilated. In her study of Sikh immigrants in a California high school, Gibson (1988) found that families developed a strategy of accommodation and acculturation without assimilation. A high degree of academic success has also been found for Cuban, Central American, and Vietnamese refugees.

Nevertheless, educators cannot expect that the cultural experiences of all immigrant students will be congruent with the norms of school. An important contributing factor is the status of the immigrant. Are the families legal immigrants, refugees, migrant workers, or undocumented workers without legal papers (Gibson, 1992/93)? School achievement is dependent on many factors: how long the family has been in the country, the student's age on arrival, parents' education and economic status in the country of origin, exposure to western and urban lifestyles, languages spoken in the family, the quality of educational experiences before immigrating, and others (Gibson). It will be important for educators to interact with immigrant families to determine the most effective instructional strategies for ensuring academic achievement. Studies indicate that "many first and second generation immigrant children are successful not because they relinquish their traditional ways but because they draw strength from their home cultures and a positive sense of their ethnic identity" (Gibson, p. 7).

Historically, some immigrant groups have established their own schools, with classes often held in the evening or on Saturday, to reinforce cultural values, traditions, and the native language. This pattern is being reinitiated by some ethnic groups. For example, a number of Native American tribes have established their own tribal-controlled public schools in which the traditional culture serves as the social and intellectual starting point (Carnegie Foundation, 1990). Although most of these schools are located in rural Native American communities, some urban areas have also established magnet Indian schools with similar goals.

A more recent and controversial development is the establishment of public school programs for African American male students. "These new programs aim to inoculate African American youth against the often hostile forces of community unemployment, drugs, violence, and poverty, by giving them a strong gender and cultural identity, and to empower these African American males as individuals and as members of a community to proceed along paths to success" (Ascher, 1991). The goals are laudable, particularly since young African American males are disproportionately murdered, arrested, and unemployed. The programs employ strong, positive role models as teachers and focus on an Afrocentric curriculum.

Thus, a number of strategies for attending to the ethnic differences of communities have evolved. There are at least two curriculum approaches to incorporating ethnic content in the school curriculum: ethnic studies and multiethnic studies. Other areas of schooling that are impacted greatly by ethnicity include desegregation and student assessment.

TEACHING CHILDREN OF UNDOCUMENTED WORKERS

Did you know that *1982 Plyler v. Doe* guarantees the rights of undocumented immigrants to free public education? What can you do as a teacher to help students adjust in your classroom?

- Refrain from asking about students' immigration status or requesting documentation at any time. Do not require undocumented students or their parents to apply for social security numbers.
- Establish school and classroom climates that all students and their parents will find open and hospitable. Parents should not be afraid to enroll their children in public schools.
- Develop strong working relationships with immigrant families. (The Mid-Atlantic Equity Center, 1992)

Ethnic Studies

Ethnic studies are an extension or special segment of the curriculum that focuses on the history and contemporary conditions of one or more ethnic groups. They allow for in-depth exposure to the social, economic, and political history of a specific group. These courses are designed to correct the distortions and omissions about an ethnic group that prevail in textbooks. Events that have been neglected in textbooks are addressed, myths are dispelled, and history is viewed from the perspective of the ethnic group as well as the dominant group. Prospective teachers and other professional school personnel who have not been exposed to an examination of an ethnic group different from their own should take such a course or undertake individual study.

Traditionally, ethnic studies have been offered as separate courses that students elect from many offerings in the curriculum. Seldom have ethnic studies been required courses for all students. Too often the majority of students who choose these courses are students from the ethnic group or groups being studied. Although the information and experiences offered in these courses are very important to these students, they are just as important for all students, regardless of their ethnic background.

Multiethnic Studies

The second approach to incorporating ethnic content affects the total curriculum of a school. A multiethnic curriculum permeates all subject areas at all levels of education, from preschool through adult education. All courses should reflect accurate and positive references to ethnic diversity. The amount of specific content about ethnic groups varies according to the course taught, but an awareness and a recognition of the multiethnic nature of the nation can be reflected in all classroom experiences. No matter how assimilated students in a classroom are, it is the teacher's responsibility to expose them to the ethnic diversity of this nation and the world.

Bulletin boards, resource books, and films that show ethnic diversity should constantly reinforce these realities, although teachers should not depend entirely on these resources for instructional content about ethnic groups. Too often, minorities are studied only during a unit on African American history or Native Americans. Too often, minorities are not seen on bulletin boards or included in the reading lists when students study biographies, the basic food groups, labor unions, or the environment. If ethnic groups are included only during a unit or a week focusing on a particular group, students do not learn to view them as an integral part of society. They are viewed as separate, distinct, and inferior to the dominant group. A multiethnic curriculum prevents the distortion of history and contemporary conditions. Without it, the perspective of the dominant group becomes the only valid and correct curriculum to which students continually are exposed.

It is the educator's responsibility to ensure that ethnic groups become an integral part of the total curriculum. This mandate does not require the teacher to discuss every ethnic group. It does require that the classroom

When students of different ethnic groups have the opportunity to develop interpersonal relationships, racial and ethnic relations also are likely to be improved.

resources and instruction not focus completely on the dominant group. It requires that perspectives of ethnic groups and the dominant group be examined in discussions of historical and current events. For example, one should consider the perspective of Native Americans as well as the majority group in a presentation and discussion of early and contemporary conflicts.

The curriculum in most schools is based on the knowledge and perspective of the West (that is, northern and western Europe). The inherent bias of the curriculum does not encourage candid admissions of racism and oppression within society. In fact, it supports the superiority of Western thought over all others and provides minimal or no introduction to non-Western cultures of Asia, Africa, and South and Central America.

In contrast, some school systems and schools in urban areas have adopted an Afrocentric curriculum to challenge Eurocentrism and confront racism and oppression. At the core of this approach is an African perspective of the world and historical events. It is conceived to "develop an African world voice as a moral and cultural necessity for understanding the behavior of Africans and Afrocentric people" (Jones, 1992). It is used in urban schools with large African American student populations to improve students' self-esteem, academic skills, values, and positive identity with their ethnic group (Ascher, 1991).

Multiethnic education should include learning experiences to help students examine their own stereotypes about and prejudice against ethnic groups. These are not easy topics to address, but should be a part of the curriculum beginning in preschool. At all levels, but particularly in junior high and secondary classrooms, students may resist discussion of these issues. Teachers can create a safe classroom climate by establishing clear guidelines for such discussions (Tatum, 1992). When students use derogatory terms for ethnic group members or tell ethnic jokes, teachers should use the opportunity to discuss attitudes about those groups. Students should not be allowed to express their hostility to other group members in any classroom.

Development of a multiethnic curriculum requires the educator to evaluate textbooks and classroom resources for ethnic content and biases. Although there have been advances in eliminating ethnic biases and adding information

PAUSE TO REFLECT

Think about your K–12 education. What ethnic group received primary attention in the curriculum? What ethnic groups other than European ones did you study? What was the content of that study? Were the contributions, experiences, or perspectives of non-European groups ever at the central, valued part of the curriculum? How can a teacher ensure that ethnic diversity is reflected in both the curriculum and the classroom?

about ethnic groups in newer textbooks, many older textbooks are still used in classrooms across the nation. With many textbook revisions, ethnic content has been added to what already existed, rather than carefully integrated throughout the text. Biased books should not prevent the teacher from providing multiethnic instruction. Supplementary materials can fill the gap in this area. The biases and omissions in the texts can be used for discussions of the experiences of ethnic groups. However, none of these instructional activities will occur unless the educator is aware of and values ethnic differences and their importance in the curriculum.

Desegregation

In its 1954 decision on *Brown v. Board of Education,* the Supreme Court declared that separate but equal schooling was no longer equal. However, it took over a decade for schools to begin serious desegregation. The early focus of these efforts was on the placement of black and white students in the same schools. Although it has been forty years since the Brown decision, current desegregation is similar to that in 1972 (Schofield, 1991). In fact, the number of students attending racially or ethnically isolated schools is increasing (Bates, 1990). Rather than schools desegregating, it appears that they are being resegregated. Bates reports that the "outlook for achieving meaningful desegregation when the minority enrollment in a school district is more than 50% is very discouraging" (p. 13).

Second-generation desegregation efforts have expanded beyond just ensuring that schools are racially/ethnically diverse. The focus has been on the inequities within schools with ethnic and gender diverse populations (Bates, 1990). Researchers have found unequal access to advanced mathematics and science classes and gifted programs. Poor and minority students are disproportionately represented in nonacademic and special education classes. Rates of school suspension and dropping out of school vary for different ethnic groups.

No longer does segregation affect primarily black students, although most urban schools in the South, the East, and the Midwest have student bodies that are predominantly African American. Hispanic students are now the most highly segregated group in schools (Valencia, 1991). Bilingual classes are very segregated. A number of Hispanic researchers believe that native language instruction should be integrated throughout the curriculum, rather than treated as a segregated, pull-out program that separates Hispanic students and others for academic study (Meier & Stewart, 1991; Donato, Menchaca, & Valencia, 1991).

The goal of desegregation has changed from the physical integration of students within a school building to the achievement of equal learning opportunities and outcomes for all students (Bates, 1990). It is recognized that effective interpersonal skills are important in achieving this goal. "The ability to work effectively with out-group members is an important skill for both majority and minority group members in a pluralistic society striving to overcome a long history of discrimination in education and employment" (Schofield, 1991, p. 340).

Clark (1991) also recommends that activities be designed to promote interracial friendships, small group teams be used to promote learning, and parents be involved to decrease the dissonance between school and home. Multicultural education is a critical component in the continued effort to desegregate schools.

Student Assessment

Schools conduct widespread testing of students for entrance into programs for the gifted, advanced courses, special education programs, colleges and universities, and professional schools. These standardized tests have limited the access of oppressed group members to more rigorous study at all educational levels, and may prevent students from entering professional schools. They are also used to assign disproportionately large numbers of minority students to special education programs for the mentally retarded, learning disabled, and emotionally disturbed.

Tests are trumpeted as measures of competence to graduate from high school, to enter upper-division college courses, to earn a baccalaureate degree, and to become licensed to teach. Many proponents of testing suggest that the tests alone can determine whether students know and perform at levels acceptable by society. Such tests are promoted as measures of quality in the nation's schools. Overwhelmingly, promoters suggest that anyone who cannot pass the appropriate test certainly cannot be qualified to move on to further study. In fact, such testing limits the access of many individuals to practice the career of their choice (Smith, 1985).

Why is it that students from oppressed groups continue to score lower on standardized tests than dominant group members? One theory suggests that minority groups have suffered socioeconomic and cultural disadvantages for generations that have prevented them from competing equally with advantaged cultural groups. Knowledgeable and sensitive educators could help make a difference. Most testing in schools is based on an Anglo-conformity model of appraisal. Psychologist Jane Mercer (1978) writes:

> In making inferences about children's "intelligence" or "aptitudes," present procedures presume that America is a culturally homogeneous society in which all children are being socialized into essentially the same Anglo tradition. . . . [Existing tests] are to be used for diagnosis, prognosis, and prescription in education so that all children can be socialized to the existing social structure, i.e., the Anglo core culture. . . . [In the Anglo-oriented view,] the greater the sociocultural distance between the individual and the dominant core culture, the lower his or her score will be. Thus, persons more culturally distant from the Anglo core culture will score lower and will be considered "subnormal," ineligible for job placement, and inadmissible to college and graduate school. (p. 15)

As educators, we must be careful not to label poor and minority children as intellectually inferior because they score poorly on standardized tests. These scores too often influence the teacher's expectations for the academic performance of students in the classroom. It is essential that we maintain high expectations for all students, regardless of ethnic background and test scores. Standardized test scores can help determine how assimilated into the majority culture one may be, but they provide little evidence of how intelligent one is. There are many other factors that can be used to provide information about intelligence, for example, ability to think and respond appropriately in different situations.

Finally, in developing tests and using the results of standardized tests, the educator must recognize the inherent cultural bias that favors dominant students. Few tests have been developed from the bias of a minority group. Test bias is a serious educational issue with devastating results to many minorities. A report of the National Alliance of Black School Educators (1984) stated:

> Testing the intellect of African American children with alien cultural content is a scientific error and is, in our opinion, professional malpractice. Testing in order to rank children by intellect, to rank them by cognitive or behavioral style, or to rank them with "non-biased" assessment procedures is malpractice, in our opinion, unless such practices can be demonstrated by valid research to result in significant and meaningful changes in achievement for our children. (p. 28)

Educators must be aware that these cultural biases exist and continually remind themselves not to rely on test scores as the only indication of students' intelligence and academic potential. There are many examples of good teachers who have helped minority students with poor standardized scores achieve at advanced levels. Poor Hispanic and African American students have outperformed other students in mathematics and other subjects after teachers have raised their expectations and changed their teaching strategies. Project SEED and the work of James Escalante in Los Angeles and Philip Uri Treisman at Berkeley are examples of successful programs.

Educators are capable of making valid decisions about ability based on numerous other objective and subjective factors about students. If decisions about the capabilities of minority students match exactly the standardized scores, the educator should reevaluate his or her own responses and interactions with these students. This is an area that none of us can afford to neglect.

Summary

Almost from the beginning of European settlement, the population of the United States was multiethnic, with individuals representing many Native American tribes and European nations, later to be joined by Africans and then Asians. Primary reasons for immigration were internal economic impoverishment and political repression in the countries of origin and the demands of a vigorous U.S. economy that required a larger labor force. The conditions encountered by different ethnic groups, the reasons they came, and their expectations about life here differed greatly and have led ethnic groups to view themselves as distinct from others.

Ethnicity is a sense of peoplehood based on national origin. Although no longer useful in describing groups of people, the term *race* continues to be used in this country to classify groups of people as inferior or superior. Its popular usage is based on society's perception that racial differences are important—a belief not upheld by scientific study. The term *minority group* is useful in understanding relationships between groups. Oppressed minority groups lack social, economic, and political power in society. Members of these oppressed groups experience discriminatory treatment and often are relegated to relatively low-status positions in society.

Prejudice is "a negative attitude toward an entire category of people" (Schaefer, 1988, p. 55). Discrimination focuses on behavior that treats individuals differently because of their membership in a minority group. When discrimination is institutionalized, inequalities are inherent in policies and practices that benefit dominant group members while appearing to be neutral in their effect on different groups.

In a classroom, students are likely to come from several different ethnic groups, although physical differences are not always identifiable. Not all people view their ethnic origins as important in understanding who they are. Their membership in other microcultures may have a greater impact on their identity than the nations from which their ancestors came. Educators must be careful of stereotyping all persons from the same ethnic group; many differences exist within the same group.

Two approaches to incorporating ethnic content in the curriculum are ethnic studies and multiethnic education. Ethnic studies are an extension or special segment of the curriculum that focuses on the in-depth study of the history and contemporary conditions of one or more ethnic groups. Often, ethnic studies are offered as separate courses. Multiethnic education is broader in scope in that it requires ethnic content to permeate the total curriculum; thus, all courses taught reflect the multiethnic nature of society. Understanding ethnicity is an advantage in developing effective teaching strategies for individual students.

Desegregation is a process for decreasing racial/ethnic isolation in schools. Although early desegregation efforts focused on ensuring that black and white students attended the same schools, today increasing number of students attend predominantly minority schools. The current emphasis is on ensuring the academic achievement of all students and eliminating the inequities in educational opportunities.

Educators must examine how they are administering and using standardized tests in the classroom. Too often, testing programs have been used for the purpose of identifying native intelligence and thus sorting people for education and jobs. If disproportionately large numbers of minority students are scoring poorly on such tests and being placed in special classes as a result, the program must be reviewed. Many factors can be used to provide information about intelligence and ability, for example, the ability to think and respond appropriately in different situations.

Questions for Review

1. Why is membership in an ethnic group more important to some individuals than to others?
2. Describe factors that cause members of oppressed groups to view ethnicity differently than dominant group members.
3. Describe differences and similarities in the immigration patterns of Africans, Asians, Central Americans, Europeans, and South Americans during the past four centuries.
4. Distinguish between prejudice and discrimination and describe their impact on oppressed group members in this country.
5. Why does race remain so important a factor in the social, political, and economic patterns of the United States?
6. What characteristics might an educator look for to determine a student's ethnic background and the importance it plays in that student's life?
7. List five ways in which an educator should be able to use ethnicity in the classroom.
8. Contrast ethnic studies and multiethnic education, and list the advantages of each.
9. If you are working in a desegregated school setting, what skills and instructional strategies should you develop to help you be an effective teacher?
10. Why is the use of standardized tests so controversial today? What are the dangers of depending too heavily on the results of standardized tests?

References

American Council on Education and Education Commission of the States. (1988). *One-third of a nation: A report of the Commission on Minority Participation in Education and American Life.* Washington, DC: American Council on Education.

Appiah, K. A. (1990). Racisms. In D. T. Goldberg (Ed.), *Anatomy of racism.* Minneapolis: University of Minnesota Press.

Appleton, N. (1983). *Cultural pluralism in education.* New York: Longman.

Ascher, C. (1991). School programs for African American male students. *Equity and Choice, 8*(1), 25–59.

Bates, P. (1990). Desegregation: Can we get there from here? *Phi Delta Kappan, 72*(1), 8–17.

Berreman, G. D. (1985). Race, caste, and other invidious distinctions in social stratification. In N. R. Yetman (Ed.), *Majority and minority: The dynamics of race and ethnicity in American life* (4th ed.) (pp. 21–39). Boston: Allyn and Bacon.

Carnegie Foundation for the Advancement of Teaching. (1990). Native Americans and higher education: New mood of optimism. *Change, 22*(1), 27–30.

Cashmore, E., & Troyna, B. (1990). *Introduction to race relations* (2nd ed.). New York: Falmer Press.

Clark, M. L. (1991). Social identity, peer relations, and academic competence of African American adolescents. *Education and Urban Society, 24*(1), 41–52.

Cross, W. E., Jr. (1991). *Shades of black: Diversity in African American identity.* Philadelphia: Temple University Press.

Derman-Sparks, L., & the A.B.C. Task Force. (1989). *Anti-bias curriculum: Tools for empowering young children.* Washington, DC: National Association for the Education of Young Children.

Donato, R., Menchaca, M., & Valencia, R. R. (1991). Segregation, desegregation, and integration of Chicano students: Problems and prospects. In R. R. Valencia (Ed.), *Chicano school failure and success: Research and policy agendas for the 1990s.* New York: Falmer Press.

Fordham, S. (1988). Racelessness as a factor in black students' school success: Pragmatic strategy or Pyrrhic victory. *Harvard Educational Review, 58*(1), 54–84.

Gans, H. J. (1985). Symbolic ethnicity: The future of ethnic groups and cultures in America. In N. R. Yetman (Ed.), *Majority and minority: They dynamics of race and ethnicity in American life* (4th ed.) (pp. 429–442). Boston: Allyn and Bacon.

Gibson, M. A. (1988). *Accommodation without assimilation: Sikh immigrants in an American high school.* Ithaca, NY: Cornell University Press.

Gibson, M. A. (Winter 1992/93). Variability in immigrant students' school performance: The U.S. case. *The Social Context of Education.* (American Educational Research Association-Division G).

Gordon, M. M. (1964). *Assimilation in American life: The role of race, religion, and national origins.* New York: Oxford University Press.

Higham, J. (1975). Toward racism: The history of an idea. In N. R. Yetman & C. H. Steele (Eds.), *Majority and minority: The dynamics of racial and ethnic relations* (2nd ed.) (pp. 207–222). Boston: Allyn and Bacon.

Jones, D. M. (1992). [Review of Kemet, *Afrocentricity and knowledge]. Harvard Educational Review, 62*(1), 88–91.

Meier, K. J., & Stewart, J., Jr. (1991). *The politics of Hispanic education.* Albany, NY: State University of New York Press.

Mercer, J. R. (1978). Test "validity," "bias," and "fairness": An analysis from the perspective of the sociology of knowledge. *Interchange, 9,* 4, 5, 14–15.

The Mid-Atlantic Equity Center. (Spring 1992). Rights of undocumented national origin minority students. *Equity Alert, 1*(1).

National Alliance of Black School Educators. (1984). *Saving the African American child.* Washington, DC: Author.

National Center for Education Statistics. (1992). *American education at a glance.* Washington, DC: Author.

Oakes, J. (1988). Tracking in mathematics and science education: A structural contribution to unequal schooling. In L. Weis (Ed.), *Class, race, and gender in American education* (pp. 106–125). Albany, NY: State University of New York Press.

Ogbu, J. (1988). Class stratification, racial stratification, and schooling. In L. Weis (Ed.), *Class, race, and gender in American education.* Albany, NY: State University of New York Press.

Omi, M., & Winant, H. (1986). *Racial formation in the United States: From the 1960s to the 1980s.* New York: Routledge & Kegan Paul.

Schaefer, R. T. (1988). *Racial and ethnic groups* (3rd ed.). Boston: Little, Brown.

Schofield, J. W. (1991). School desegregation and intergroup relations: A review of the literature. In G. Grant, *Review of research in education.* Washington, DC: American Educational Research Association.

Schuman, H., Steech, C., & Bobo, L. (1985). *Racial attitudes in America: Trends and interpretations.* Cambridge, MA: Harvard University Press.

Smith, P. (1985). The impact of competency tests on teacher education: Ethical and legal issues in selecting and certifying teachers. In M. Haberman (Ed.), *Research in teacher education*. To be published.

Solomon, R. P. (1988). Black cultural forms in schools: A cross national comparison. In L. Weis (Ed.), *Class, race, and gender in American education* (pp. 249–265). Albany, NY:. State University of New York Press.

Takaki, R. (1989). *Strangers from a different shore*. Boston: Little, Brown.

Tatum, B. D. (1992). Talking about race, learning about racism: The application of racial identity development theory in the classroom. *Harvard Educational Review, 62*(1), 1–24.

Teper, S. (1977). *Ethnicity, race, and human development: A report on the state of our knowledge*. Chicago: Institute on Pluralism and Group Identity.

Valencia, R. R. (Ed.) (1991). The plight of Chicano students: An overview of schooling conditions and outcomes. In R. R. Valencia, *Chicano school failure and success: Research and policy agendas for the 1990s*. New York: Falmer Press.

Violence on rise in America's schools. (July 1992). *SPLC Report, 22*(3).

Willis, P. E. (1977). *Learning to labour: How working class kids get working class jobs*. Farnborough, England: Saxon House.

Yancey, W. L., Ericksen, E. P., & Juliani, R. N. (1985). Emergent ethnicity: A review and reformulation. In N. R. Yetman (Ed.), *Majority and minority: The dynamics of racial and ethnic relations* (4th ed.) (pp. 185–194). Boston: Allyn and Bacon.

Yetman, N. R. (Ed.). (1985). *Majority and minority: The dynamics of racial and ethnic relations* (4th ed.). Boston: Allyn and Bacon.

Suggested Readings

Derman-Sparks, L., Gutierrez, M., & Phillips, C. B. (Undated). *Teaching young children to resist bias: What parents can do*. Washington, DC: National Association for the Education of Young Children.

This pamphlet provides recommendations for helping primary age students and their parents understand ethnic, race, gender, and disability biases.

Edelman, M. W. (1992). *The measure of our success: A letter to my children and yours*. Boston: Beacon Press.

Written by the founder and president of the Children's Defense Fund, this book is a compassionate message for parents trying to raise moral children. It includes twenty-five recommendations to guide young people.

Educators for Social Responsibility. (Undated). *Dealing with differences: Conflict resolution in our schools*. Cambridge, MA: Author

This pamphlet describes ESR's program for helping educators manage conflict within schools. It includes a number of recommendations for teachers.

FairTest. (1990). *Standardized tests and our children: A guide to testing reform*. Cambridge, MA: National Center for Fair and Open Testing.

Available in Spanish and English, this guide addresses the national movement to replace standardized, multiple-choice testing with performance-based assessments. It includes sections on the use of standardized tests, alternative evaluations, parents' rights, the history of testing, commonly used tests, and the meaning of test scores.

Hale, J. (1982). *Black children: Their roots, culture, and learning styles*. Provo, UT: Brigham Young University Press.

This book provides a conceptual framework for examining the development of African-

American children. It includes curriculum recommendations with implications for early childhood education.

Kotlowitz, A. (1991). *There are no children here: The story of two boys growing up in the other America.* New York: Anchor Books.

This book chronicles the lives of two brothers growing up in a Chicago housing project. It highlights the politics of inertia, hopelessness, and greed that encompasses poverty.

Tafolla, C. (1992). *Sonnets to human beings and other selected works.* Santa Monica, CA: Lalo Press.

This book contains the author's award-winning manuscript, "Sonnets to Human Beings," *and other poems and stories written from a Chicana perspective.*

Teaching Tolerance. (Published by the Southern Poverty Law Center, 400 Washington Ave., Montgomery, AL 36104).

This semi-annual magazine provides teachers with resources and ideas to promote harmony in the classroom. Articles are written from the perspectives of multiple ethnic groups. It is available at no cost to teachers.

Terkel, S. (1992). *Race: How blacks and whites think and feel about the American obsession.* New York: The New Press.

Nearly 100 black and white men and women of different ages describe their experiences and expose their attitudes as members of a racist society. The stories show honest and changing opinions about race in this country.

CHAPTER 4

Gender

The girls in Abdul Rashid's science class are talking about what they plan to wear to the dance on Friday. However, he had planned to introduce them to ecology. Since school began seven months ago, he has not been able to interest most of the females in the science content.

Most of his female students are capable of understanding and using science, but they show no interest. Sometimes he thinks that they just do not want to upstage the boys in the class. He knows that some of them should be in an advanced science class because they score extremely well on the written tests, but they show no interest in class discussions and experiments.

For the ecology orientation, he decided last night to take a different approach. Perhaps he could relate the subject to something meaningful in their real lives—maybe even their families' or their own social activities. He wanted to find examples that they would care about. He decided to focus on the toxic chemicals that are found in the creek that runs behind many of their homes. Premature births in that area are being blamed on the chemical dumping that has been going on for over twenty years.

Why do most of the females in Mr. Rashid's class appear to be uninterested in science? What are the participation rates of females in advanced mathematics and science courses? What are the reasons for the lack of participation by girls and young women? What do you think of Mr. Rashid's approach to introducing ecology? What would you do to increase the interest and participation of females in science and mathematics?

Gender and Culture

Although there are few differences between males and females, the popular, and sometimes "scientific," beliefs about differences between the genders have not always matched reality. At the beginning of this century some scientists and many individuals thought that men, particularly those with ancestors from northern and western Europe, were intellectually superior to women and thus generally more capable of most professional and administrative work. It was believed that women's nature made it imperative that men give orders and women take orders in the workplace. Because their strength was not comparable to that of men, women were also unable to obtain many manual or working-class jobs except for the most menial and lowest paid. Well-adjusted women were expected to be married homemakers, performing services for the family without remuneration.

Even though there is now clear evidence that women and men do not differ in intelligence, the percentage of men in the best-paying and most demanding professional jobs is disproportionately higher than the percentage of women in those jobs. Because of technological advances, brute strength is usually no longer a requirement for most manual jobs, but the percentage of women in those jobs still falls far behind the percentage of men. Many men and women still believe that there are biological differences that prevent gender equality in the home and the workplace.

In response to the patriarchical arrangements that have kept women subordinate to men within the home and in our capitalist system, strong women's movements have developed at different periods in our history. A number of the women and men in the antislavery movements prior to the Civil War raised concerns about women's issues, including divorce, property rights, the right to speak in public, abuse by husbands, work with little or no pay, and suffrage. At the Seneca Falls Convention in 1848, women organized to fight against their oppression. In this effort, there were some male supporters, including Frederick Douglass and white abolitionists who were fighting against slavery and for human and civil rights for all. At the same time, many women did not view their conditions as oppressive and were not supportive of the movement for equality.

During the last half of the nineteenth century, protective legislation for women and children was enacted. This legislation made some manual jobs inaccessible to women because of the danger involved and limited the number of hours that could be worked and the time at which one could work. However, such legislation did little to extend equal rights to women. Unfortunately during this period, feminists segregated their fight for equal rights from the struggles of other oppressed groups and refused to take a stand against Jim Crow laws and other violations of the civil rights of African and Asian Americans. Women's groups, which were predominantly white, also pitted themselves against black men in the fight for the right to vote.

The most significant changes in the status of women were initiated in the 1960s, when feminists were able to gain the support of more women and men than at any previous time in history. As in the previous century, this movement developed out of the struggle for civil rights by African Americans. In an attempt to defeat the Civil Rights Bill in Congress, a southern congressman added the words "or sex" to Title VII, declaring that discrimination based on "race, color, national origin, or sex" was prohibited. This legislation, which was approved in 1964, was the first time that equal rights had been extended to women. Nevertheless, in 1983 Congress refused to adopt the one-sentence Equal Rights Amendment (ERA), *Equality of rights under the law shall not be denied or abridged by the United States or by any state on account of sex,* even though two-thirds of the U.S. population supported it.

The women's movements that were initiated in the nineteenth century were, and continue to be, dominated by middle-class white women. They have, for the most part, limited the struggle to women's issues rather than broader civil rights for all oppressed groups. This focus has prevented the widespread involvement in the movement of both men and women who are African Americans, Asian Americans, Hispanic Americans, and Native Americans. Support from the working class has also been limited. The 1990s appear to be ushering in a change toward broader support for civil rights for all groups and greater inclusion of men and women from diverse ethnic groups in the feminist movement. A growing number of articles and books on equity by feminists and others address the interaction of race, gender, and class in the struggle for equity for all groups.

Why do equal rights for women continue to be unmet? There are different views about the equality of the sexes. Feminists fight for equality in jobs, pay, schooling, responsibilities in the home, and the nation's laws. They believe that women and men should have a choice about working in the home or outside of the home, having children, and acknowledging their sexual orientation. They believe that women should not have to be subordinate to men at home, in the workplace, or in society. They fight to eliminate the physical and mental violence that has resulted from such subordination by providing support groups and shelters for abused women and children as well as pushing our judicial system to not tolerate such violence. In addition, they promote shared male and female responsibilities in the home and the availability of child care to all families. At the same time, feminists struggle with identifying the special qualities of being a woman, not succumbing to the undesirable qualities of the male world, and seeking solutions to make society more equitable (Noddings, 1990).

On the other hand, there is a vocal group of antifeminists that includes both men and women who have fought against the Equal Rights Amendment and other equality issues. This group is led by political conservatives, especially those from a fundamentalist religious background. They believe that the primary responsibilities of a woman are to be a good wife and mother; employment outside of the home is viewed as interfering with these expected roles. Homemaking is in itself a viable career that should be pursued. The male is to be the primary breadwinner in the family, and a woman's dependency on the husband or father is expected. They believe that feminism and equal rights will lead to the disintegration of the nuclear family unit. Homosexuality and abortion are rejected. The men and women who support these positions have effectively organized themselves politically to defeat the ERA, promote positions against gays and lesbians, and curtail dissemination of information on sexuality.

Regardless of one's identification with feminism, "most human beings live in single-sex worlds, women in a female world and men in a male world, and the two are different from one another in a myriad of ways, both subjectively and objectively" (Bernard, 1981, p. 3). Differences can be observed in gender segregation at schools and social gatherings; concentrations in different occupations; dress and gender-specific grooming; and types of relationships, both between and within the genders, such as dating behavior, gender-specific leisure activities, and stereotyped perceptions by members of each gender about themselves and the other gender (Safilios-Rothschild, 1979). "All human languages make a definite distinction between the genders, and all societies use sex as the basis for assigning people to different adult roles" (Stockard & Johnson, 1980, p. 3). Men and women disproportionately enter different occupations and have different activities and opportunities in the economic world. "At school, at church, at work, at play, boys and girls and men and women are governed by different norms, rules of behavior and expectations; they are subject to different eligibility rules for rewards and different vulnerability to punishments" (Bernard, 1981, p. 4).

In all known cultures, men's work is assigned higher prestige in society than women's work, regardless of the nature of the work. Male activities and roles are recognized as more important and given more authority and value than those undertaken by women (Rosaldo & Lamphere, 1974). This superior status is reflected in the inequities that exist in the prestige of different jobs held by men and women, the difference in wages earned by men and women, and the differential prestige and economic rewards for housework and childrearing compared to nonhousehold work. Of course, the range of social and economic differences within one gender is as great as it is between them. There is no doubt that some women are economically and socially better off than many men. Women often assume the same class role as their spouses and are able to maintain that status unless it is disrupted by divorce or death. Nevertheless, women as a group have not been allowed a status equal to men in economic, social, and political spheres. In addition, differences between men and women are influenced by class, ethnicity, race, religion, and age.

Men are also greatly affected by society's view of gender expectations. The masculine characteristics that are rewarded in our society are independence, assertiveness, leadership ability, self-reliance, and emotional stability (Bornstein, 1982). However, Filene (1986) observes that "in reality, few men truly extinguished the need to be comforted, the fear of loneliness, the anxiety of being inept or wrong or unloved. But they had learned to hide those vulnerabilities behind tight lips and dry eyes—the masculine armor" (p. 213). Some men have established their own male liberation groups to promote choices beyond the traditional male roles. While occupation is still very important in a man's identification of who he is, the desire to be more involved in childrearing and housekeeping is gaining support.

Unlike the women's movement, which became social action, male liberation remains a personal, not political, matter. When a group holds power and privilege in society, it is difficult to relinquish it. "Men cannot be liberated from conventional male roles until institutions permit part-time and flexible work schedules as well as abundant, inexpensive child-care facilities. And men will not liberate themselves until they resolve the culturally entrenched definitions of control achievement and self-esteem" (Filene, 1986, p. 221).

Are there biological differences that prevent male- and female-assigned roles from being interchanged? Although women alone can bear offspring, does that also mean that only they can rear a child? Do biological differences suggest that we do different types of work?

Differences Between Males and Females

We do not choose to be born female or male. Gender is determined before birth and is one of the first characteristics noticed at birth. Ethnicity, religion, and class status are automatically the same as our parents'. However, the baby's gender elicits different responses from both society and the family.

Although newborns are described by their gender, there are few observable differences in physical characteristics other than reproductive organs. Boys tend to be slightly longer and heavier than girls. Girls have a lower percentage of their total body weight in muscle, and their lungs and heart are proportionally smaller. However, in a comparison of thirty newborns of the same length, weight, and Apgar scores (i.e., rating of the infant's color, muscle tone, reflexes, irritability, and heart and respiratory rates), researchers found that parents described girls and boys differently. Girls were more likely to be described as little, beautiful, pretty, and cute, whereas boys were described as big, strong, and hardy (Rubin, Provenzano, & Luria, 1974). More importantly, many parents and other individuals begin to treat their children differently from birth, based primarily on their gender (Safilios-Rothschild, 1979).

Most of us can easily identify physical differences between men and women by appearance alone. Girls tend to have lighter skeletons and different shoulder and pelvic proportions. Although the proportion of different hormones in the body differs by gender, boys and girls have similar hormonal levels and similar physical development during the first eight years (Barfield, 1976). The onset of puberty marks the difference in hormonal levels that controls the physical development of the two genders. At this time, the proportion of fat to total body weight increases in girls and decreases in boys. The differences in physical structure contribute to a female's diminished strength, lower endurance for heavy labor, greater difficulty in running or overarm throwing, and better ability to float in water. Of course, environment and culture greatly influence the extent of these physical differences for both males and females. Thus, the feminine characteristics listed here can be altered with good nutrition, physical activity, practice, and different behavioral expectations (Barfield, 1976).

There are a number of other reported physical differences between the genders. Because of different expectations and behaviors of males and females in the past, it is difficult to determine how many of these differences are actually biological. Some may result from different cultural expectations and lived experiences rather than from different biological makeup. For example, gender differences in the incidence of cardiovascular disease may decrease as more women enter jobs associated with stress. However, researchers at the University of North Carolina found that childless, single, and married women working in demanding careers suffer the lowest incidence of stress-related disease of all men and women. The highest incidence of heart disease was found in women who are mothers and work in clerical positions (Radl, 1983).

Researchers have found gender differences in mathematical, verbal, and spatial skills. Some researchers have attributed these differences to biological determinism, especially hormones affecting hemispheral specialization in the brain. They argue that the right hemisphere of the cerebral cortex controls spatial relations and the left hemisphere controls language and other sequential skills. Since males perform better on tests of spacial visualization, these researchers conclude that males have greater right-hemisphere specialization and thus achieve better in mathematics and science.

Other researchers attribute the gender differences in these areas to socialization patterns in childrearing and schooling rather than biological factors. After an extensive review of the research, Sadker, Sadker, and Klein (1991, p. 309) reported that "differences in math, verbal, and spatial skills have been declining over recent years. These changes in gender differences over a small period of time speak against a heavy reliance on biological arguments" (Halpern, 1989). These researchers found that:

- *On quantitative abilities*: There are no differences until the age of ten. During the middle school years, researchers have found slight differences in favor of girls, slight differences in favor of boys, and no differences. Differences favoring males occur at the high school level. Female students do indicate less interest in mathematics. However, the magnitude of differences in performance in both math and science has declined since 1974.

- *On spatial abilities*: Gender differences are declining and spatial ability can be improved with training.
- *On verbal abilities*: Although past research found that females began to develop verbal superiority at age eleven, more recent research finds little significant difference between males and females.

The factor that complicates discussions about gender differences is the tendency to equate women with the natural world and men with culture, which controls and transcends nature (Moore, 1990). In this view women are associated with childbearing and childrearing while men work to support a nuclear family. However, recent research analyses of gender differences provide little support for a biological explanation. Anthropologists report that differences vary greatly from culture to culture. They find that "the images, attributes, activities, and appropriate behavior associated with women [and men] are always culturally and historically specific" (Moore, 1990, p. 7) as opposed to biologically specific.

The term that describes the differences that separate male and female worlds is *gender.* It includes aspects that separate masculinity and femininity like clothes, interests, attitudes, behaviors, and aptitudes (Delamont, 1990). These characteristics are determined by culture, not by biology, and are those used most often to describe differences between females and males.

Gender Identity

Most people take their gender identity for granted and do not question it because it agrees with their biological identity. One's recognition of the appropriate gender identity occurs unconsciously early in life. It becomes a basic anchor in the personality and forms a core part of one's self-identity (Stockard & Johnson, 1980). By the age of two years, children realize that they are either a boy or a girl and begin to learn their expected behaviors. By the time they are five or six years old, they have already learned their gender and stereotypical behavior (Bernard, 1981).

Researchers are unsure how gender identity develops, but the most important factor is the assignment of gender to an individual at birth by the doctor, parents, family, and friends. Appropriate gender behavior is reinforced by reading, watching television, and playing with peers and toys (Safilios-Rothschild, 1979). In this socialization process children develop social skills and a sense of self in accordance with socially prescribed roles and expectations. The gender typing by parents is reflected in the personality attributes, intellectual performance, and occupational choices of their children.

Appropriate gender behavior is reinforced throughout the life cycle by social processes of approval and disapproval, reward and punishment. Studies show that there are substantive differences in the ways parents treat children of different genders. Because mothers have primary responsibility for raising most children, the mother-child relationship in the early years is important in determining the male or female personality. The mother provides a girl an easily accessible model from the beginning. It is easy and natural for a girl to know and learn appropriate behavior by being with her mother much of the time during the preschool years. However, boys are not as likely to have readily available male models or masculine activities. At some point, the boy must break from his mother and establish his maleness separately from her (Rosaldo & Lamphere, 1974).

Socialization does not end with parents and relatives. When the child enters school, the socialization process continues. In fact, achievement studies show that schooling is most effective when the values of school and family are similar. Generally, schools convey the same standards for gender roles as most parents in our society. The attitudes and values about appropriate gender roles

From an early age, most children adhere to the gender behavior and identity expected by society.

are embedded in the curriculum of most schools. Elementary schools appear to imitate the mothering role with a predominance of female teachers and an emphasis on obedience and conformity. In classrooms, boys and girls tend to receive different feedback for their work, similar to the patterns used at home.

In a four-year study of peer interactions in the elementary school, Best (1989) found than boys and girls separated themselves from teachers at different ages. During the second grade, boys began to develop peer solidarity, which influenced their gender development in a way compatible with society's expectations for males. Girls did not establish peer solidarity until the fourth grade. The importance of the peer group for the boys was reflected in their segregation in the rest rooms, lunchroom, and playground, and the emphasis on hierarchical order within the group. "But not all boys were equally involved. There were some who never made it 'in'" (Best, 1989, p. 17). By the third grade these excluded boys showed their hostility by stealing, throwing stones, and killing birds and fish for fun.

The socialization of boys has been oriented toward achievement and self-reliance, that of girls toward nurturance and responsibility. Traditionally, it was believed that girls naturally learned their roles as wife and mother. The knowledge required to carry out these roles was not as highly valued by society as the knowledge required to achieve manhood. Especially in the middle class, girls learned to share and boys learned to compete (Filene, 1986).

During socialization, we internalize the social norms considered appropriate for our gender, including gender-appropriate behavior, personality characteristics, emotional responses, attitudes, and beliefs. These characteristics become so much a part of our self-identification that we forget they are learned and are not innate characteristics. Individuals who demonstrate characteristics inappropriate to their gender are often chastised by society.

The fact that gender identity is learned becomes clear when males and females from other cultures are observed. During her field work in New Guinea, Margaret Mead (1935) observed three variations of male and female personalities. Both male and female Arapesh were cooperative, unaggressive, and responsive to the needs and demands of others. In contrast, the Mundugumor males and females were ruthless and aggressive, with few signs of a maternal cherishing aspect of personality. The Arapesh ideal was the mild, responsive man married to the mild, responsive woman; the Mundugumor ideal was the violent, aggressive man married to the violent, aggressive woman. In the third tribe, the Tchambuli, Mead found a genuine reversal of the gender attitudes of our own culture. The Tchambuli woman was dominant, impersonal, and the managing partner, while the man was less responsible and the emotionally dependent person. Mead's observations suggest that there is no basis for regarding aspects of behavior as inherently either male or female.

In our society women are supposed to be feminine and men masculine, with society tolerating little crossover. However, biology does not necessarily equate with an individual's gender feeling. There are some men and women who prefer to behave like the opposite gender, sometimes in overt ways like cross-dressing. Daytime talk shows thrive on talking with individuals who do not accept or follow society's gender categories. Generally, females are allowed more flexibility in their gender identification than males in that the female with masculine traits is more acceptable in society then the male with feminine traits.

Gender should no longer be viewed in the traditional bipolar fashion as if masculine and feminine traits never coexist in an individual. "An individual is not more or less masculine, or more or less feminine, but rather more or less aggressive, sexual, nurturant, ambitious, verbal, spatial, and so on" (Barfield, 1976, p. 109).

Impact of Perceived Differences

Anthropologists have found that there are some universal practices related to gender roles. First, in all societies, men have clear control of political and military apparatus; there is no known society in which men are "systematically excluded from political rights and authority" (Moore, 1990, p. 22). Second, no society fosters achievement and self-reliance in females more than in males. Third, boys tend to seek dominance more than girls do and are significantly more physically and verbally aggressive. However, there is no clear evidence that these characteristics are universal gender role characteristics rather than a function of a near-universal cultural practice (Lee, 1976). The fact that these universal practices exist is the result of a historical development rather than the superiority of the male (de Beauvoir, 1974).

Every society reflects characteristic tasks, manners, and responsibilities associated with either women or men. Traditionally, women have had the primary responsibility for childrearing; men have had the responsibility for waging wars and being the primary breadwinners (Rosaldo & Lamphere, 1974).

Today, men are still likely to have the primary responsibility for earning the income to support the family, although both the wife and husband work in 40 percent of all families and in 60 percent of middle-income families (Filene, 1986). Many women continue to fulfill the roles of mother and wife; the husband fulfills the roles of wage earner, father, and husband. However, these male and female roles are expanding and changing. Almost half of the nation's work force is female, and 90 percent of all women will work outside the home at some time. Today, a growing number of women are divorced, widowed, or otherwise alone. Unable to depend on a male wage earner, they are forced economically to fulfill that role alone. Although both men and women now work in a variety of careers and share many roles and activities that were formerly gender-typed, many adults still retain their traditional gender roles as well.

Traditional feminine roles have less status than masculine roles. This female inferiority often leads to ambivalence, especially in the adolescent girl. There is growing evidence that "women who lack a sense of social and sexual entitlement, who hold traditional notions of what it means to be female—self-sacrificing and relatively passive—and who undervalue themselves, are disproportionately likely to find themselves with an unwanted pregnancy and to maintain it through to motherhood" (Fine, 1988, p. 48). Teenagers from low-income families are particularly susceptible to fulfilling their female role through childbearing, no matter what their racial or ethnic backgrounds. In some cases, having a baby is the passage from childhood to adulthood. The educational and occupational achievements of the mothers are often halted or delayed. As a result, the children of teenage mothers are disproportionately poor.

Teaching and nursing continue to be identified as female professions. Although women comprise 87 percent of our elementary teachers and 67 percent of all teachers, they are only 20 percent of the elementary school principals (Apple, 1989). In a study of women teachers in an urban area, Weiler found that their choice of teaching as a career was based, in part, on the use of their nurturing and caring qualities. Because of their oppressed status, they found reasons not to pursue the math, science, or other professional careers that they had envisioned when they started college. The realities of racism and sexism influenced their final career decision. Weiler (1988) concludes:

> It is the internalization of a male hegemony that leads women to devalue their own worth and to assume that the career of a man is more important than their own, or that they are somehow "incapable" of doing math or science. Thus even when choices are freely made, they are choices made within a kind of logic of existing social structures and ideology. And this logic is learned very early and is reinforced through many institutions. Thus we see in these stories [of women teachers] the valuing of female nurturance, and at the same time women's sense of inadequacy; an acceptance that men are the real people and that girls and women are there to support them. (p. 89)

Gender role expectations are also reflected in schools. Girls and young women are expected to be well behaved and to do well. Males are expected to be less well behaved and not to achieve academically as well as females prior to puberty. Many working-class males develop patterns of resistance to school and its authority figures because it is feminine and emphasizes mental rather than manual work (Willis, 1977).

Stereotyping of Gender Roles

Although gender roles are gradually changing, they continue to be projected stereotypically in the socialization process. Stereotyping narrowly defines the male and female roles and defines them as quite distinct from one another. It leads children to generalize that all persons within a group behave in the same way. Men and women become automatically associated with the characteristics and roles with which they are constantly endowed by the mass media and by classroom materials. Careers are not the only areas in which stereotyping occurs. Male and female intellectual abilities, personality characteristics, physical appearance, social status, and domestic roles have also been stereotyped. Persons who differ from the stereotype of their group, especially gay men and lesbians, are ostracized by the dominant group. Such role stereotyping denies individuals the wide range of human potential that is possible.

Television is one of the great perpetuators of gender stereotyping. Studies show that by three years of age, children have already developed tastes in television programs related to age, gender, and race. By the time of high school graduation, the average child will have spent eleven thousand hours in the classroom and fifteen thousand hours in front of the television. Few children are exempt from this practice, since most homes in this country have one or more television sets.

The stereotypical roles portrayed on television do not reflect the realities of life for most males and females in today's society. The ideals and ideas of dominant America are incorporated into program development as symbolic representations of American society. They are not literal portrayals, yet these representations announce to viewers what is valued and approved in society.

A study by the National Commission on Working Women found that "viewers are likely to see girls with no visible skills, no favorite subjects in school, no discussions about college majors or vocational plans. . . . These images create the impression that one can magically jump from an adolescence of dating and shopping to a well-paid professional career. . . . On TV, girls' looks count for more than their brains" (Sidel, 1990). Adult working women are portrayed on television, but both they and adolescent women are predominantly rich or middle class (Sidel). Except for the popular *Roseanne,* strong, intelligent working- class women are invisible. Female heroines are not social workers, teachers, or secretaries.

Although a number of TV men in the early 1980s were caring and sensitive, today's heroes tend to eliminate evil antagonists by shooting them, are womanizers and/or chauvinists, or are the authoritative, all-knowing heads of households. Sidel (1990) reports that "the introspective male hero who sees many sides of an issue and is torn apart by his understanding of individuals and their limitations and society and its limitations is being replaced by characters who see issues in starker terms and who believe in individual accountability rather than societal accountability" (pp. 106–107).

The written media is another area in which women and men continue to be stereotypically portrayed. Most newspapers have women's pages that include articles on fashion, food, and social events—pages specifically written for what is believed to be the interests of women alone. Many magazines are directed at predominantly male or female audiences. Women's magazines often send contradictory messages by indicating that "women should achieve in the workplace and take greater control of their lives but that they should also look great, feel great, consume ceaselessly, and play the old roles of gender object, dependent woman, and devoted mom" (Sidel, 1990, p. 102).

Whereas the average adult spends about one hour daily reading newspapers, magazines, and books (Stockard & Johnson, 1980), children spend much

CHECK FOR YOURSELF

Over the next week, keep a record of how males and females are portrayed in the mass media with which you come into contact. For this study, choose your favorite mass media (e.g., television news and/or sitcoms, popular magazines, movies, the newspaper, videos, the radio, etc.).

of their reading time with school textbooks and assigned readings. How do the genders fare in the resources used in classrooms across the nation? Studies show that both children and adults in textbooks are assigned rigid traits and roles based on gender stereotypes.

In a review of sixty-two elementary readers, Purcell and Stewart (1990) found that males and females were represented in equal numbers. Although girls were shown in a wide range of activities, they were often portrayed as more helpless than boys. Similar findings were found in elementary arithmetic and science textbooks. However, women's contributions continue to be minimized in history texts (Sadker, Sadker, & Klein, 1991). In a study of the five most widely used primary and intermediate basal readers, King (1989) found that female minority representation in stories ranged from 7 to 15 percent. African American characters were found the most often. Least often seen were Asian American characters—they appeared a total of two times.

Award-winning children's literature is generally sensitive to issues of ethnic and gender diversity. Other popular children's books do not reflect the same multicultural sensitivity. Although there are equal numbers of female and male main characters, they are often gender-stereotyped. Sadker et al. (1991) report that

> New books appear to be more fair and inclusive than those of the past. However, because most teachers themselves grew up with older books representing highly traditional gender roles, the influence of these more sexist books remains pervasive. For example, Smith, Greenlaw, and Scott (1987) interviewed 254 elementary teachers concerning their favorite books to read aloud in the classroom. Of these teachers' top ten favorites, eight books had male main characters, one had a female protagonist, and one had both male and female main characters. (p. 177)

Although males appear to be blessed with more desirable characteristics in books, they also suffer from stereotyping. For the most part, females are allowed more flexible roles. Many males do not fit the confining stereotype of textbooks, in which they are expected to be strong, brave, and intelligent at all times. Some boys (and men, too) show emotions in real life, but they almost never do in textbooks. Any sign of weakness may prevent them from becoming

EDUCATIONAL ISSUE

A number of studies report that boys prefer stories in which the main character is male while girls are not as particular about the gender of the main character. At the same time, children seem to develop a better understanding of persons who are different from themselves through reading stories with them as characters. If you were selecting children's books for your elementary classroom, what kind of balance of main characters would you try to provide? Why?

a "real man" because they lack the necessary characteristics. Although men change diapers, wash dishes, clean the house, and cook meals, they seldom do these chores in textbooks. Men are seldom shown in nurturing roles in the home or as a career. Some men today choose nonstereotyped careers, such as nursing or preschool teaching, but these careers do not exist in textbooks, where men are limited to rigid attributes, emotions, and responsibilities in textbooks, making them victims of sex stereotyping, too (Gollnick, Sadker, & Sadker, 1982).

The gender stereotypes portrayed in the mass media do not accurately reflect the nation in which we live. The stereotypical household with a full-time working father, stay-at-home mother, and one or more school-age children at home was typical in 1950 of 70 percent of all U.S. households. Today, however, only 4 percent of all households fit the stereotype (Hodgkinson, 1986). About 30 percent of the families in this country are headed by a female, and one of every four American children lives in a single-parent family. The greatest change in the stereotypical family has been the wife entering the labor force. By 1991, the two-income family had become the norm rather than the exception; over 58 percent of all wives were working, and over half of these working wives had children under eighteen years old (U.S. Bureau of the Census, 1992). The 1950 nontraditional family became the traditional family of 1980, but the 1950 family is the one continually portrayed in the mass media and in classroom materials. The fact that one type of household has been portrayed as more favorable is not the concern here. The major concern is the reflection of reality in our society—the recognition and portrayal of the variety of households that in fact do exist.

Of course, it is not only the type of household that is stereotyped. In contemporary society, the male and female traditional roles are practiced interchangeably in a growing number of families. Both men and women work in nontraditional careers and share many of the formerly gender-typed roles. Even the portrayal of the woman who stays at home is stereotyped; the reality and difficulty of juggling the care of children and a husband, cleaning, cooking, shopping, doing laundry, repairing a leaky faucet, entertaining, and bookkeeping are seldom presented.

Young men are often expected to prove their masculinity through macho behavior. They face peer pressure to take risks to prove themselves worthy of being male. Thus, many of them race cars, brag of sexual prowess, and fight for honor—characteristics that are the central themes of popular adolescent films and books (Whatley, 1991). Their hobbies are limited to sports, machines, hunting, and other masculine interests. These behavioral and emotional constraints extend to adulthood, usually as internalized patterns that lead to the stigmatization of men who choose to work in traditionally feminine roles such as nurses, librarians, or preschool teachers. Men who pursue traditionally feminine careers and hobbies are often ridiculed unless they have already proved their masculinity. These constraints prevent males from developing their nurturing traits in a way that would allow them to be as competent at childrearing as many women are.

Consciousness-raising activities to help men and women understand and evaluate the stereotyped roles for which they have been socialized have been extremely helpful in opening options for both groups. In many communities, one no longer has to have only feminine or masculine characteristics, behavior, or job options; it is becoming easier to have both. More couples are sharing the role of wage earner—a traditionally gender-typed role for men. It is possible that in the future, a growing number of men will share more equally in the responsibilities of childrearing and homemaking. Optimistically, both men and women will be able to choose roles with which they are comfortable rather than having to accept a gender role determined by society.

We are living in an era of changing norms, in which old, unequal roles are being rejected by many. These changes are resulting in many new uncertain-

Today, a few men are taking on job roles that were previously accepted as women's work only.

ties in which the norms of the appropriate gender role are no longer so distinct. As new norms develop, more flexible roles, personalities, and behaviors are evolving for both females and males.

Gender Discrimination

Throughout history, women have been assigned a subordinate role to men. Only a century ago, most women could not attend college, had no control of either their property or their children, could not initiate a divorce, and were forbidden to smoke or drink. Because these outrageous inequities no longer exist and there are now laws to protect the rights of women, many people believe that men and women are treated equally in society. However, society continues to hold deep-rooted assumptions about how men and women should think, look, and behave. These societal expectations lead to discriminatory behavior based on gender alone.

"Sex discrimination is the denial of opportunity, privilege, role, or reward on the basis of sex" (Bornstein, 1982, p. 1). Often this discrimination is practiced by individuals in personal situations of marriage and family life as well as in their occupational roles as manager, realtor, secretary, or legislator. Socialization patterns within the family are discriminatory when children are taught self-differentiated behaviors. For example, girls are taught to be more obedient, neat, passive, and dependent, while boys are allowed to be more disobedient, aggressive, independent, exploring, and creative. These gender-differentiated behaviors prepare each for gender-specific jobs and severely limit the options available to an individual. Aggressive and independent individuals (usually men) are likely to manage those who are obedient and dependent (usually women).

Many of us discriminate on the basis of gender without realizing it. Because we are raised in a sexist society, we think our behavior is natural and acceptable, even when it is discriminatory. Women often do not realize the extent to which they do not participate equally in society—a sign that they internalize their distinct roles well during the socialization process. Most parents do not directly plan to harm their daughters by teaching them to be feminine. They do not realize that such characteristics may prevent their daughters from achieving societal benefits comparable to men. Too often, girls are encouraged to gain such societal rewards through marriage rather than by their own achievement and independence.

Many individuals outside the family also practice gender discrimination. The kindergarten teacher who scolds the boy for playing in the girls' corner is discriminating. The personnel director who hires only women for secretarial positions and only men as managers is overtly discriminating on the basis of gender. Such behavior prevents men from entering female occupations and vice versa. Educators have the opportunity to help all students break out of group stereotypes and to provide opportunities to explore and pursue a wide variety of options in fulfilling their potential as individuals.

Gender discrimination is practiced not only by individuals; it has also been institutionalized in policies, laws, rules, and precedents in society. These institutional arrangements benefit one gender over the other. What are the results of individual and institutional gender discrimination?

When physical strength determined who performed certain tasks, men conducted the hunt for food, which required them to leave the home, while women raised food close to the home. With industrialization, this pattern of men working away from home and women working close to home was translated into labor market activity for men and nonlabor market activity for women. Men began to work specific hours and receive pay for that work. By contrast, women worked irregular and unspecified working periods in the home and received no wages for their work. The value of a woman's work was never rewarded by money paid directly to her. It certainly was not as valued as the work of men, who contributed in labor market production. In our society, individuals who provide services for which they are paid have a higher status than those who are not paid for their work, such as homemakers.

Unlike men, most working women maintain dual careers. In addition to their labor market activities, they generally have the responsibility for the home, including child care and housekeeping chores. Studies of family time allocation have found that few husbands increase their participation in work at home when the wife enters the labor force. The typical husband helps out with about 20 percent of the homemaking and childrearing activities, regardless of whether the wife also works outside the home (Filene, 1986). Women who work outside the home usually have little reduction in their work at home. Instead, they reduce their amount of free time or the amount of time spent in homemaking activities.

Teenage pregnancy complicates even further women's participation in the labor force. "Young women with poor basic skills are three times more likely to become teen parents than women with average or above-average basic skills" (Fine, 1988, p. 48). Further, the children of these single teenage mothers are more likely than other children to be poor for long periods of their childhood. Many of these mothers must depend on welfare and/or work in low-paying jobs. This issue has been exacerbated by discrimination against pregnant teenagers in many of the nation's high schools.

Does the amount of education influence a person's participation in the labor market? Regardless of their education, men are expected to work. For women, however, the acquisition of more education does not increase the likelihood of working after completing school. At the same time, the amount of education obtained by women does little to close the gap between the earnings of men and women. The more education received, the greater expected earnings for both genders, but women with four years of college earn only slightly more than men who have only finished elementary school.

The difference in income between men and women generally increases with age. The difference shown in Figure 4-1 is not impacted by women who do not work. It reflects the income of male and female full-time workers. Why do these differences exist and continue to increase throughout life?

These discrepancies in income are due in part to the types of jobs held by the two groups. Women first entered the labor market in jobs that were similar to those performed in the home, such as sewing, teaching, nursing, and doing household services. Therefore, the stereotypes about the capabilities and roles of women in the domestic setting were transferred to the labor market. Jobs were defined according to their gender appropriateness. Women workers continue to be heavily concentrated in a few occupations. These jobs are accompanied by neither high prestige nor high income. Women continue to be extremely underrepresented as managers and as skilled workers.

It has been difficult for women to enter administrative and skilled jobs. There are fewer entry-level positions for these jobs than for the less prestigious ones. The available openings are often for jobs where there are short or nonexistent promotion ladders, few opportunities for training, low wages, few chances for stability, and poor working conditions. Clerical and sales positions are examples of such jobs, but even professions such as teaching and nursing offer little opportunity for career advancement. To earn the comfortable living

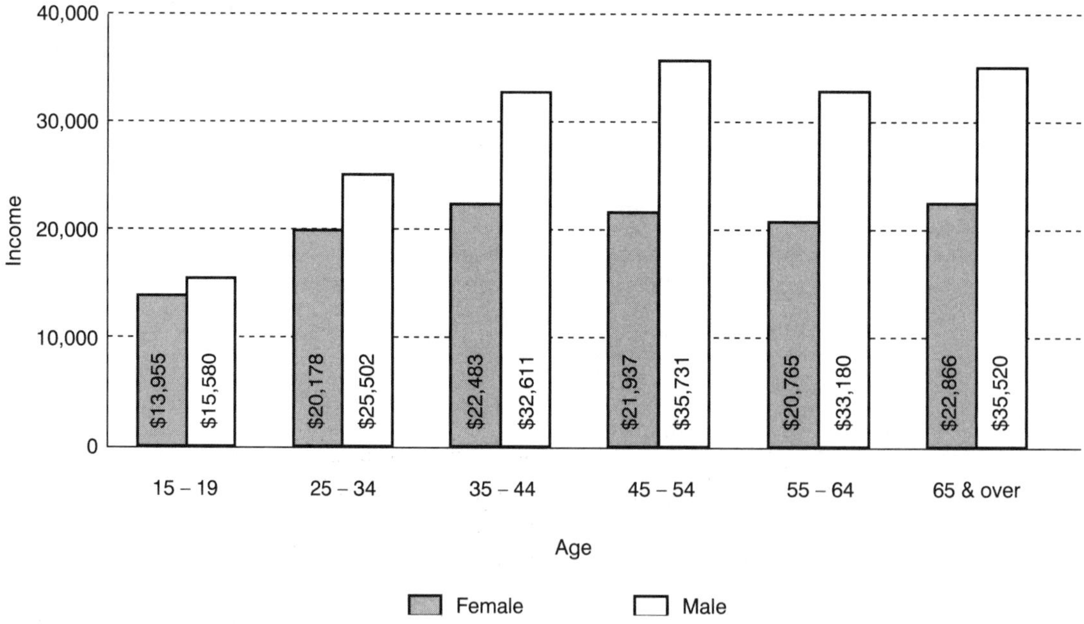

Figure 4-1. Median annual income of year-round, full-time workers over fifteen years old by gender in 1990. (No data were available for twenty- to twenty-four-year-olds.)

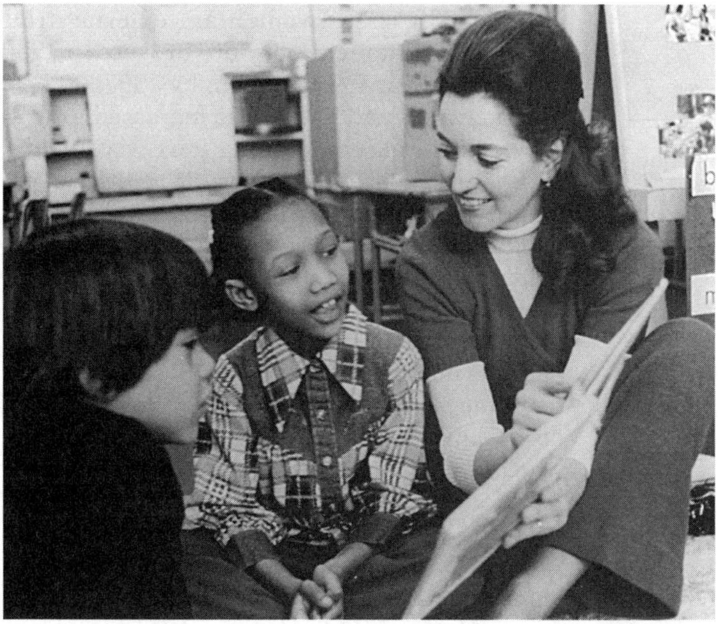

Women still work disproportionately in traditionally female jobs. For example, they make up nearly 99 percent of the preschool teachers in this country.

that is the *American dream* requires women to seek either a traditionally male job or husband with a *good* job. Unfortunately, society does not currently value traditional female jobs, which are essential to society, enough to afford them the prestige and salary that they deserve.

When men enter traditionally female fields, they often do not hold the same positions as women in the field. For example, in 1990 men comprised less than 15 percent of all elementary teachers, 46 percent of all high school teachers, and 62 percent of all principals (U.S. Bureau of the Census, 1992). Male social workers are more often community organizers rather than group workers or caseworkers. Although the percentage of men participating in traditionally female jobs has increased over the years, they have become overrepresented in the higher status, administrative levels of these occupations. For example, 74 percent of all preschool through grade twelve teachers are women, whereas over 41 percent of the teachers in colleges and universities are women (U.S. Bureau of the Census, 1992).

Gender segregation and wage discrimination also affect women in blue-collar and white-collar jobs. The majority of women enter the labor force at the lowest entry level of these categories, with unstable employment opportunities and low wages. Much of the discrimination against women in the labor force results from decisions of employers concerning promotions and wage increases. In addition, many of the occupations in which women are concentrated have not been organized by unions that might help change poor working conditions and low wages.

Gradually, more women are entering traditionally male occupations, as barriers against their entry are broken. In 1950, for example, only 6.5 percent of all physicians were women; by 1991, 20 percent were women. The percentage of lawyers and judges has increased from 4 percent to 19 percent, but only 8 percent of all engineering jobs were held by women as recently as 1991 (U.S. Bureau of the Census, 1992). Even in education, the percentage of female principals has increased from 20 percent in 1982 to 38 percent in 1990. Although more women are entering the traditionally male-dominated fields, they continue to face discrimination in wages earned. In 1955, women working full time earned 65 cents for every dollar earned by men; in 1990, they were still earning only 71 cents for every dollar earned by men. This disparity is due in part to the lower-status jobs held by many women, but is also due to lower salaries for women holding comparable positions to men. Such discrimination greatly affects the quality of life for women, particularly those who are single heads of household, and their children.

Homophobia

Homophobia is another area of discrimination of which educators should be aware. Heterosexuality is the valued sexual orientation that is promoted by the dominant power group in this country. It is so highly valued that laws and social practices have developed to try to prevent any other sexual orientation. Until recently, laws in most states forbade sexual liaisons between members of the same sex; some states still have laws against sodomy. In many areas of the country where overt discrimination against homosexuals remains, gay men and lesbians may not be able to find housing or jobs. Often they are not admitted to "straight" clubs and are vulnerable to attacks on city streets. The National Gay and Lesbian Task Force collects data on reports of harassment and violence against gays, and such incidents have increased dramatically over the past few years.

Many people have little knowledge about homosexuality, but they know many myths about it. As a result, they often develop an irrational fear of homosexuals, which is manifested in feelings of disgust, anxiety, and anger. Individuals who harbor these negative feelings usually have had little or no personal contact with gays and lesbians, have participated in little or no homosexual behavior themselves, hold a conservative religious ideology, and/or have little knowledge about the social, medical, and legal issues related to homosexuality (Sears, 1992). In the past many people viewed homosexuality as a sin, a sickness, or a crime (Harbeck, 1992). Only recently did the American Psychological Association drop homosexuality from its list of mental disorders.

As early as 1948, Kinsey estimated that 10 percent of the population is exclusively homosexual (Uribe and Harbeck, 1992). However, two studies released in 1993 suggest that the number is less than 5 percent. Although there is disagreement on the number, experts agree that sexual orientation is established very early in life, rather than being learned from others in adolescence and adulthood. In *Joseph Acanfora v. Board of Education of Montgomery County, et al.* [359 F. Supp. 843 (1973); aff'd 491 F. 2nd 498 (4th Cir. 1974); cert. denied, 419 U.S. 836 (1974)], the judge agreed with the testifying experts that a child's sexual orientation is firmly established by age five or six at the latest.

Prior to the 1970s, most lesbians and gay men hid their homosexuality from their families, landlords, and the people with whom they worked because of the fear of rejection and retaliation. Following the 1969 Stonewall Inn riot in Greenwich Village, in which gays fought back against police, it became somewhat easier for many of them to openly admit their homosexuality. They, like other oppressed groups, extended the fight for civil rights to include their own struggle. As a result, "more than half of the states repealed sodomy laws, the Civil Rights Commission lifted its ban on hiring homosexuals, and the 1980 Democratic Party platform endorsed gay rights" (Filene, 1986, p. 218). Nevertheless, discrimination and prejudice against gay men and women remain, as evidenced by policies to prevent them from organizing clubs on some college campuses or to openly declare their homosexuality in the armed services. Derogatory terms (e.g., *sissy, faggot,* and *dyke)* are used by many adults and students in schools. Much work is still required to overcome prejudices and discrimination based solely on sexual orientation.

Even though a growing number of gays and lesbians are coming out of the closet, many still fear reprisal. In many areas of the country and in many classrooms, they are harassed and abused if they openly acknowledge their sexual preference. At the same time, they suffer loneliness and alienation by not acknowledging it. "Adolescent homosexuals are either treated as though they do

CONTROVERSIAL ISSUE

Assume that you are teaching a high school class. You are leading a discussion about current events and today's topic is AIDS. After several minutes of give-and-take discussion among students in the class, the following dialogue occurs:

MARY: I think it's too bad that all these people are so sick and are going to die. I just think . . .

PAUL (interrupting): Those fags get what they deserve. What makes me mad is that we're spending money trying to find a cure. If we just let God and Nature take its course, I won't have to worry about any queer bothering me.

MARY: I never thought about it that way before.

Mary then faces you and asks, "What do you think about Paul's comments?" Briefly state how you would respond. (Sears, 1992, pp. 63–65)

not exist or as objects of hate and bigotry. The traditional support structures that serve all other children do not serve gay, lesbian, and bisexual youth" (Uribe and Harbeck, 1992, p. 12). Gay and lesbian educators strictly separate their personal and professional lives for fear of losing their jobs (Griffin, 1992).

Professional educators have the responsibility for eradicating sexism in the classroom and school. Their role requires that they not limit the potential of any student because of gender or sexual orientation. However, in a study of school counselors and teacher candidates, Sears (1992) found that "educators, in general, lack the sensitivity, knowledge, and skills to address effectively the needs of students with the same-sex feelings" (p. 39). Classroom interactions, resources, extracurricular activities, and counseling practices must be evaluated to ensure that students are not being discriminated against because of their sexual orientation.

Interaction of Gender with Ethnicity, Class, and Religion

The degree to which a student adheres to a traditional gender identity is influenced by the family's ethnicity, class, and religion. It is impossible to isolate gender from one's ethnic background. For many women who are not members of the dominant group, their ethnic identity takes precedence over their gender identity. In some religions gender identity and relations are strictly controlled by church doctrine. Thus, gender inequality takes on different forms among different ethnic, class, and religious groups.

Although the evidence is not conclusive, many studies indicate that working-class children are more aware of distinct gender roles than are middle-class children (Safilios-Rothschild, 1979). In addition, middle-class women are more likely to attend college immediately after high school than are women from working-class families. In an ethnographic study of high school women in a business work study program, Valli (1988) found that

> COOP [cooperative education program] students dissatisfied with the minimal challenge of office jobs did not, like middle-class young women, decide to pursue higher education. Even though many of them were clearly capable of college success, their working-class backgrounds exerted a strong influence on their life plans. Instead of college they projected part-time or temporary futures in beauty shops, travel agencies, nursery schools, and shopping malls. Nor did they, like working-class boys, have culturally-defined monetary reasons for staying in dissatisfying work environments. (p. 101)

Young women, especially working-class ones, may not be clear about their future work lives. However, most young women take for granted that they will work outside the home as adults (Sidel, 1990).

Black and white working-class women value common-sense knowledge that they have gained through their lived experiences. "Their ways of knowing are embedded in community, family, and work relationships and cannot be judged by dominant academic standards" (Luttrell, 1989, p. 33). Although these women believe that both men and women have common sense, more value is placed on that of men. Working-class men gain their knowledge collectively in the workplace, while the women learn theirs individually as mothers and homemakers. It is accepted that individuals with accumulated academic knowledge seldom have the common sense that is required for working-class life. Still, many working-class women pursue additional education, most often in community colleges, to increase their ability to find better employment. After this, education usually is not sought until the women are older and have children. However, such academic achievement puts a strain on the working-class family, where men's knowledge has been more valued (Luttrell, 1989).

Ethnic group membership also influences the socialization patterns of males and females. The degree to which traditional gender roles are accepted depends, in large part, on the degree to which the family maintains the traditional patterns and on the particular experiences of the ethnic group in this country. Puerto Rican, Mexican American, Appalachian, and Native American families that adhere to traditional religious and cultural patterns are more likely to encourage adherence to rigid gender roles than families that have adopted bicultural patterns.

For example, labor market opportunities for Appalachian women who had moved into an urban area were found to be more influenced by their roles as Appalachian women than any other factor, including talent. These women "possess a strong cultural heritage emphasizing their identification with place [i.e., the mountains], their emotional strength, and their ability to manage family and other social relations with particular ability and energy. . . . Such an environment contributes to the image of the strong, independent woman" (Borman, Mueninghoff, & Piazza, 1988, p. 234). Because the Appalachian heritage does not easily fit into middle-class schools, students become alienated. In the poor Appalachian culture, a female's transition from childhood to adulthood is noted by having a baby, which often leads to dropping out of school and going on welfare; later she might return to school to gain the skills necessary for employment. Most young women who break this pattern and choose academic achievement, completion of high school, and possible college attendance have adopted middle-class values and developed friendships outside the ethnic community. In many cases, they have sacrificed their ethnic heritage in order to seek well-paying jobs and professional careers (Borman et al., 1988).

On the other hand, women in African American families historically have worked outside the home and are less likely to hold strict traditional views about their roles. They have learned to be both homemaker and wage earner. They are more likely than African American men to complete high school and college. At the same time, African American women who are poor and working class attain less schooling than any other ethnic group except Hispanics and Native Americans. Unlike many middle-class white women, middle-class black women do not necessarily perceive marriage as a route to upward mobility or out of poverty.

African American women of all classes have current and historical experiences of discrimination based on their race. Both black feminists and gays often feel forced to choose between a racial or gender identity, which has led to the lack of attention to the divisions of class and sexual orientation within the African American community (West, 1992). The 1991 Anita Hill/Clarence Thomas hearings began to open up discussions about the inequalities both within the African American community and in society as a whole. It is likely that similar discussion will be held within other ethnic groups as well.

It is dangerous to assume that students will hold certain views or behave in gender-typed ways because of their ethnicity or class level. Individual families within those two microcultures vary greatly in their support of gender-typed roles for men and women and their subsequent behavior along a continuum of gender identity.

Religions, however, generally recognize and include masculine and feminine principles as part of their doctrine. Regardless of the specific religion, rituals usually reflect and reinforce systems of male dominance:

> Because religion defines the ultimate meaning of the universe for a people, the impact may be deep and often emotional rather than intellectual. When male dominance is embodied within religion, it enters the arena that a society considers sacred. This may make it even less open to question and more resistant to change than other social areas. (Stockard & Johnson, 1980, p. 8)

Most people define the appropriate behaviors of males and females through their own ethnic, class, and religious orientations. Males are not supposed to exhibit female characteristics and vice versa. In addition, individuals who choose homosexuality over heterosexuality are often not accepted as real men or real women, even though they may exhibit the same degree of masculinity or femininity as heterosexuals. They often "find themselves torn between their racial identity and their sexual identity, with little chance of finding an open community that welcomes both aspects of their identities" (Porche, 1992, p. 568).

Gay men share with heterosexual men a dominant position in relation to women, but are subordinate in relation to heterosexual men. As a result of the isolation and discrimination forces on homosexuals, gay cultural forms have developed. These include gay newspapers, magazines, churches, health clinics, and social clubs. Equality has yet to be extended to many females and males who openly define their sexual orientation against the national norm.

It is the more fundamentalist groups that support a strict adherence to gender-differentiated roles. Their influence extends into issues of sexuality, marriage, and reproductive rights. They sometimes have successfully organized politically to control state and federal policies on family and women's affairs.

At the same time, the more liberal religious groups support the move toward equality of the genders.

The classroom teacher is likely to find students at different points along the gender identity continuum, both in their beliefs about female and male roles and in their actual behavior. It is also important to know that "no woman's [or man's] experience is generic, and that there is no generic experience of racial-ethnic, class or gender oppression. Liberatory knowledge demands awareness of our privileges as well as of the different forms of oppression which we and others experience" (Amott & Matthaei, 1991, p. 354). We must understand the influence of the microcultural memberships of our students as we try to open up the possibilities for all of them, regardless of their gender.

Educational Implications

Education is seen by many people as a key to upward mobility and success in adulthood. The occupational roles that individuals pursue in adulthood are greatly influenced by their education in elementary and secondary schools. By the time students reach the secondary level, they have chosen, or been helped to choose, either a college preparatory program, a general education program, or a specific vocational training program. Males and females often select different secondary programs, especially in the vocational areas. When college students select a major, disproportionate numbers of males select technical and business majors over females selecting those fields of study. These early choices can make a great difference in later job satisfaction and rewards.

Educational experiences and outcomes continue to differ for males and females at all levels of experience:

- At ages nine, fourteen, and seventeen, girls perform higher on assessments of reading achievement, but by ages twenty-one to twenty-five, males perform at the same level as females in reading and literary proficiency (Mullis, 1987).
- On all subsections of the SAT and ACT, males score higher than females (Dauber, 1987).
- Females receive 36 percent of the National Merit Scholarships (PEER, 1987).
- Males score higher on admission tests for graduate and professional schools [i.e., the Graduate Record Examination (GRE), the Medical College Admissions Test (MCAT), and the Graduate Management Admissions Test (GMAT)] (Brody, 1987).

Many persons believe that if the experiences of boys and girls are changed in school, they will achieve greater equality as adults. However, there is not common agreement even among feminists on how to accomplish this goal. Historians Tyack and Hansot (1988) found that

> Some feminists believe that schools should consciously strive to create a gender-blind pedagogical order that will enlarge aspiration for both girls and boys and promote greater equality of opportunity by eliminating differential treatment of the sexes. Other feminists argue that male-defined values and practices permeate schools and that affirming and strengthening feminine qualities and ethical principles—making schools gender-sensitive rather than seemingly gender-neutral—is a worthier goal. Meanwhile, traditionalists, equally passionate, believe that schools should reflect and strengthen the separate spheres of men and women. (p. 34)

Programs designed to end gender stratification focus on education rather than on other societal institutions, probably because it is easier to effect change in schools than in many other institutions. Teachers, counselors, teachers' aides, coaches, and principals all have roles in eradicating the inequities that result from sexism. Schools have utilized two approaches in this process: women's studies and nonsexist education. In addition, laws have been passed at the federal level that influence education in this area.

Women's Studies

Women's studies programs are similar to ethnic studies programs in their attempt to record and analyze the historical and contemporary experiences of a group that has usually been ignored in the courses taken by the majority of students. Courses in women's studies include concepts of consciousness-raising and views of women as a separate group with unique needs and disadvantages in schools and other institutions. They examine the culture, status, development, and achievement of women as a group (Sexton, 1976).

Women's studies have evolved in secondary and higher education as units in history, sociology, and literature courses; as separate courses; and as programs from which students can choose a major or minor field of study. Similar to the ethnic studies programs, the experiences and contributions of women and related concepts have been the focus.

For all students, women's studies often provide a perspective that is foreign. Historical, economic, and sociological events are viewed from the perspective of a group that has been in a position subordinate to men throughout history. Until students participate in such courses, they usually do not realize that 51 percent of the population has received so little coverage in most textbooks and courses. These programs allow students to increase both their awareness and knowledge base about women's history and contributions. Sometimes women are taught skills for competing successfully in a man's world or for managing a career and a family. In addition, many women's studies programs assist in developing a positive female self-image within a society that has viewed women as inferior to men. Psychological and career assistance to women is also a part of some programs.

Although the content of women's studies is desperately needed to fill the gaps of current educational programs, it usually is a program set aside from the regular or general academic offerings. Instead of being required, it is usually an elective course. Thus, the majority of students may never integrate the information and concepts of women's studies into their academic work. The treatment of women as a separate entity also subtly suggests that the study of women is secondary to the important study of the world—a world that is reflected in textbooks and courses as one of males from a male perspective. All students need to learn about a world in which there are both male and female participants.

Nonsexist Education

When women's studies programs are a part of nonsexist education, they become an integral part of the total education program rather than a separate luxury. Teachers may be required to use specific textbooks and materials, but in general, they have control of the curriculum taught in their classrooms. Even with sexist materials, alert teachers can point out the discrepancies that exist between the genders, discuss how and why such inequities are portrayed, and supplement the materials with information that provides a more balanced view of the roles and contributions of both men and women. Required readings should include the writings of women as well as of men. At minimum, nonstereotypical male and female examples can appear on bulletin boards and in teacher-prepared materials.

All students should be exposed to the contributions of women as well as men throughout history. For example, history courses that focus primarily on wars and political power will almost totally focus on men; history courses that focus on the family and the arts will more equitably include both genders. Science courses that discuss all of the great scientists often forget to discuss the societal limitations that prevented women from being scientists. (Women scientists and writers often had to use male names or give their work to men for publication.) Students are being cheated of a wealth of information about the majority of the world's population when women are not included as an integral part of the curriculum. Because teachers control the information and concepts taught to students, it is their responsibility to present a view of the world that includes women and men and their wide ranges of perspectives.

Educators also should incorporate factual information on homosexuality. The contributions of gays to society should not be ignored. Homophobic name-calling by students could be used to provide facts and correct myths about homosexuality. "If adults criticize other forms of name-calling, but ignore anti-gay remarks, children are quick to conclude that homophobia is acceptable because gay men and lesbians deserve to be oppressed" (Gordon, 1983, p. 25).

In addition to helping all students correct the myths they have about gays and lesbians, educators should promote the healthy development of self-identified homosexual youngsters in the school setting. Key to this approach is breaking the silence that surrounds discussion of homosexuality. The classroom and the school should provide a safe and supportive atmosphere for adolescents to discuss their sexual preference in a nonthreatened way. Finally, teachers and other school personnel need to develop a nonjudgmental posture on this topic.

It is also the responsibility of the teacher to provide each student the opportunity to reach his or her potential. If girls constantly see boys as more active, smarter, more aggressive, and exerting more control over their lives, female students are being cheated. Boys who are always expected to behave in stereotypically masculine ways also suffer. Students are bombarded by subtle influences in schools that reinforce the notion that boys are more important than girls. This unplanned, unofficial learning—the hidden curriculum—has an impact on how students feel about themselves and others. Sexism is often projected in the following ways: in the messages that children receive in the illustrations, language, and content of texts, films, and other instructional materials; in the interaction of school authorities with male and female students; in the different roles of the two genders in school rituals; and in the presence of influential role models (Bornstein, 1982).

One of the goals of nonsexist education is to allow girls and young women to be heard and to understand the legitimacy of their experiences as females. Young men should have the opportunity to explore their privileged role in our inequitable society and learn to "speak unproblematically on behalf of women" (Lewis, 1990, p. 486). Teachers will not find this an easy task. Many females and males resist discussions of power relations and how they benefit or lose within those relations. The value to students and society is worth the discomfort that such discussions may cause to students, and perhaps to the teacher. The classroom may be the only place in which students can confront these issues and be helped to make sense of them.

An area over which all educators have control is their own interactions with students. Consistently, researchers find that educators react differently to boys and girls in the classroom, on the athletic field, in the hall, and in the

EDUCATIONAL ISSUE

During a presentation on the topic of violence against women by a female student, a frustrated young man demands to know why we had to talk about women and men all the time, and why the presenter does not offer "the other side of the story." As the teacher, how do you respond? (Lewis, 1990)

counseling office. Research studies in the past decade have shown the following:

- in preschool, the teachers asked girls significantly more personal-social questions than boys;
- girls in early childhood classes were found less likely to participate in block play, climbing, sand play, and construction play;
- teachers in the same early childhood classes spent nearly two-thirds of their time with male students;
- at all levels of schooling, teachers have a greater number of interactions with male students;
- the discrepancy in teacher interactions with male and female students becomes greater as students move from the seventh to the eighth grade;
- 79 percent of the teacher-organized demonstrations in science were carried out by males;
- not all males are equal recipients of a high level of teacher attention—the few *star* students receive the attention with one or two students receiving about 20 percent of the teacher interactions; and
- minority group students, both male and female, receive less teacher attention than majority group students (Sadker, Sadker, & Klein, 1991).

When asked if they discriminate in the way they react to boys and girls in the classroom, most teachers respond "no." Once they critically examine their interactions, however, most find that they do respond differently. The most important factor in overcoming gender biases in the classroom is the recognition that subtle and unintentional biases exist. Once these are recognized, the teacher can begin to make changes in the classroom and in the lives of the students in that classroom.

Nonsexist education is reflected in the school setting when students are not sorted, grouped, or tracked by gender in any aspect of the school program or environment. The teacher can develop a curriculum that does not give preferential treatment to boys over girls; that shows both genders in aggressive, nurturing, independent, exciting, and emotional roles; that encourages all students to explore traditional and nontraditional roles; and that assists them in developing positive self-images about their sexuality. One's actions and reactions to students can make a difference.

Science and Mathematics Participation

An American Association of University Women Educational Foundation (1992) study of how girls are treated in schools found that

- Differences between girls and boys in math achievement are small and declining. Yet in high school, girls are still less likely than boys to take the most advanced courses and be in the top-scoring math groups.
- The gender gap in science, however, is not decreasing and may, in fact, be increasing.

- Even girls who are highly competent in math and science are much less likely to pursue scientific or technological careers than are their male classmates. (p. 4)

These and other findings suggest that the participation of females in mathematics and science in schools deserves some special attention. In an extensive review of the research on achievement by females and minorities in these areas, Oakes (1990) found that "when they do receive encouragement and are exposed to opportunities, they respond in much the same way as white males—with interest and participation" (p. 154). This optimistic finding suggests that different approaches to schooling and teaching may increase the participation rates of minorities and females in math and science.

Generally, researchers have found that the percentage of class time spent on mathematics did not differ, nor did the mathematics activities in which students participated. However, teacher interactions with the two groups did differ in most cases. Teachers initiated more interactions with boys than with girls concerning classroom behavior. They more often worked individually with boys on classroom management, directions, and procedures. More social interactions were initiated with boys than with girls. In response to low-level mathematics questions, more called-out responses were received and accepted from boys. Teachers engaged boys in significantly more low-level and high-level interactions related directly to mathematics. At the same time, the researchers found that "the more that teachers asked high-level mathematics questions and interacted about mathematics at a high cognitive level with girls, the more girls learned about a higher cognitive level of mathematics" (Fennema & Peterson, 1987, p. 118).

Girls and most minorities were more likely to learn in cooperative mathematics activities; boys, on the other hand, learned better in competitive activities. Girls were influenced positively by the teacher's praise of a correct answer. Boys achieved better when the teacher corrected a wrong answer, but girls achieved better when the teacher prompted them for the correct answer. The differences between the achievement of girls and boys in mathematics classes appears to be related to the difference between dependence and independence (Fennema & Peterson, 1987). To help both girls and boys achieve well in mathematics will require different teaching strategies for boys than for girls.

Oakes (1990) found that a major difference in math and science achievement is the result of courses taken. Poor and minority students are more likely to attend schools with fewer math and science courses, especially at the advanced level. Regardless of ability, girls are less likely to choose advanced math classes than boys. Minority students, with the exception of many Asian Americans, often do not have opportunities to take advanced courses or lack the background to take them.

Males also have more experience with science than females throughout most of their schooling. Teachers interact more with boys and encourage them more. Another factor in the lack of female participation in science is related to inadequate and limited time for science instruction in elementary schools (Oakes, 1990).

In summary, Oakes (1990) found that

> Factors such as prior achievement, course taking, expectations of parents and school adults, academically oriented peers, interest in science and math, perceived future relevance of these subjects for career and life goals, and confidence in ability emerge as related to the achievement and participation for all groups of students. In other words, what produces educational attainment for white boys also works well for girls, minorities, and poor students. (p. 203)

The most critical factor in math and science achievement is placement in an academic track in high school (Oakes, 1990). As educators, we may be able to improve minority and female participation in these areas through encouragement of students, attention to science in our classrooms, and counseling students into advanced mathematics and science classes.

Nondiscrimination and Title IX

One law—Title IX of the 1972 Education Amendments—addresses the differential, stereotyped, and discriminatory treatment of students based on their gender. Title IX states that "no person shall, on the basis of sex, be excluded from participation in, be denied the benefits of, or be subjected to discrimination under any education program or activity receiving federal financial assistance." It protects students and employees in virtually all 16,000 public school systems and 2,700 postsecondary institutions in the United States. The law prevents gender discrimination in (1) the admission of students, particularly to postsecondary and vocational education institutions; (2) the treatment of students; and (3) the employment of all personnel.

What does Title IX require of teachers, counselors, principals, and other educators in kindergarten through twelfth-grade settings? The law clearly makes it illegal to treat students differently or separately on the basis of gender. It requires that all programs, activities, and opportunities offered by a school district be equally available to males and females. All courses must be open to all students. Boys must be allowed to enroll in home economics classes and girls allowed in industrial arts and agriculture courses. Regarding the counseling of students, Title IX prohibits biased course or career guidance; the use of biased achievement, ability, or interest tests; and the use of college and career materials that are biased in content, language, or illustration. Schools cannot assist any business or individual in employing students if the request is for a student of a particular gender. There can be no discrimination in the type or amount of financial assistance or eligibility for such assistance. Health and insurance benefits available to students cannot be discriminated against or excluded from any educational program or activity.

Membership in clubs and other activities based on gender alone is prohibited in schools, with the exceptions of YWCA, YMCA, Girl Scouts, Boy Scouts, Boys' State, Girls' State, Key clubs, and other voluntary and tax-exempt youth service organizations that have been traditionally limited to members nineteen years of age or younger of one gender. Rules of behavior and punishments for violation of those rules must be the same for all students. Honors and awards may not designate the gender of the student as a criterion for the award.

Probably the most controversial program covered by Title IX has been the area of athletics. Provisions for girls to participate in intramural, club, or interscholastic sports must be included in the school's athletic program. The sports offered by a school must be coeducational with two major exceptions: (1) when selection for teams is based on competitive skill and (2) when the activity is a contact sport. In these two situations, separate teams are permitted but are not required. Although the law does not require equal funding for girls' and boys' athletic programs, equal opportunity in athletics must be provided.

The law alone will not change the basic assumptions and attitudes people hold about appropriate female and male roles, occupations, and behaviors; but it will equalize the rights, opportunities, and treatment of students within the school setting. Experience has shown that once discriminatory practices are eliminated and discriminatory behavior is altered, even unwillingly, changes in prejudiced attitudes often follow (Kearse, 1980). Equal treatment of students from kindergarten through college will more adequately encourage all students to explore available career options.

Summary

Our culture determines in large part how parents and others treat boys and girls. Although girls and boys are members of all other microcultures, the culture at large has different expectations of them based solely on their gender. Culture establishes the norms of acceptable gender-typed behavior. Two distinct gender groups are influenced greatly by a person's membership in other microcultures, such as ethnicity, religion, class, and age.

Anthropologists have observed many cultural differences in sexual behavior and in the division of labor between the genders. However, research indicates that the biological differences between males and females have little influence on their behavior and roles in a culture. Instead, the differences within a society are primarily culturally determined rather than biologically determined.

Socialization is the process of learning to behave in accordance with socially prescribed roles and expectations. It is during this period that children learn to be male or female. Male and female roles in our society are usually defined as quite distinct from one another and are often portrayed stereotypically by the media and reinforced in many families. Consciousness-raising activities over the past decade have helped men and women understand and evaluate the stereotyped roles for which they have been socialized, opening new options for both groups.

Gender discrimination has kept women in less prestigious and lower-paying jobs. Even the amount of education obtained by a woman does little to close the gap between the earnings of men and women—now at 71 cents earned by a woman for every dollar earned by a man. Such discrimination greatly affects the quality of life for women and their children.

One has no choice about gender identity, but an individual can have either feminine or masculine characteristics or a combination of the two. The degree to which an individual adheres to a traditional gender identity varies as a result of past socialization patterns and is influenced by the family's ethnicity, socioeconomic level, or religion.

Women's studies and nonsexist education represent educational approaches to combating sexism in schools and society. Women's studies programs attempt to record and analyze the historical and contemporary experiences of women and usually are offered as separate courses. On the other hand, nonsexist education attempts to make the total school curriculum less sexist by incorporating content that reflects female as well as male perspectives. Nonsexist education also incorporates positive and supportive interactions of teachers with students. Educators are asked to be aware of behavior that discriminates against one of the genders in a way that prevents equitable benefits from schooling.

The federal government provides support for aspects of nonsexist education through Title IX of the 1972 Education Amendments. This law protects against the differential, stereotyped, and discriminatory treatment of students based on their gender.

Questions for Review

1. In what ways are differences between the sexes culturally rather than biologically determined?
2. How does socialization into stereotyped roles harm females and males in our changing society?
3. Explain how gender discrimination has disproportionately impacted on women.
4. Contrast women's studies and nonsexist education, and explain the advantages of both.
5. How can teachers learn whether they are discriminating against students based on their gender?
6. How does homophobia manifest itself in schools? What can educators do toward eliminating the prejudice and discrimination that occur?

7. How can you as an educator help increase the participation of minorities and females in mathematics and science careers?
8. What impact has Title IX had on schooling over the past twenty years?

References

American Association of University Women Educational Foundation. (1992). *How schools shortchange girls: Executive summary*. Washington, DC: Author.

Amott, T. L., & Matthaei, J. A. (1991). *Race, gender, and work: A multicultural economic history of women in the United States*. Boston: South End Press.

Apple, M. W. (1989). *Teachers and texts: A political economy of class and gender relations in education*. New York: Routledge.

Barfield, A. (1976). Biological influences on gender differences in behavior. In M. S. Teitelbaum (Ed.), *Sex differences: Social and biological perspectives* (pp. 62–121). Garden City, NY: Anchor Press.

Bernard, J. (1981). *The female world*. New York: Free Press.

Best, R. (1989). *We've all got scars: What boys and girls learn in elementary school*. Bloomington, IN: Indiana University Press.

Borman, K. M., Mueninghoff, E., & Piazza, S. (1988). Urban Appalachian girls and young women: Bowing to no one. In L. Weis (Ed.), *Class, race, and gender in American Education* (pp. 230–248). Albany, NY: State University of New York Press.

Bornstein, R. (1982). *Sexism in education*. Washington, DC: U.S. Department of Education, Women's Educational Equity Act Program.

Brody, L. (1987). *Gender differences in standardized examinations used for selecting applicants to graduate and professional schools*. Paper presented at the annual meeting of the American Educational Research Association, Washington, DC.

Dauber, S. (1987). *Sex differences on the SAT-M, SAT-V, TWSE, and ACT among college-bound high school students*. Paper presented at the annual meeting of the American Educational Research Association, Washington, DC.

de Beauvoir, S. (1974). *The second sex*. New York: Vintage Books.

Delamont, S. (1990). *Sex roles and the school* (2nd ed.). New York: Routledge.

Fennema, E., & Peterson, P. L. (1987). Effective teaching for girls and boys: The same or different. In D. C. Berliner and B. V. Rosenshine (Eds.), *Talks to teachers* (pp. 111–125). New York: Random House.

Filene, P. G. (1986). *Him/her/self* (2nd ed.). Baltimore: The Johns Hopkins University Press.

Fine, M. (1988, February). Sexuality, schooling, and adolescent females: The missing discourse of desire. *Harvard Educational Review, 58*(1), 29-53.

Gollnick, D. M., Sadker, M., & Sadker, D. (1982). Beyond the Dick and Jane syndrome: Confronting sex bias in instructional materials. In M. Sadker & D. Sadker (Eds.), *Sex equity handbook for schools* (pp. 60–95). New York: Longman.

Gordon, L. (1983). What do we say when we hear "faggot"? *Interracial Books for Children Bulletin, 14*(3, 4), 25-27.

Griffin, P. (1992). From hiding out to coming out: Empowering lesbian and gay educators. In K. M. Harbeck (Ed.), *Coming out of the classroom closet: Gay and lesbian students, teachers and curricula* (pp. 167–196). Binghamton, NY: Harrington Park Press.

Halpern, D. (1989). The disappearance of cognitive gender differences: What you see depends on where you live. *American Psychologist, 44*, 1156–1157.

Harbeck, K. M. (Ed.) (1992). *Coming out of the classroom closet: Gay and lesbian students, teachers and curricula*. Binghamton, NY: Harrington Park Press.

Hodgkinson, H. (1986). *The schools we need for the kids we've got.* Paper presented at the 1987 annual meeting of the American Association of Colleges for Teacher Education, Washington, DC.

Kearse, E. E. T. (1980). Affirmative action required to sever deep roots of sexism. *Jobs Watch, 1*(2), 1–2, 9, 23.

King, Y. M. (1989, March). *Equity in basal readers.* Paper presented at the annual meeting of the American Educational Research Association, San Francisco.

Lee, P. C. (1976). Introduction. In P. C. Lee & R. S. Stewart (Eds.), *Sex differences: Cultural and developmental dimensions* (pp. 1–5). New York: Urizen Books.

Lewis, M. (1990, November). Interrupting patriarchy: Politics, resistance, and transformation in the feminist classroom. *Harvard Educational Review, 60*(4), 467–488.

Luttrell, W. (1989, January). Working-class women's way of knowing. Effects of gender, race, and class. *Sociology of Education, 62*(1), 33–46.

Mead, M. (1935). *Sex and temperament in three primitive societies.* New York: Morrow.

Moore, H. L. (1990). *Feminism and anthropology.* Minneapolis: University of Minnesota Press.

Mullis, I. (1987). *Trends in performance for women taking the NAEP reading and writing assessments.* Paper presented at the annual meeting of the American Educational Research Association, Washington, DC.

Noddings, N. (1990). Feminist critiques in the professions. In C. B. Cazden (Ed.), *Review of research in education* (pp. 393–424). Washington, DC: American Educational Research Association.

Oakes, J. (1990). Opportunities, achievement, and choice: Women and minority students in science and mathematics. In C. B. Cazden (Ed.), *Review of research in education* (pp. 153–222). Washington, DC: American Educational Research Association.

PEER (Project on Equal Educational Rights). (1987, May 29). Equal education alert 7.

Porche, M. V. (1992, Winter). Review of growing up gay in the south: Race, gender, and journeys of the spirit. *Harvard Educational Review, 62*(4), 567–570.

Purcell, P., & Stewart, L. (1990). Dick and Jane in 1989. *Sex Roles, 22,* 177–185.

Radl, S. R. (1983). *The invisible women: Target of the religious new right.* New York: Dell.

Rosaldo, M. Z., & Lamphere, L. (Eds.). (1974). *Woman, culture, and society.* Stanford, CA: Stanford University Press.

Rubin, J. Z., Provenzano, F. J., & Luria, Z. (1974). The eye of the beholder: Parents' views on sex of newborns. *American Journal of Orthopsychiatry, 44*(4), 512–519.

Sadker, M., Sadker, D., & Klein, S. (1991). The issue of gender in elementary and secondary education. In G. Grant (Ed.), *Review of research in education.* Washington, DC: American Educational Research Association.

Safilios-Rothschild, C. (1979). *Sex role socialization and sex discrimination: A synthesis and critique of the literature.* Washington, DC: National Institute of Education.

Sears, J. T. (1992). Educators, homosexuality, and homosexual students: Are personal feelings related to professional beliefs? In K. M. Harbeck (Ed.), *Coming out of the classroom closet: Gay and lesbian students, teachers and curricula* (pp. 29–79). Binghamton, NY: Harrington Park Press.

Sexton, P. C. (1976). *Women in education.* Bloomington, IN: Phi Delta Kappa.

Sidel, R. (1990). *On her own: Growing up in the shadow of the American dream.* New York: Viking.

Smith, N., Greenlaw, M., & Scott, C. (1987, January). Making the literate environment equitable. *Reading Teacher,* 400–407.

Stockard, J., & Johnson, M. M. (1980). *Sex roles: Sex inequality and sex role development.* Englewood Cliffs, NJ: Prentice-Hall.

Tyack, D., & Hansot, E. (1988, April). Silence and policy talk: Historical puzzles about gender and education. *Educational Researcher, 17*(3), 33–41.

U.S. Bureau of the Census. (1992). *Statistical Abstract of the United States.* Washington, DC: Government Printing Office.

Uribe, V., & Harbeck, K. M. (1992). Addressing the needs of lesbian, gay, and bisexual youth:

The origins of PROJECT 10 and school-based intervention. In K. M. Harbeck (Ed.), *Coming out of the classroom closet: Gay and lesbian students, teachers and curricula* (pp. 9–28). Binghamton, NY: Harrington Park Press.

Valli, L. (1988). Gender identity and the technology of office education. In L. Weis (Ed.), *Class, race, and gender in American education* (pp. 87–105). Albany, NY: State University of New York Press.

Weiler, K. (1988). *Women teaching for change: Gender, class, and power.* South Hadley, MA: Bergin & Garvey.

West, C. (1992). Black leadership and the pitfalls of racial reasoning. In T. Morrison (Ed.), *Race-ing, Justice, En-gendering power: Essays on Anita Hill, Clarence Thomas, and the construction of social reality* (pp. 390–401). New York: Pantheon.

Whatley, M. H. (1991). Raging hormones and powerful cars: The construction of men's sexuality in school sex education and popular adolescent films. In H. A. Giroux (Ed.), *Postmodernism, feminism, and cultural politics* (pp. 119–143). Albany, NY: State University of New York Press.

Willis, P. E. (1977). *Learning to labour: How working class kids get working class jobs.* Farnborough, England: Saxon House.

Suggested Readings

Amott, T. L., & Matthaei, J. A. (1991). *Race, gender, and work: A multicultural economic history of women in the United States.* Boston: South End Press.

The interaction of race, class, and gender in the economic experiences of groups is explored. Labor histories of Native American, Chicana, European American, African American, Asian American, and Puerto Rican women are described.

Faludi, S. (1991). *Backlash: The undeclared war against American women.* New York: Anchor.

This book explodes many myths about women and their lives that have been perpetuated in the popular press. Antifeminism and obstacles to women's equality are described.

Miller, N. (1989). *In search of gay America: Women and men in a time of change.* New York: Harper & Row.

A journalist reports the lived experiences of gays and lesbians across the United States, including experiences in rural, suburban, and urban areas.

Morrison, T. (Ed.). (1992). *Race-ing, justice, engendering power: Essays on Anita Hill, Clarence Thomas, and the construction of social reality.* New York: Pantheon.

This collection of eighteen essays by black and white males and females reflects on what was learned from the testimony of Anita Hill at the Senate hearings on the confirmation of Clarence Thomas as Supreme Court Justice. The authors address gender and class differences within a political, historical, and cultural context.

Sadker, M., & Sadker, D. (1982). *Sex equity handbook for schools.* New York: Longman.

This resource for prospective teachers includes chapters that address sex differences, sexism in education, sex bias in classroom interactions, sex bias in instructional materials, and sex equity in school organizations. Sample lessons and classroom activities are provided.

Sears, J. T. (1991). *Growing up gay in the south: Race, gender and journeys of the spirit.* New York: Harrington Park Press.

The narratives of thirteen young men and women and data from a large research study portray the isolation and prejudice experienced as they grew up in the South. The insights are especially helpful to educators who have had no contact with gays and lesbians.

Sidel, R. (1990). *On her own: Growing up in the shadow of the American dream.* New York: Viking.

Young women describe their hopes for the future, which focus on their desire for material wealth and the need to make it on their own. The accompanying analysis focuses on the mixed messages being sent to young women in our society.

Skolnick, J., Langbort, C., & Day, L. (1982). *How to encourage girls in math and science: Strategies for parents and educators.* Englewood Cliffs, NJ: Prentice-Hall.

Practical strategies are provided for teachers to use in helping girls develop math and science skills and an interest in related careers. It includes descriptions and examples of sex role socialization and specific strategies and activities for kindergarten through eighth-grade students.

CHAPTER 5

Exceptionality

Travis Yamashita, a third-grade teacher at the Martin Luther King Elementary School, has been asked to see the principal, Erin Wilkerson, after the students leave. Mr. Wilkerson explains that the district is experimenting with a full-inclusion program in which children with severe disabilities will be fully integrated into regular education classrooms. Because he was a nominee for the district's teacher of the year award two years ago and because of his outstanding classroom skills, it has been recommended that Yamashita be a part of this early attempt at full inclusion.

"What this will involve, Travis, is two students with severe disabilities. One has developmental disabilities and is a child with Down Syndrome. He has some severe learning problems. The other child has normal intelligence but is nonambulatory, with limited speech and severe cerebral palsy. If you are willing to be a part of this program, you will have a full-time aide with a special education background. Maria Harris, the resource room teacher, will assist you with instructional plans and strategies. What is important is that you prepare the students in your class and their parents so that a smooth transition can be made when the program begins in January—in just two and a half months. If you

agree to do this, I'd like you and Ms. Harris to map out a plan of action and give it to me in two weeks."

This is a scenario that has been played out in schools across the country in recent years. What are Yamashita's and Harris's plan of action to include? What are some critical elements in a successful plan to move into full inclusion?

Exceptionality

A significant segment of the population in the United States is made up of exceptional individuals. Twenty-five million or more individuals from every ethnic and socioeconomic group fall into one or more of the categories of exceptionality. Nearly every day, educators come into contact with exceptional children and adults. They may be students in our classes, our professional colleagues, our friends and neighbors, or individuals we meet in our everyday experiences.

Exceptional individuals include both individuals with disabilities and gifted individuals. Some, particularly persons with disabilities, have been rejected by society. Because of their unique social and personal needs and special interests, many exceptional individuals become a part of a microculture composed of individuals with similar exceptionalities. For some, this cultural identity is by ascription; they have been labeled and forced into enclaves by virtue of the residential institutions where they live. Others live in such communities by their own choosing. This chapter will provide an examination of the exceptional individual's relationship to society. It will address the struggle for equal rights and the ways the treatment of individuals with disabilities often parallels that of other oppressed groups.

Definitions for exceptional children vary slightly from one writer to another, but Heward and Orlansky's (1992) is typical of most:

> The term *exceptional children* includes both children who experience difficulties in learning and children whose performance is so superior that special education is necessary if they are to fulfill their potential. Thus *exceptional children* is an inclusive term that refers to children with learning and/or behavior problems, children with physical disabilities, and children who are intellectually gifted. (p. 8)

This definition is specific to school-age children who are usually referred, tested to determine eligibility, and then placed in special education programs. Included in the process is the labeling of the child. At one end of the continuum are the gifted and talented children; at the other end are children with disabilities (some of whom may also be gifted). These disabilities are categorized with labels such as mental retardation, learning disability, speech impairment, visual impairment, hearing impairment, emotional disturbance (or behavioral disorders), and physical and health impairments.

Labeling

The categorizing and labeling process has its share of critics. Opponents characterize the practice as demeaning and stigmatizing to people with disabilities, with the effects often carried through adulthood. Earlier classifications and labels, such as *moron, imbecile,* and *idiot,* have become so derogatory that they are no longer used in a professional context. Some individuals, including many with learning disabilities and mild mental retardation, were never considered to have disabilities prior to entering school. The school setting, however, intensifies their academic and cognitive deficits. Many, when they return to their homes and communities, do not seem to function as individuals with disabilities. Instead, they participate in activities with their neighborhood peers until they return to school the following day, where they attend special classes (sometimes segregated) and resume their role in the academic and social structure of the school as children with disabilities. The problem is so pervasive that it has led to the designation of "the six-hour retarded child." These are children who spend six hours a day in schools where they are treated as individuals with mental retardation. During the remaining eighteen hours a day away from the school setting, they are not considered to have mental retardation by the people they interact with (President's Committee on Mental Retardation, 1969). Heward and Orlansky (1992) suggest that the demands of the school seem to "cause" the mental retardation.

The labels carry with them connotations and stigmas of varying degrees. Some disabilities are socially more acceptable than others. Visual impairment carries with it public empathy and sometimes sympathy. The public has for years given generously to causes for the blind, as evidenced by the financially well-endowed Seeing Eye Institute, which produces the well-known guide dogs. The blind are the only group with a disability permitted to claim an additional personal income tax deduction by reason of their disability. Yet the general public looks upon blindness as one of the worst afflictions imposed on humankind.

On the other hand, mental retardation and, to some extent, emotional disturbance, are often linked to lower socioeconomic status. Both labels are among the lowest socially acceptable disabilities and perhaps the most stigmatizing. This is due in part to the general public's lack of understanding of these two disabilities and the sometimes debilitating impact they can bring to the family structure.

Learning disabilities, the newest category of exceptionality, is one of the more socially acceptable conditions. While mental retardation is often identified with lower socioeconomic groups, those with learning disabilities tend to be more middle-class in their identity. Whether these perceptions are accurate or not, middle-class parents accept learning disabilities more readily than mental retardation as a cause of their child's learning deficits. What has been observed is a reclassification of many children from mentally retarded to learning disabled (Ortiz & Yates, 1983). It has sometimes been said that one person's mental retardation is another's learning disability and still another's emotional disturbance. The sometimes fine line that distinguishes one of these disabilities from another is at times so difficult to distinguish that individuals could be identified as a student with mild emotional disturbance by one school psychologist and as a student with learning disabilities by another.

While the labeling controversy persists, even its critics often concede its necessity. Federal funding for special education is predicated on the identification of individuals in specific handicapping conditions. These funds, which total over $1 billion each year, are so significant that many special education programs would all but collapse without them, leaving school districts in severe financial distress. Consequently, the labeling process continues, sometimes even into adulthood, when university students may have to be identified with learning disabilities to receive necessary accommodations to their learning needs. Others are placed in jobs by vocational rehabilitation counselors, with labels more indicative of their learning problems than their work skills. This, in turn, tends to stigmatize, enhancing the likelihood of social isolation.

There is now an effort to recognize an individual with a disability primarily as a person, and to view the disability as only secondary to the personhood. Consequently the reader will note that individuals with disabilities are not referred to as "handicapped individuals," "handicapped children," "mentally retarded persons," or "physically handicapped students" in this text. Instead they are referred to as an "individual with a disability" or as a "student with a physical disability." They are first an individual or a student who happens to have a disability. They are more like nondisabled individuals than unlike them. They have a disability which may or may not be a handicap to them. A university student who chooses to pursue a career as an English teacher may have a disability if she is born without her left hand. But it may not be much of a handicap to her as a teacher. To refer to her as a handicapped student emphasizes her disability when it is unnecessary and perhaps detrimental to do so.

Historical Antecedents

The plight of persons with disabilities has in many instances closely paralleled that of oppressed ethnic groups. The history of the treatment of those with disabilities has not shown society eager to meet its responsibilities. Prior to 1800, with a few exceptions, those with mental retardation, for example, were not considered a major social problem in any society. Those with more severe retardation were simply killed or died early of natural causes (Drew, Logan, & Hardman, 1992).

The treatment and care of individuals with mental and physical disabilities has typically been a function of the socioeconomic conditions of the times. In addition to attitudes of fear and disgrace brought on by superstition, early nomadic tribes viewed individuals with disabilities as nonproductive and as a burden, draining available resources. As civilization progressed from a less nomadic existence, individuals with disabilities were still often viewed as non-productive and expendable (Drew, Logan, & Hardman, 1992).

They were frequently shunted away to institutions designated as hospitals, asylums, and colonies. Many institutions were deliberately built great distances from the population centers, where the residents could be segregated and more easily contained. For decades, American society did not have to deal with its conscience with respect to its citizens with severe disabilities—we simply sent them far away and forgot about them. Most Americans did not know of the cruel and inhumane treatment that existed in many facilities, and they did not really want to know. Those individuals with mild disabilities were generally able to be absorbed into society, sometimes seeming to disappear, sometimes contributing meaningfully to an agrarian society, often not even being identified as having a disability.

As society became more industrialized and educational reforms required school attendance, the academic problems of students with disabilities became increasingly more visible. Special schools and special classes were designated to meet the needs of these children. Thus, society segregated these individuals, often in the guise of acting in their best interests.

The earlier attempts to provide for the educational needs of those with disabilities often fell short. Personnel lacked training, and school districts accepted students on a selective basis. For the most part, only those with mild disabilities were considered acceptable for the educational process. Children with moderate and severe disabilities were simply denied educational services. Parents were forced to pay for private services, keep the children at home, or institutionalize them.

Society's treatment of some groups with disabilities, such as those with mental retardation, has frequently been questionable with respect to their civil rights. Krishef (1972) indicates that one-fourth of all states surveyed reported prohibitions against marriage between individuals with retardation. Another third of the states either reported that no information was available or did not respond. Furthermore, twenty-four states permitted sterilization of individuals with retardation, while only two states prohibited such sterilization. The Congressional Record reports fifteen states as having statutes authorizing compulsory sterilization of individuals with mental illness or retardation.

Edgerton (1967) found that forty-four out of forty-eight individuals with mental retardation released from a state institution had undergone eugenic sterilization. During the time of their institutionalization, sterilization was considered a prerequisite to release. Form letters sent to parents or guardians to gain consent for the procedure implied that sterilization could permit parole and would be in the individual's best interest. Follow-up interviews of the subjects indicated strong negative feelings regarding the sterilization that had been imposed on them. They viewed sterilization as an indelible mark of their institutionalization. Some felt deprived of the children they wanted, and there was a fear on the part of many that the secret they kept of their forced sterilization would be discovered by their partners.

This issue of marriage prohibitions and eugenic sterilization raises serious social and ethical questions. The nondisabled segment of society, charged with the care and education of persons with disabilities, apparently views as its right and responsibility those matters dealing with sexual behavior, marriage, and procreation. In a similar way, educators determine the means of communication for the blind individual, either an oral/aural approach or a manual/total communication approach. Such decisions have profound implications, as they not only determine how these individuals will communicate, but to a great extent with whom they will be able to communicate. Too often, society seeks to dehumanize people with disabilities by ignoring their personal wishes, making their critical decisions for them, and treating them as children throughout their lives.

Litigation and Individuals with Disabilities

In the last two decades, the U.S. Congress has passed several major pieces of legislation that will forever change the rights of individuals with disabilities in the United States. Not unlike the treatment of ethnic minorities, many individuals with disabilities throughout the country were disenfranchised of a meaningful education from the time educational services were first provided.

Section 504 was enacted through the legislative vehicle of Public Law 93-112, the Vocational Rehabilitation Act Amendments of 1973. This legislation is a counterpart to the Civil Rights Acts of 1964. It does for individuals with disabilities essentially what the earlier legislation did for ethnic minorities. It is the basic civil rights provision with respect to prohibiting discrimination against a person with disabilities. Though brief in its actual language, it has far-reaching implications. The statute states that "No otherwise qualified handicapped individual in the United States . . . shall, solely by reason of his [her] handicap, be excluded from the participation in, be denied benefits of, or be subjected to discrimination under any program or activity receiving federal financial assistance."

In essence, Section 504 prohibits exclusion from programs solely on the basis of one's disability. This means that a coach cannot bar a student with a disability from trying out for a team sport because he or she has mental retardation or learning disabilities. Nor can the band director stop another student with disabilities from trying out for the school marching band. If, however, the first student cannot learn or remember the plays, or the second student cannot follow the marching formations, then the student with a disability can be cut from the team or the band in the same manner as a student who does not have a disability.

For years, students with disabilities were routinely excluded from teacher education programs. Programs, schools, or colleges of education have admissions criteria to determine a student's eligibility to enter a teacher education program. Prior to the advent of Section 504, many of these programs required students to pass physical examinations that included hearing and vision tests, which effectively eliminated any student with hearing or visual impairment from consideration for admission. As in athletics, any student who cannot learn essential skills or perform essential teaching tasks can be eliminated from the program. But if barriers have been artificially created to exclude students with disabilities, federal funds can be withheld, not only from the guilty program, but from the entire institution.

Public Law 94-142, the Education for All Handicapped Children Act, was passed by the U.S. Congress and signed into law by President Gerald Ford on November 29, 1975. The thrust of P.L. 94-142 is fivefold: (1) to provide a free and appropriate education for all children with disabilities; (2) to ensure that school systems provide safeguards to protect the rights of children with disabilities and their parents; (3) to educate children with disabilities with non-disabled children to the maximum extent possible in the least restrictive environment; (4) to require that an Individualized Education Program (IEP) be developed and implemented for each child with a disability; and (5) to ensure that parents of children with disabilities play an active role in the process used to make any educational decision about their children. States complying with the requirements of P.L. 94-142 receive federal funds to assist in providing services (Heward & Orlansky, 1992). While P.L. 94-142 applies to all children with disabilities, ages three to twenty-one inclusive, who require special education or related services, Section 504 applies to all Americans with disabilities, regardless of age.

P.L. 94-142 guarantees the right of a free and appropriate education. It provides for due process safeguards to ensure the educational rights of children with disabilities. The heightened sensitivity of many educators to the rights as well as the capabilities of students with disabilities have been coupled with the threat of litigation for noncompliance of the law.

In 1990, Congress amended the Education for All Handicapped Children Act and renamed it the Individuals With Disabilities Education Act (IDEA), making it Public Law 101-476. Under the amendments, the definition of special education was expanded to include instruction in all settings, including the workplace and training centers. In addition to the students included in P.L. 94-142, IDEA now includes students with autism and traumatic brain injury. Related services now include rehabilitation counseling and social work services.

In addition, IDEA now requires that the IEP be expanded to include a transition services statement for students by age sixteen, or younger when it is appropriate. The U.S. Department under IDEA is now required to address the issue of providing services to children with attention deficit disorders.

AWARENESS EXERCISE

Throughout the coming weekend, keep track of the buildings that you enter, streets you cross, activities in which you participate, etc., in which access or mobility would be near impossible if you were in a wheelchair, blind, or deaf. How could these areas be made more accessible to the disabled? How should the Americans with Disabilities Act help?

The Americans with Disabilities Act (ADA) (P.L. 101-336) was signed into law on July 26, 1990, by President George Bush. The ADA was the most significant U.S. civil rights legislation since the Civil Rights Act of 1964; it was designed to end discrimination against individuals with disabilities in private sector employment, public services, public accommodations, transportation, and telecommunications.

Among the many components of this legislation, the efforts to break down barriers for individuals with disabilities include:

- Employers cannot discriminate against individuals with disabilities in hiring or promotion if they are otherwise qualified for the job.
- Employers must provide reasonable accommodations for individuals with disabilities, such as attaching an amplifier to the individual's telephone.
- New buses, bus and train stations, and rail systems must be accessible to persons with disabilities.
- Physical barriers in restaurants, hotels, retail stores, stadiums must be removed; if not readily achievable, alternative means of offering services must be implemented.
- Companies offering telephone services to the general public must offer telephone relay services to those using telecommunication devices for the deaf.

Consequently, more than ever, children with disabilities and adults are becoming an integral part of the nation's educational system and are finding their rightful place in society. While the progress that has been made in recent years is indeed encouraging, society's attitudes toward individuals with disabilities has not always kept pace with their legal rights. As long as individuals are motivated more by fear of litigation than by a moral ethical response, we cannot consider our efforts in this arena a success.

Exceptionality and Society

Even in modern times, the treatment and understanding of any type of deviance have been limited. Society has begun to accept its basic responsibilities for the individuals with disabilities by providing for their education and care, but social equality for these individuals has yet to become a reality.

Society's view of people with disabilities can perhaps be illustrated by the way the media portray our population with disabilities. In general, when the media wish to emphasize persons with disabilities, they are portrayed as (1) children, usually with severe mental retardation and obvious physical stigmata, or (2) persons with crippling conditions, either in a wheelchair or on crutches. Thus, society has a mind-set on who the people with disabilities are. They are children or childlike, and they have severe disabilities—mentally, physically, or both.

Because society often views those with disabilities as children, they are denied the right to feel and want like normal individuals. Teachers and other professional workers can often be observed talking about individuals with disabilities in their presence, as if they are unable to feel any embarrassment. Their desire to love and be loved is often ignored, and they are often viewed as asexual, without the right to the same sexual desires as the nondisabled. Gliedman and Roth (1980) make the following statement:

> The able-bodied person sees that handicapped people rarely hold good jobs, become culture heroes, or are visible members of the community and concludes that this is "proof" that they cannot hold their own in society. In fact, society systematically discriminates against many perfectly capable blind men and women, cripples, adults with reading disabilities, epileptics, and so on. In other instances—and again the parallel with white racism is exact—beliefs about the incompatibility of handicap with adult roles may be not more than a vague notion that "anyone that bad off" cannot possibly lead an adult life, and not more respectable than the view that a handicapped person is mentally or spiritually inferior because he is physically different or that "people like that" have no business being out on the streets with "us regular folks." Like race prejudice, a belief in the social incapacity of the handicapped disguises ignorance or bigotry behind what we "see" to be an obvious biological fact. For, like Tycho Brahe (Danish astronomer) watching the sun "move" around the earth, we do not see our belief. We see a handicapped person. (pp. 22–23)

Gliedman and Roth (1980) suggest that with respect to discrimination, individuals with disabilities are in some ways better off than African Americans in that there is no overt discrimination, no organized brutality, no lynch mob "justice," and no rallies by supremist groups. However, in some ways people with disabilities are worse off. African Americans and other groups have developed ethnic pride. African Americans started with "black is beautiful," and the Asians followed with "yellow is beautiful," the Native Americans with "red is beautiful," and the Mexican Americans with "brown is beautiful." In contrast, it is unlikely that one has ever heard a "cerebral palsy is beautiful" cry. Society opposes racism with the view that blacks are not self-evidently inferior, but at the same time takes for granted the self-evidently inferior status of those who have disabilities.

Stereotypes of individuals with disabilities deny them a place in normal society. The disability dominates our perception of the person's social value. It creates a mind-set, and all perceptions are clouded by our view of deviance. Individuals with disabilities are viewed as vocationally limited and socially inept.

Persons with disabilities are tolerated and even accepted as long as they maintain the roles ascribed to them. They are often denied basic rights and dignity as human beings. They are placed under the perpetual tutelage of those more knowledgeable and more capable than they. They are expected to subordinate their own interests and desires to the goals of a program decreed for them by the professionals who provide services to them.

Racists may be required by law to allow the African American child in the public schools. They may have to work with an ethnic minority individual. They do not have to allow their children to play with the African American child after school. The racist does not have to like the ethnic coworker or invite this person home to socialize. Likewise, the general public may be required by law to provide educational and other services for individuals with disabilities. The general public is prohibited by law against certain aspects of discrimination against our citizens with disabilities. No one, however, can require the person on the street to like a person with a disability and to accept him or her as a social equal—and many do not accept a person with a disability. Just as racism leads to discrimination or prejudice against other races because of the belief in one's racial superiority, handicappism leads to stereotyping of and discrimination against individuals with disabilities because of attitudes of superiority of some nondisabled individuals.

Exceptional Microcultures

Because of insensitivity, apathy, or prejudice, many of those responsible for implementing and upholding the laws that protect individuals with disabilities fail to do so. The failure to provide adequate educational and vocational opportunities for individuals with disabilities may preclude the possibility of social and economic equality. These social and economic limitations are often translated into rejection by nondisabled peers and ultimately into social isolation.

Not unlike many ethnic minority groups who are rejected by mainstream society, individuals with disabilities often find comfort and security with each other, and in some instances they may form their own enclaves and social organizational structures. Throughout the country, one can find microcultures of groups of individuals such as those who are visually or hearing impaired and those who have mental retardation. In some instances, they congregate in similar jobs, in the same neighborhoods, and at various social settings and activities. For example, near Frankfort Avenue in Louisville, Kentucky, there are three major institutions providing services for individuals who have visual impairments. The American Printing House for the Blind, the Kentucky School for the Blind, and the Kentucky Industries for the Blind are all within close proximity to each other. The American Printing House for the Blind, the leading publisher of materials for individuals with visual impairments, employs a number of individuals who are blind. The Kentucky School for the

Persons with a disability sometimes live in the same communities, share social activities and support systems, and develop their own microculture with characteristics that are not familiar to others.

Blind is a residential school for students with visual impairments, and it also employs a small number of individuals with visual impairments, including teachers. Finally, the Kentucky Industries for the Blind operates as a sheltered workshop for individuals who are blind. With the relatively large number of persons who are blind employed by these three institutions, it is understandable that there are large numbers of individuals with visual impairments in the surrounding residential area.

Living in this area allows them to live close enough to their work to minimize the many transportation problems related to their visual limitations. It also provides a sense of emotional security for the many who, in earlier years, attended the School for the Blind and lived on its campus and thus became a part of the neighborhood. The neighborhood community can also provide social and emotional security and feelings of acceptance. A few years ago, a mailing was sent from the Kentucky School for the Blind to its alumni. Ninety percent of the mailings had the same zip code as the school.

The Gifted

The gifted and talented usually do not experience the same type of discrimination and social rejection that many individuals with disabilities experience. Yet, like individuals with disabilities, they may suffer isolation from mainstream society and seek others with equal abilities, who may provide a feeling of acceptance as well as intellectual or emotional stimulation. Rejection of the gifted and talented may differ from that of individuals with disabilities because the roots may stem from a lack of understanding or jealousy rather than from the stigma that may relate to certain disabilities.

Unfortunately, many gifted and talented students are not properly identified and as a result are not appropriately provided for in educational programs.

Unchallenged and bored with the routine of school, a few of these gifted children may resort to negative forms of behavior that jeopardize acceptance by classmates and teachers. This rejection may lead to social isolation that in turn may contribute to the development of alliances with other gifted and talented individuals who can provide understanding and acceptance and who have similar interests. Some gifted and talented individuals may not be rejected by others, but nevertheless seek others with similar talents and interests to provide the necessary or desired stimulation. The existence of Mensa, an organization whose membership prerequisites include high scores on intelligence tests, attests to the apparent need of some gifted individuals to be with others of their own kind.

Individuals with Mental Retardation

It has been estimated that approximately 3 percent of the general population has mental retardation. Translating this percentage into actual numbers suggests that there are 6.5 million or more individuals with mental retardation living in the United States (Drew et al., 1992).

Many of the individuals with mild retardation live independently or in community-based and community-supported group homes, which provide a family-like atmosphere, and are supervised by houseparents. Most of the individuals with moderate retardation who do not live in institutions tend to live at home. Many individuals with severe and profound retardation and some with moderate retardation are institutionalized and are thus forced into their own cultural group or enclave, isolated from the rest of society.

Because of their intellectual limitations, frequent poverty, and minority status, individuals with mental retardation are often discriminated against and rejected. And because of their alienation from society, those individuals may seek their own cultural identity.

Individuals with Visual or Hearing Impairments

Deaf or blind communities may exist when individuals who are sensory impaired live in the same neighborhood, work together, socialize, and marry one another. In other cases, the microcultural group of persons who are sensory impaired may consist of individuals from different communities. Because they do not feel part of the mainstream society and because they share many commonalities, such as language (sign language or braille), and may have similar interests, they find comfort, satisfaction, and security in one another.

Of the various disabling conditions, those with visual impairments and hearing impairments are among those most likely to form their own cultural groups. There are a number of overriding factors that contribute to the need for individuals in these groups to seek out one another and to form cultural groups. The blind have limited mobility. Living in cultural enclaves allows them easier access to one another. They share the same forms of communication—oral language, braille, and talking books. Social and cultural interests created partly by their physical limitations can often be shared. The hearing impaired have communication limitations within the hearing world. Their unique means of communication provide them with an emotional as well as functional bond. Religious programs and churches for individuals with hearing impairments have been formed to provide services in total communication and social activities.

Individuals with Physical and Health Impairments

Individuals with physical and health impairments often have conditions that interfere with their mobility. These limitations may have an impact on school, work, and social interactions.

Advances in biomedical science have in some instances eliminated or reduced problems associated with these conditions. On the other hand, advances in medical science have also contributed to the existence of these conditions. Infants and children who previously would not have survived the physical trauma resulting from severe disease or accidents are often spared the loss of life through advanced medical techniques. They are, however, sometimes left with permanent physical impairments, such as cerebral palsy, or experience a life as a paraplegic with limited wheelchair mobility.

The range and variety of conditions related to physical and health impairment are numerous, and it would serve no useful purpose in this chapter to attempt to list them. However, it is important to note the impact of physical disability on the individual, the family, and society. Contemporary American society places great emphasis on physical beauty and attractiveness. Individuals who deviate significantly from physical norms are subject to possible rejection, even if their physical deviations do not interfere with their day-to-day functioning.

Society tends to place behavioral expectations on both men and women. Boys and men have specific masculine roles they are expected to assume. Boys are expected to be athletic. Physical impairments, however, may preclude athletic involvement. Unable to fulfill this role, the young paraplegic male may develop devalued feelings of self-worth or a feeling that he is less than a man. Feminine roles are also assigned, and women with physical disabilities who are unable to assume these roles may suffer from feelings of inadequacy. With the increased participation of women in athletics, some women may also suffer the frustration of being unable to be competitive in some athletic programs.

Individuals with physical disabilities may or may not become a part of a microcultural group related to the disability. Some function vocationally and socially as part of the mainstream society. With adequate cognitive functioning and adequate communication patterns, normal social interaction is possible. However, socialization may be a function of the degree of impairment and the individual's emotional adjustment to the disability. Some individuals with physical disabilities may function in the mainstream world and also maintain social contacts with others with similar disabilities. Social clubs for individuals with physical disabilities have been formed to provide experiences commensurate with functional abilities as well as a social climate that provides acceptance and security. Athletic leagues for competition in sports, such as wheelchair basketball and tennis, have been formed. Many marathon events (e.g., the Boston Marathon) now include competition for wheelchair entries.

Individuals with Emotional Disturbance and Those with Delinquent Behaviors

Emotional disturbance and delinquency significantly affect the adequate functioning of the individual's family as a unit, as well as social contacts beyond the family. The behavior exhibited by these individuals is often negative and excessive, and the response to this behavior is typically rejection. Because the behavior may grossly affect the well-being of society, the individual and the family are often held accountable for these actions, even if they are, in reality, beyond willful control.

It is clear that adverse environmental conditions contribute greatly to emotional disturbance. Where individuals are subjected to extreme stress, there is a greater likelihood for the development of emotional problems. Extreme poverty, for example, may subject an individual to constant stress, and the inability to cope with the stress results in emotional disturbances. Problems with delinquency, particularly in childhood and adolescence, may be related to lower socioeconomic circumstances, including being on public welfare, living in low-rent housing, and being a member of a minority group that tends to be caught in the low-income poverty cycle. Extreme stress caused by environmental deprivation can contribute to delinquent behaviors. However, it would be wrong to assume that children and adolescents faced with poverty-related stress are necessarily predisposed to delinquent behavior.

Gelfand, Jenson, and Drew (1988) suggest that poverty, malnutrition, homelessness, family discord, divorce, childrearing practices, and child abuse are a function of the behaviors we see in children. While some emotional problems in children stem from early negative interactions between parents and children, there are no solid research findings that would allow the blame for children's behavioral problems to be attributed primarily to their parents. It has become increasingly evident that influences are transactional and interactional, and children affect their parents as much as their parents affect them.

It has been speculated that some delinquent children are rebelling against social standards that are different from those of their own minority or disadvantaged group. In other instances, the resentment and negative behaviors may be directed against their own social and economic system, such as the maladjustment problems observed among individuals in middle and higher socioeconomic groups.

Some individuals who have no viable means to attain their goals may develop social alienation and maladjustment. Individuals from low-income groups, for example, are often confronted with the problem of wanting the material comforts of the middle and upper classes but not having a legitimate means to achieve these desires. Frustrated and disillusioned with their attempts to achieve through socially acceptable means, they may begin to seek less legitimate means that seem to bring more satisfying results.

The delinquent often forms or becomes part of a gang. The gang members form their own cultural group with their own values, morals, and standards. This may involve substance abuse with alcohol or other drugs. Those who are incarcerated in correctional institutions become a part of a larger microcultural group that also develops its own standards, values, and way of life.

Gang life has become a highly visible part of the urban scene in the 1980s and 1990s. Gang membership may include individuals from all ethnic groups, but it consists primarily of young people from oppressed minority groups. Gang life is often violent; major cities such as Washington, DC, and Los Angeles report hundreds of gang-related deaths each year. We will not devote extensive coverage here to examining the motivation for gang participation. However, it is important for educators to realize that for most of the young Americans who choose gang membership with its risk of violent death, their perception is that society offers them no better alternative. This could be interpreted to mean that our schools cannot convince these gang members that the educational system in this country does offer them a better choice.

Disproportionate Placements in Special Education

In 1968, Dunn, in his seminal article, "Special Education for the Mildly Retarded: Is Much of It Justifiable?" pointed out the phenomenal increase of classes for students with mental retardation. Perhaps the most profound revelation was that 60 to 80 percent of the pupils taught in classes for those with retardation were minority-group children from low socioeconomic backgrounds. Questioning the proliferation of classes for students with mental retardation, Dunn asserted that the extensive placement of these minorities in classes for children who had mental retardation raised serious educational and civil rights issues. In a classic study, Mercer (1973) documented the disproportionate placement of minorities in the Riverside, California, public school classes for students with mental retardation. While Mexican American students there constituted only 11 percent of the general school population sampled, they made up 45.3 percent of the students in classes for those with mild retardation. African American children were placed in the same classes at a rate three times greater than their numbers in the school population at large. Whites, on the other hand, constituted 81 percent of the general school population but only 32.1 percent of the special education classes for students with mental retardation.

Chinn and Hughes (1987) analyzed the 1978–1984 U.S. Office of Civil Rights Surveys of Elementary and Secondary Schools. These surveys provided data regarding student enrollment and placement in special education classes. While Hispanics are no longer overrepresented in classes for students with mild mental retardation in the national data, African Americans continue to be. They are also overrepresented in classes for students with moderate retardation and the seriously emotionally disturbed (SED). Native Americans are overrepresented in classes for students with moderate mental retardation and learning disabilities. Hispanics, African Americans, and Native Americans are all significantly underrepresented in classes for the gifted and talented. In the 1986, 1988, and 1990 Office of Civil Rights Surveys, the same trends persist (OCR, 1988, 1990, 1992). Chinn and Hughes emphasized that the national data obscure some state data, where minority groups may be over- or underrepresented in certain categories.

The issues of ethnicity, social class, and gender appear to be intricately intertwined with the issues of exceptionality. It is apparent that significant numbers of children from African American, Native American, and Hispanic families, many of whom come from lower socioeconomic backgrounds, are systematically excluded from classes for the gifted and talented. Large numbers of African Americans, twice their numbers in the general school population, are placed in classes for those with mild mental retardation (EMR). The extent of disproportionate placement of African Americans in classes for students with serious emotional disturbance (SED) is not as great as in classes for students with mild mental retardation, but enough to question the reasons for placement.

Other disturbing statistics include the facts that males are placed in SED classes three and a half times more often than females (Office of Civil Rights, 1992), and that children of lower-class backgrounds are also overrepresented in SED classes (Kauffman, 1993).

There are no simple solutions to the problems of disproportionate placement in special education classes. What is clear is that there are direct relationships to ethnicity, class, and gender. Laws related to special education have increased the law suits for alleged inappropriate placement, and school districts have responded by exercising more caution when making placements; yet the problem persists.

What is known is that when a referral (usually from classroom teachers) is made for special education, the likelihood of placement is high. High and Udall (1983) suggest that teacher attitudes toward culturally diverse students affect their referral rates.

Teachers, most of whom are white middle class, often have values that are incongruent with that of ethnic minority and lower-socioeconomic students. Behaviors that may be considered within acceptable ranges in a child's home or community may be viewed as unacceptably aggressive by educators. These teachers may be prone to make referrals to special education in order to have the students removed from their classrooms (Chinn & Harris, 1990).

Differences in cognitive style may also result in perceiving children as less competent, particularly if the teacher is field-independent and the student is field-sensitive. Since field-independent teachers prefer greater independent learning styles in their students, the more interactive and group-learning style preferred by the field-sensitive students is likely to be viewed less favorably when the teaching and learning styles are incongruent. Kitano and Kirby (1986) suggest that gifted children from culturally diverse backgrounds may go unnoticed because they express their talents in ways different from children in the dominant culture.

Males are also placed in classes for students with mild retardation, moderate retardation, speech impairment, serious emotional disturbance, and learning disabilities at higher percentages than females. They are placed in classes for students with mild retardation at one and a half times, for speech impairment at one and three-quarter times, for serious emotional disturbance at three and a half times, and for learning disabilities at two and a half times the rate of placement for females. Males may indeed be more prone to some disabilities; however, the circumstances operating in the classroom with males may be similar to the situation with ethnic minorities and children from lower-class backgrounds. The majority of our teachers, particularly in the elementary school years, are female. They are socialized differently from males. In some instances, the teacher tolerance level for assertive or aggressive male students may preclude effective teacher-pupil relationships and may precipitate special education referrals.

The disproportionate placement of African Americans and other minority groups has also been attributed to the assessment process. Special education placement is at least partially predicated on test scores. No test is culture-free, and some are inherently biased against children from culturally and linguistically different groups.

In *Diana v. California State Board of Education,* a class action suit was brought on behalf of nine Mexican American children against the California

PAUSE TO REFLECT

It is the time of year when your school district tests the basic skills of its students at the third, fifth, and eighth grades. In previous years you had not thought much about the standardized tests that you distributed and monitored. However, this year you have several students who have limited proficiency in English. You know that they are not yet comfortable enough in English to perform well on this test. Why should you be concerned about the performance of these students? What might be the impact of poor performance on these students? What steps could you take to intervene on behalf of the students who have limited proficiency in English?

State Board of Education. The suit alleged that the children were inappropriately tested in a language (English) which was not their primary language. In addition, the suit alleged that parts of the test were biased against the children. For example, one question in the test asked, "Is it better to pay bills by cash or by check?" The children in the suit selected cash as their response. According to the test key, check was the correct response. The attorneys for the plaintiffs asserted that none of the parents of these children had checking accounts. When retested by a bilingual psychologist who used English and/or Spanish and allowed responses in either language, the results were dramatically different from the initial findings. Seven of the children tested were above the special education cutoff, one at the cutoff, and one only three points below. As a result of the suit, the defendant agreed to testing in the child's primary language, the use of nonverbal tests, and the use of extensive supporting data.

Lack of skill or sensitivity on the part of test administrators has also been blamed for incorrect assessment results. *Larry P. v. Riles* (1972) was a major court case that found that some African American children placed in special education classes for the retarded were victims of inappropriate assessment. The findings of the court have changed the entire placement process in California and have impacted on practices throughout the country.

The Office of Civil Rights (OCR) findings of disproportionate placement of African Americans in classes for children with moderate retardation is particularly distressing. The majority of the children in these classes have known central nervous system impairment. Consequently, there are few challenges to the referral, assessment, or placement practices. Prior to the collection of data regarding special education placement and ethnicity, it was often assumed that moderate and severe mental retardation had no respect for ethnicity or social class. The OCR findings refute such an assumption. African Americans are placed in these classes at a rate one and a half times their representation in the general population. Chinn and Hughes (1987) state

> The existence of poverty among some minority groups is a reality which cannot be logically disputed. The extent to which poverty and its concomitant problems contribute directly or indirectly to learning and behavior problems is difficult to determine. However, it is generally recognized that poverty, at least in extreme forms, may preclude adequate pre- and postnatal care, nutrition, and other environmental advantages. Absence of these favorable environmental conditions may place a child at greater risk. (p. 45)

In addition, there is a positive correlation between poverty and teenage pregnancies along with unwed motherhood (Berger, 1983). These situations, in turn, are directly related to children born preterm, which places the fetus and infant at risk. Children born at risk are in greater likelihood of sustaining physical insult or injury, sometimes permanent. Children who live in poverty are often subjected to extreme stress related to coping with the day-to-day demands of obtaining food and shelter. Stress is a major contributor to emotional disturbance. Thus it should not be surprising when children who live in poverty or in crime- and drug-infested neighborhoods, sometime witnessing firsthand violent deaths, develop serious emotional problems.

Educational Implications

The educational implications for working with exceptional individuals are numerous, and entire chapters could be devoted to each exceptionality. Educators should remember that exceptional children, those with disabilities and those who are gifted, are more like than unlike normal children. Their basic needs are the same as all children's. Abraham Maslow's theory on self-actualization is familiar to most students in education. To be self-actualized, or to meet one's full potential, Maslow (1954) theorized that one's basic needs must be fulfilled. That is, to reach self-actualization, one's physiological needs, safety needs, belongingness or love needs, and esteem needs must first be met. Although many individuals with disabilities may never match the accomplishments of their normal peers, they can become proficient at whatever they are capable of doing. Educators can assist them by helping to ensure that their basic needs are met, allowing them to strive toward self-actualization.

Teachers must be constantly cognizant of the unique needs of their exceptional children. The exceptional adult may choose to become a part of, or may be forced by society to become a part of, a microcultural group. The interactions between educators and the exceptional child may not change what will eventually take place. Even if exceptional adults are a part of a microcultural group, they also will interact with the mainstream society on a regular basis. The efforts on the part of the educator to meet the needs of the child may ultimately affect the exceptional adult's interaction with society.

Teachers of children with physical and other health impairments may find it advantageous to check their student records carefully to determine potential problem situations with these students in the classroom. If the child has particular health problems that may surface in the classroom, teachers need to be prepared for such situations so that they will know precisely what to do should the child have, for example, an epileptic seizure. The parents will most likely be able to provide precise instructions, and the school nurse could also provide additional recommendations. If the children are old enough to understand, they themselves can be a valuable source of information. Ask them what kind of adaptations, special equipment, or teaching procedures work best for them. Teachers should not be afraid of their own uncertainties. They should feel free to ask the student when they do or don't want help. Teachers should treat their students with disabilities as normally as feasible, neither overprotecting them nor giving or doing more for them than is needed or deserved. Allowing them to assume responsibility for themselves will do much to facilitate their personal growth.

There are many variables affecting the learning, cognition, and adjustment of individuals with disabilities. Educators and others who work with students with disabilities can do much to ensure that these variables impact in a positive manner.

The range and variety of experiences imposed on or withheld from persons with disabilities may result in undue limitations. Too often, parents and teachers assume that a child's visual limitation precludes the ability to appreciate the typical everyday experiences of sighted children. Children who are blind may not be able to see the animals in a zoo, but they can smell and hear them. They may not be able to enjoy the scenes along a bus route, but they can feel the stop-and-go movements, hear the traffic and people, and smell their fellow travelers. The child who is deaf may not be able to hear the sounds at the symphony or the crowd's roar at a football game. Both events, however, offer the possibility of extraordinary sensory experiences that the child needs exposure to. The child with cerebral palsy needs experiences such as going to restaurants, even if there is difficulty using eating utensils in a socially acceptable manner.

Well-adjusted individuals with a sensory disability usually attain a balance of control with their environment. Individuals who depend completely on other members of the family and friends may develop an attitude of helplessness and a loss of self-identity. Individuals with disabilities who completely dominate and control their environment with unreasonable demands sometimes fail to make an acceptable adjustment and could become selfish and self-centered.

It is critical to remember that children who are exceptional are first and foremost children. Their exceptionality, although having an influence on their lives, is secondary to their basic needs as children. Chinn, Winn, and Walters (1978) identify three of those needs: communication, acceptance, and the freedom to grow.

Communication Needs

Exceptional children are far more perceptive than many adults give them credit for being. They are sensitive to nonverbal communication and hidden messages that may be concealed in half-truths. They, more than anyone, need to deal with their exceptionality, whether it is a disability or a giftedness. They need to know what their exceptionality is all about so that they can deal with it. They need to know how it will impact on their lives in order to make appropriate adjustments to make the best of their lives and reach their full potential. They need straight, honest communication tempered with sensitivity.

Acceptance Needs

The society in which we live often fails to provide the exceptional child with a positive and receptive environment. Even the educational setting can be hostile and lacking in acceptance. The teacher can facilitate the acceptance of a child in

J.B., a first-grade student who suffered from a hearing loss, was fitted with a hearing aid. When he came to school with the hearing aid, the students in the class immediately began whispering about the "thing" J.B. had in his ear. After observing the class behavior, the teacher assisted J.B. in a "show and tell" preparation for the next day. With the teacher's assistance and assurances, J.B. proudly demonstrated his hearing aid to the class. By the end of the demonstration, J.B. was the envy of the class, and any further discussion of the hearing aid was of a positive nature.

a classroom by exhibiting an open and positive attitude. Students tend to reflect the attitude of the teacher. If the teacher is hostile, the students will quickly pick up these cues. If the attitude is positive, the students are likely to respond and provide a receptive environment for their classmates with disabilities.

Freedom to Grow

Students with disabilities need acceptance and understanding. Acceptance implies a freedom for the exceptional child to grow. There are times when it may seem easier to do things for a child rather than to take the time to teach the child.

At other times, it may be tempting for teachers and parents to make extra concessions for the exceptional child. Often these exceptions preclude the emotional growth of the child and may later cause serious interpersonal problems.

S.B. was a nine-year-old girl who was blind and who had an orthopedic disability. She attended a state residential school for the blind. She wore leg braces but had a reasonable amount of mobility with crutches. To save time and effort, fellow students or staff members transported her between the cottage where she lived and the classroom building in a wagon. One day her teacher decided she needed to be more independent in her travel to and from her cottage. To S.B.'s surprise, the teacher informed her after school that she would not ride back in the wagon but that he was walking her back. Angered, she denounced him as cruel and hateful in front of the entire class. She complained bitterly the full thirty minutes of their walk back to the cottage. After a few days the complaining subsided and the travel time was curtailed. Within a few weeks S.B. was traveling on her own in ten minutes or less with newfound self-respect. (Chinn, Winn, & Walters, 1978, p. 36)

Normalization and Mainstreaming

Much effort is directed today toward the concept of normalization. Normalization means "making available to the mentally retarded patterns and conditions of everyday life which are as close as possible to the norms and patterns of mainstream society" (Nirje, 1969, p. 181). Normalization was expanded and advocated in the United States by Wolfensberger (1972). He has subsequently suggested a rethinking of the term *normalization* and introduced the concept of "social role valorization"—giving value to individuals with mental retardation. He suggested that the "most explicit and highest goal of normalization must be the creation, support, and defense of valued social roles for people who are at risk of social devaluation" (Wolfensberger, 1983, p. 234).

Drew et al. (1992) suggest that normalization and social valorization have brought about an emphasis on deinstitutionalization, whereby individuals from large residential facilities for individuals with retardation are returned to the community and home environments. They add that the concept is not limited to the movement away from institutions to a less restrictive environment, but also pertains to those individuals living in the community for whom a more "normal" lifestyle may be an appropriate goal.

The principles of normalization as they were first introduced were developed with the mentally retarded as the target group. In more recent years, the concept has broadened, so that all categories of individuals with disabilities are now targeted.

Mainstreaming seemed to undergo a natural evolutionary process from the concept of normalization. While IDEA mandates educating children with disabilities in the "least restrictive environment," nowhere in the statute is the word *mainstream* used. However, "least restrictive environment" means that children with disabilities are to be educated with nondisabled children whenever possible, in as normal an environment as possible. While the concept of least restrictive environment does not necessarily mean integration into regular education classes, the term *mainstreaming,* through common usage, refers to the practice of integrating children with disabilities into regular education classes for all or a portion of the day. A goal in special education, therefore, is to mainstream as many children with disabilities as is feasible.

Initially, mainstreaming was intended for students with milder disabilities; a more current movement seeks to provide children with moderate and severe disabilities with similar opportunities (Stainback & Stainback, 1985). While resistance to mainstreaming students with mild retardation is far less intense than it once was, resistance from some educators toward those with more severe disabilities is often still intense. The arguments against integrating children with severe disabilities have often been centered on the presumed inability of normal children to accept their peers with disabilities. In reality, some of the reservations may be more a reflection of educators who themselves are unable or unwilling to accept the dignity and worth of individuals with severe disabilities.

Most individuals with disabilities would like to participate in the same activities as the nondisabled. By removing barriers that limit access to them, they have found ways to participate fully in society, including taking part in athletics.

The Constitution mandates that every citizen has a right to life, liberty, and property. They cannot be denied these without due process. *Brown v. Board of Education* (1954) determined that education was a property right. While there is no constitutional guarantee of a free public education, Brown found that if a state undertakes the provision of free education for its citizenry, then the property right of an education is established. Brown did not involve children with disabilities. However, as the precedent was set to guarantee equal educational opportunity for ethnic minority children, it too sets a precedent in the argument of guaranteeing the rights of students with disabilities. Not only have the courts supported rights of students with disabilities to have a free education, but litigation and legislation have sought to bring them an appropriate education.

Brown found "separate but equal" education to be unequal. Separate education denied African American students an equal education; it denied them a fully integrated education, free from the stigma of segregation. Chief Justice

Warren stated that segregation "generates a feeling of inferiority as to their [children's] status in the community that may affect their hearts and minds in a way unlikely ever to be undone." Supporters of children with moderate and severe disabilities argue that the same thing has happened to students with disabilities who are denied an integrated education (Will, 1984).

Opponents of integration use many of the same arguments that segregationists used forty years ago. Perhaps some of their arguments are valid, perhaps not. As educators, we must be aware of the fact that our fear of change and our fear of the unknown have often prevented us from making changes for the better. The purpose of this chapter is not to persuade integration of students with moderate and severe disabilities into regular education. Rather, it is important for us as educators to see the parallels that exist with this group of students and those over forty years ago that Brown addressed. It is important that as educators we maintain an open mind so that perhaps we ourselves can be educated.

The legal mandates do not eliminate the special schools or classes, but they do offer a new philosophical view. Instead of the physical isolation of disabled individuals, an effort to enable students with disabilities to assume a more appropriate place in the educational setting is being promoted. There are still many children with disabilities who apparently may not benefit appreciably from an integrated setting and may be better educated in a special setting. As attitudes become more congruent with the laws, individuals with disabilities may have more of an option in the decision to be a part of the mainstream or to form their own cultural groups.

Summary

The concerns related to the disproportionate placement of ethnic minorities, males, and students from low-income families in special education programs have been addressed to focus on a long-standing educational problem. The issues raised are not intended to negate the fact that there are students who are retarded as well as seriously emotionally disturbed and other children with disabilities from both majority and minority groups. Rather, they are raised to call attention to problems in referral and assessment as well as the problems associated with poverty.

Adults with disabilities often become a part of a microculture for individuals with disabilities by ascription or by individual choice. They do not choose to have a disability, and their situation often precludes full acceptance or integration into the world of those who are perceived to be physically, socially, or mentally normal. Their adjustment to their environment may be in part a function of the way they are perceived, treated, and accepted by educators. Consequently, teachers and other educators may have a greater influence on children with disabilities than they themselves realize.

Public Law 94-142, IDEA, and Section 504 of Public Law 93-112 and the Americans with Disabilities Act guarantee all exceptional children the right to a free and appropriate education and freedom from discrimination resulting from their disability. In spite of these mandates, equality still eludes millions of individuals with disabilities in this country. Insensitivity, apathy, and prejudice contribute to the problems of those with disabilities. Because of prejudice, institutionalization, or a desire to meet their own needs, some exceptional individuals form their own microcultures and some their own enclaves, where they live and socialize with one another. The laws can force services for individuals with disabilities, but only time and effort can change public attitudes.

Questions for Review

1. What are some of the objections to labeling children with disabilities?
2. In what ways has the treatment of individuals with disabilities paralleled treatment of oppressed minorities?
3. In what ways have ethnic minority children been disproportionately placed in special classes for students with disabilities and students who are gifted?
4. What are some of the variables contributing to the disproportionate placement of minorities in special education?
5. What are the major implications of Public Law 94-142, IDEA, and Section 504 of Public Law 93-112 and the Americans with Disabilities Act?
6. Explain the concepts of normalization, social role valorization, and mainstreaming.
7. What are some of the negative ways that individuals with disabilities are portrayed by the media and viewed by some members of society?
8. What are some of the ways in which exceptional individuals form their own microcultures?
9. What are some of the needs of exceptional children?

References

Berger, K. S. (1983). *The developing person through the life span.* New York: Worth.

Brown v. Board of Education of Topeka. (1954). 347 U.S. 483, 74 S. Ct. 686, 91, L. Ed. 873.

Chinn, P. C., & Harris, K. C. (1990). Variables affecting the disproportionate placement of ethnic minority children in special education programs. *Multicultural Leader, 3*(1), 1–3.

Chinn, P. C., & Hughes, S. (1987). Representation of minority students in special education classes. *Remedial and Special Education, 8*(4), 41–46.

Chinn, P. C., Winn, J., & Walters, R. H. (1978). *Two-way talking with parents of exceptional children: A process of positive communication.* St. Louis: Mosby.

Drew, C. J., Logan, D. R., & Hardman, M. L. (1992). *Mental retardation: A life-cycle approach* (5th ed.). New York: Merrill/Macmillan.

Dunn, L. (1968). Special education for the mildly retarded: Is much of it justifiable? *Exceptional Children, 7,* 5–24.

Edgerton, R. B. (1967). *The cloak of competence.* Berkeley: University of California.

Gelfand, D. M., Jenson, W. R., & Drew, C. J. (1988). *Understanding child behavior disorders* (2nd ed.). New York: Holt, Rinehart & Winston.

Gliedman, J., & Roth, W. (1980). *The unexpected minority.* New York: Harcourt Brace Jovanovich.

Heward, W. L., & Orlansky, M. D. (1992). *Exceptional children* (4th ed.). New York: Merrill/Macmillan.

High, M. H., & Udall, A. I. (1983). Teacher ratings of students in relation to ethnicity of students and school ethnic balance. *Journal of Education and the Gifted, 6,* 154–166.

Kauffman, J. M. (1993). *Characteristics of emotional and behavioral disorders of children and youth* (5th ed.). New York: Merrill/Macmillan.

Kitano, M. K., & Kirby, D. F. (1986). *Gifted education: A comprehensive view.* Boston: Little, Brown.

Krishef, C. H. (1972). State laws on marriage and sterilization of the mentally retarded. *Mental Retardation, 10*(3), 136–38.

Larry P. v. Wilson Riles. (1979). C-71-2270, FRP. Dis. Ct.

Maslow, A. (1954). *Motivation and personality.* New York: Harper.

Mercer, J. (1973). *Labeling the mentally retarded.* Los Angeles: University of California Press.

Nirje, B. (1969). The normalization principle and its human management implications. In R. B. Kugel & W. Wolfensberger (Eds.), *Changing patterns in residential services for the mentally retarded* (pp. 227–254). Washington, DC: President's Committee on Mental Retardation.

Office of Civil Rights. (1988). *1986 elementary and secondary schools civil rights survey.* Washington, DC: Department of Education.

Office of Civil Rights. (1990). *1988 elementary and secondary schools civil rights survey.* Washington, DC: Department of Education.

Office of Civil Rights. (1992). *1990 elementary and secondary schools civil rights survey.* Washington, DC: Department of Education.

Ortiz, A., & Yates, J. R. (1983). Incidence of exceptionality among Hispanics: Implications for manpower planning. *National Association of Bilingual Education Journal, 7*(3), 41–53.

President's Committee on Mental Retardation. (1969). *The six hour retarded child.* Washington, DC: U.S. Department of Health, Education and Welfare.

Stainback, S., & Stainback, W. (1985). *Integration of students with severe handicaps into regular schools.* Reston, VA: Council for Exceptional Children.

Will, M. C. (1984). "Let us pause and reflect but not too long." *Exceptional Children 51*(1), 11–16.

Wolfensberger, W. (1972). *Normalization: The principle of normalization in human services.* Toronto: National Institute on Mental Retardation.

Wolfensberger, W. (1983). Social role valorization: Proposed new form for the principle of normalization. *Mental Retardation, 21*(6), 234–239.

Suggested Readings

Drew, C. J., Logan, D. R., & Hardman, M. L. (1992). *Mental retardation: A life-cycle approach* (5th ed.). New York: Merrill/Macmillan.

An excellent developmental approach to mental retardation. Includes a sensitive view of mental retardation and its impact on the family. A chapter on legislative and legal issues related to individuals with mental retardation is also included.

Edgerton, R. B. (1967). *The cloak of competence: Stigma in the lives of the mentally retarded.* Berkeley: University of California Press.

A detailed follow-up of the lives of individuals released from Pacific State Hospital in California. Includes detailed portraits of selected subjects and concerns of these individuals living outside the institution. Considered a classic in the field of mental retardation.

Gliedman, J., & Roth, W. (1980). *The unexpected minority.* New York: Harcourt Brace Jovanovich.

An examination of how social rather than biological aspects of disability doom handicapped children and adults to stunted and useless lives. Demonstrates how discrimination against the handicapped is the result of stereotypes and misconceptions that distort the attitudes of both professionals and society at large.

Heward, W. L., & Orlansky, M. D. (1992). *Exceptional children* (4th ed.). New York: Merrill/Macmillan.

One of the few survey texts to include a chapter on culturally diverse exceptional children. An overview of all exceptionalities that will provide a good basic understanding of the gifted and talented as well as the various handicapping conditions.

Stainback, W., & Stainback, S. (Eds.). (1992). *Controversial issues confronting special education: Divergent perspectives.* Boston: Allyn and Bacon.

An excellent treatment of major issues in special education. There are twelve sections, and twenty-four chapters. In each section, there are two chapters that take different points of view.

CHAPTER 6

Religion

Congress shall make no law respecting an establishment of religion, or prohibiting the free exercise thereof; or abridging the freedom of speech, or of the press; or the right of the people peaceably to assemble, and to petition the Government for a redress of grievances.

FIRST AMENDMENT TO THE UNITED STATES CONSTITUTION, 1791

In a suburb of San Francisco, the teacher and administrators of the Edison Onizuka middle school were putting the finishing touches on their plans for the school's honors convocation. The principal, Dr. Margaret Moennich, had suggested the event to recognize the school's high academic achievers in each grade. This effort to stimulate and reinforce student academic efforts was enthusiastically endorsed by the faculty. Guadalupe Gutierrez and Rebecca Weintraub were tied with the highest grades in the eighth grade and were to be recognized and asked to make a seven- to ten-minute speech on the importance of an education. Because the faculty and Dr. Moennich wanted the school district superintendent to be part of the ceremony, they had agreed to schedule the event at 3:00 P.M. on the fourth Saturday in May. This was the superinten-

dent's only available time; she was participating in high school commencement ceremonies at all of the other times that were proposed.

Dr. Moennich called the Gutierrez and Weintraub families herself to inform them of their daughter's selection as convocation speakers. As expected, both sets of parents were delighted at the news of their daughter's accomplishments and selection. However, Mr. Weintraub indicated that Saturday was quite impossible since it was the Sabbath for their family, who were Orthodox Jews. The event would have to be rescheduled to any day but the Sabbath. It was impossible, Dr. Moennich pleaded. All the plans were made and there were no satisfactory alternate dates. "Would you plan the event on a Sunday?" Mr. Weintraub exclaimed. "I would not ask you to. Then why do you schedule it on our Sabbath? You must change the day." At an impasse, Dr. Moennich knew she had to come up with another plan in a hurry. What would you do in Dr. Moennich's place?

Religion and Culture

In the United States, close to 150 million individuals are affiliated with some religious group. In an average week, 42 percent of the adults attend a church or synagogue. Religion is clearly an important aspect of the lives of many individuals. Some individuals have little, if anything, to do with religion, but for others, including many children in U.S. classrooms, their religion influences the way they think, perceive, and behave. The forces of religious groups are far from dormant. They can influence the election of school board members as well as the curriculum and textbooks used in the schools. Principals, teachers, and superintendents have been hired and fired through the influence of religious groups. This chapter will provide an overview of religion in the United States and its influence in the educational system.

The pluralistic nature of the school in which one teaches will be determined in great part by its geographical location in the United States. Because of various immigration and migration patterns throughout history, ethnic and religious groups have settled in different parts of the country. Although few areas remain totally homogeneous, a school community may be dominated by families that identify with a particular ethnic group. More often, families identify with the religious orientation of one or more denominations in the community. The perspective of a particular religious doctrine often influences what a family expects from the school and thus from the teacher. In an area where the religious perspectives and school expectations differ greatly, educators face numerous challenges. A look at the religious composition of schools in various sections of the country will provide a sense of the diversity one might face throughout a career in education.

A consolidated rural high school in the South may be attended primarily by students whose families are conservative Southern Baptist or Pentecostal. The church serves as the center of most community activities, and many families spend several nights a week at church or serving the church. Sex education is not allowed in the public school curriculum. Teachers may face harsh criticism if they teach about evolution or lifestyles that conflict with those acceptable in that community. Textbooks and assigned readings are often scrutinized to ensure that the content does not stray far from the beliefs of this fundamentalist community.

At a middle school in northeastern Indiana, most students are from the same European background, but they dress and behave differently. Some of the students are from a local Old Order Amish community with strict dress codes for its members, while the majority of the other students are Mennonites. The former are very respectful and well behaved, but some are ridiculed by non-Amish students. After completing the eighth grade, the Amish students will no longer be part of the school system because their families withdraw them to work full-time on their farms.

Students from Catholic, Jewish, Protestant, and Buddhist families attend a suburban school on the West Coast. Some of the students in the school are from families that have no religious affiliation. Although the religious backgrounds of the students differ, they seem to share many of the same values. The school projects a generally liberal curriculum that includes sex education and ethnic studies. Except for the students' celebration of various religious holidays, religion seems to have little impact on the students or the school.

At an inner-city school on the East Coast, the religious backgrounds of students vary greatly. Some students attend Catholic services; others attend Baptist churches or storefront Pentecostal churches; some belong to a cult that has been established in the community; and others have no religious affiliation. Thus, some students are constantly involved in religious activities during their nonschool time. The school reflects little of these diverse religious perspectives in the curriculum or the school environment.

Moving to the state of Utah, the educator will find a school in a moderate-size community dominated by members of the Church of Jesus Christ of Latter-Day Saints (Mormons). Many Mormon families serve their ward several nights every week and socialize almost solely with other Mormon families. Mormon beliefs do not allow smoking or drinking of alcohol, coffee, or tea. In that Utah community, many major institutions and businesses are controlled by members of this religious group. Religion itself is not taught as part of the school curriculum, but the perspective of the dominant religious group in this community is reflected in school and curriculum practices. Many students leave during school hours to receive religious instruction at a Mormon seminary adjacent to the school. Most of the elected officials are members of the Mormon church; thus, state and local laws affecting education reflect a Mormon influence.

People differ greatly in their beliefs about the role that religious perspective should play in determining school curriculum and environment. Like all other institutions in this country, schools have a historical background of rural, white, Protestant domination. Such domination has determined the holidays, usually Christian holidays, that are celebrated by schools. Moreover, the Protestant majority has determined the moral teachings that have been integrated into our public schools.

While the First Amendment to the U.S. Constitution affirms the principle of separation of church and state, it is one of the most controversial parts of the Constitution, as various individuals and groups tend to interpret it to meet their own needs and interests. For some, religious emphasis is appropriate in the public schools as long as it is congruent with their own religious persuasion. These same individuals, however, may be quick to cite the constitutional safeguards for separation of church and state if other groups attempt the infusion of their religious dogmas.

In most communities in this country, schools close in observance of Christmas and sometimes Easter (although Easter break may now be referred to as spring break). The Christian residents in these communities may realize that others may not observe these Christian holidays, but they may also expect everyone to recognize their right to close the schools during their religious holy days. These individuals, however, may vigorously resist any attempts by other religious groups to close the schools in observance of their special religious days.

Equity and propriety are often in the eye of the beholder, and one's religious orientation may strongly influence one's perception of what constitutes objectivity, fairness, and legality.

Parents and churches disagree about the separation of church and state as required in the First Amendment. Since the removal of prayer from the schools by a 1963 Supreme Court decision, parent groups have continued to fight (sometimes successfully) to restore prayer in the schools through state and federal legislation. Parent groups have fought on religious grounds to prevent the teaching of sex education and evolution. Coming from different religious backgrounds, parents have fought verbally and physically over what books their children should read in literature courses and what curriculum should be used in social studies and science classes. Members of more liberal Protestant, Catholic, and Jewish denominations often argue that they want their children exposed to the perspectives of different religious and ethnic groups. Members of the more conservative, especially fundamentalist, groups argue that they do not want their children exposed to what they consider immoral perspectives and the language inherent in such instructional materials.

Community resistance to cultural pluralism and multicultural education has at times been led by some individuals associated with conservative religious groups. Because cultural pluralism inevitably involves religious diversity, multicultural education is sometimes viewed as an impediment to efforts to maintain the status quo or, better yet, to return to the religious values of the past.

Sometimes maligned as a bedfellow of the Secular Humanist movement, multicultural education is erroneously accused of supporting movements that detract from basic moral values. What multicultural education does is to provide a basis for understanding and appreciating diversity and to minimize the problems inherent in people being different from one another.

Of all the microcultures examined in this book, religion may be the most problematic for educators. In one school, the religious beliefs of students appear to have little influence on what is taught in a classroom; in fact, the teacher is expected to expose students to many different perspectives. In another school, the teacher may be attacked for asking students to read *The Catcher in the Rye*.

Educators themselves vary in their beliefs about the role of religious perspective in education. If one shares the same religion or religious perspectives as the community, there will probably be little conflict between one's own beliefs and the beliefs reflected in the school. If the educator is from a religious background different from that prevalent in the community or has a perspective about the role of religion that differs from that of the community, misunderstanding and conflicts may arise that prevent effective instruction. If an educator does not understand the role of religion in the lives of the students, it may be difficult to develop appropriate instructional strategies. In some cases, it would be difficult to retain one's job.

This chapter will examine religion and its impact on a student's life, the various religions existing in the United States, the degree to which an individual identifies with a particular religious doctrine, and the educational implications of religion.

Religion as a Way of Life

Religious pluralism has its foundation in the U.S. Constitution, as there were no ties between the government and a state or favored church. Although the separation of church and state is an integral part of our heritage, the two usually support each other. In many churches, the U.S. flag stands next to the church flag, and patriotism is an important part of religious loyalty. On the other hand, God has been mentioned in all inaugural addresses except Washington's second address and it is not an uncommon practice for politicians and preachers to refer to the United States as the promised land. The secular ideas of the American dream also pervade many religions in this country. In fact, religions often reflect the dominant values of our society (Greeley, 1982).

For most individuals, religion serves as a looking glass in which "humanity beholds its own image, its ideal portrait of itself, its highest intentions, its destiny" (Raschke, Kirk, & Taylor, 1977, p. 7). Western religions tend to emphasize individual control over life—an emphasis that prompts believers to blame the disadvantaged for their disadvantage (Stark & Glock, 1974). Many religions are particularistic in that members believe that their own religion is uniquely true and legitimate and all others are false (Wilson, 1978). Other religions accept the validity of various faiths that have grown out of different historical experiences. The values and lifestyles of families are affected by their religious beliefs (Greeley, 1982).

Nine out of ten Americans regard their religious beliefs as very, or at least fairly, important to them (*Emerging Trends,* 1992). Although less than half of the population attends church weekly, most identify with a religious perspective that is reflected in their daily living (Bezilla, 1993). Religion appears to have an influence in patterns of gender roles, marriage, divorce, birthrates, child training, sexual activity, friendships, and political attitudes. It may affect one's dress, social activities, and dietary habits, including alcohol consumption and smoking.

If the religious group is tightly knit, a member may have little chance to interact on a personal level with anyone other than another member of the same religion, especially if a religious school is maintained. Tight control over criteria for membership in the group and little contact with nongroup members are often key factors in maintaining the integrity of religious sects. The Hutterites and, to a great extent, the Amish have been able to survive in this way. Mormons, a much larger group, were able to grow with little outside interference once they were established in Salt Lake City. Even in suburban areas, friendship patterns are largely based on religious preference (Mueller, 1974).

Churches and their religious programs serve as a strong socialization mechanism in the transmission of values from one generation to another. Rituals, parables, and stories reinforce these values, and Sunday schools serve as primary agents for transmitting them. Religious institutions are also responsible for reinterpreting social failure in spiritual terms, compensating for the lack of value realization, and functioning as an agent of social control by reward and punishment (Wilson, 1978).

All but 2 percent of the parents in this country believe that their children should have religious training for character building and as a means of keeping the family together (Gallup Poll, 1984). Children become aware of their religious identity as Protestant, Catholic, or Jew by five years of age, although they tend to equate religion with national and racial identities. By nine years of age, they are able to distinguish between religion and irreligion, and they can identify denominations by their practices. As one might expect, children of religious parents are more likely to be religious than children of nonreligious parents (Greeley, 1982).

In the United States, adults (42 percent) attend church or synagogue as regularly as did their counterparts in 1939 (41 percent). Although not equal to the all-time high of 49 percent in 1955 and 1958, attendance from 1969 to 1991 deviated a maximum of three percentage points throughout that period (Bezilla, 1993). Church and synagogue attendance patterns are listed in Table 6-1.

Table 6–1. Church/Synagogue Attendance Among U.S. Adults: Percentage Attending in Average Week

Year	Percentage	Year	Percentage
1991	42	1970	42
1990	40	1969	42
1989	43	1968	43
1988	42	1967	43
1987	40	1966	44
1986	40	1965	44
1985	42	1964	45
1984	40	1963	46
1983	40	1962	46
1982	41	1961	47
1981	41	1960	47
1980	40	1959	47
1979	40	1958	49[a]
1978	41	1957	47
1977	41	1956	46
1976	42	1955	49[a]
1975	40	1954	46
1974	40	1950	39
1973	40	1940	37[b]
1972	40	1939	41
1971	40		

[a]High points
[b]Low points

From Gallup Report (1987), *Religion in America, 259*(38), and from Bezilla (1993) *Religion in America, 42.*

Weekly attendance at church or synagogue interacts with other microcultural memberships. In 1990, more women (46 percent) attended weekly services than men (39 percent). Blacks (55 percent) attended more regularly than whites (41 percent). College graduates attended to a greater extent than nongraduates, and 14 percent more individuals fifty and older attended than those in the eighteen to twenty-nine age group. Southerners (48 percent) had a 14 percent higher attendance rate than Westerners (34 percent) (*Emerging Trends,* 1992b).

Thus, religious behavior is learned as a normal part of the socialization pattern. Religion and religious differences are important in our study of this pluralistic nation because they are a way of life for many people, as described by Wilson (1978):

> Religion is much more than a voluntary association of people with a common hobby or pastime. A denomination, sect, or church is also a community of people who intermarry, worship together as a family, choose their friends along religious lines, and socialize their children according to the teachings of their

faith. Each faith, even each denomination, is a separate subcommunity as well as a voluntary association. It is a way of life, with social clubs, athletic leagues, insurance companies, professional societies, publishing houses, veterans groups, and even movie-rating committees. (p. 278)

Religious Pluralism in America

Four decades ago, few Americans would have envisioned their country led by a Catholic president or foreseen an African American minister elected as the majority whip in the U.S. House of Representatives. In very recent years, we have seen Jesse Jackson, an African American minister, make a strong and serious bid for the Democratic Party's presidential nomination. In the same election year, 1988, Pat Robertson, a popular televangelist, was a serious candidate for the Republican nomination and received strong support financially and otherwise. Again in 1992, Jesse Jackson made a significant showing in the presidential campaign.

In recent years, we have observed thousands of young people, many white, led by a Korean minister and leader of the Unification church; we have seen African Americans leaving traditional African American Protestant churches and joining the ranks of the Black Muslims; we have witnessed tens of thousands of Hispanics leaving the Roman Catholic Church for Pentecostal churches, and we have seen college students embracing Zen Buddhism.

Today, the electronic church (televangelism) reaches the homes of millions of Americans, influences their lives and their voting patterns, and has helped to elect or defeat politicians and change the face of America for years to come. Thus, religious groups are mediating structures that link families and individuals to the larger social order (Roof and McKinney, 1985).

Americans tend to identify not only with major groups, such as Protestants, Catholics, and Jews, but also with smaller groups or denominations within these major religious microcultures. For example, former president Jimmy Carter, a Southern Baptist, identified himself as a "born-again" Christian. Others may identify themselves as charismatic Catholics. It is important to note that within each major group, there is considerable heterogeneity. Conservative Protestants, for example, differ in many respects from their liberal counterparts. It is not unusual today to find conservative Protestants joining forces with conservative Catholics and Jews over moral or political issues, such as the pro-choice/right to life debate.

Of the U.S. population, 84 percent identify themselves as belonging to one of three major faiths—Protestant, Catholic, or Jewish (see Table 6-2). Until early in this century, however, Protestantism was by far the dominant religious force in the country, and most of our institutions continue to bear the mark of the white Protestants who established them. After the great immigrations from southern and eastern Europe, Catholic Ireland, and Asia, however, pluralism

Table 6–2. Religious Preference in 1986

	Major Faiths			
	Protestant	Catholic	Orthodox Catholic	Jewish
Nationally	56%	25%	1%	2%
Age				
Under 30	45	29	1	2
30-49 years	54	25	1	2
50 and older	64	23	1	2
Gender				
Men	52	25	1	2
Women	58	25	1	2
Region				
East	41	40	1	4
Midwest	57	27	1	1
South	71	13	1	1
West	49	22	1	2
Race				
Whites	55	26	1	2
Blacks	72	10	1	*
Non-Whites	59	20	1	*
Education				
College graduates	51	25	1	5
College incomplete	52	27	1	2
High school graduates	58	26	1	1
Non-high-school graduates	63	20	1	1
Household income:				
$50,000 and over	50	29	1	4
$49,999–$30,000	55	27	1	2
$29,999–$20,000	58	24	1	1
Under $20,000	60	22	1	1

*Less than one half of one percent.

From Bezilla (1993), *Religion in America, 37.*

described the religious diversity of the nation. Protestants as a group are still in the majority, with 56 percent of the population; 26 percent of the population identify themselves as Catholic, 2 percent as Jewish, 0.2 percent Muslim, 0.1 percent Hindu, and 11 percent as no preference (*Emerging Trends,* 1992).

The fact that Americans place themselves in one of these three major faiths is misleading in understanding the great diversity of religious beliefs in this country. These three categories describe three historical religious groups that share the same Old Testament heritage, but they do not attest to the diversity of beliefs and interpretations of the Bible. Wilson (1978) states that there are 280 different religious bodies in the United States. Catholics compose the largest single denomination. Protestants as a group are the largest in numbers, followed by Catholics and Jews (Jacquet, 1991). See Table 6–3.

A number of denominational differences have their origin in ethnic differences. The English established the Anglican (Episcopalian) and Puritan (later Congregational) churches here; the Germans established some of the Lutheran, Anabaptist, and Evangelical churches; the Dutch, the Reformed churches; the Spanish, French, Italians, Poles, and others, the Roman Catholic church; and the Ukrainians, Armenians, Greeks, and others, the Eastern Orthodox church. Over time, many of these separate ethnic denominations have united or expanded their membership to include other ethnic groups, although they may still be dominated by the original group. On the other hand, a different pattern has developed for black Americans because they often were not included in the expansion of membership. For example, 8 percent of all African Americans are Methodist, and 54 percent are Baptists (Gallup Report, 1987). Although many African Americans attend integrated churches, the majority attend racially segregated ones.

Most denominations have remained in their traditional regional strongholds, with Catholics in the Northeast, liberal and moderate Protestants in the Northeast and Midwest, and conservative Protestants in the South. Some groups, however, have expanded their base considerably. Episcopalians, Presbyterians, and members of the United Church of Christ are no longer as concentrated in the Northeast as they once were; some numerical base shifts have been made

Table 6–3. Number of U.S. Churches and Members, by Religious Groups

Religious Group	Number of Churches	Number of Members
Buddhist	67*	19,441*
Eastern Churches	1,705	4,057,339
Jews[a]	3,416	5,944,000
Old Catholic, Polish National Catholic, Armenian Churches	442	979,831
Protestants[b]	320,039	79,386,506
Roman Catholic	23,000	57,019,948
Miscellaneous[c]	1,168	200,329
Totals	350,337	147,607,394

[a]Including Orthodox, Conservative, and Reform branches

[b]Some bodies included here are, strictly speaking, not Protestant in the usual sense, including, for example, Latter-Day Saint groups and Jehovah's Witnesses.

[c]This is a grouping of bodies officially non-Christian, including those such as Spiritualists, Ethical Culture Movement, and Unitarian-Universalists.

*100,000 were reported in 1987 with 100 churches. The actual figure may be greater than that reported.

into the Sun Belt. Conservative Protestants, such as the Southern Baptists, are growing in all regions, including the Northeast and the West. Twenty-nine percent of Mormons are now in regions other than the West. Those without a religious preference are well represented in all regions, but continue to have the largest concentrations in the West (Roof & McKinney, 1985). The Jewish population tends to be located in metropolitan areas throughout the country, with the largest concentration in the mid-Atlantic region (Bezilla, 1993).

Although religious pluralism has fostered the rapid accommodation of many American religious movements toward a mainstream of acceptability and respectability by society, groups such as the Jehovah's Witnesses and Seventh-Day Adventists have maintained their independence. Those smaller groups that maintain their distinctiveness historically have been victims of harassment by members of mainstream religious groups. Christian Scientists, Jehovah's Witnesses, Children of God, and the Unification Church are minority groups that have been subjected to such treatment in the past (Appel, 1983). Conflict among the three major faiths has also been intense at different periods in our history. Anti-Semitic and anti-Catholic sentiments are still perpetuated in some households and institutions in this country. Although religious pluralism in our past has often led to conflict, the hope of the future is that it will lead to a better understanding and respect for religious differences. In this section, we will examine in greater detail the three major faiths and then briefly discuss others that the educator may find in various communities.

Protestantism

Traditionally, Protestantism has stressed individualism, activism, and pragmatism for its members (Wilson, 1978). Many sects that separated from the Catholic church after the Reformation are now recognized as established Protestant denominations. There is no one doctrine or one church that is representative of Protestantism.

The history of Protestantism in this country is integrally mixed with the development of capitalism and the expansion of the West. Most of the better-known Protestant groups began as transplants of nonconformist European groups, including the Pilgrims and Puritans, Baptists and Quakers, Presbyterians, Mennonites, Moravians, and many Lutherans (Moseley, 1981). Jews and Catholics from England and Ireland were also among the early settlers, but they were clearly outnumbered by the Protestant groups.

Throughout the nineteenth and early twentieth centuries, Protestant groups maintained separate social communities based on common tradition and identity. The church served as the chief locus of social life in small towns and rural communities, bound by a common religious belief and national origin (Moseley, 1981). As these separate groups accommodated to Americanization, English replaced the immigrant language, and ethnic differences blurred. As these distinctions among religions diminished, doctrinal and liturgical distinctions were often accentuated. Although Protestantism has become characteristically American, remnants of ethnic identity remain in many Lutheran churches and the German sects of Mennonites, Moravians, and Brethren. Segmentation remains with the Protestant denominations, but segregated from them, the black church has been the major institution over nearly two centuries that has allowed African Americans the opportunity for self-expression. Over two hundred different sects and denominations that currently flourish in this country grew from these various sectional divisions.

The Dominant Protestant Influence

The western Europeans who immigrated into this country in large numbers brought with them their various forms of Protestantism. Consequently, the political and social systems in the country still reflect the heavy influence of Protestantism. Although Protestants are no longer as dominant a force as they once were, they still claim 56 percent of the population *(Emerging Trends,* 1992c). Even that majority is divided along racial lines of black and white churches and denominations.

Has the political structure reflected the religious diversity that has developed over the past century? Table 6–4 shows the trends in the House of Representatives by denomination. In 1986, Protestants led the group with 64.2 percent, which is 6.2 percent higher than the 58 percent of the general population that indicated that they were Protestants that year (Gallup Report, 1987).

Table 6–4. Religious Affiliation of Members of the U.S. House of Representatives

Religious Group		Number	Percentage
Roman Catholic		141	(26.7%)
Jewish		37	(7.0%)
Eastern Orthodox		7	(1.3%)
Protestant (including Mormon and Unitarian)		339	(64.2%)
Methodist	74		
Episcopalian	60		
Presbyterian	57		
Baptist	54		
Lutheran	37		
Not Identified	23		
United Church of Christ	16		
Mormon	11		
Unitarian	10		
Church of Christ	5		
Disciples of Christ	3		
Bible Church	2		
Christian Science	2		
No Religious Affiliation		4	(0.8%)

Extracted from "Where Congress Goes to Church," *Christianity Today, 30*(44), December 12, 1986.

Roman Catholics followed with 26.7 percent, which is almost identical to the Gallup poll's findings of 27 percent of the general population. Jewish congressional members made up 7 percent of the congressional seats, which was 5 percent higher than that of the general population. Those with no affiliation held less than 1 percent, considerably less than the general population's 9 percent. Eastern Orthodox congressional members held 1.3 percent of the House seats.

It is interesting to note, however, that the Protestant breakdown differs considerably from that revealed in the Gallup poll that year. Episcopalians, who made up only 2 percent of the general population in 1986, made up 11.4 percent of Congress. Presbyterians also made up 2 percent of the general population, but 10.8 percent of Congress; Methodists, 9 percent of the general population, but 14 percent of Congress; and Baptists, 20 percent of the general population, but only 10.2 percent of Congress. The two groups with the highest disproportionate representation are considered among the more politically liberal to moderate and from higher socioeconomic groups. The Methodists, who are also overrepresented, are generally considered moderates and in the middle socioeconomic group. The Baptists (particularly Southern Baptists), who are significantly underrepresented, are usually more conservative and likely to be in the lowest socioeconomic group of the four denominations mentioned here.

Members of liberal churches and Jews may be disproportionately overrepresented because historically, they have felt a responsibility for public issues. Another factor is probably related to the social class of members of these various denominations. Because holding political office can be quite costly, religious groups whose members are typically upper middle class are overrepresented in political offices (Carroll, 1979). In the past decade, evangelical churches also have actively entered the political arena, taking advantage of the fact that they are large, identifiable forces in society. In elections—from local school boards to national offices—since 1975, coalitions of these evangelical groups have pursued campaigns to elect persons with ultraconservative political views and free-enterprise economic principles.

Protestantism maintains not only the major religious influence on society, but also the dominant control of political leadership. Because Protestants continue to represent the majority of the population, such influence is to be expected. However, pluralism increasingly forces the sharing of power and resources among diverse groups of people in society.

Similarities Amidst Diversity

As one visits various Protestant services and listens to the different doctrines espoused by members, one often wonders how such a diverse conglomeration can be classified into one faith. This great diversity is reflected in the following examples:

> In one church, the priest, resplendent in his embroidered robes, raises a golden chalice and consecrates the wine within it. This is an Episcopal service in which

the priest, who is a Protestant, begins the communion portion of the service. Across town the pastor leads her congregation in healing those with afflictions through the "slaying of the spirit." Toward the end of the service, she will lead them in the "speaking of tongues." This too is a Protestant church, a charismatic Pentecostal church. In a Pennsylvania community the men are dressed in black suits and broad-brimmed hats. Most have beards. The women are dressed in old-fashioned bonnets and long black dresses. They enter their horse-drawn buggies to attend an all-day worship service. They use no electricity, no tractors for their farms, nor do they use automobiles. They are Amish and are also Protestants.

Let us look first at some commonalities among what appear to be very different beliefs and practices. Probably the most binding factor is that Protestants share a common faith that emanates from the Reformation, when there was a separation from the Catholic tradition. They reject the authority of the Pope and believe that they individually communicate with God. Other similarities have little to do with religious doctrine, but are based instead on a shared American experience and its accompanying values.

To understand the differences that exist in Protestantism and that are often reflected in the classroom, the faith can be divided into two broad categories—liberal and conservative. Liberal Protestants make up approximately 9 percent of the population (Roof & McKinney, 1985). They attempt to rethink Christianity in forms that are meaningful for a world dominated by science and rapid change. They stress the right of individuals to determine for themselves what is true in religion. They believe in the authority of Christian experience and religious life rather than dogmatic church pronouncements of the Bible. Many liberal Protestants reject the traditional emphasis on the supernatural events of Jesus' recorded life, and they stress human dignity. They are most likely to support and participate in social action programs because of their belief that what individuals become depends greatly on an environment over which they have little control. The mainline, traditional denominations are included in this group. The United Church of Christ and Episcopalian churches are examples, although the degree of liberalism depends on the individual congregation. Methodists and Disciples of Christ represent more moderate denominations within this category. They make up approximately 24 percent of the population (Roof & McKinney, 1985).

In the 1970s and 1980s several Protestant churches identified as liberal or moderate experienced staggering membership losses. In the 1970–1980 period, the United Presbyterian church lost 19 percent of its members; Disciples, 17 percent; Episcopalians, 15 percent; United Church of Christ, 11 percent; and United Methodists, 9 percent. The declines were rather abrupt, affecting all groups at about the same time. The losses were more the result of decreasing numbers of new members rather than increasing dropout rates. Younger adults were conspicuously absent among new members, raising speculation about a lost generation in these churches. In the liberal churches, the average age is noticeably high. Forty-two percent of the Disciples of Christ, 41 percent of the United Methodists, and 43 percent of the United Church of

Christ are fifty-five years of age or older. By comparison, none of the conservative Protestant groups has more than 40 percent of its membership over fifty-five years of age. Some (e.g., Assemblies of God) have less than a third over that age. It is apparent that in comparison to their conservative counterparts, liberal Protestant groups are less successful in attracting and holding onto young members (Roof & McKinney, 1985).

Conservative religious groups generally believe that the Bible is inerrant, that the supernatural is distinct from the natural, that salvation is essential, and that Jesus will return in bodily form during the Second Coming. They emphasize personal morality rather than social ethics (Woodward, Barnes, & Lisle, 1977). The conservative branch can be divided further into the fundamentalists, who are literalistic and inflexible, and the evangelicals, who are somewhat less literalistic and not so inflexible. Billy Graham's ministry would fit more appropriately into the second category.

Conservative churches include the Churches of Christ and Southern Baptists. Assembly of God, other Pentecostal groups, and Church of the Nazarene also represent fundamentalist denominations. Some sects of the more liberal denominations have reacted to liberalism and established themselves as conservative groups, such as Wesleyan Methodist and Orthodox Presbyterian. Conservative Protestants make up approximately 15 percent of the population (Roof & McKinney, 1985).

Although the fundamentalist groups strictly and literally interpret the Bible, the different groups do not necessarily interpret it or practice their faith in the same way. The various sects and denominations are unrelenting in their belief that they are the one true church. Some groups, such as the Pentecostals, believe that their lives have been dramatically changed by infusion of the Holy Spirit—a spiritual baptism that results in the individual's being able to speak in other tongues (Marty, 1975). Although the Pentecostals historically have come and gone in storefront ghetto churches and rural areas across the country, the Pentecostal church has been adopted as a charismatic sect by branches of many mainstream churches during the last decade (Briggs, 1977).

Some fundamentalist groups, such as the Mormons and Jehovah's Witnesses, do not classify themselves as Protestants. These two groups and the Seventh-Day Adventists stand out from many other groups because the practice of their religion thoroughly pervades their way of life. Members of these groups proselytize as a part of their commitment to their beliefs. *The Watchtower,* a publication, is distributed door-to-door by Jehovah's Witnesses, and Mormon missionaries often work door-to-door. Members are unrelenting in their beliefs and in their commitment to prepare themselves for future fulfillment in the establishment of a latter-day sainthood and a life in heaven (Mormons), or in life after the Armageddon (Jehovah's Witnesses), or in the millennium after Christ's Second Coming (Adventists).

The conservative groups have in recent years experienced rapid growth, often exceeding population growth rates. By 1967, Southern Baptists were the largest Protestant denomination. By 1990, they had nearly 38,000 churches and a membership well in excess of fifteen million (Jacquet, 1991). In addition to increased church membership, church school enrollments, missionary support, book publications, and the establishment of private Christian schools attested to the movement toward and growth of conservatism (Roof & McKinney, 1985).

An examination of the responses of various Protestants to some basic doctrinal questions from a University of California survey conducted in the 1970s shows how great church differences are. In response to a question that asked if it is "absolutely necessary to believe in Jesus to be saved," 97 percent of the Southern Baptists and 38 percent of the Congregationalists responded affirmatively. Thirty-two percent of the Episcopalians and 80 percent of the Missouri Synod Lutherans "believe every word of the Bible is literally true." Finally, 99 percent of the Southern Baptists said they "believe in a real live devil" compared to 22 percent of the Congregationalists ("Protestantism—World Religions," 1977).

These differences in beliefs among Protestants themselves have resulted in many court cases to determine what can or cannot be taught to or asked of students in public schools. Fundamentalism versus liberalism came to the forefront in the 1925 Scopes Trial, in which a biology teacher was convicted for teaching Darwin's theory of evolution. Although the teacher's conviction was later reversed, the argument continues today as fundamentalists push for state legislation preventing the teaching of evolution or instituting the teaching of creationism. Jehovah's Witnesses have been taken to court because their children have refused to salute the flag. The Amish have fought in courts to remove their children from public schools after they have completed the eighth grade. Finally, some of these religious groups continue to fight against the 1963 Supreme Court decision that disallowed prayer in public schools.

Thus, Protestants represent a pluralistic group that includes over two hundred different sects and denominations. Their beliefs range from very liberal to very fundamentalist. Members of the traditional churches can be located along the continuum from very fundamentalist to very liberal, with many of the liberal churches having sects that are fundamentalist and sometimes charismatic. The educator is expected to respect students and their beliefs no matter where they fall along this continuum or how they differ from the educator's own beliefs.

Catholicism

In 1992, the Roman Catholic Church was the largest U.S. denomination, with over fifty-eight million members (Bezilla & Jones, 1992). Approximately 25 percent of the U.S. population identified themselves as Roman Catholic (Bezilla, 1993). Unlike the Protestant faith, which includes denominational pluralism, the Catholic faith is one denomination under papal authority. In this country, the Catholic faith has developed from Catholicism practiced by many different ethnic groups in the "old" countries. Although the doctrine and pattern of worship are somewhat uniform among churches, the individual parishes differ according to the race, ethnic background, and social class of their members.

Generally, a larger percentage of Catholics than non-Catholics have always attended church. In 1988, for example, the attendance figure for Catholics was 48 percent, compared to 45 percent for Protestants and 20 percent for Jews (Gallup Report, 1989). The religion has not spread significantly beyond the ethnic boundaries of the Catholic immigrations during the past two centuries. Over the past three decades, Catholics have increased in numbers from 22 percent of the population to 27 percent. This has been accomplished primarily through high birthrates and through immigration. In recent years, Catholics have made spectacular gains in education, occupational status, and income. In 1986, Catholics (16 percent) compared favorably to Protestants (17 percent) with respect to college graduates and exceeded Protestants in household income (Gallup Report, 1987).

The movement toward conservatism has not been limited to Protestants. Some Catholics have objected to changes in liturgy and other areas of modernization instituted by Vatican II.

By becoming a uniquely American church, members of the Catholic church have not rejected the belief that they belong to the one universal church. Instead, they have accepted the facts that American society is intrinsically pluralistic and that their religion is one of the three major faiths in this country.

Judaism

Herberg (1960), in his now classic text, indicates that Judaism is one of the oldest religions known to humanity and that it provides the historical roots of both Catholicism and Protestantism. Among the three major faiths in this country, Judaism represents only about 2 percent of the population. It has become one of the three major faiths primarily as a result of Jews from many different countries amalgamating under the identification of Jewish American.

Jewish immigrants were among the early settlers in this country, arriving here in small numbers with the 1654 New Amsterdam settlers. Those first American Jews were largely Sephardic Jews (i.e., Spanish and Portuguese Jews), who were gradually joined by other Jews from central Europe and Poland. Their numbers were small. By 1825, there were only about five thousand American Jews living along the East Coast. They established synagogues and auxiliary institutions to maintain their religion. In other areas of American life, they were rapidly acculturated and soon found that they also had to adapt their religious institutions and patterns in a way that was uniquely American (Herberg, 1960).

The remainder of the nineteenth century, however, changed the ethnic composition of the American Jewish population. Between 1820 and 1870, their ranks increased from five thousand to over two hundred thousand as a result of the many Germans immigrating to the United States. In a pattern similar to Catholic immigrations, the German immigrants did not immediately fuse with the native Jews. In fact, they initially identified themselves primarily as Germans rather than as Jews. With their Protestant counterparts, these German immigrants moved with the advancing frontier rather than remaining in the cities along the coast. When there were enough German Jews settled together, they established Jewish institutions and movements that coexisted with those of their German neighbors. By the last quarter of the century, the roots of Reform and Conservative Judaism had emerged from the adaptation of the religion to American ways. They followed closely the Protestant-American pattern of decentralization and volunteerism (Herberg, 1960).

The final major change in the composition of the Jewish population in this country occurred between 1870 and 1924. By 1920, 80 percent or more of the Jewish population in the United States was eastern European in origin. The majority belonged to Orthodox synagogues as compared to those who adhered to reformed Judaism (Hudson & Corrigan, 1992). Those five and a half decades brought nearly 2.5 million eastern European Jews, who settled in a few large cities. In addition to representing many nationalities with different languages, these Yiddish-speaking immigrants were strangers to the native Jews as well as to other Americans. World events, especially the increased persecution of Jews abroad, soon helped to unite the ethnically separate Jews in this country. Ethnic differences subsided as religion became the most salient feature of their self-identification (Herberg, 1960).

"The emergence of the third generation changed the entire picture of American Jewry and Judaism in America" (Herberg, 1960, p. 186). Ethnic and religious identity merged. The lifestyle evolved into the microculture of the American middle class. Education, including higher education, played an important role in the Jewish community by advancing young people from the working class into white-collar and professional positions. Religious practices and patterns were modified in ways that made them characteristically American. "The central place of the sermon, congregational singing, mixed choirs, organs, responsive readings, abbreviated services, the concluding benediction, and many other commonly accepted features obviously reflected the influence of familiar Protestant practice" (Herberg, 1960, p. 191). The three denominations, or divisions, of Jewish thought and practice—Orthodox, Conservative, and Reform—continued to meet the needs of the Jewish population.

Compared to Protestants and Catholics, the Jewish population has declined, partly a result of intermarriage and low birthrates. Yet, as a group, they remain a distinctive, identifiable religious minority whose social standing and influence are disproportionate to their numbers.

Jews in this country and throughout the world have been the target of prejudice and discrimination, sometimes leading to attempted annihilation of the population. The Jewish Holocaust, which resulted in the brutal deaths of millions of European Jews, was systematically conducted by one of the most economically and technically advanced nations. The civilized world cannot complacently sit back and ignore the fact that in spite of overwhelming evidence of what was being done by the Nazis, nothing was done to stop one of the greatest atrocities ever committed against humankind. As we approach the twenty-first century, other attempts at genocide persist. It is the responsibility of educators to help their students understand that even today, other holocausts are taking place in countries such as Bosnia.

Anti-Semitism is rooted in Jewish-Gentile conflicts that have existed for centuries. In this country Jews and Catholics were also targets of the Ku Klux Klan in the 1920s (Williams, 1990). Discrimination has occurred in both occupational and social life. Jews have often been denied high-level corporate management positions and have been barred from membership in social clubs. There is evidence "that overall, religious people tend to be more anti-Semitic than non-religious people" (Wilson, 1978, p. 316). The form and degree of anti-Semitism vary with world and national events; when non-Jews believe that events are the result of Jewish action, prejudices resurface in word and deed. Current events in the Middle East that involve Israel often initiate these reactions.

The conservative movement has involved American Judaism as well. Orthodox Judaism has seen a resurgence, growing more rapidly than either Reformed or Conservative groups in the 1970s. Growing numbers of Jews have turned to the more traditional faith, rejecting what some consider lax

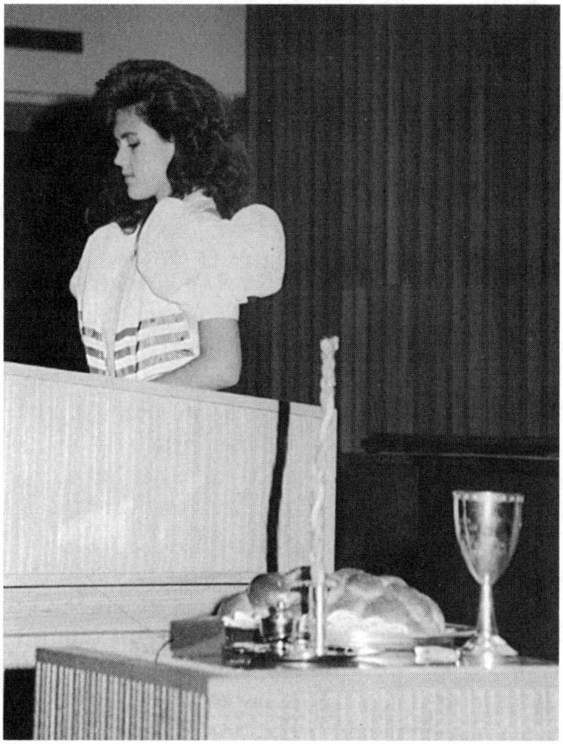

A thirteen-year-old Jewish female observes her Bat Mitzvah by reading from the Torah in Hebrew. The event marks her entry into religious adulthood.

observance and permissiveness among the non-Orthodox groups. This is an apparent reversal from the earlier movement away from Orthodoxy toward the more liberal groups (Roof & McKinney, 1985).

About 75 percent of the nation's Jews live in five metropolitan communities (Herberg, 1960); one-third live in New York City (Marty, 1979). Although Jews strongly identify with their religion, their practice of religion is relatively low regarding synagogue attendance and home religious observance (Carroll, 1979). Nevertheless, the American synagogue is the strongest agency in the Jewish community. Although they may not attend services as regularly (20 percent) as their Catholic and Protestant counterparts, a large percentage (44 percent) of Jews retain affiliation with the synagogue (Gallup Report, 1987). Many feel that Jewish identity does not require attendance at the synagogue; attending religious services and studying Jewish texts hold little interest for much of the Jewish population (Sklare, 1974). Attendance on High Holidays, however, is always at a maximum. The synagogue in America serves not only as a place of religious worship, but also as a primary base for Jewish identity and survival (Carroll, 1979).

Judaism, like the other two major faiths, has become an integral part of American society. "The American Jew . . . establishes his Jewishness not apart from, not in spite of, his Americanness, but precisely through and by virtue of it" (Herberg, 1960, p. 198). American Judaism emphasizes Jewishness as peoplehood and nationality more than as religion.

Other Religions

In addition to the three major faiths in this country, 4 percent of the population in 1986 indicated that they preferred another religion, and 8 percent responded "none" when asked about a religious preference (Gallup Report, 1987). What are the other religions that an educator might encounter in a community? They range from Christian religions that do not fall into the discrete categories of Protestantism or Catholicism to Islam, Eastern religions, and religions based on current psychological thinking.

One of the Christian religions that does not fall into the two major groupings is the Eastern Orthodox church. With four million members in the United States, Eastern Orthodoxy probably claims about one-fourth of all Christians worldwide. One of the reasons that the Eastern Orthodox church is less known in this country may be that its members, from Syria, Greece, Armenia, Russia, and the Ukraine, only immigrated during the last century. Although they split with the Roman Catholic church in 1054 over theological, practical, jurisdictional, cultural, and political differences, to many outsiders they appear very similar to the pre-Vatican II Catholic church. As the name suggests, Eastern Orthodoxy is steeped in tradition, as is apparent in its Divine Liturgy—a highly formal service of worship (Marty, 1975).

At least two other religions have a Christian heritage but seem to fall through the cracks of discrete categorization because of their beliefs. The

Christian Scientists are one of these groups, with probably less than half a million members. Like some of the fundamentalist Protestant groups and others described in this section, their beliefs are so different from conventional religious beliefs that they attract public attention. They exist "to dispel illusion and bring people into harmony with mind, with God as All—away from what others call disease, sin, evil, matter, and death" (Marty, 1975, p. 205). Although they do not proselytize, they maintain reading rooms in business and shopping centers of many communities. *The Christian Science Monitor* is a highly respected general newspaper.

Another group that defies categorization is the Unitarian Universalists—a church that connotes liberalism to most people. Their membership has included several U.S. presidents (William Howard Taft, Thomas Jefferson, John Adams, and John Quincy Adams) and several New England writers (Henry Wadsworth Longfellow, James Russell Lowell, and William Cullen Bryant), helping to make the church an influence beyond that expected of a relatively small group. Unitarians are often found in suburbs, small towns, and college communities; many of the members could be described as political liberals. While many members have the highest respect for Jesus Christ, the church is "most open to the wisdom of non-Christian religions and may draw many of its readings from scriptures of Buddhism, Hinduism and religious philosophies" (Marty, 1975, p. 217). As an expression of this openness, Unitarianism houses both Christian and non-Christian wings. The denomination follows no imposing standards of dogma or membership. Thus, their worship services appear extremely simple and are often experimental (Marty, 1975).

Islam now has more than two million followers in the United States. Some are immigrants from every area of the world, including the Mideast and Africa, or the children of these immigrants (Jacquet, 1991). However, this is not solely an immigrant religion. As early as the 1930s, black Americans in Detroit were establishing the Nation of Islam (better known as the Black Muslims) as an alternative expression of black religion for African Americans who populated the city's ghettos. Mosques now exist in cities across the country, and members are drawn from various religious and class lines. The religion addresses cultural identity, the acceptability and respectability of blackness, and economic self-help (Haddad, Haines, & Findley, 1984). The past emphasis on racial awareness, the fight against white oppression, and hostility toward whites placed the church in a leadership role of the black power movement during the 1960s. Many have been drawn by the simple egalitarian teachings of Islam, which provide for self-identity and a clear purpose in life (Jacquet, 1991). The religion stresses self-determination for African Americans, and members have been able to develop a successful economic program in the tradition of American capitalism. Until recently, membership had been limited to nonwhites.

Conversion to Islam usually requires a change in one's self-identity, and membership demands a high level of commitment (Haddad et al., 1984). "The individual Muslims themselves are their own best currency of proselytism;

they are clean, confident, prosperous, and respected" (Lincoln, 1974, p. 168). The strict dietary habits and other rules of living sometimes come into conflict with the public schools. Educators should be aware of the importance of such rules to believers in the Islamic religion.

The recent influx of Indochinese, Chinese, Koreans, and other groups has increased the religious pluralism in this country. These groups have brought their religions with them, in addition to other aspects of their culture. The Laotians and Cambodians are primarily Buddhists, as are the Vietnamese. Some of the Vietnamese, however, are Taoists and Roman Catholics, and many, like the majority of the Chinese, Japanese, and Korean immigrants, adhere to the teachings of Confucianism, which is more a philosophy than a religion. Most Koreans are likely to be Buddhists. However, a large minority are Protestants, and a smaller but still significant group are Roman Catholics. The majority of Hong Kong immigrants are Buddhists, with some Taoists. Many of the recent immigrants from India and Pakistan have brought their Hindu and Moslem beliefs with them. The increasing religious diversity in this country is evident in the 1988 completion of the largest Buddhist temple/monastery in the Western Hemisphere, located in Hacienda Heights, a Los Angeles suburb.

The Fo Kuang Shan Hsi Lai Temple opened in Hacienda Heights, California, in 1988. This Los Angeles County temple is the largest Buddhist temple in the Western Hemisphere.

Young people in many communities practice religions based on an Eastern religious tradition. This grouping includes the Hare Krishna, the Divine Light Mission, and the Unification Church. Members of some of these groups are very visible to the public. The Hare Krishna can be seen dancing with tambourines on sidewalks in larger cities, and members of the Unification Church may approach travelers in airports for donations. "The basic intent of each group is to help the individual become a part of a group seeking meaning and purpose for life" (Johnson, 1979, p. 99). Members of these religious movements are often well educated, young, and from different backgrounds. Many were involved with protest movements in the 1960s and sought a new religious consciousness. "In nearly all cases the life being shaped is disciplined, committed to the group, and devoted to discovering a dynamic inner self. The groups also demand that some expression of the religious feelings be demonstrated or shared with society at large" (Johnson, 1979, p. 99).

These various religions are practiced by a small minority of the population, but their presence in a community is often exaggerated beyond that warranted by their numbers. This notoriety often stems from the fact that their doctrine and practices are viewed as heretical by members of the major faiths, yet orthodox by the believers. In addition, members of the majority faiths, especially parents, fear the attraction of some of these groups because young people may desert the majority ranks.

Religion and Gender

There can be little doubt that religion can and does often profoundly influence gender issues. It has already been established that in the United States (and in many other countries and regions in the world) religion is viewed as very important to its citizenry. Religion often has an impact on a person's daily activities, decision making, and the way an individual interacts with others. Many religious bodies have clearly defined roles for males and females. In the Roman Catholic church and in the Church of Jesus Christ of Latter-Day Saints (Mormons), for example, women cannot attain the priesthood and, therefore, cannot assume the highest positions in those religious bodies. Such limitations are by no means confined to these two religious groups; many other groups either prohibit or limit participation of women in certain activities.

Religion may be used to define the parameters of male and female participation; it may also be used to prescribe male and female roles outside of the religious context. Such prescriptions may be done either directly or indirectly. In religious groups where women are given a less prominent status, this may carry over into general family life and other aspects of society as a natural course. In other instances the pronouncements may be more direct. Religious writings with great importance such as the Bible are continuously interpreted, studied, and analyzed. In the United States, the Bible (or at least the Old Testament) is viewed as very sacred by most of its citizens who claim church membership, and, consequently, it has a profound influence on many Americans. Biblical scholars and interpreters have been debating the meaning of the writings for centuries. Van Leeuwen (1990) suggests that some biblical interpreters believe that God gave man, through Adam (Genesis 1:26–27), dominion over Eve and, therefore, over women. At the same time, there are biblical scholars who argue that such an interpretation is incorrect and that both Adam and Eve (Man and Woman) were given dominion over every other living thing.

Many churches play a significant role in shaping attitudes toward homosexuality. While some religious groups openly condemn homosexuality, other churches welcome gay and lesbian members and some have ordained homosexual priests or ministers. What is important to understand is that ministers, priests, and other church and religious authorities have considerable influence on the people they lead. They—and the writers and theologians who influence them—often get their inspiration, or their justification, for their positions through religious writings. These writings are then interpreted for lay persons and may be used to shape their perceptions of themselves and of others. Children growing up in a religious environment may learn that in religious settings and in some lay settings there are limitations imposed on them because of their gender. They may learn that homosexuality is an abomination, or they may learn that homosexuality is an alternative lifestyle of choice.

While some religions or segments within a religious body may assume more liberal or conservative sex equity positions, there is no correct or incorrect position. Religion is a matter of choice and religious diversity is a valued entity in this country.

Religion and Race

As with gender issues, religion has had a profound impact on race and ethnic diversity issues. The modern day civil rights movement was centered in southern African American churches. Many of the civil rights leaders were or are ministers or church leaders—Martin Luther King, Jr., Ralph Abernathy, Andrew Young, Jesse Jackson, and Malcolm X, to name but a few. From their pulpits, these religious leaders have been able to direct boycotts and organize civil disobedience and nonviolent confrontations.

In earlier times, spirituals provided comfort, hope, or a promise of a better life after death. Today many of these spirituals are still sung in the churches, but those who sing and those who listen to them seek more immediate response to the demands for equity. Clearly, African American churches deserve much credit for bringing about many of the civil rights gained in the last three decades. Alienated and disillusioned by mainstream politics, few African Americans have in the past registered to vote. Recent data suggest that well over 90 percent of the African American clergy nationwide advocate church involvement in social and political issues. In recent years the black church has been extremely successful in registering well over a million voters and becoming an important voice in the electoral process (Lincoln & Mamiya, 1990).

While African American churches did much to achieve civil rights for many Americans, other religious bodies have helped mold attitudes toward African Americans. As with gender equity issues, the Bible is interpreted and used to teach and shape positive attitudes and justify equity for all ethnic racial groups. At the same time, others use the same religious writings, particularly the Bible, in interpreting and justifying differential treatment based on race. Consequently many churches, particularly in the South, have a history of segregation in membership or in seating.

In some religions African Americans were permitted membership but prohibited from attaining high positions of church leadership. These prohibitions were justified through biblical interpretations or through divine revelations received by church leaders. While nearly all such racial limitations on membership and church leadership have been removed in recent years, the effects of these religious prohibitions remains to be seen. Many individuals who read or listened to leaders justifying segregation or bans against leadership positions, cannot readily dismiss some of the attitudes developed through years of prolonged exposure to negative points of view.

Like the gender issues that have become a center of religious debate, race issues have been debated for decades. As the courts and society as a whole have turned their back on segregation and racially limiting practices, so too have most religious bodies taken an official position of openness. While the official position and the actual position may differ somewhat, hopefully—at least in churches that advocate brotherly love—the two may be moving to a higher level of congruence.

Beliefs—A Function of Class and Education

Surveys conducted by the Princeton Religion Research Center (Bezilla, 1993) strongly suggest that religious beliefs are related to one's education and socioeconomic class. For example, the higher an individual's educational level, the less likely he or she is to accept the Bible literally. While 58 percent of those who had not graduated from high school accepted the Bible literally, only 14 percent of college graduates did. Likewise, 49 percent of those with household incomes below $20,000 accepted the Bible literally, while only 14 percent of those with household incomes above $50,000 did. College graduates relied more on self and on science and less on their clergy as believable authorities in matters of truth. However, for those with less education, greater authority was placed in the scriptures and religious leaders and considerably less on self and science. It appears that the more education one receives, the greater the self-dependence and reliance on scientific data for determining one's belief structures.

Individual Religious Identity

Most Americans are born into their religion, baptized in the church of their parents, and later join that same church. Within the context of the religious freedom espoused in this country, however, individuals are always free to change their religion or to choose no religion. The greatest pressure to retain membership in the religious group in which one was born usually comes from the family and other members of that same religious group. Often it is more difficult for individuals to break away from their religious origins than to make breaks from any of the other microcultures of which they are members. Parents whose children have joined groups such as Hare Krishna or the Unification Church sometimes feel that their children (usually young adults) have been brainwashed by members of these religious cults, and some of these parents pay experts to remove their children from these religious groups by *deprogramming* them. Families have been known to disown their children who marry outside of the faith. Thus, individual freedom of choice may be extremely limited by religious group membership.

Herberg's (1960) study of the three major faiths suggests that Americans are more likely to identify themselves by their membership in a religious microculture than by membership in any other subculture.

> To find a place in American society increasingly means to place oneself in one or another of these religious communities. And although this process of self-identification and social location is not in itself intrinsically religious, the mere fact that in order to be "something" one must be a Protestant, a Catholic, or a Jew means that one begins to think of oneself as religiously identified and affiliated. (p. 56)

While it has been over three decades since Herberg's study, it is likely that one's religious microculture is still one of the most important. While a person's ethnicity, class, or gender may have considerable influence on behavior, religion may well be the primary microculture with which many individuals identify themselves. When one's ethnic identity is very important to an individual, it is often combined with a religious identification. Irish Catholic, Russian Jew, and Norwegian Lutheran are examples of dual identification, and understanding the individual's relationship to both microcultures is important in understanding who the individual is.

The region of the United States in which one lives also affects the strength of identification with a specific religious group. In much of Georgia, many people will have the same or similar views; religious diversity is limited. On the other hand, religious diversity in New York is common. "At a party one is careful not to be critical of other religious groups, because the other partner to a conversation may be a member of one, an alumnus of another, and married to a member of a third" (Marty, 1979, p. 88). In many areas of the country, any deviation from the common religious beliefs and practices is considered heretical, making it very difficult for the nonadherent to be accepted by most members of the community. In other areas, the traditionally religious individual may not be accepted as a part of a community that is religiously liberal. Educators, as well as students, are usually expected to believe and behave according to the mores of the community—mores that are often determined by the prevailing religious doctrine and the degree of religious diversity.

Most communities have some degree of religious diversity, although the degree of difference may vary greatly. Often, students whose beliefs are different from those of the dominant group are ostracized in school and in social settings. Jews, atheists, Jehovah's Witnesses, and Pentecostals are among those groups whose members are sometimes shunned and discriminated against for their beliefs. Educators must be careful that their own religious beliefs and memberships do not interfere with their ability to provide equal educational opportunity to all students, regardless of their religious identification.

Religion Switching

Changing from one religious faith to another has been a common practice in this country. One-fourth of all Americans do not belong to the religious group to which they were born. As a group, Protestants have gained members through religious switching often at the expense of the Catholics. There are nine times as many Protestants who were formerly Catholics, than Catholics who were previously Protestants (Bezilla, 1993). Forty percent of Protestants today have changed religious affiliation at some time in their life (Roof & McKinney, 1985).

Switching from conservative to liberal Protestant churches has often accompanied upward mobility. Theologically liberal and higher-status churches have been in keeping with advances in education and occupation. Thus, the liberal churches have typically benefited from upward mobility; Episcopalian and Congregationalist churches have gained memberships at the expense of the moderate and conservative denominations. Baptists and Methodists have suffered the greatest losses to religious switching; they account for 19 and 11 percent respectively of those who have changed religions. The Roman Catholics have also shown heavy losses, with religious switching accounting for 18 percent of those who have left the church. In recent years, the proselytizing of Hispanics by Pentecostal churches has accounted for many of the Catholic church's losses (Bezilla, 1993).

Those shifting to the liberal churches have tended to be older, more educated, in higher-status occupations, and, as might be expected, with more liberal views on moral issues. As a group, they tend to be less active in their new churches than the members of the conservative churches they have left (Roof & McKinney, 1985).

A second group of individuals involved in changing churches includes those who have switched to more conservative churches. As a group, they tend to be young and of lower socioeconomic status. While liberal churches have tended to have larger net gains, the conservatives have been able to attract and maintain members who are generally more loyal and active.

A third group is switching to nonaffiliation. For every person who is raised with no religious affiliation and who later becomes involved in organized religion, more than three people leave churches and become nonaffiliated with religious bodies. While all religious groups lose to nonaffiliation, moderate groups within the three major religious bodies are the major losers. The individuals involved in switching to nonaffiliation are predominantly males who are well educated (Roof & McKinney, 1985). The movement to nonaffiliation or unchurched, as it is sometimes designated, may be due in part to increasing social acceptance of nonparticipation in organized religion. Whereas those who did not belong to or did not attend a church may have at one time been considered immoral or amoral, society appears to be increasingly more accepting, or at least tolerant, of the individual's right to determine the degree, if any, of religious participation. (It might be noted here that there was a time when some school districts required church attendance of their teachers.)

In some respects, the religious institutions (even those with a net loss) may gain from this switching behavior. Choices relating to churches or religious bodies have become based more on genuine preference. Consequently, religious groups may tend to become more homogeneous, with clearer social and religious identities.

Declining Memberships

While church attendance has remained fairly constant, all three of the major religious communities have experienced membership declines in recent years. In 1974, 76 percent of adults in the United States identified themselves as church or synagogue members. By 1978, the figure had dropped to 68 percent, and remains there in 1993 (Bezilla, 1993; Roof & McKinney, 1985). Approximately 80 percent of Catholics and 73 percent of Protestants are church members, and 45 percent of Jews are members of a synagogue. In reality, many who say they are church members are effectively unchurched because of their lack of attendance or involvement. Using a more rigorous criteria, a major study in 1978 identified 41 percent of the adult population as unchurched because of lack of involvement in religious institutions. That same year, the Gallup poll found that 68 percent claimed church membership, a 9 percent discrepancy with the previously cited study (Gallup Report, 1989; Roof & McKinney, 1985). It is likely that if the more stringent criteria were applied today, a little over half of the adult population would qualify as active church members.

Roof and McKinney (1985) suggest that many of the unchurched are believers and are quite religious in many respects, but choose to express their beliefs apart from organized institutions. As a group, they tend to welcome social change, hold less to conservative values, and are less rooted in stable social networks in their communities (Roof & McKinney, 1985). About 32 percent of the population does not belong to a church or synagogue (Bezilla, 1993). The decline of religious membership in recent years about equals the increase of those indicating no religious affiliation. This decrease in members may suggest a growing secular constituency that may be more irreligious than antireligious and which Roof and McKinney (1985) suggest is a force of growing cultural importance in a pluralistic society.

Influence of the Religious Right

Court cases involving religion became very significant in the 1970s and 1980s. The numerous laws that reinforced Protestant morality were challenged and some were repealed. However, the attempts to legislate the public's morality dates back several decades. In 1919 the Eighteenth Amendment was ratified, bringing prohibition to the United States in an attempt to address the welfare of the American people. However, after thirteen years this law was repealed and the courts began to protest the freedoms of those outside of the Protestant mainstream. Laws restricting behavior (such as divorce and "deviant" sexual practices) on moral grounds were repealed and the courts began to reinforce the principle of separation of church and state. One of the most dramatic examples of the Supreme Court's new attitude was the decision rendered in 1973 in *Roe v. Wade,* which protected a woman's right to seek abortion in the early stages of pregnancy. This and other decisions, which protected the rights of the Amish and the Unification Church, were not welcomed by the religious conservatives. The battle lines were drawn (Hudson & Corrigan, 1992).

By the late 1970s, the ideologies of a conservative and increasingly influential group referred to as the Religious Right were clashing head-on with the ideologies of secular humanism. The battle was waged on two fronts: the family and the school. Controversies centered on the family and gender roles and on issues such as abortion, the Equal Rights Amendment, and gay rights. The conservatives supported a return to traditional roles for men and women and opposed equal protection for women and homosexuals, such as the hiring of homosexuals as public school educators (Roof & McKinney, 1985).

The New Christian Right, referred to at times as evangelicals, became a potent force in the 1970s and 1980s partly because of the effective television ministries (dubbed the electronic church) of individuals such as Jerry Falwell, Pat Robertson, Robert Schuller, Jim Bakker, and Jimmy Swaggert. With their ability to reach millions in their own homes, these religious leaders have encouraged political involvement and have mounted efforts on issues such as school prayer, abortion, pornography, and national defense. The Religious Right has provided strong support or opposition for political candidates based on their voting records or position on issues (Roof & McKinney, 1985). In 1980 and 1984, they were a strong factor in the election of Ronald Reagan. It is interesting to note that in 1960 John Kennedy assured the American electorate that he would not allow American politics to be influenced by his faith. In 1980 and again in 1984 Ronald Reagan experienced the exact opposite, assuring fundamentalist groups that he was a creationist and that he would seek to bring prayer back to the public schools (Colombo, 1984).

In 1982 an Arkansas law specifying that creation science be taught in the schools—as well as evolution—was struck down in a U.S. District Court. By the end of the 1980s Ronald Reagan and George Bush had been successful in placing conservative judges on the federal benches and on the Supreme Court, and groups outside the mainstream began losing cases in which they sought support for exercising their religious beliefs (Hudson & Corrigan, 1992).

By 1987, the electronic church had suffered staggering setbacks. Robertson had resigned from his ministry to pursue an unsuccessful presidential bid; Bakker was forced to resign as head of his PTL (Praise the Lord) Club in the wake of sexual and financial improprieties and subsequently served a prison term. Swaggert was suspended from the Assemblies of God after revelations of his sexual improprieties (William, 1990). However, televangelism remains a significant part of the religious life of many Americans and continues to be an influence politically and otherwise. In the 1992 elections the influence of the conservative television ministries was diminished somewhat as George Bush, the more conservative of the candidates, lost to Bill Clinton, a Southern Baptist.

The efforts of the Religious Right have, however, altered the course of American history and will impact on the judicial systems in this country for decades. Ronald Reagan succeeded in appointing conservative justices to the Supreme Court. In the late 1980s and early 1990s, the remaining liberal justices were of advanced age and President Bush appointed conservatives to match his own agenda. However, with a more liberal president elected in 1992, the balance of power is likely to tilt in the Supreme Court as new appointments are made.

The religious conservatives have put pressure on the American educational system to return the schools to what they once were, to once again include the study of creation according to the Book of Genesis in addition to the previously mentioned school prayer. They have allied themselves with political conservatives, and together they work diligently to impose their convictions and values in the schools. Today's educators cannot ignore the influence of these groups, which in some communities is very powerful.

Nationally, our adherence to the principle of separation of church and state has obviously been schizophrenic at best. Oaths are typically made on Bibles and often end with the phrase, "so help me God." Our coins and currency state "In God we trust." We have military chaplains and congressional chaplains, and we hold congressional prayer breakfasts. This has been interpreted by some to mean that the separation of church and state simply means that there will be no state church (Welch, Medeiros, & Tate, 1981).

Complete separation of church and state, as defined by strict constitutionalists, would have a profound effect on our socioreligious life. It is likely that the American public wants some degree of separation of these two institutions, but it is equally likely that it would be outraged if total separation were imposed. Total separation would mean no direct or indirect aid to religious groups, no tax-free status, no tax deductions for contributions to religious groups, no national Christmas tree, no government-paid chaplains, no religious holidays, no blue laws, and so on. The list of religious activities, rights, and privileges that might be eliminated seems almost endless (Klein, 1983).

Educational Implications

Religious groups place different emphases on the need for education and have different expectations of what children should be taught. The Amish usually want to remove their children from formal schooling after they complete the eighth grade. The Hutterites do not want their children to attend school with non-Hutterite students, although the teacher is usually not a member of the religious community. Catholics, Lutherans, Episcopalians, Hutterites, and Seventh-Day Adventists have established their own schools to provide both a common education (i.e., the general, nonreligious skills and knowledge) and a religious education.

Public schools should be free of religious doctrine and perspective, but many people believe that schools without such a perspective do not provide a desirable value orientation for students. There is a constant debate about the public school's responsibility in fostering student morality and social responsibility. A major point of disagreement focuses on who should determine the morals that will provide the context of the education program in a school. Because religious diversity is so great in this country, that task is nearly impossible. Therefore, most public schools incorporate commonly accepted American values that transcend most religions. In response, some students are sent to schools operated by a religious body; other students attend religion classes after school or on Saturdays; and many students receive their religious training at Sunday school.

Although the U.S. Constitution requires the separation of state and religion, this does not signify that public schools and religion have always been completely separated. Until the 1962 and 1963 Supreme Court decisions determined that these practices were unconstitutional, some schools included religious worship and prayer in their daily educational practices. Although schools should be secular, they are influenced greatly by the predominant values of the community. Whether evolution, sex education, and values clarification are part of instruction in a school is determined in great part by the religious beliefs of a community. Educators must be cognizant of this influence before introducing certain readings and ideas that stray far from what the community is willing to accept within their belief and value structure. Among the controversial issues that surround the efforts of the New Right and fundamentalist religious groups are school prayer, tuition tax credits, and censorship. While cognizant of the interests of conservative religious groups, educators must also be mindful of the interests of those who strongly adhere to the principle of separation of church and state. Even a seemingly harmless question as to whether or not the children had attended church and Sunday school could foster strong negative reactions.

School Prayer

In spite of the 1962 and 1963 Supreme Court decisions regarding school prayer, conservative groups have persisted in their efforts to revive prayer in the schools. The present law is in essence a voluntary prayer law, which in no way prevents teachers or students from praying privately in school. Any teacher or student can offer his or her own private prayer of thanks before the noon meal or meditate or pray between classes and before and after school. Public group prayer is forbidden by law. Advocates of school prayer sometimes advance their efforts under the term "voluntary" prayer. The interpretation of what constitutes voluntary school prayer has become one of the main issues in the prayer controversy. Some proponents advocate mandated school prayer, with individuals voluntarily choosing to participate or not participate. It is likely that if such laws were ever enacted, there would be considerable social pressure to participate that would be particularly difficult for younger children to resist (Welch et al., 1981).

Tuition Tax Credits

Tuition tax credits have been a major controversy within education. Proponents support income tax credits for parents who enroll their children in private schools. Many of those who support these tax credits believe that since the children in private schools reduce the number of students in public education and thereby reduce public education costs, their parents are entitled to some tax relief. Proponents support the tax credits as a matter of social equity, encouraging greater pluralism, diversity, and competition in the American education system. The decision to send children to private schools is usually precipitated by parental desires to provide an education coupled with a religious environment, to provide an education superior to that available in the public schools, or, in some cases, to segregate their children from other children in the public schools.

Opponents to tuition tax credits see them as a weakening of the public education system and an encouragement for some parents to abandon public education for the exclusiveness of the private education sector. It was attacked by two U.S. senators as "segregation sanctioning—rip-off for the rich, creating a dual system of education: public schools for the poor, the handicapped and disadvantaged and private schools for the rest" ("Senate Scuttles," 1984, p. 13).

In 1983, the Supreme Court, in *Mueller v. Allen*, upheld Minnesota's allowance of income tax deductions for the cost of tuition and related education expenses. The Minnesota law provides for income tax deductions regardless of whether a child attends public or private school—parochial or secular. Minnesota was able to convince the court that the purpose of the law was to ensure a well-educated citizenry and to relieve the burden on public schools. The court applied a three-part test that it often used to determine the unconstitutional establishment of religion, and determined that (1) the purpose of the tax law was not to aid religion; (2) the law did not have the primary effect of aiding religion; (3) the law did not promote excessive entanglement between church and state (Lines, 1983). With the Mueller decision, it is likely that other groups will attempt to emulate Minnesota's success through both federal and state tax laws.

Censorship

The discussion of censorship is included in this section because the censorship movement tends to be heavily influenced by many individuals from fundamentalist and conservative religious groups. Censorship of textbooks, library books, and other learning materials has become another major battleground in education for the New Right and other fundamentalist groups. Jenkinson (1979) estimates that there are no less than two hundred groups involved in public school censorship.

The impact of censorship in the public schools cannot be underestimated. It is a serious matter. Censorship, or attempts at censorship, have resulted in violence, where involved parties have been beaten and even shot. It has resulted in the dismissal or resignation of administrators and teachers. It has split communities and in the past thirty years has created nearly as much controversy as the desegregation of schools. Few can doubt the sincerity of censors and their proponents. Most, if not all, are absolutely certain that the cause they support is just and morally right and that for the sake of all, they are obligated to continue their fight.

At the other end of the continuum, opponents of the censors also tend to share a conviction that they are the ones who are in the right and that censors infringe on academic freedom, seeking to destroy meaningful education. Opponents feel that their antagonists thrive on hard times, when schools come under fire because of declining Scholastic Aptitude Test (SAT) scores, rising illiteracy rates, escalating costs of education, and increasing concern about violence and vandalism in the schools (Jenkinson, 1979). Other factors that prompt the activities of censors are the removal of school prayer, teaching methods that are branded as secular humanism, and programs such as values clarification, drug education, and sex education. Books written specifically for teenagers about subjects that are objectionable to some parents and in language others consider too realistic are often a source of concern. The emergence of African American literature, sometimes written in the black vernacular, is sometimes the source of irritation or concern (Jenkinson, 1979).

Targets for the censors are those books and materials that are identified as disrespectful of authority and religion, destructive of social and cultural values, obscene, pornographic, unpatriotic, or in violation of individual and familial rights of privacy. Books written by homosexuals are frequently attacked.

Among the materials attacked by censors are those considered nonracist or nonsexist. Magazines such as *Time, Newsweek,* and *U.S. News and World Report* are sometimes attacked because they publish stories about war, crime, death, violence, and sex. In a conservative community, a teacher can anticipate a negative reaction to the teaching of evolution without presenting the views on creationism.

In 1977, a survey of a selected number of secondary school teachers was conducted by the National Council of Teachers of English. One aspect of the survey requested the titles of books that were the focus of objections by would-be censors. A total of 145 titles were reported. Here is a list of the ten books receiving the most complaints, with *The Catcher in the Rye* receiving more than twice as many complaints as the two Steinbeck books tied for second place. The number of objections or complaints is listed in parentheses (Burgess, 1979).

1. *The Catcher in the Rye* (25)
2. *Of Mice and Men* (12)
3. *The Grapes of Wrath* (12)
4. *Go Ask Alice* (10)
5. *One Flew Over the Cuckoo's Nest* (8)
6. *Lord of the Flies* (7)
7. *My Darling, My Hamburger* (6)
8. *One Day in the Life of Ivan Denisovich* (6)
9. *Flowers for Algernon* (5)
10. *Love Story* (5)

In addition, certain dictionaries with words and definitions described as offensive have been forced off adoption lists. Curricula such as MACOS (Man—A Course of Study), a social studies course published by the National Science Foundation, a federal agency, have felt the full force of the censors' attack, which focused on topics such as wife swapping and cannibalism. Its defenders accused the censors of fostering misunderstanding by taking materials out of context. The battles over censorship continue, with both sides certain that they are right.

One can understand the concern of parents who are often influenced by censors. They believe that unless they choose sides and act, their children will be taught with materials that are anti-God, anti-family, anti-authority, anti-country, anti-morality, and anti-law and order.

The failure to communicate effectively with parents has been cited as a major contributing source of alienation between educators and parents (Jenkinson, 1979; Kamhi, 1981). Failure to communicate the objectives of new curricula and to explain how these programs enrich the educational experience may cause suspicion and distrust. Many administrators and librarians indicate that communication with parents is more crisis-oriented than continuous. Information about programs, policies, and procedures tends to be offered in response to inquiries or challenges rather than as part of an ongoing public relations effort.

A small Ohio community faced with parental challenges and rumors about a "dirty" book assigned to their children set up an evening course for parents entitled, "Books Our Children Read." In the class, parents read and discussed the book in question and others like it. As a result, the teachers learned something from the parents, and the parents, in turn, learned to respect and trust the teachers (Berkley, 1979).

Secular humanism has been one of the direct targets of the censors, particularly those affiliated with fundamentalist religious groups. The emphasis in secular humanism is a respect for human beings, rather than a belief in the supernatural. Its objectives include the full development of every human being, the universal use of the scientific method, affirmation of the dignity of humans, personal freedom combined with social responsibility, and fulfillment through the development of ethical and creative living (Welch et al., 1981).

The groups opposed to secular humanism cite two Supreme Court cases as evidence that secular humanism is a religion: *Torcaso v. Watkins* and *United States v. Seeger.* These cases were not heard by the court to determine whether or not secular humanism is a religion; nevertheless, the wording in the court findings has been frequently used to support the position that the Supreme Court recognizes secular humanism as a religion (Jenkinson, 1979).

However, secular humanism is not an organized religion like Roman Catholicism, Protestantism, and Judaism. It does not have rituals, a church, or professed doctrines. Its existence is in the minds of individuals who align themselves with these perspectives. The specific beliefs and manifestations of beliefs vary from one believer to another.

Teachers new to the profession or new to a community should never underestimate the determination of those involved in the censorship movement. All teachers would be well advised to make certain that they are fully aware of the climate within the community before introducing new, innovative, or controversial materials, teaching strategies, and books. Experienced colleagues and supervisors can usually serve as barometers as to how students, parents, and the community will react to the new materials or teaching techniques. With this type of information, the new teacher can proceed with a more realistic anticipation of the reception that can be expected.

PAUSE TO REFLECT

The faculty at your school has been working for several months on a new integrated curriculum across subject areas. For the first time, they have really collaborated in this effort. At the presentation to the school board, one member accused them of being secular humanists and not providing proper moral direction to their children. The faculty members were shocked. Why were these accusations made by the school board member? Why do some members of the community think that secular humanism is a religion? How should the faculty have approached their new curriculum project to prevent the backlash from the community?

Classroom Implications

Although religion and public schooling are to remain separate, religion can be taught in schools as a legitimate discipline for objective study. A comparative religion course is part of the curriculum offered in many secondary schools. In this approach, the students are not forced to practice a religion as part of their educational program. They can, however, study one or more religions.

As part of the curriculum, students should learn that the United States (and indeed the world) is rich in religious diversity. Educators portray their respect for religious differences by their interactions with students from different religious backgrounds. Understanding the importance of religion to many students and their families is an advantage in developing effective teaching strategies for individual students. Instructional activities can build on students' religious experiences to help them learn concepts. This technique helps students recognize that their religious identity is valued in the classroom and encourages them to respect the religious diversity that exists.

At the same time, educators should avoid stereotyping all students from one denomination or church. There is diversity within every religious group and denomination. In each group, there are likely to be differences in attitudes and beliefs. For example, Southern Baptists may appear to be conservative to outsiders. However, among Southern Baptists, some would be considered part of a liberal or moderate group, whereas others may be identified as conservative. Some Southern Baptist churches may hold services so formal in nature that they might even be described as resembling an Episcopalian service, while others are by comparison extremely informal.

It is the responsibility of educators to be aware of the religious diversity and the influence of religion in the community in which they work. They must also understand the influence of religion on the school's curriculum and climate in order to teach effectively. Finally, educators must periodically reexamine their own interactions with students to ensure that they are not discriminating because of differences in religious beliefs. It is imperative that educators recognize the influence of membership in a religious microculture in order to help students develop their potential.

Summary

One's religion has considerable impact on how one functions on a day-to-day basis. Education may be greatly influenced by religious groups. Some private schools are established on religious principles, and in those schools, religion is an integral part of the curriculum. Even in public schools, attempts by religious groups are made regularly to influence the system. The degree of religious influence in the schools varies from one community to another. Educators should not underestimate the influence and strategies of conservative religious groups and would be well advised to know their community before introducing controversial materials.

Questions for Review

1. Discuss how the religious atmosphere of a community can influence curriculum and instructional methodology.
2. To what extent does religion influence American life with respect to its importance to the individual and to church or synagogue attendance?
3. What is the relationship of religion to public office?
4. What are the present trends with respect to membership in conservative, moderate, and liberal religious groups? What are the implications of these trends for the political and legal directions of the country?
5. What do present laws permit with respect to school prayer? How does the Religious Right want to change these laws?.
6. Discuss censorship in the schools, including the targets of the censors.
7. How have Protestantism, Catholicism, and Judaism influenced American culture?
8. In what ways does gender impact religion and religion impact gender issues?
9. What is the relationship of religion to race?

References

Appel, W. (1983). *Cults in America: Programmed for paradise.* New York: Holt, Rinehart & Winston.

Berkley, J. (1979). Teach the parents well: An anti-censorship experiment in adult education. In J. E. Davis (Ed.), *Dealing with censorship.* Urbana, IL: National Council of Teachers of English.

Bezilla, K. B., & Jones, A. M. (Eds.) (1992). *Yearbook of American and Canadian Churches.* Nashville, TN: Abingdon Press.

Bezilla, R. (Ed.). (1993). *Religion in America.* Princeton, NJ: Princeton Religion Research Center.

Briggs, K. A. (1977). Charismatic Christians. In H. L. Marx, Jr. (Ed.), *Religions in America.* New York: Wilson.

Burgess, L. (1979). A brief report of the 1977 NCTE censorship survey. In J. E. Davis (Ed.), *Dealing with censorship.* Urbana, IL: National Council of Teachers of English.

Carroll, J. W. (1979). Continuity and change: The shape of religious life in the United States—1950 to the present. In J. W. Carroll, D. W. Johnson, & M. E. Marty (Eds.), *Religion in America: 1950 to the present.* New York: Harper & Row.

Colombo, F. (1984). *God in America—religion and politics in the United States.* New York: Columbia University Press.

Emerging Trends. (1992a). Final 1991 Data Show an Upswing in the Importance of Religion in Peoples Lives, 14(3), p. 1.

Emerging Trends. (1992b). Church Attendance Constant, 14(3), p. 4.

Emerging Trends. (1992c). Only One American in Nine Expresses No Religious Preference, 14(4), p. 1.

Gallup Poll. (1984). *Religion in America.* Princeton, NJ: Gallup International.

Gallup Report. (1987, April). *Religion in America,* 259.

Gallup Report. (1989, September). *Religion in America.*

Greeley, A. M. (1982). *Religion: A secular theory.* New York: Free Press.

Haddad, Y. Y., Haines, B., & Findley, E. (1984). *The Islamic impact.* Syracuse, NY: Syracuse University Press.

Herberg, W. (1960). *Protestant—Catholic—Jew: An essay in American religious sociology.* New York: Anchor Press.

Hudson, W. S., & Corrigan, J. (1992). *Religion in America* (5th ed.). New York: Macmillan.

Jacquet, C. H., Jr. (Ed.). (1991). *Yearbook of American and Canadian churches, 1991.* Nashville, TN: Abingdon Press.

Jenkinson, E. B. (1979). *Censors in the classroom.* Carbondale, IL: Southern Illinois University Press.

Johnson, D. W. (1979). Trends and issues shaping the religious future. In J. W. Carroll, D. W. Johnson, & M. E. Marty (Eds.), *Religion in America: 1950 to the present.* New York: Harper & Row.

Kamhi, M. M. (1981, December). Censorship vs. selection: Choosing the books our children shall read. *Educational Leadership,* 211–213.

Klein, J. P. (1983). Separation of church and state: The endless struggle. *Contemporary Education, 54*(3), 166-170.

Lincoln, C. E. (1974). *The Black church since Frazier.* New York: Schocken Books.

Lincoln, C. E., & Mamiya, L. H. (1990). *The Black Church in the African American Experience.* Durham, NC: Duke University.

Lines, P. M. (1983, August 24). Impact of Mueller: New options for policymakers. *Education Week.*

Marty, M. E. (1979). Interpreting American pluralism. In J. W. Carroll, D. W. Johnson, & M. E. Marty (Eds.), *Religion in America: 1950 to the present.* New York: Harper & Row.

Marty, M. E. (Ed.). (1975). *Our faiths.* Royal Oak, MI: Cathedral Publications.

Moseley, J. G. (1981). *A cultural history of religion in America.* Westport, CN: Greenwood Press.

Mueller, S. A. (1974). The new triple melting pot: Herbert revisited. In P. H. McNamara (Ed.), *Religion American style.* New York: Harper & Row.

Protestantism—world religions. Pt. 6. (1977, April 7). *Senior Scholastic, 109,* 22–24.

Raschke, C. A., Kirk, J. A., & Taylor, M. C. (1977). *Religion and the human image.* Englewood Cliffs, NJ: Prentice-Hall.

Roof, W. C., & McKinney, W. (1985, July). Denominational America and the new religious pluralism. *Annals of the American Academy of Political and Social Science, 480,* 24–38.

Senate Scuttles. (1984). *Religion and Public Education, 11*(1), 13.

Sklare, M. (1974). The American synagogue. In P. H. McNamara (Ed.), *Religion American style.* New York: Harper & Row.

Stark, R., & Glock, C. Y. (1974). Prejudice and the churches. In P. H. McNamara (Ed.), *Religion American style.* New York: Harper & Row.

Van Leeuwen, M. S. (1990). *Gender and grace.* Downers Grove, IL: Intervarsity Press.

Welch, D., Medeiros, D. C., & Tate, G. A. (1981, December). Education and the New Right. *Educational Leadership,* 203–207.

Williams, P. W. (1990). *American's religions—traditions and cultures.* New York: Macmillan.

Wilson, J. (1978). *Religion in American society: The effective presence.* Englewood Cliffs, NJ: Prentice-Hall.

Woodward, K. L., Barnes, J., & Lisle, L. (1977). Born again! In H. L. Marx, Jr. (Ed.), *Religions in America.* New York: Wilson.

Suggested Readings

Bach, J., & Modl, T. (Eds.). (1989). *Religion in America.* San Diego, CA: Greenhaven Press, Inc.

Provides opposing viewpoints to questions such as: Is America a religious society? Should religious values guide public policy? Does religious discrimination exist in America? Is television evangelism positive?

Colombo, F. (1984). *God in America—religion and politics in the United States.* New York: Columbia University Press.

An in-depth portrait of contemporary United States from a religious point of view. Asks the relevant question: Will the fine line between church and state survive the new era of religious involvement in moral judgment and political affairs?

Herberg, W. (1960). *Protestant—Catholic—Jew: An essay in American religious sociology.* New York: Anchor Press.

A sociological study of the three major faiths in the United States. Describes Americans as "melting" into one of those three groups rather than a one-model American. Includes a brief history of each group. Considered a classic by some.

Hudson, W. S., & Corrigan, J. (1992). *Religion in America* (5th ed.). New York: Macmillan Publishing Co.

A look at the history of religion in this country and its profound influence on the formation of culture in America. Includes the pluralistic nature of religion today.

Lincoln, C. E., & Mamiya, L. H. (1990). *The black church in the African American experience.* Durham, NC: Duke University.

An examination of the history and role of the black church in American society.

Podell, J. (Ed.) (1987). *Religion in American life.* New York: Wilson.

Contains a number of interesting and provocative articles and essays regarding religion in the United States. Includes Roof and McKinney's excellent article related to religious pluralism in the country.

Van Leeuwen, M. S. (1990). *Gender and grace.* Downers Grove, IL: Intervarsity Press.

An examination of gender issues in a Christian biblical context.

Williams, P. W. (1990). *America's religions—traditions and cultures.* New York: Macmillan.

An examination of American religion, its historical antecedents, and the current state of religious pluralism.

66

CHAPTER 7

Language

To devalue his language or to presume Standard English is a better system is to devalue the child and his culture and to reveal a naiveté concerning language.

BARATZ, 1968, P. 145

Theresa Lobb, a kindergarten teacher at Waialeale School in Honolulu, had finished welcoming her new kindergarten class. As she wrote her name and the name of the school on the blackboard, she felt a slight tug on the back of her skirt and heard a faint voice just above a whisper say, "Teacha, I like go pee pee." As she turned around she saw the pleading face of Haunani Sousa. "What did you say?" Ms. Lobb asked disgustedly. In a slightly louder voice, Haunani repeated herself, "I like go pee pee." With some in the class beginning to giggle, Ms. Lobb exclaimed, "You will go nowhere, young lady, until you ask me in proper English. Now say it properly." "I no can," pleaded Haunani. "Then you can just stand there until you do." With the students giggling and Haunani standing as ordered, Ms. Lobb proceeded with her lesson.

A few minutes later, the occasional giggle exploded into a chorus of laughing. As Ms. Lobb turned to Haunani, the child was sobbing as she stood in the middle of a large puddle of urine on the classroom floor.

The above incident actually happened in a school in Hawaii many years ago. Haunani (not her real name) spoke only pidgin English when she entered school. She is now an adult and describes the incident as one of the most painful and humiliating of her life. The insensitivity of the teacher, who knew precisely what the child was asking for, resulted in lasting emotional scars on a child, now a woman.

Language and Culture

Some students come to school barely speaking English, some are bilingual, some speak a nonstandard dialect, and some use sign language. As the scene changes from school to school, the languages and dialects spoken also change. The scene, however, is indicative of the multilingual nature of the United States, a result of our multicultural heritage.

Students exhibit cultural similarities and differences related to language as well as to gender, class, ethnicity, religion, exceptionalities, and age. Because they speak one or more languages, as well as dialects of these languages, they are a part of another microcultural group. Of course, not all African American children speak black English, nor do all Hispanic Americans speak Spanish. Within most microcultures, members will vary greatly in the language or dialect used.

Unfortunately, society often attaches a stigma that characterizes bilingual students as "low-income, low-status persons who are educationally at risk" (Hakuta, 1986, p. 7). Rather than valuing and promoting the use of two or more languages, we expect students to replace their native language with English as soon as possible. Movements to establish English-only policies and practices bestow "official blessing upon state residents who speak English, and a repudiation of those residents who do not" (Spencer, 1988, p. 142). Individuals who have limited English proficiency frequently suffer institutional discrimination as a result of the limited acceptance of languages other than English.

Language is the means by which we communicate. It is that which makes our behavior human. It can incite anger, elicit love, inspire bravery, and arouse fear. It binds groups of people together. Language and dialect serve as a focal point for cultural identity and provide a common bond for individuals with the same linguistic heritage, who often share the same feelings, beliefs, and behaviors. Individuals traveling abroad are often pleased to find other travelers speaking their language or their dialect. The dialect or language used in the right situation can provide an individual with immediate acceptance or credibility (Chinn, 1985).

However, language is much more than just a means of communication. It is used to socialize children into their linguistic and cultural communities, developing patterns that distinguish one community from another. In an ethnographic study of the use of language in three culturally different communities in the Piedmont area of North Carolina, Heath (1983) discovered that:

> 1. Patterns of language use in any community are in accord with and mutually reinforce other cultural patterns, such as space and time orderings, problem-solving techniques, group loyalties, and preferred patterns of recreation.
> 2. Factors involved in preparing children for school-oriented, mainstream success are deeper than differences in formal structures of language, amount of parent-child interaction, and the like. The language socialization process in all its complexity is more powerful than such single-factor explanations in accounting for academic success.
> 3. The patterns of interactions between oral and written uses of language are varied and complex, and the traditional oral-literate dichotomy does not capture the ways other cultural patterns in each community affect the uses of oral and written language. In the communities [in the study] occasions for writing and reading of extended prose occur far less frequently than occasions for extended oral discourse around written materials. (p. 344)

Thus, the interaction of language and culture is complex but central to the socialization of children into acceptable cultural patterns.

Exactly how a language is learned is not known, but almost all children have the ability to learn one or more native languages. They learn gradually, in part through imitating older persons. They learn to select almost instinctively the right word, the right response, and the right gesture to fit the situation. By age five, children have learned the syntax of their native language, and they know that words in different arrangements mean different things (Neisser, 1983). The average adult has fifty thousand words at his or her disposal and, in addition, can communicate through numerous vocal sounds and gestures.

Native speakers of a language unconsciously know and obey the rules and customs of their language community. Society and language interact constantly. To make a wrong choice in word selection may come across as rude, crude, or ignorant. Children who are learning a new language or who are unfamiliar with colloquialisms may make wrong choices or even be surprised at the use of certain words that are incongruent with their perceptions of what is proper. An Australian student in a southwestern U.S. university was shocked when a girl in his class responded to his query of what she had been doing during the summer, "Oh, just piddling around." Her response was meant to convey the message that she had been passing her time in idle activities. However, from his frame of reference, the Australian student understood her to say that she had been urinating. It is important for classroom teachers to recognize that students who are new to a language may not always be able to make appropriate word selections or comprehend the meaning of particular dialects or colloquialisms.

The subtle and complex nature of the interaction between language and culture sometimes makes it difficult for the student whose first language is not English to fully master the English language as it is used in schools and institutions. Instruction, practice, and exposure do assist in the mastery of vocabulary and grammar; however, total immersion in the new linguistic community may make it easier to master the finer points of language usage and the associated subtleties that allow for alternative and appropriate ways of saying things at the appropriate times.

In the 1930s Fiorello La Guardia was the mayor of New York City. He was of mixed Jewish and Italian ancestry and was fluent in both Yiddish and Italian, as well as the New York dialect of English. When speaking to Italian audiences, La Guardia used the broad and sweeping gestures characteristic of the people of southern Italy. When speaking Yiddish to Jewish audiences, he utilized the forearm chop identified with many eastern European Jews. When speaking English, he used softer, less emphatic gestures more typical of English-speaking individuals. The example of La Guardia not only suggests different communication styles among different ethnic groups, but also suggests that individuals adjust their communication style, whenever possible, to suit the needs of the intended audience.

At an early age, a child acquires the delicate muscle controls necessary for pronouncing the words of the native language or for signing naturally if the child is deaf. As the child grows older, it becomes increasingly more difficult to make the vocal muscles behave in the new, unaccustomed ways necessary to master a foreign language. For example, some Filipinos are unaccustomed to the sounds associated with the letter *f*, which makes it difficult, if not impossible, for them to pronounce the word *four* properly. Perhaps even more difficult to learn are the vocabulary and structure of the new language.

All this tends to inhibit people from learning new languages and as such encourages them to maintain the one into which they were born. Although the United States is primarily an English-speaking country, there are many other languages spoken. Spanish, Italian, and sign language are the most commonly used languages other than English. Among the English-speaking, there are numerous dialects—from the Hawaiian pidgin to the southern drawl of Atlanta to the Appalachian white dialect to the Brooklyn dialect of New York. Each is distinctive, and each is an effective means of communication for those who share its linguistic style.

In the United States, it has been estimated that there are approximately 32 million individuals whose native language is not English (U.S. Bureau of Census, 1990). This figure does not include the millions of English-speaking individuals whose dialects are sometimes labeled as nonstandard.

The multilingual nature of American society reflects the rich cultural heritage of its people. Such language diversity is an asset to the nation, especially in its interaction with other nations in the areas of commerce, defense, education, science, and technology. There is an advantage to being bilingual or multilingual that is often overlooked because of our ethnocentrism. In many other nations, children are expected to become fluent in two or more languages and numerous dialects.

The Nature of Language

As humans, we communicate in order to share ourselves with others. Language is our medium of exchange for sharing our internal states of being with one another. Through language we reach out and make contact with our surrounding realities. Through language we share with others our experiences with that reality (Samovar & Porter, 1991).

According to Samovar and Porter (1991), language is not simply a means of reporting experience. They suggest that it is also a way of defining experience. Different languages represent different social realities. Thus, to understand what is being said, we must also understand the social context of the language itself. Language goes beyond the simple understanding of one another. It helps us to understand culture itself. Language itself represents culture. Each language provides us with a means to perceive the world and a means to interpret experiences.

Language usage is culturally determined. In addition to influencing the order of words to form phrases, language influences thinking patterns. "Time" is described differently from culture to culture. Western societies view time as something that can be saved, lost, or wasted. Punctuality is highly valued. In other societies, time assumes different values and is reflected in the language of the group. In the language of Sioux Indians, for example, there are no words to convey "late" or "waiting" (Samovar & Porter, 1991).

Some Asians tend to be circular in their speaking patterns. One of the reasons for this is the feeling that for a point to be understood and appreciated, a foundation or background must be fully laid out. In this manner the point of the discussion is put in its proper context. However, for Westerners and others who are accustomed to getting directly to the issue at hand, the point could be lost in the circular presentation of the concept—or the frustrated listener has just tuned out the speaker.

In order for effective communication to take place, it is important that there are enough cultural similarities between the sender and the receiver for the latter to decode the message adequately. Even when one is familiar with a word or phrase, comprehension of the intended meaning may not be possible unless there is similarity in the cultural backgrounds. In certain cultural groups, *bad* takes on an opposite meaning and may denote "the best." A "candy man" is not one who sells sweets, but one who sells drugs. *Bad* and *candy man* are examples of *argot,* a more or less secretive vocabulary of a co-culture group, in which some words take on different meanings. Co-cultures are groups of people that exist outside of the dominant culture and are often alienated in some way from the dominant culture. Users of argot include some working-class ethnic groups, homosexuals, gang members, and hobos (Samovar & Porter, 1991).

From a linguistic point of view, there is no such thing as a good language or a bad language. All languages developed to express the needs of their users, and, in that sense, all languages are equal. Although languages do not all have the same amounts of grammar, phonology or semantic structure, they are equal in the sense that there is nothing limiting, demeaning, or handicapping about any of them. All languages meet the social and psychological needs of their speakers and as such, are arguably equal (Crystal, 1987).

Language is very cultural. It, together with dialects, is usually related to one's ethnic, geographic, gender, or class origins. Speakers from a particular background often downgrade the linguistic styles of others. For example, Easterners, citing the use of slow, extended vowels and the term *y'all,* may be critical of the speech of Southerners. Southerners, on the other hand, may be critical of the speech and language patterns of people from Brooklyn, who seem to speak through their nose and use phrases such as *youse guys.* The eastern dialect of English is appropriate in the East, the southern dialect appropriate in the South, and black English appropriate in many African American communities.

Language changes because society changes. Language change is inevitable and rarely predictable. For example, a third-generation Japanese American born and raised in Maryland learned Japanese from his grandparents and his parents. Because of particular pride in his cultural and linguistic heritage, he continued to use his Japanese, teaching and speaking the language to his American-born Japanese wife and children. On his first trip to Japan, he had no difficulty in conversing with the people, but noticed smiles, grins, and giggles when he spoke. When he asked if he has said anything humorous, the people politely explained that he was speaking as if he were someone out of the 1800s. He realized that his grandparents had immigrated to the United States in the 1800s and had maintained the language of that period. The language in Japan, however, had changed sufficiently to make his language patterns stand out as archaic.

In some areas, language changes are so gradual that they go unnoticed. In other circumstances, changes are more easily noted. There are expressions and words that tend to be identified with a particular period. Sometimes the language is related to particular microcultures for certain periods. For example, words and phrases such as *chilling, hyped,* and *def* may be a part of our language for a time, only to be replaced by other expressions.

All languages are systems of vocal sounds and/or nonverbal systems by which group members communicate with one another. Some languages do not have a written system. Sign language is a system of communication that is used primarily by the deaf to talk to each other. However, the fact that the language is not written or is not oral does not make it inferior to French, German, or English.

Language Differences

There are literally thousands of known languages in the world today. Most reference books suggest that there are four to five thousand, but there are estimates as high as ten thousand (Crystal, 1987). Language differences ultimately reflect basic behavioral differences between groups of people. Physical and social separation inevitably leads to language differences. The constant movement and settlement patterns of people, as well as natural barriers like mountains and rivers, isolated many of the early settlers in the United States. The lack of communication across communities in the early years of the country further contributed to the isolation. Thus, as language changes took place, different dialects of the same language developed in different communities.

Social variables also contribute to language differences, with both class and ethnicity reflecting such differences. The greater the social distance between groups, the greater the tendency toward language differences. Upwardly mobile individuals often adopt the language patterns of the dominant society, since it may at times facilitate social acceptance.

Sign Language

Not all language is oral. Individuals who are deaf are not able to hear the sounds of oral language and have developed their own language for communication. American Sign Language (ASL) is a natural language that has been developed and used by deaf persons. Only in the past thirty years have linguists come to recognize ASL as a language with complex grammar and well-regulated syntax. A growing number of colleges and universities will accept fluency in ASL to meet a second-language requirement.

Like oral languages, different sign languages have developed in different countries. ASL is used by the majority of adults who are deaf in Canada and the United States. Children who are deaf are able to pick up the syntax and rhythms of signing as spontaneously as hearing children pick up their oral languages. They learn to think in it and to translate other sign languages and lip reading into it. Children who are born into deaf families—both children who hear and children who are deaf—usually learn ASL from birth. Deaf children who have hearing parents do not have the opportunity to learn ASL until they attend a school for the deaf, where they learn it from their peers.

ASL is the only sign language that is recognized as a language in its own right, rather than a variation of spoken English. With its own vocabulary, syntax, and grammatical rules, ASL does not correspond completely to spoken or written English (Heward & Orlansky, 1992). Signed English is often used by the deaf to communicate with the hearing. Rather than having its own language patterns like ASL, it translates the English oral or written word into sign. Few hearing individuals know ASL because they rarely observe it. Individuals who are deaf use it to communicate with each other. When one sees an interpreter on television or at a meeting, it is usually signed English that is being used.

The use of sign language is one of the components of the deaf microculture that sets its users apart from the hearing. In part because of the residential school experiences of many individuals who are deaf, a distinct cultural community has developed. As a cultural community, they are "highly endogamous, with in-group marriages estimated at between 86 and 90 percent of all marriages involving individuals who are deaf" (Reagan, 1988, p. 2). Although ASL is the major language of the deaf community, many individuals are bilingual in English and ASL.

Bilingualism

> In its short history, the United States has probably been host to more bilingual people than any other country in the world. One of the most fascinating aspects of bilingualism in the United States is its extreme instability, for it is a transitional stage toward monolingualism in English. Each new wave of immigrants has brought with it its own language and then witnessed the erosion of that language in the face of the implicitly acknowledged public language, English. (Hakuta, 1986, p. 166)

Language diversity in the United States has been maintained primarily because of continuing immigration from non–English-speaking countries. However, the incessant move toward monolingualism is a very rapid process (Hakuta, 1986), in which schools have assisted. Prior to World War I, native languages were used in many schools where a large number of ethnic group members were trying to preserve their language. In this country, the maintenance of native languages other than English now depends on the efforts of members of the language group through churches and other community activities. Now, even our bilingual education programs are designed to move students quickly into English-only instruction.

A major reason for learning English quickly is economic. The acquisition of a second language is important when it serves one's own social and economic needs. If immigrants have available only the most menial jobs in society, the need to learn English is minimal (Spencer, 1988).

During the civil rights movement of the 1960s, language-minority groups, especially Hispanics, began to celebrate their native language tradition. Other ethnic groups decried the loss of their native languages over a few generations and blamed the schools' Americanization process for the loss. The passage of federal legislation for bilingual education resulted. Many of those early advocates, however, hoped that the bilingual programs would help maintain and promote the native language while teaching English skills.

What constitutes bilingualism? The word implies the ability to use two different languages; however, there are differences of opinion about the degree of fluency required. Whereas some maintain that a bilingual individual must

Continuing immigration to the United States has helped to maintain language diversity. The challenge for educators is to help immigrants learn English without abandoning their native languages.

have nativelike fluency in both languages, others suggest that measured competency in two languages constitutes bilingualism (Baca & Cervantes, 1989).

Hakuta (1986) has identified two types of bilingualism: subtractive bilingualism and additive bilingualism. Subtractive bilingualism occurs when the second language replaces the first. Additive bilingualism occurs when the two languages are of equal value and one does not dominate the other. The latter has the more positive effect on academic achievement.

Accents

An accent generally refers to how an individual pronounces words. Since the Japanese do not have the sound of *l* in their language, many tend to pronounce English words that begin with the letter *l* as if they began with the letter *r*. Thus, the word *light* may be pronounced as if it were *right*, and *long* as if it were *wrong*. Note that an accent differs from the standard language only in pronunciation. A dialect, however, may involve differences both in pronunciation and in grammatical patterns of the language system. For example, in Hawaiian pidgin English, "Don't do that" may evolve into "No make like dat." Teachers should be aware that persons who speak with an accent often speak standard English, but at this level of their linguistic development are unable to speak without an accent.

Dialect Differences

There is no agreement on the number of dialects of English spoken in this country. There are at least ten regional dialects— Eastern New England, New York City, Western Pennsylvania, Middle Atlantic, Appalachian, Southern, Central, Midland, North Central, Southwest, and Northwest (Owens, 1992). However, social, ethnic, age, and gender considerations complicate any attempt to isolate areas completely.

Dialects

Although English is the primary language in the United States, numerous English dialects are used by identifiable groups throughout the country. Dialects are language rule systems that vary in some manner from the language standard considered ideal. Each dialect shares a common set of grammatical rules with the standard language. Theoretically, dialects of a language are mutually intelligible to all speakers of the language; however, some dialects enjoy greater social acceptance and prestige. No dialect is better than any other, nor should a dialect be characterized as substandard, deviant, or inferior (Owens, 1992).

Certain languages are sometimes improperly referred to as dialects. Examples are the labeling of African languages as African dialects or the languages of the various American Indians as Indian dialects. This improper practice would be synonymous to labeling French and German as dialects spoken in the different countries of Europe.

Dialects differ from one another in a variety of ways. Differences in vowels are a primary means of distinguishing regional differences, whereas consonant differences tend to distinguish social dialects. However, regional and social dialects cannot be divorced from one another because an individual's dialect may be a blend of both. In northern dialects, for example, the *i* in words such as *time, pie,* and *side* is pronounced with a long *i* sound that Wolfram and Christian (1989) describe as a rapid production of two vowel sounds, one sounding like *ah* and the other like *ee.* The second sound glides off the first so that *time* becomes *taheem, pie* becomes *pahee,* and *side* becomes *saheed.* Southern and southern-related dialects may eliminate the gliding *e,* resulting in *tahm* for *time, pah* for *pie,* and *sahd* for *side.*

In social dialects, consonants tend to distinguish one dialect from another. Common examples of consonant pronunciation differences are in the *th* sounds and in the consonants *r* and *l.* In words such as *these, them,* and *those,* the initial *th* sound may be replaced with *d,* resulting in *dese, dem,* and *dose.* In words such as *think, thank,* and *throw,* the *th* may be replaced with *t,* resulting in *tink, tank,* and *trow.* Wolfram and Christian (1989) suggest that middle-class groups may substitute *d* for *th* to some extent in casual speech, whereas working-class groups make the substitution more often.

In some groups, particularly the African American working class, the *th* in the middle or at the end of a word—as in *author* and *tooth* may be replaced with *f,* as in *aufor* and *toof.* In words such as *bother* and *smooth, v* may be substituted for *th,* resulting in *bover* and *smoov.* In regional and social dialects, *r* and *l* may be lost, as in *ca* for *car* and *sef* for *self.*

Among the various dialects, differences in various aspects of grammatical usage can also be found. Wolfram and Christian (1989) suggest that nonstandard grammar tends to carry with it a greater social stigma than nonstandard pronunciation.

A common example of grammatical differences in dialect is in the absence of suffixes from verbs where they are usually present in standard dialects. For example, the *-ed* suffix to denote past tense is sometimes omitted, as in "Yesterday we play a long time." Other examples of grammatical differences include the omission of the *s* used in the present tense to denote agreement with certain subjects. "She have a car" may be used instead of "She has a car." The omission of the suffix has been observed in certain Native American communities, as well as among members of the African American working class. In the dialect of some African American working-class groups, the omission of the *s* in the plural forms of certain words and phrases, as in "two boy" rather than "two boys," has been observed. *Two* is plural, and an *s* after *boy* is viewed as redundant. Also often omitted in these dialect groups is the possessive *s*, as in "my friend car" instead of "my friend's car."

Variations in language patterns among groups are significant when compared by age, socioeconomic status, gender, ethnic group, and geographical region (Wolfram & Christian, 1989). For example, individuals in the forty- to sixty-year-old age group tend to use language patterns different from those of teenage groups. Teenagers tend to adopt certain language patterns that are characteristic of their age group. Slang words, particular pronunciation of some words, and certain grammatical constructions are often related to the teenage and younger groups. As the individual grows older, social pressures may encourage the dropping of those speech patterns. Although a teenager may refer to a good idea as "real bad," few fifty-year-old Madison Avenue executives would choose to use such an expression in a board meeting.

Social factors play a role in the choice of language patterns. The more formal the situation, the more formal the speech patterns. The selection of appropriate speech patterns appears to come naturally and spontaneously. Individuals are usually able to "read their environment" and to select from their large repertoire the language or speech pattern that is appropriate for the situation.

Wolfram and Christian (1989) also indicate that while the evidence is not conclusive, the range between high and low pitch used in African American communities is greater than that found in white communities. Such differences would, of course, be the result of learned behavior. African American males may tend to speak with a raspiness in their voice. American women, it has been suggested, may typically have a greater pitch distribution over a sentence than do men.

Other differences in dialects exist as well. Since educators are likely to find dialect differences in the classroom, additional reading in this area may be appropriate. The Suggested Readings at the end of this chapter include some helpful resources.

Bidialectalism

Certain situations, both social and professional, may dictate adjustments in dialect. Some individuals may have the ability to speak in two or more dialects, making them bidialectal. In possessing the skills to speak in more than one dialect, an individual may have some distinct advantages and may be able to function and gain acceptance in a greater number of cultural contexts. A large-city executive from an agrarian background may quickly abandon his three-piece suit and put on his jeans and boots when visiting his parents' home. When speaking with the hometown folks, he may put aside the standard English necessary in his business dealings and return to the hometown dialect that proves he is still the old country boy they have always known.

Likewise, an African American school psychologist who speaks standard English both at home and at work may elect to include some degree of black English in her conference with African American parents at the school. The vernacular may be used to develop rapport and credibility with the parents. This strategy may allow the psychologist to show the parents that she is African American in more than just appearance and that she understands the problems of black children and parents. She may choose, however, not to use as much of the dialect as the parents in order to maintain her credibility as a professional. On the other hand, in a conference with white parents, the same psychologist may choose to be scrupulously careful to speak only standard English if she feels that this is necessary for effective communication.

Children tend to learn adaptive behaviors rapidly, a fact that is often demonstrated in the school. Children who fear peer rejection as a result of speaking standard English may choose to use their dialect even at the expense of criticism by the teacher. Others may choose to speak with the best standard English they possess in dealing with the teacher but use the dialect or language of the group when outside the classroom.

Educators must be aware of the child's need for peer acceptance and balance this need with realistic educational expectations. Pressuring a child to speak standard English at all times and punishing him or her for any use of dialects may be detrimental to the overall well-being of the child.

Standard English

Although standard English is often referred to in the literature, no single dialect can really be identified as such. In reality, however, the speech of a certain group of people in each community tends to be identified as standard. Norms vary with communities and there are actually two norms, informal standard and formal standard. The language that is considered proper in a community is the informal standard. Its norms tend to vary from community to community. Formal standard is the acceptable written language that is typically found in grammar books. Few individuals speak formal standard English.

Since no particular dialect is inherently and universally standard, the determination of what is and what is not standard is usually made by people or groups of people who are in positions of power and have the status to make such a judgment. Teachers and employers are among the individuals who decide what is and what is not acceptable in the school and in the workplace.

Thus, people seeking success in school and in the job market often tend to use the standard language as identified and used by those in positions of power. Moreover, certain individuals may be highly respected in the community. Just as hairstyles are often influenced by people who are respected and admired, the language of those who are admired also serves as a model. Generally speaking, standard American English is a composite of the language spoken by the educated professional middle class. With the wide variations of dialects, there are actually a number of dialects of standard American English (Wolfram & Christian, 1989).

Perspectives on Black English

Black English, sometimes referred to as Vernacular Black English, is one of the best known and one of the most controversial dialects spoken in the United States. Its use is widespread; it is the primary form of communication for the majority of African Americans. It is the linguistic system used by working-class African Americans within their speech community (Owens, 1992; Fairchild & Edwards-Evans, 1990).

Woffard (1979) estimates that approximately 80 percent of African Americans use Black English consistently and another 19 percent of African Americans use speech that, with the exception of slight differences in vocal quality and pronunciation, is undistinguishable from standard English. The remaining one percent use other dialects.

Black English is considered by most linguists and African Americans to be a legitimate system of communication. It is a systematic language rule system of its own and not a substandard, deviant, nor improper form of English. While there are differences between Black English and standard English, they both operate to the same type of structural rules as any other type of language or dialect (Fairchild & Edwards-Evans, 1990). There is considerable overlap between Black English and Southern English and southern white nonstandard English. Much of the distinctiveness of the dialect is in its intonational patterns, speaking rate, and distinctive lexicons (Owens, 1992).

Teacher bias against Black English is common among majority group educators and among some African American educators as well. While Black English is an ethnically related dialect, it is also a dialect related to social class. Dialects that are related to lower social classes such as Hawaiian pidgin, Appalachian English, and Black English are typically stigmatized in our multidialectal society. As such, the use of these dialects without the ability to speak standard American English leaves the speaker with a distinct social, educational, and sometimes occupational disadvantage. Unfortunately many people attach relative values to certain dialects and to the speakers of those dialects. Stereotyped responses are often made to the speakers of those dialects (Owens, 1992). The refusal to acknowledge Black English as a legitimate form of communication may be considered Eurocentric. Insofar as teachers endorse this rejection, they are sending a message to many of their African

American students that the dialect of their parents, grandparents, and significant others in their lives is substandard and unacceptable.

Nonverbal Communication

Although most individuals think of communication as being verbal in nature, nonverbal communication can be just as important in the total communication process. Because it is so clearly interwoven into the overall fabric of verbal communication, nonverbal communication often appears to be inseparable from it. Samovar and Porter (1991) suggest that "nonverbal communication involves all those stimuli (except verbal stimuli) within a communication setting, generated by both the individual and the individual's use of the environment, that have potential message value for the sender or receiver" (p. 179).

Nonverbal communication can serve several functions. It conveys messages through one's attitude, personality, manner, and even dress. It augments verbal communication by reinforcing what one says. A smile or a pat on the back reinforces the positive statement made to a student. It contradicts verbal communication, as a frown accompanying a positive statement to a student sends a mixed or contradictory message. Nonverbal communication can replace a verbal message. A finger to the lips or a teacher's hand held in the air may communicate to a classroom that there is to be silence.

The total meaning of communication includes not only the surface message as stated (content), but also the undercurrent (emotions or feelings associated with that content). The listener should watch for congruence between the verbal message and that which is sent nonverbally, such as by body language.

There are a number of physical features that relate directly to nonverbal communication. These features themselves communicate messages, sometimes inaccurately, although much depends on the perceptions of the observer. When first introduced to an individual, people instinctively form some type of impression before any words are actually spoken. These first impressions are often communicated by features such as body build, height, weight, skin color, and other noticeable physical characteristics.

Often the impressions are functions of the observer's cultural background. Research has supported the contention that definite prejudices are based on body characteristics; for example, physical attractiveness plays a part in the way we perceive other people. Physical attractiveness is viewed by society as so important that billions of dollars are spent each year on clothing, cosmetics, hair grooming supplies, and physical fitness clubs and equipment. Even very young children tend to seek out attractive friends over less attractive playmates (Samovar & Porter, 1991). The study of nonverbal behavior is usually divided into three major areas: proxemics, kinesics, and paralanguage.

Proxemics

Proxemics is the language of social space. It is concerned with the spatial distance between people. Cultural variables affect proxemics. The normal conversational distance between white Americans, for example, is about twenty-one inches. A distance much greater than this may make the individuals feel too far apart for normal conversation and a normal voice level. Individuals of other cultural groups, such as Arabs, Latin Americans, and southern Europeans, are accustomed to standing considerably closer when they talk. In contrast to these contact cultures, Asians, Indians, Pakistanis, and northern Europeans have been identified as noncontact cultures. They may maintain a greater distance in conversation. In addition, there are differential distances maintained in cross-cultural relationships. White Americans tend to maintain a greater distance when conversing with blacks than when conversing among themselves. Women tend to allow a closer conversational space than do men. Straight students distance themselves farther from conversational partners they perceive to be gay (Samovar & Porter, 1991).

Among some cultural groups, physical contact is a common means of greeting. The English and French are separated by only twenty-one miles of water, yet there are vast differences in the way they greet their friends. A Frenchman may greet his male friends by kissing them on both cheeks. An Englishman, who typically avoids body contact, may avoid even a handshake.

At times, individuals protect their space by deliberately placing a barrier between themselves and those to whom they are speaking. A desk is an effective barrier. Moreover, a large chair behind the desk, in contrast to a smaller office chair on the other side, reinforces the individual's superior position.

Kinesics

Kinesics is the study of body language. It includes facial expressions, posture, gestures, and any other body movements that might carry some type of message. Body movements and gestures carry feelings and attitudes between people. The body language of students may tell the teacher whether what is being communicated is accepted or rejected. A student leaning forward in his or her seat may indicate receptiveness, whereas a student slouched in his or her seat with arms crossed could indicate rejection or boredom (Bull, 1983). However, the teacher should be careful not to assume that the student's body language means the same thing to both the student and the teacher. These responses are culturally determined and must be interpreted within the student's cultural context rather than the teacher's.

In some Asian cultures a bow takes the place of a handshake. However, a bow is much more complex than a handshake and conveys a deeper meaning. A person who holds a lower status must begin the bow and that person's bow must be lower than the other person's. When two individuals are of equal status, the bow is simultaneous and of equal depth.

Communication is more complex than the stated words. Hand movements, facial expressions, and distance between the speakers have different meanings in different cultures.

In the United States casualness may be viewed as an expression of friendliness. Slouching in a chair or when standing may be acceptable. In formal European cultures (e.g., German) such body posture in a conversation would convey rudeness and disrespect (Samovar & Porter, 1991).

Paralanguage

Nonverbal communication is not necessarily nonvocal. Often what is being said depends on the manner in which it is said. For example, the single word *yes* can carry a message of defiance, resignation, acknowledgment, interest, agreement, or enthusiasm. Vocal cues such as the rise or fall of the voice provide us with information with which we can make judgements about an individual's personality or emotional state (Samovar & Porter, 1991).

Paralanguage includes all production of sound that is vocal but nonverbal. It includes voice quality, ways of verbal expression, and sounds that are not verbal, such as laughing and crying. It is that which is communicated through sounds that are not contained in the words themselves (Samovar & Porter, 1991; Malandro & Barker, 1983).

There are two categories of paralanguage: vocalizations and vocal qualities. Vocalizations are sound and noises that are not words. Vocalizations are broken into three types: (1) vocal characterizers, which include sounds such as laughing, crying, sighing, and coughing; (2) vocal qualifiers, which include characteristics of sounds such as intensity (loud or soft) and pitch (high or low); and (3) vocal segregates, which are sounds other than words, such as *uh-huh, mmmm,* and *shhh.* Among African Americans, *um-huh-um-huh-um-huh-um-huh-um* may be used to express surprise, admiration, or total frustration, depending on the context in which it is used. *Uh-uh-uh-uh-h-h-h* and *um-m-m-m-m-m-uh* are similar expressions (Samovar & Porter, 1991).

Vocal qualities include resonance, tempo, articulation control, and rhythm control. These different characterizations of voice can be manipulated as one speaks to communicate various messages. Anger, for example, tends to be expressed by a faster rate of speech, louder volume, and higher pitch; sadness through slower speech, lower volume, and lower pitch (Malandro & Barker, 1983).

Vocal cues provide listeners with remarkable amounts of information; they can enable listeners to distinguish between male and female speakers, African American and white speakers, and older and younger speakers, as well as distinguishing educational level and area of residence within a certain dialect region. A speaker's social class and status can often be determined based on his or her vocal characteristics.

In any discussion of nonverbal behavior, there are inherent dangers. As examples are given, the reader must realize that these are gross generalizations, and it should not be assumed that any given behavior can immediately be interpreted in a certain way. Nonverbal communications are often a prominent part of the context in which verbal messages are set. Although context never has a specific meaning, communication is always dependent on context.

Educational Implications

Language is an integral part of life and an integral part of our social system. The diversity and richness of our language systems in this country are a reflection of the richness and diversity of American culture. The ability of American educators to recognize and appreciate the value of different language groups will to some extent determine the effectiveness of our educational system.

All children bring to school the language systems of their culture. It is the obligation of each educator to ensure the rights of each child to learn in the language of the home until he or she is able to function well enough in English. This may imply the use of English as a Second Language (ESL) or bilingual programs for limited English-proficient children. Equally important is the responsibility to understand cultural and linguistic differences and to recognize the value of these differences while working toward enhancing the student's linguistic skills in the dominant language. While it is important to appreciate and respect the child's native language or dialect, it is also important that the teacher communicate the importance and advantages of speaking standard English in certain vocational and social situations.

Language and Educational Assessment

There are few issues in education that are as controversial as the assessment of culturally diverse children. The problem of disproportionate numbers of ethnic minority children in special education classes for the handicapped has resulted from such assessment. The characteristics of language have a direct relationship to the assessment of linguistically different children. Many of the educational and intelligence tests used to assess ethnic and linguistic minority children use norms for children primarily from white, middle-class backgrounds. Thus, such tests are often biased against the minority student.

Most intelligence tests rely heavily on language, yet there may be little attempt to determine a child's level of proficiency in the language or dialect in which a test is administered. For example, a Hispanic child may be able to perform a task that is called for in an intelligence test, but may not be able to understand the directions given in English. Even if a Spanish translation were available, it might not be in a dialect with which the child is familiar. Using an unfamiliar Spanish dialect would place a student in an extreme disadvantage and might yield test results that are not a true indication of a child's abilities. The same may be true for Asians, African Americans, or Native Americans who are being tested. The refusal to acknowledge the importance of the value of linguistic differences has resulted in inadequate services and in the inappropriate placement of children through highly questionable assessment procedures.

In 1970, the class action suit *Diana v. the California State Board of Education* was filed in a federal court on behalf of nine Mexican American children from Spanish-speaking homes. The nine children had been placed in classes for children with mental retardation. Their diagnoses were based on IQ tests that relied heavily on verbal English, thereby ignoring the children's native language skills. In addition, test items were clearly biased against the chil-

Standardized testing is common in our schools and influences classes in which students are placed and colleges they can attend. At the same time, many tests are culturally and linguistically biased against students who are not from the dominant cultural group.

dren's cultural backgrounds. One question asked if it were better to pay bills by check or with cash. Since none of the children's parents had checking accounts, all selected cash (the incorrect response according to the key) as their answers. The court determined that there was inherent cultural bias in the tests that discriminated against the plaintiffs. The case was eventually settled out of court with stipulated improvements in testing procedures and reevaluation of Mexican American children already placed in classes for children with mental retardation.

Guadalupe Organization, Inc., v. Tempe Elementary School District No. 3 et al. (1972) was a suit filed in Arizona that resulted from the disproportionately high placement of Yaquii Indian and Mexican American children in classes for students with mental retardation. Placement had been based on the results of IQ tests given in English rather than in the children's native language. The out-of-court settlement required reevaluation of the students in these classes and testing in the primary language.

Dialects and Education

The issue of requiring a standard American English dialect in the schools is both sensitive and controversial. Since there is a close relationship between ethnic minority groups and dialects that are often considered nonstandard, this issue also has civil rights implications.

To require that standard English be spoken in the schools is considered discriminatory by some who think that such a requirement places an additional educational burden on the nonstandard-English-speaking students. As such, the insistence on standard English may hinder the acquisition of other educational skills, making it difficult for these students to succeed. It is argued that such practice denies the nonstandard-English-speaking students the same educational opportunities as others and thus morally, if not legally, denies them their civil rights.

Others argue that the school has the responsibility to teach each student standard English to better cope with the demands of society. There is little doubt that the inability to speak standard English can be a decided disadvantage to an individual in certain situations, such as seeking employment.

Dialect differences in the school may cause problems beyond the interference with the acquisition of skills. A second problem tends to be more subtle and involves the attitude of teachers and other school personnel toward students with nonstandard dialects. Too often, educators as well as other individuals make erroneous assumptions about nonstandard dialects, believing at times that the inability to speak a standard dialect reflects lower intelligence.

In a university classroom experiment by one of the authors, segments of two tape recordings in the area of language and culture were played. Neither speaker was identified; however, both are nationally prominent individuals in the field of linguistics. Both hold earned doctoral degrees, and both are from ethnic minority backgrounds. One individual speaks in standard English with no ethnic accent whatsoever. The other individual speaks in a combination of standard English and a slight trace of black dialect. His speech patterns leave little doubt that he is African American.

After the two tape segments were played, students were asked to indicate which of the two speakers in their opinion was the more intelligent. The class, which included a number of African American students, was unanimous in selecting the individual who spoke with the standard English dialect.

This simple classroom experiment suggests that most people have distinct preconceived notions about individuals who speak nonstandard English. If teachers and other school personnel react in this manner to students, the consequences could be serious. Students may be treated as less intelligent than they are, and they may respond in a self-fulfilling prophecy in which they function at a level lower than they are capable of. In cases where children are tracked in schools, they may be placed in groups below their actual ability level. This problem surfaces in the form of disproportionately low numbers of African American and Hispanic children being placed in classes for the gifted and talented (Office of Civil Rights, 1990). School administrators have cited the inability to appropriately identify these gifted and talented ethnic minority children as one of their biggest challenges. Teachers who have negative attitudes toward children with nonstandard dialects may be less prone to recognize potential giftedness and less inclined to refer these children for possible assessment and placement.

There are several alternatives for handling dialect in the educational setting. The first would be to accommodate all dialects, based on the assumption that they are all equal. The second would be to insist that only a standard dialect be allowed in the schools. This alternative would allow for the position that functional ability in such a dialect is necessary for success in personal as well as vocational pursuits.

A third alternative is a position between the two extremes, and it is the alternative most often followed. Native dialects are accepted for certain uses, but standard English is encouraged and insisted on in other circumstances. Students in such a school setting may be required to read and write in standard English, since this is the primary written language they will encounter in most work settings. They would not be required to eliminate their natural dialect in speaking. Such a compromise allows the student to use two or more dialects in school. It tends to acknowledge the legitimacy of all dialects while recognizing the social and vocational implications of being able to function in standard English.

The issue that seems to be at stake with some individuals who support the right to use nonstandard dialects is the recognition of the legitimacy of the particular dialect. Few, if any, will deny the social and vocational implications of dialects. Some parents may prefer to develop or have their children develop a standard dialect. However, the arrogant posture of some school officials in recognizing standard dialects as the only legitimate form of communication is offensive to many and may preclude rational solutions to this sensitive issue.

CONTROVERSIAL ISSUE

Some activists have suggested that the language of instruction should be in the dialect of students' cultures. Others argue that standard English should be the only acceptable language within the classroom. What are the advantages and disadvantages of both approaches? Do you think teachers should at least be familiar with the dialects used by students in the classroom? Why or why not? How do you plan to respond to different dialects in your classroom?

Second Language Acquisition

The annual arrival of immigrants to this country adds to the numbers of language minority students in our schools. Most of these students are able to move quickly from bilingual education programs to English-only instruction. Motivation is usually high. The acquisition of English skills serves both social and economic needs. Without linguistic acculturation, assimilation into mainstream society may be impossible. This in turn effectively closes the non-English speaking or limited English speaking out of many job markets.

The Role of First Language in Second Language Acquisition

Most children acquire their first language naturally through constant interaction with their parents or significant others. The knowledge of their first language plays an important role in the process of acquiring and learning a second language. Some concepts acquired through their first language (e.g., Spanish) can be transferred to a second language (e.g., English), when a comparable concept in the second language exists.

In the study of second language acquisition, various occurrences have been observed. When a limited English proficient (LEP) child's language development is interrupted or is replaced due to instruction in a second language in school prior to the development of his or her first language proficiency skills, the following may result: (1) a loss of first language (Lambert & Freed, 1982); (2) a mixing or combining of the first and second languages, resulting in the child's own unique (idiosyncratic) communication system (Ortiz & Maldonado-Colon, 1986); (3) limited proficiency in both first and second languages (Skutnabb-Kangas & Toukomaa, 1976); and (4) an inability to develop English language proficiency in their school years (Cummins, 1984).

The implications of these observed language behaviors suggest that LEP children should be allowed to develop a firm grasp of basic concept in their home language prior to the instruction of academic concepts in an English-only environment.

Language Proficiency

Cummins (1984) found that large numbers of LEP students failed academically after they had completed English as a second language (ESL) and were placed in monolingual English class settings. Many of these students were subsequently referred and placed in special education classes. In carefully studying the language characteristics of these students, Cummins found that in two years they were able to acquire adequate English communication skills to suggest to their teachers that they were adequately prepared to function in a monolingual English class placement. Cummins found, however, that the basic language skills, which he labeled "basic interpersonal communicative skills (BICS)," were inadequate to function in high-level academic situations. While two years was adequate for everyday conversational usage, an addition of five to seven years of school training was essential to develop the higher levels of proficiency required in highly structured academic situations. Cummins (1984) labeled this higher level of proficiency "academic/cognitive language proficiency (CALP)." Cummins's framework for conceptualizing language proficiency has been widely adopted by many ESL and bilingual special education programs and has profound implications for language minorities.

Bilingual Education

The language diversity that exists in the United States is naturally extended into the schools. In large urban and metropolitan school districts, there may be nearly one hundred different native languages spoken. Some students are bilingual in English and their native language. Others enter school speaking no English. Still others (2.26 million students) have limited English proficiency skills (OBEMLA, 1992). Further, it is projected that the number of students with limited English proficiency will continue to increase by as much as 35 percent by the end of this century (Council for Chief State School Officers, 1987). The challenge to provide an effective education for these students is met, in part, through the provision of bilingual education.

In 1974, a class action suit on behalf of eighteen hundred Chinese children was brought before the Supreme Court. The plaintiffs claimed that the San Francisco Board of Education failed to provide programs designed to meet the linguistic needs of those non-English-speaking children. The failure, they claimed, was in violation of Title VI of the Civil Rights Act of 1964 and the Equal Protection Clause of the Fourteenth Amendment. They argued that if the children could not understand the language used for instruction, they were deprived of an education equal to that of other children and were, in essence, doomed to failure.

The school board defended its policy by stating that the children received the same education afforded other children in the district. The position the board assumed was that a child's ability to comprehend English when entering school was not the responsibility of the school but rather the responsibility of the child and the family. In an unanimous decision, the Supreme Court stated that "Under state imposed standards, there was no equality of treatment merely by providing students with the same facilities, textbooks, teachers, and curriculum; for students who do not understand English are effectively foreclosed from any meaningful education" *(Lau v. Nichols,* 1974). Although the court did not mandate bilingual education for non-English-speaking or limited-English-speaking students, it did stipulate that special language programs were necessary if schools were to provide equal educational opportunity for such students. Hence, the Lau decision gave considerable impetus to the development of bilingual education.

In 1975 the Education for All Handicapped Children Act (amended in 1990 as Individuals with Disabilities Education Act) required each state to avoid the use of racially or culturally discriminating testing and evaluation procedures in the placement of children with disabilities. It also required that placement tests be administered in the child's native language. In addition, communication with parents regarding such matters as permission to test the child, development of individualized education programs, and hearings and appeals must be in the parents' native language.

Throughout the 1970s, the federal government and the state courts sought to shape the direction of bilingual education programs and mandate appropriate testing procedures for students with limited English proficiency (LEP). The Lau Remedies were developed by the U.S. Office of Education to help schools implement bilingual education programs. These guidelines prescribed transitional bilingual education and rejected English as a Second Language (ESL) as an appropriate methodology for elementary students. With a change of the federal administration in 1981, a shift to local policy decisions began to lessen federal controls. Emphasis was placed on the transition from the native language to English as fast as possible and the methodology for accomplishing the transition became the choice of the local school district. Thus, ESL programs began to operate alongside bilingual programs in many areas. While the future level of federal involvement in bilingual education is uncertain, there is little doubt among educators that some form of bilingual education is needed.

The definition of bilingual education that is generally agreed upon is "the use of two languages as media of instruction" (Baca & Cervantes, 1989, p. 24). Bilingual education has been supported, in part, by federal funds provided by the Bilingual Education Act of 1968 and reauthorized in 1974, 1978, and 1984. Hernandez (1989) reports that "federal policy encourages the establishment of programs using bilingual educational practices, techniques, and methods or of alternative instructional programs in school districts in which bilingual programs are not feasible" (p. 83).

Thus, federal legislation defines bilingual education more broadly than Baca and Cervantes. Methods other than the use of two languages are allowed and even encouraged. However, the Bilingual Education Act accounts for less than 10 percent of the total services provided to limited-English-proficient students (Secada, 1987).

Children who speak little or no English cannot understand English-speaking children or lessons that are presented in English. Not only are these children faced with having to learn new subject matter, but they must also learn a new language and often a new culture. It is likely that many of these children will not be able to keep up with the schoolwork and will drop out of school unless there is appropriate intervention. Approximately 45 percent of Mexican American children drop out of school before the twelfth grade, and the attrition rate of Native American students is as high as 55 percent. Although language differences may not be the sole contributor to the academic problems of these children, they are considered by many to be a major factor.

The primary goal of bilingual education is not to teach English or a second language per se, but to teach children concepts, knowledge, and skills in the language that they know best and to reinforce this information through the use of English (Baca & Cervantes, 1989). Two different philosophies currently shape programs in bilingual education: the transitional approach and the maintenance approach.

Transitional programs emphasize bilingual education as a means of moving from the culture and language most commonly used for communication in the home to the mainstream of American language and culture. It is an assimilationist approach in which the LEP student is expected to learn to function effectively in English as soon as possible. The native language of the home is used only to help the student make the transition to the English language. The native language is gradually phased out as the student becomes more proficient in English.

In contrast, maintenance bilingual programs provide a pluralistic orientation. The goal is for the LEP student to function effectively in both the native language and English. The student's native language and culture are taught concurrently with English and the dominant culture. The student actually becomes bilingual and bicultural in the process, with neither language surfacing as the dominant one.

Bilingual education can be justified as (1) the best way to attain maximum cognitive development for LEP students, (2) a means for achieving equal educational opportunity and/or results, (3) a means of easing the transition into the dominant language and culture, (4) an approach to educational reform, (5) a means of promoting positive interethnic relations, and (6) a wise economic investment to help linguistic minority students become maximally productive in adult life for the benefit of our society and themselves (Baca & Cervantes, 1989).

Whereas most bilingual educators favor maintenance programs, the majority of the programs in existence are transitional. Lack of trained personnel and the cost for maintenance programs are frequently cited for the predominance

PAUSE TO REFLECT

When there are only two native languages (e.g., Spanish and English) used by students in a school, bilingual programs conducted in both languages are appropriate. However, you may be assigned to a school in which there are a dozen languages used. What are the advantages and disadvantages to using different approaches to bilingual education? What approach do you think will be the most appropriate? What knowledge and experiences would help you prepare to work effectively with students from a number of different language groups?

of transitional programs. Bilingual educators, however, strongly support the use of bicultural programs even within the transitional framework. A bicultural emphasis provides students with a recognition of the value and worth of their family's culture and enhances the development or maintenance of a positive self-image.

Bilingual education is not without controversy. It is an issue that stirs the emotions of many people—as advocates or opponents. After analyzing letters to the editors of newspapers and testimony before Congress, Hakuta (1986) summarized the charges against bilingual education:

> That there is no historical precedent for bilingual education; that most existing programs follow the maintenance model; that there is no popular support for bilingual education; that young children learn a second language in a very short period of time, so not much time is lost if they are placed in English-only classes; that education in the native language takes away valuable time that would otherwise be spent in English; that bilingual education is not effective; and that the number of eligible students is far smaller than originally estimated. [However,] there is research evidence that bears on all these points, evidence with which all too few of those who voice their opinions are familiar. (p. 210)

In a telephone survey, Hakuta and his students sampled the attitudes toward bilingual education in New Haven, Connecticut. Seventy percent of the respondents had favorable attitudes. They were also able to identify three distinguishing characteristics of those individuals who were against bilingual education. "First, men were more likely than women to oppose bilingual education. Second, men and women aged fifty or older tended to be more opposed. And third, men and women who had grown up using a non-English language at home were more opposed" (Hakuta, 1986, p. 212).

The opposition to bilingual education is due, in part, to the open acknowledgment of the legitimacy of non-English languages (Hakuta, 1986). Some people believe that it threatens the dominance of English as the national language. As a result, local and state laws to support two languages for official business often become emotional issues in a community.

Parents of LEP students also vary in their support for bilingual and ESL programs. Recent immigrants usually place high priority on their children's learning English in school; less importance is given to studying the native language. In a study of Punjabis and Mexican American students in a California high school, Gibson (1988) concluded that:

> Immigrant minorities are less likely than involuntary minorities to favor bilingual education as an integral part of the regular instructional program of the public schools. . . . Those who equate an all-English curriculum with forced assimilation and Anglo conformity favor bilingual-bicultural education. These same groups tend also to be those that feel most exploited by the dominant group and that view majority-group teachers with suspicion. (194–195)

Even this observation should not be generalized to all subordinate and new immigrant group members. Ethnic groups differ in their support for bilingual education, and individual families within the group may have different opinions about what is best for their children. Educators must be attuned to the beliefs of the community as they decide what strategies will be most effective in serving LEP students.

Advocates of bilingual education see the advantages in being bilingual. Although bilingual education programs have primarily been established to develop English skills for LEP students, some offer opportunities for English-speaking students to develop proficiency in other languages. In its position statement on bilingual education, the American Association of Colleges for Teacher Education (1985) states:

> It is desirable for native English-speaking children to participate in bilingual instruction programs, too. . . . Two advantages of dual language proficiency in this case include the learning that there are other equally valid ways of expressing ideas, and the development of respect for students who speak a different language at home, in the country, and the world. (p. 5)

In addition, bilingualism provides an individual with job market advantages. As our country becomes less parochial, there are more business and other contacts with individuals from other countries, providing decided advantages to bilingual individuals. Nevertheless, the controversy will continue as the dialogue develops about how pluralistic the nation should be.

English as a Second Language

English as a Second Language (ESL) is a program often confused with bilingual education. In this country, the learning of English is an integral part of every bilingual program. But the teaching of English as a second language in and by itself does not constitute a bilingual program. Both bilingual education and ESL programs promote English proficiency for Limited English Proficiency (LEP) students. The approach to instruction distinguishes the two programs. Bilingual education accepts and develops native language and culture in the instructional process. Bilingual education may use the native language as well as English as the medium of instruction. ESL instruction, however, relies exclusively on English for teaching and learning. ESL programs are used extensively in this country as a primary medium to assimilate LEP children into the linguistic mainstream as quickly as possible. Hence, some educators place less emphasis on the maintenance of home language and culture than on English language acquisition, and they view ESL programs as a viable means for achieving their goals.

English-Only Controversy

In 1981, U.S. Senator S. I. Hayakawa, a strong and harsh critic of bilingual education and bilingual voting rights, introduced a constitutional amendment to make English the official language of the United States. The measure sought to prohibit federal and state laws, ordinances, regulations, orders, programs, and policies from requiring the use of other languages. Hayakawa's efforts seemed to be in support of English, but they were primarily against bilingualism. Had the amendment been adopted, Hayakawa's proposal would have reversed the efforts that began in the 1960s to accommodate linguistic minorities in this country. The English Language Amendment died without a hearing in the 97th Congress (Crawford, 1992).

In 1983, Hayakawa helped to found *U.S. English*, and began lobbying efforts resulting in a 400,000-member organization and an annual budget of $6 million. The movement—also referred to as "Official English" or "English Only"—has yet to come to a vote in Congress, but by 1990, it had been adopted as statutes or constitutional amendments in seventeen states (Crawford, 1992).

Official English has become a polarizing issue. William Bennett, Secretary of Education during the Reagan administration, leveled an attack on the Bilingual Education Act as "a failed path, a bankrupt course, and a waste of tax dollars." Bennett received considerable amounts of mail supporting his position. However, an examination of these letters by Crawford (1992) found that they contained little with respect to the education of non-English-speaking students. Instead the letter writers used the opportunity to vent their frustrations with illegal aliens on welfare, Asians and Hispanics overrunning communities, and other complaints such as the out-of-control birthrates of linguistic minorities. They were offended by the use of tax dollars to support what they viewed as the perpetuation of foreign language.

For the supporters of the English Only movement, English has always been the common language in this country. It is a means to resolve conflict in a nation with diverse ethnic, linguistic, and religious groups. English is an essential tool of social mobility and economic advancement (Crawford, 1992).

Individuals such as former Education Secretary Bennett cite failures in bilingual education itself (Bennett, 1992).

Opponents of the English Only movement readily agree on the importance of learning English. However, they view their adversaries as individuals trying to force Anglo-conformity by ending essential services in foreign languages. They view the attacks on bilingual education as unjustified because good bilingual education has been shown to be effective. Poor bilingual education, they concede, is ineffective; poor programs are seldom bilingual, except in name. Opponents of bilingual education, they argue, have seen to it that programs fail by giving inadequate support or resources to programs, by staffing programs with unqualified personnel, by obtaining faulty test results on bilingual education students by testing them in English, and by other means that cast negative outcomes on bilingual education (Fillmore, 1992).

The realities are that the numbers of language minority students are increasing dramatically in this country. States such as California, which have been in the forefront nationally in providing for the linguistic needs of students, are unable to recruit and train adequate numbers of bilingual and ESL teachers.

It is true that many of our earlier immigrants did not have the benefit of bilingual education programs. Thrust into sink-or-swim situations, many ended up swimming, succeeding in school and finding their niche in society. However, it is also true that many were unable to swim and sank in their efforts to acculturate in school. Our numbers of language minority students today are greater and we cannot afford massive numbers of students who would end up sinking if thrust into sink-or-swim situations. Cummins's (1984) (see section on language proficiency) research suggests that educators may very well unwittingly thrust students (at the basic interpersonal communications skill level) into academic settings where they are over their heads linguistically and prone to failure.

Sign Language and Education

Historically, most students who are deaf have been segregated from hearing students for their schooling experiences. Most states support one or more residential schools for students who are deaf. However, PL 94-142 (the Education for All Handicapped Children Act) calls for exceptional students to be mainstreamed into regular classrooms rather than being segregated in their own schools or classrooms. Because the residential schools have traditionally served as the place where American Sign Language (ASL) is learned and where the deaf culture is developed, there is concern among individuals who are deaf that the movement to mainstream them into regular classrooms may seriously hamper the transmittal of the culture (Reagan, 1988).

The major controversy in deaf education is between the use of an oral approach and the use of a manual approach. In the oral approach, students learn how to speak. Signing is used in the manual approach, but it is usually not ASL and is combined with speaking English. During the nineteenth century, sign language was used as a means of instruction. At the turn of the century, the oral approach took precedence and students were not permitted to sign in or out of the classroom. During the civil rights movements of the 1960s, the oral approach began to be replaced again by a manual approach (Neisser, 1983). Total communication is now the predominant means of communicating with and instructing severely hearing impaired students in the United States. Those who practice total communication speak and sign (including finger spelling when necessary) simultaneously.

With the shift to mainstream deaf students into regular classrooms, more teachers will have students with hearing impairments in their classes. It will be important to become aware of the silence in which these students live and to develop strategies to make them an integral part of the class. Strategies could include helping all of the students learn about deafness and manual ways to communicate with each other. The culture of the deaf should be valued and extended into the classroom as much as possible. Paternalistic treatment should be avoided.

Nonverbal Communication in the Classroom

Cultural differences in appropriate nonverbal communications between students and teachers can be very frustrating to both. To begin to overcome such differences, the teacher must try to analyze particular nonverbal communications when students, especially those who are from a different cultural background, are not responding as the teacher expects. What teachers sometimes perceive as inattention on the part of the student, or interruptions by the student at times considered inappropriate by the teacher, or even a tendency on the part of the student to look away from the teacher while being addressed may in fact be cases of miscommunication.

Too frequently, we jump to the conclusion that the student is not showing us respect when in fact he or she is simply not following the informal rules of classroom etiquette. In most school settings, students from subordinate groups are expected to become bicultural and adopt the nonverbal communication patterns of the dominant group while in school. A more positive approach to avoiding miscommunication would be for teachers also to learn to operate biculturally in the classroom.

Erickson (1979) suggests that teachers should reflect on what is occurring in the classroom when communications are not as expected. The first step is to "become more aware of what the nature of the trouble is" (p. 122). In the school setting, students should have access to teachers, counselors, or administrators who are from a culturally similar background. Teachers, meanwhile, could learn in a recipe fashion what the cultural cues of students mean and react appropriately. However, a more effective approach is to be able to analyze what is happening in the classroom and to respond based on what is known about the student and his or her cultural background.

Summary

The Lau decision of 1974 ensures non-English-speaking children the right to an appropriate education that meets their linguistic needs. Even with a legal mandate, appropriate services may not always be delivered because of lack of tolerance or insensitivity to language or dialects other than that which is considered standard English. Because nonstandard dialects tend to have a negative stigma attached to them, some educators may refuse to view them as legitimate forms of communication. While they may indeed be legitimate forms of communication and may serve the speaker well in certain contexts, the use of nonstandard English dialects may preclude certain social and vocational opportunities.

Bilingual education has both its supporters and its detractors. Through proper educational programming, however, children with limited English proficiency can have the education to which they are entitled.

Questions for Review

1. How is language a function of culture?
2. Explain why American Sign Language is considered a language parallel to English, German, Chinese, etc.
3. What are the advantages of being bilingual in the United States? How is bilingualism encouraged and discouraged within most educational settings?
4. What are dialects? What factors generally determine whether an individual becomes bidialectal?
5. Why is Black English a controversial issue in education? How should it be handled in the classroom?
6. Why is it important to be sensitive to nonverbal communications between the teacher and student and among students?
7. Why is it unwise to assume that a student is ready for academic instruction in English as soon as he/she has some basic English conversational skills?
8. Contrast maintenance and transitional bilingual education. Which do you think is more appropriate? Why?
9. When might the English as a Second language approach be the most appropriate strategy to use in a classroom?
10. What are some of the issues in the English Only/U.S. English Controversy?
11. What changes in your teaching methodology should you make when a deaf student is in your classroom? What changes should you make when you have a student or students whose native language is not English?

References

American Association of Colleges for Teacher Education. (1985). *Educating a profession: Bilingual education.* Washington, DC: Author.

Baca, L. M., & Cervantes, H. T. (1989). *The bilingual special education interface.* New York: Merrill/Macmillan.

Baratz, J. (1968). Language in the economically disadvantaged child: A perspective. *ASHA, 10,* 145–146.

Bennett, W. (1992). Bilingual education: A failed path. In J. Crawford (Ed.), *Language loyalties.* Chicago: University of Chicago Press.

Bull, P. (1983). *Body movement and interpersonal communication.* New York: Wiley.

Chinn, P. C. (1985). Language as a function of culture. *Social Education, 48*(5), 101–103.

Council for Chief State School Officers. (1987, December). *Model interdepartmental state education agency strategies to meet the educational needs of limited English proficient students: Project summary.* Participant's Notebook for the conference on "Improving the Educational Achievement of Limited English Proficient Students."

Crawford, J. (Ed.). (1992). *Language loyalties.* Chicago: University of Chicago Press.

Crystal, D. (1987). *The Cambridge encyclopedia of language.* Cambridge, England: Cambridge University Press.

Cummins, J. (1984). *Bilingualism and special education: Issues in assessment and pedagogy.* San Diego, CA: College Hill Press.

Erickson, F. (1979). Talking down: Some cultural sources of miscommunication in interracial interviews. In A. Wolfgang (Ed.), *Nonverbal behavior: Applications and cultural implications* (pp. 99–158). New York: Academic Press.

Fairchild, H. H., & Edwards-Evans, S. (1990). "African American dialects and schooling: A review." In A. M. Padilla, H. H. Fairchild, and C. M. Valadez (Eds.), *Bilingual education, issues and strategies.* Newberry Park, CA: Sage Publications.

Fillmore, L. W. (1992). Against our best interest: The attempt to sabotage bilingual education. In J. Crawford (Ed.), *Language loyalties.* Chicago: University of Chicago Press.

Gibson, M. A. (1988). *Accommodation without assimilation: Sikh immigrants in an American high school.* Ithaca, NY: Cornell University Press.

Hakuta, K. (1986). *Mirror of language: The debate on bilingualism.* New York: Basic Books.

Heath, S. B. (1983). *Ways with words: Language, life, and work in communities and classrooms.* New York: Cambridge University Press.

Hernandez, H. (1989). *Multicultural education: A teacher's guide to content and process.* New York: Merrill/Macmillan.

Heward, W. L., & Orlansky, M. D. (1992). *Exceptional children* (3rd ed). New York: Merrill/Macmillan.

Lambert, R., & Freed, B. (Eds.) (1982). *Loss of language skills.* Rowley, MA: Newbury House.

Lau v. Nichols, 414, U.S., 563–572. (1974, January 21).

Malandro, L. A., & Barker, L. (1983). *Nonverbal communication.* Reading, MA: Addison-Wesley Publishing Co.

Neisser, A. (1983). *The other side of silence: Sign language and the deaf community in America.* New York: Knopf.

OBEMLA. (1992). *Condition of bilingual education in the nation. Report to Congress and the President.* Washington: Office of Bilingual Education and Minority Language Affairs.

Office of Civil Rights. (1990). *1988 Elementary and secondary civil rights survey.* Washington, DC: Government Printing Office.

Ortiz, A. A., & Maldonado-Colon, E. (1986). Reducing inappropriate referrals of language minority students in special education. In A. C. Willig and H. F. Greenberg (Eds.), *Bilingualism and learning disabilities: Policy and practice for teachers and administrators.* New York: American Library Publishing Co.

Owens, R. E., Jr. (1992). *Language development.* New York: Merrill/ Macmillan.

Reagan, T. (1988, Fall). Multiculturalism and the deaf: An educational manifesto. *Journal of Research and Development in Education, 22*(1), 1–6.

Samovar, L. A., & Porter, R. E. (1991). *Communication between cultures.* Belmont, CA: Wadsworth.

Secada, W. G. (1987). This is 1987, not 1980: A comment on a comment. *Review of Educational Research, 57*(3), 377–384.

Skutnabb-Kangas, T., & Toukomaa, P. (1976). *Teaching migrant children's mother tongue and learning the language of the host country in the context of the socio-cultural situation of the migrant family.* Helsinki: The Finnish National Commission for UNESCO.

Spencer, D. (1988, May). Transitional bilingual education and the socialization of immigrants. *Harvard Educational Review, 58*(2), 133–153.

U.S. Bureau of the Census. (1990). *Language spoken at home and ability to speak English for U.S. regions and states: 1990.* Washington, DC: U.S. Department of Commerce (CPH-L133)

Woffard, J. (1979). Ebonics: A legitimate system of oral communication. *Journal of Black Studies, 9*(4), 367–382.

Wolfram, W., & Christian, D. (1989). *Dialects and education, issues and answers.* Englewood Cliffs, NJ: Prentice Hall Regents.

Suggested Readings

Baca, L. M., & Cervantes, H. T. (1989). *The bilingual special education interface.* New York: Merrill/Macmillan.

An excellent overview of bilingual special education. Contains basic but important information on general bilingual education, including litigation and legislation related to the rights of children with limited English proficiency.

Crawford, J. (Ed.) (1992). *Language loyalties.* Chicago: University of Chicago Press.

An excellent treatment of the "Official English/English Only" controversy. Contains essays, speeches, and articles for and against the "Official English" issue. Includes articles supporting bilingual education and articles against it.

Owens, R. E., Jr.(1992). *Language development.* New York: Merrill/Macmillan.

An excellent overview of language development including language differences.

Samovar, L. A., & Porter, R. E. (1991). *Communication between cultures.* Belmont, CA: Wadsworth Publishing Co.

An excellent treatment of language and culture. Includes chapters on intercultural communication and the communication of the nonmainstream group.

Wolfram, W., & Christian, D. (1989). *Dialects and education, issues and answers.* Englewood Cliffs, NJ: Prentice Hall Regents.

An excellent overview of dialects in a question-and-answer format. Answers questions such as, "What is a dialect?" "What are the main differences between dialects of English?" and "What are the consequences of dialects in education?"

CHAPTER 8

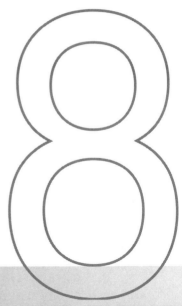

Age

Crystal Rossi wears two streaks of bright magenta in her hair. They hang, stains of Kool-Aid, down her loose, long strands of blonde like a seventh grader's twist of punk: "Don't come too close. Don't mess with me. Don't tell me what to do. I'm not like you."

At her Brooklyn public school, a kaleidoscope of teenage rage, Crystal's teachers see a young girl with an attitude. They focus on her slouch, her Kool-Aid streaks, her grunge clothes and sullen anger and see all the signs of trouble. But those vivid slashes say the most, communicating a basic paradox of adolescence, the double-edged message: "bug off" and "LOOK AT ME."

This is the time, this tender age of twelve, when every major decision on the treacherous road to adulthood looms. It is also the time, in the sixth and seventh grades, when some students start a long, slow fall away from school. (Manegold, 1993, p. A1)

Age and Culture

Each individual who lives long enough will become a part of every age microculture. Without choice, we must all go through the various stages in life and eventually join the ranks of the elderly. Like other microcultures, we feel, think, perceive, and behave in part because of the age-group to which we belong. Although many adolescents behave differently from one another, the way they think, feel, and behave is at least partly because they are adolescents. At the same time, age does not stand alone in affecting the way a person behaves or functions. Ethnicity, socioeconomic status, religion, and gender interact with age to influence an individual's behavior and attitudes.

Adolescence is perhaps one of the most challenging times in the life of the individual and the family. It is a long transitional period (six years or so) during which the individual is "suspended" between childhood and adulthood. During adolescence, emancipation from the primary family unit is the central task of the individual. It is a difficult period for the young person, who is attempting to be free from the role of a child but is not fully equipped to assume the responsibilities of adulthood.

In some cultures, entry into adulthood begins immediately after childhood. In these cultures, adolescence as a stage of behavioral development does not exist. However, in Western culture, an individual is seldom allowed or expected to make an immediate transition from childhood to adulthood. It is interesting to note that the anticipated state of extreme disequilibrium associated with adolescence and the period of "storm and stress" does not exist in some cultures in which adolescence does not exist. Cultural definitions of the role of the adolescent along with social attitudes have created a number of circumstances that cause this period of life to be what it is in our Western culture.

There has been speculation that the behavioral turmoil associated with adolescence in Western cultures is related to the physiological changes that take place within the individual during this period. However, studies have provided little support for this contention. Rather, the changes that take place are gradual and fluctuate little on a day-to-day basis. These changes may contribute to the problems of the adolescent, but do not by themselves cause the problems associated with thirteen- to eighteen-year-olds.

To many, the adult years represent the best years of their lives. To others, it is a time of important decision making coupled with stress and sometimes pain. Young adults are faced with some of the greatest decisions they will ever make in their lives. Decisions must be made regarding the possibility of education beyond high school. Vocational choices must be determined. If the individual chooses to marry, the critical decision of choosing a mate must be made, as well as the decision of whether or not to have children.

Physical vitality, the excitement of courtship, marriage, the birth of children, and career satisfaction can bring considerable pleasure to individuals during this period of life. At the same time, unwise choices in education or vocation, along with frustration in courtship and failure in marriage, can bring frustration and grief. To many of America's poor, adulthood brings to them the reality that they are among the disenfranchised in this country. If they are among the minority groups frequently targeted for discriminatory practices, life can be particularly difficult. Lack of financial resources may make the reality of a higher education elusive. Good jobs are particularly difficult to find since preference is often given to majority group individuals and to individuals from more favored minority groups. During a recession, these individuals tend to be the most affected, suffering from abject poverty, unemployment, poor living conditions, and little likelihood of escape from their life. Frustration and anger appear to be inevitable along with an intense feeling of impotence.

The Baby Boomers

The "baby boomers," 76 million strong, are likely the most influential cohort group in the United States. Born during the post-WWII years, between 1946 and 1964, the oldest of this group are now in their mid- or late forties. Together, the "boomers" set the moral and political tone of the country as well as family styles and career patterns (Roof, 1990). President Bill Clinton and Vice President Al Gore and their spouses are part of this group, as are many of the advisors who surround them. Many of the boomers are in, or approaching, their professional prime and as such are able to exert considerable influence on others.

As the most educated cohort group in the history of this country, 85 percent of baby boomers have high school degrees and 36 percent have completed college. This is the generation that was surrounded by the civil rights movement, the issues related to the Vietnam War, and the changing moral, sexual, and familial values associated with the countercultural years.

The boomers are divided into two age-groups. Those who were born in the late 1940s tend to form a group different from those in the early 1960s. The older group experienced or witnessed the freedom marches, the Kennedy assassination, and the Vietnam War. They participated in or witnessed the political turmoil of the period. The younger group experienced less social unrest and is more likely to have been impacted by the gasoline shortages of 1970 and the incidents at Three Mile Island and Chernoble, and may as a group be more prone toward inwardness (Roof, 1990). Members of this group may have been more a part of the "me generation" of the 1980s than the older boomers.

Whereas many of the boomers dropped out of church involvement for two or more years, 43 percent of the older and 38 percent of the younger boomers have returned to active involvement. The younger boomers tend to be more religious with respect to personal faith and practice. As a group they adhere to traditional Judeo-Christian beliefs and practices more than the older group.

This group voted for George Bush in greater numbers and considers themselves more as political conservatives and hold more traditional views on moral issues than the older group (Roof, 1990).

More of the older boomers, than most Americans, tend to endorse alternative religious beliefs, believe in reincarnation, practice meditation and view other religions as equally viable alternatives to their own. Because more of this group is married and have children, they tend to be involved with religious institutions to a greater extent. Roof (1990) suggests that while married persons with children tend to be more involved with religious activities, the opposite is true for married individuals without children. They tend to have lower levels of religious involvement, and have views sometimes characterized as more liberal than singles, on views such as the legalization of marijuana and abortions, and acceptance of alternative lifestyles.

It is apparent that the social and political views of one's youth often leave an indelible imprint on the individual, often affecting one's attitudes, beliefs, and religious involvement. In addition, these attitudes and experiences are communicated to *their* children. As a result, these beliefs are likely to become evident in our schools.

The Baby Busters

After the baby boomers—the "busters"! Forty-one million in number and born between 1965 and 1976, this cohort group has been tagged the "baby busters" or the "X Generation." While the average number of babies born during the 1946 to 1964 baby boomer years was 4 million a year, the average number of children born each year during the buster years was 3.4 million.

Susan Mitchell (1993) of American Demographics describes the busters as resentful of the baby boomers. These young adults feel that the boomers had a party and didn't clean up their mess. They ran the country into a huge deficit, created job scarcity, and the 1993 college graduates faced one of the worst job markets in recent years. As the baby busters entered the job market, they found themselves competing not only among themselves, but with previous graduates who had not yet found jobs and others laid off from their jobs.

While many of the boomers, particularly the younger ones, have faced financial hardship in recent years, they generally remain optimistic that they will do as well, if not better, than their parents. Twenty percent of the 1984-1990 college graduates have jobs that do not require a college education. There have been fewer jobs opened in the 1990s requiring a college education than in the 1980s. As the number of college graduates increases, the result may be as many as 30 percent of college graduates underemployed or unemployed. High school graduates entering the job market today make less than their counterparts in 1979 (Mitchell, 1993).

Born into a more diverse world, the busters tend to be more accepting than older Americans in matters related to ethnicity, national origin, family structure and lifestyle. They have grown up in an age of AIDS, latchkey kids, divorce, economic decline, and increased violence. They realize that danger is always present and stability may be difficult to come by (Mitchell, 1993).

Politically, nearly 50 percent of the busters identify themselves as independent compared to only 38 percent of the rest of the Americans. They are often more liberal on social issues than those who are older—including the boomers. They are less likely than others to support book bannings from libraries or firings of gay teachers. They tend to be accepting of interracial dating and have a more positive view of the women's movement. They are more likely than other Americans to support affirmative action for minorities (Mitchell, 1993).

As a group, the busters were counted on more heavily by Bill Clinton than by George Bush in the 1992 presidential election; the efforts apparently paid off for Clinton that year. The youngest of the busters, as well as the oldest of the post-buster group, will be eligible to vote in the 1996 elections. Since 1977, the national birth rate has averaged 3.7 million per year, a rate higher than that of the buster group. Therefore, in the next two decades the busters and post-busters combined will have the potential for considerable impact on the nation's political focus.

As individuals mature in age, they will eventually move through a number of different age-groups, and as such, they will become members of different microcultures. As individuals join new age-group cultures they bring with them other aspects of culture, such as ethnicity, socioeconomic status, and gender. As these various cultures interface with one another and blend their individual unique qualities, they add to the rich pluralistic nature of American society.

Development of Ethnic Identity

Aboud (1988) defines ethnic awareness as a "conscious recognition of ethnicity in individuals or groups. . . . being able to assign correctly the labels to the actual faces or pictures of various people indicates a basic form of perceptual ethnic awareness" (p. 6). Among young children, ethnic awareness and prejudice tend to increase with age. At some point prejudice may decline, while ethnic awareness may remain high. While it may be necessary for a child to be aware of ethnic differences before he or she can develop prejudice, ethnic awareness in itself is not bad in a child. Attempts to discourage children from noticing that people are different, that they have different pigmentation, different hair and eye colorization, or that they speak differently denies an accurate perception of reality in children (Aboud, 1988). Unprejudiced children are also aware of differences, but respond differently to them.

To be able to recognize differences in others, a child must also be able to be involved in self-identification, as the child must be aware of what he or she is like before recognizing how other children differ. Children as young as three are able to identify with others of the same color or racial group (Aboud, 1988). There is also evidence that three-year-olds can respond to different skin pigmentation (Morland, 1972). By three or four years of age, white children tend to have positive associations with the color white and with white individuals. Minority group children tend to be more sensitive to racial cues and develop racial awareness earlier than their majority group peers (Katz, 1982).

At four and five years of age, a significant number of children (about 75 percent) are able to correctly identify ethnic groupings. By ages six and seven, children are able to make the identification at close to 100 percent accuracy. Some minority group children demonstrate an early preference for whites. Similarly, some white children indicate a preference for minority group children (Aboud, 1988).

Prejudice

After years of work in improving race relations in this country there was growing optimism as we moved into the 1980s and 1990s that the United States had turned the corner on race relations. However, the hate crimes and racial violence that have emerged in recent years have served to remind us that the ugly head of racism has not been defeated. While we as educators expect to see racism among adults and, to some extent, adolescents, we are sometimes shocked and often dismayed when it is evidenced in the behavior of young children. In spite of the overall improvement in race relations and the lower level of prejudice among parents, the level of prejudice among young children ages four to seven has not declined in the last forty years and continues to remain high.

It is often assumed that children who hold biased attitudes toward other groups are simply reflecting their parents' attitudes. People assumed that children who are prejudiced were taught these attitudes by their parents. In analyzing the available research on children and prejudice, Aboud (1988) has concluded that such assumptions are unjustified. Children who are under the age of seven are often more prejudiced than their parents and often do not adopt the open and unbiased attitudes of their parents. Children who are over the age of seven are influenced by their parents to a greater extent than when they were younger, but the influence does not rest solely from the parents. Parents, unaware that the accusations of parental influence are unjustified, are defensive about any suggestions that their child is prejudiced. They are, therefore, resistant to suggestions to confirm the child's prejudicial attitudes and to attempt intervention.

Variables Affecting Attitudes and Prejudice

One of the proposed theories of prejudice in children is a *social reflection theory*. This theory suggests that the prejudice we see in children is a reflection of the values of society. Research studies have, in general, shown that the higher status groups of society are preferred by both white and minority children. Whites are typically members of the higher status groups. Where there is social stratification in a community, young children develop negative attitudes toward the lower status groups. This tends to be true even if the parents hold positive or open attitudes toward minority groups who are typically a part of the lower status groups (Aboud, 1988).

As children grow older, usually around age seven or eight, major cognitive changes develop and attitudes are often altered. Many white children become less prejudiced around this age and more neutral toward their own group. At the same time, many minority group children develop a more positive attitude toward their own group. After the age of seven, children are influenced more by their parents' attitudes and the racial mix in their school. Aboud (1988) suggests that a critical change takes place in the prejudice in children around the age of seven when they reach Piaget's (1932) concrete operational ways of thinking. Prior to age seven, when they are at Piaget's preoperational stage, their cognitive limitations may preclude a full understanding of the basis of ethnicity and the individuals who make up ethnic groups. Aboud (1988) states that, "the prejudice of four- to seven-year-olds is qualitatively different from the prejudice of seven- to twelve-year-olds" (p. 22). From four to seven years of age, children are egocentric and are unaware of ethnic groups. Preferences tend to be based on random personal considerations. At ages seven to ten, Aboud suggests that children become sociocentric instead. At this stage, the focus is on their own group rather than solely on themselves. This focus, Aboud suggests, tends to prevent them from understanding other groups. Rather, other groups tend to be recognized in ways that contrast with the child's own group. At ages ten to fifteen, children are usually able to distinguish among other groups. At this stage, they are capable of accepting the validity of different perspectives.

The available research suggests that if children adopt the ethnic attitudes of their parents, it is usually after the age of seven. Aboud (1988) suggests that parents who are characterized as prejudiced are often authoritarian in their child-rearing practices and tend to use more punitive strategies in ensuring their status as parents while creating hostility in their children. Parents with these characteristics tend to produce prejudiced children. It has been theorized that such parental practices instill low self-esteem in children as a message is conveyed to them that they are bad. The children, in turn, project their negative qualities onto others (minorities) who are the object of their parent's attacks. Bagley's two studies found authoritarian prejudiced fathers having prejudiced children with low self-esteem. These children selected friends who were also prejudiced (Bagley, Mallick, & Verma, 1979; Bagley, Verma, Mallick, & Young, 1979). Whether or not this theory is viable as a variable in the development of prejudiced behavior, it does raise concerns about child-rearing practices.

PAUSE TO REFLECT

Students in your kindergarten class made several prejudiced comments about the characters of color in a storybook that you read to them. How would you respond? What activities should you introduce to help the students deal with their biases? How would you handle a similar situation if the students were teenagers?

Since prejudice appears to be somewhat prevalent among young children (ages four to seven), and since children are cognitively capable of becoming less prejudiced, it would appear to be very appropriate to develop activities that have been shown to reduce prejudice (e.g., Katz & Zalk, 1978; Bowers & Swanson, 1988) during the early years of elementary school. This is a time when some children may choose to be influenced by prejudiced parents or by their peers. Schools should intervene at this stage and exert their influence through programs that foster socially acceptable behaviors.

Peer Influence

During infancy and the earliest years of childhood, children's companions are most likely to be parents, siblings, other close members of the family, and children in the immediate neighborhood. As the child's first social group, the family plays an integral part in the establishment of attitudes and socialization skills. The family, therefore, greatly influences how the child perceives and relates to other groups in the ensuing years.

The middle childhood years mark a change in the focus of socialization. The influence from the school and peers begins to predominate. The shift is neither sudden nor complete. For those attending day care and preschool programs, the change begins earlier. The influence of the family remains significant throughout childhood, but the focus shifts from the immediate family to the school setting, where peers form a microcultural setting. The peers at this point become a dominant source of influence of lifestyle, dress habits, speech patterns, and standards of behavior and performance. Peer group standards become vitally important, and an effort is made to conform. Acceptance by the peer group becomes paramount, even above that of family acceptance. This is often a trying time for children, who must cope with peer group pressures that may be incongruent with the standards in their home. Success or failure in meeting peer group standards may be judged more harshly than previous judgments made in the home environment. The devastation that comes from not being accepted by the group may be the most severe that children have experienced. On the other hand, the feelings of success that come from achieving group approval are powerful and gratifying.

This period may be a difficult time for an immigrant family. Children seeking peer acceptance may wish to become more acculturated than what is considered acceptable by parents seeking to maintain traditional cultural values. The conflicting values may emanate from the teachers as well as from peers. It is not uncommon to find children at this level resisting the language of the home as well as family values related to dress and behavior. During this period, children begin to identify with significant adults in their lives who serve as role models. This identification allows children to strengthen, direct, and control their own behavior in such a manner that it approximates the behavior of those they hold in esteem. Children often choose as role models individuals of the same sex who have similar physical traits, often their mother or father. Identification may also be with the parent of the opposite sex, or they may adopt other adult models with whom they can identify.

Children in their middle childhood tend to develop a code of behavior based on their perceptions of right and wrong, justice, and fairness. As they begin to try out their developing behaviors, they may find that it is contrary to that deemed acceptable by the family but congruent with the values of their peers. Clothing and hairstyles are typically influenced by the peer group. Small, close-knit groups of friends are formed, and nonmembers (both children and adults) are usually excluded. Group standards of loyalty and behavior are clearly delineated, and any members who violate the standards may be severely criticized and even excluded.

Children in this age-group begin to recognize socioeconomic differences. While the choice of friends may or may not be a function of socioeconomic levels, the type of playmates available may be. With the exception of the children transported away from their neighborhood schools, most children in their earlier years attend schools that are somewhat homogeneous in terms of socioeconomic level. Neighborhood playmates are even more homogeneous. During this period, however, an increasing awareness develops regarding the differences in material possessions found in different homes. The child begins to understand what is meant by rich and poor.

Children in their late childhood (ages nine to eleven years) are usually quite adjusted to the change from family-oriented activities to peer-oriented activities. The peer group has considerable influence on attitudes, desires, and behavior—an influence that increases as children grow older. Children in this age-group are not prepared to abandon parental control. Although they may complain about parental restrictions, they need and want the security of parental authority to assist them in coping with the ever-expanding problems of their environment.

The late childhood period is also characterized by the formation of cliques. The peer group provides a sense of belonging. The effects of exclusion from the peer group may be devastating. Children who fail to make entry into some group may enter adolescence without some of the necessary socialization skills and may be branded as misfits. Younger children who are unable to gain full entry into the peer group tend to hang around the periphery of the group—watching, learning, and practicing skills, and participating whenever they are allowed to or deemed worthy. Often, as children get older, full participation rights are granted.

Because children tend to have a strong need *not* to be different, group structure may be intolerant of those who are different. Children with disabilities, children who are ethnically different, or children who do not conform to group standards may be excluded from membership. While group identification and association are important to children's socialization process, there are some inherent problems. Peer pressure may induce behaviors that violate their personal standards. Smoking, drinking alcoholic beverages, experimenting with drugs, stealing, and engaging in sexual activity have often been initiated by peer group pressure. Not only do some of the behaviors involve risks of personal health and safety, but they also result in emotional trauma for both parents and children.

Three factors continually impact children as microcultural groups are established. Gender, ethnicity, and socioeconomic status interface with other variables and often determine what the nature of the microcultural group will be. Among some children, religion, exceptionality, and language may determine the choice of friends and composition of their peer groups. In Utah, for example, the Mormon church exerts considerable influence over social as well as religious life. As such, peer groups or cliques may form in which religious background is an overriding element in determining membership. One clique may consist of children who are all of Mormon background, whereas another peer group may consist of all non-Mormon children.

In childhood and adolescence, peers begin to be a dominant source of influence on social behavior, sometimes causing alienation from parents and other family members.

In some instances, children with disabilities may be treated somewhat like younger children in terms of peer group membership. This is more likely to be true of children with mental retardation than of children with other disabilities. If they are not totally excluded from peer group membership, they, like younger children, may remain on the periphery, watching and participating if they are allowed. However, unlike younger children who eventually gain entry as they get older, children with mental retardation may remain on the periphery indefinitely, because advancement in chronological age is not likely to be accompanied by commensurate advancement in social skills.

Language may also be a factor in either exclusion from or formation of peer groups among children. Children with limited English proficiency may be excluded from peer group participation. Other children may form cliques with Spanish or nonstandard English as a criteria for membership. In some instances, the peer group may influence members regarding language patterns. Children who talk in nonstandard English may work diligently toward developing standard English skills if standard English is valued by the peer group. Conversely, the peer group may reinforce the use of a dialect and devalue the use of standard English.

Alienation from Family

Alienation is disturbing to families, to adult members of the community, and to the adolescents themselves. In their efforts to achieve autonomy, sexual functioning, and identity, some adolescents think that they must turn away from the family. There is considerable ambivalence, since young persons are usually unprepared to yield family support systems in the quest for independence. As adolescents assert their rights to assume adult behaviors, there is sometimes an inability to assume complementary adultlike responsibility. Recognizing this, parents are understandably reluctant to grant them adult privileges, further adding to the alienation.

Many young people reach a higher level of education than their parents. Most parents support the intellectual and educational development of their children and often encourage their children to achieve a higher level than they did. Parents may find that their children sometimes develop the typical "intellectual" approach, viewing as worthy only the most vital aspects of life (as defined by them). They develop an attitude of superiority, looking down on anyone (including their parents) who, in their opinion, has a more mundane view of life. Often, neither parents nor children are able to comprehend the developing dynamics. Rejection and lack of communication develop. Problems can also develop if the parents are high achievers and if family and social pressure is present for the children to achieve in the same manner. If these standards cannot be met, alienation may result.

When family values are incongruent with those of adolescents' peer groups, the family standards may then be rejected to maintain peer group acceptance. Many adolescents, therefore, reject the validity and desirability of their family expectations. They view their family standards as wrong. If they do not meet the family standards, they do not consider themselves as failures, because it is not possible to fail if the standards are wrong in the first place.

Some ethnic minority adolescents can have unique problems. They may become alienated from society if they recognize the inequities of our social system as they relate to minority groups. They see how their parents have been unable to achieve, and they may become angry for their parents and for what they feel is in store for themselves. At times, parents assume a more passive acceptance of the social system or do not share in the same degree of frustration as their children. This difference in attitude or perception may alienate these children from their parents as well as from society.

As the adolescent shifts emotional ties from the family to peers, there may be a restructuring of the parent-adolescent relationship. Parents may be viewed more objectively. Parents may become more concerned about peer influence as they have increasingly less interaction with their child (Newman & Newman, 1986). These changes have the potential for turning the period of adolescence into one of dissonance and alienation from parents and other members of the family. However, one need only observe a few adolescent-family situations to realize that the degree of dissonance and alienation varies greatly.

The attitude of the parents may contribute to the alienation. Parents who expect problems with their children in the adolescent period sometimes fall into the trap of a self-fulfilling prophecy. Their expectation of alienation generates a hostile attitude on their part. This attitude is quickly sensed by the adolescents, and a vicious cycle is started. On the other hand, parents who have confidence in their children may promote a feeling of confidence and trust. These children often develop sufficient self-confidence to resist peer pressure when it is appropriate.

Sexuality

During adolescence, physical development occurs to the point of sexual competence. This can be a difficult time for young persons, particularly if sexual development is either early or late. According to Gispert (1981), "Biologically, sexual maturation occurs at an earlier chronological age than in previous generations, while the sociological period of adolescence has been extended upward into the twenties by prolongation of studies, financial dependence on parents, and the trend toward marriage at a later age" (p. 32a). Menstruation often begins at age twelve for girls. Fourteen was once the typical age of onset; however, each decade, the onset has dropped by an average of three months. Meanwhile, women have been delaying marriage. The typical age of a first marriage for women is now twenty-five—up from twenty-one in the 1950s. This has given females an additional four years of sexual maturity prior to marriage (Gibbs, 1993).

A major psychological task facing adolescents is the integration of their perceptions of their developing bodies with their desire to develop their femininity or masculinity in the context of the expectations of their parents, peers, and society. There is no doubt that adolescents are, as a group, sexually active. In 1982, 19 percent of fifteen-year-old girls were sexually active. Today, 27 percent of girls that age are sexually active, as are a third of the boys. Sixty-one percent of sexually active teenage girls have had multiple partners. By age twenty, three-fourths of American youth have been sexually active.

Twenty percent of the AIDS patients in this country are under the age of thirty. Because the incubation period for AIDS is eight or more years, the Centers for Disease Control believes that many were infected as teenagers (Gibbs, 1993). While the threat of the AIDS virus may now inhibit the sexual activity of some adolescents, it is apparent that this group is still sexually active. Some teens take a fatalistic view on AIDS and seem to be willing to take their chances. Some believe that there will be a cure for AIDS before they will contract it and die from it. Others have indicated that with the streets so violent, they will either be killed or incarcerated by the time they are twenty, so they might as well take their chances (Gibbs, 1993). While studies show that AIDS awareness tends to be high among adolescents, they persist in engaging in high-risk sexual behavior (Sidel, 1990).

Today's adolescents operate in a social environment that is considerably more liberal and permissive in sexual attitudes than that of their parents. Adolescents are continuously exposed to sexually oriented material in the media, with movies, television, and newspapers presenting the more permissive and liberal views. Gibbs (1993) suggests that with teenagers watching an average of five hours of television a day, they are exposed to thousands of sexual encounters on the screen each year. One study found 65,000 references to sexual behavior in one television season in the three major television networks alone (Sidel, 1990). Peers may also encourage adoption of liberal views. On the other hand, parents may continue to hold the more conservative views of their generation.

When adolescents adopt liberal attitudes toward sexual behavior and their parents maintain conservative attitudes and values, dissonance and alienation are inevitable. Unable or unwilling to turn to their parents, and often lacking adequate sex education at school, adolescents may turn to their peers for support. Although they may be able to provide sympathetic understanding and support, the peers often are neither knowledgeable nor able to respond in an objective manner. The lack of appropriate information and knowledge may explain why half of all the illegitimate births in the United States involve adolescents.

Sex education and school clinics that provide information on sexuality and birth control can provide adolescents with the background to deal with their increased sexual awareness. They can, however, be a source of considerable controversy, and parents in some communities may resist these efforts or endeavors. This is an issue which may see conservative Protestants joining forces with Catholics as was the case in New York City where the Chancellor was dismissed for his stand on condom distribution and the effort to teach students about gay lifestyles.

In an attempt to combat what they believe to be moral decay in this country, conservative parents, educators, and religious groups have provided the impetus for the *abstinence-only* movement. Advocates of this movement teach that sex outside of marriage is wrong. They believe that sex education that teaches young people about birth control or abortion encourages immoral behavior and leads the young down the path of self-destruction. This movement has had considerable success in having their approach adopted as official curriculum throughout the United States. With roots in the Reagan presidency period, the abstinence-only movement has considerable finances to develop classroom materials. The curriculum tries to help teens to understand pressure situations and provide alternatives to having sex on dates. Even if individuals have been sexually active, they are encouraged to stop and wait until they are married (Elmer-Dewitt, 1993).

Because the movement disapproves of sexual activity and is concerned that birth control discussions will only encourage illicit behavior, such information is conspicuously absent from the curriculum. Proponents argue that the program works. For those who do adhere to it faithfully, it is naturally the most effective means to protect a teen against venereal disease or pregnancy. Further, proponents argue that those who study the curriculum have a substan-

CONTROVERSIAL ISSUE

Educators and communities disagree on the distribution of information about sexuality and birth control to students both inside and outside of schools. Recommendations about how to handle these issues range widely. Three dominant strategies include:

(1) Providing no instruction or counseling in helping students understand their sexuality.
(2) Including sex education, including information about AIDS and birth control, in the school curriculum.
(3) Establishing birth control clinics in or near the school with professionals available for counseling and distributing information and birth control devices.

What are the arguments for and against each strategy? What factors must be considered by educators before the implementation of the second and third strategies?

tially lower pregnancy rate. Critics of these statistics question their accuracy. Critics also question the accuracy of the materials used for instruction. They assert that there are incorrect statements or outright falsehoods in the materials. Other criticisms center around the fact that some of the instructional materials were originally religious tracts which have been rewritten to replace specific references to "God" and "Jesus" (Elmer-Dewitt, 1993).

Opponents further argue that in communities where teens are very active sexually, abstinence-only curricula are unlikely to change behaviors. Critics contend that the failure to provide information on birth control and AIDS prevention is irresponsible on the part of officials who know that teens are at risk for unwanted pregnancy or AIDS infection. It is self-evident that abstinence is 100 percent effective to those who adhere to it. In communities where abstinence is socially reinforced, it may have some merit as a curricular approach. In communities where sexual activity is viewed as socially appropriate and encouraged by peers, the task of convincing adolescents to adhere to abstinence may be formidable. Cranston (1992) suggests that adolescents need a comprehensive health education program. Young people, he contends, need to have a broad understanding of personal health and wellness, particularly of related high-risk behaviors. This should be a planned and sequential approach to a broad range of health issues and should be included across all grade levels. However, he advises that the self-esteem of our young people underlies this approach. Young people cannot be expected to choose healthy behaviors if they do not have a strong sense of personal worth (Cranston, 1992).

Crises Faced by Students

Growing up is a dangerous time for many students. Safety is one of the concerns often expressed by students today. School sometimes is the only safe haven for them. They suffer from child abuse at home, worry constantly about attacks from others enroute to and from school, and are often tempted with drugs and gang membership. It is a difficult period that they hope to survive.

Child Abuse

Child abuse is a tragedy faced by an increasing number of the nation's students. In 1985, there were nearly two million reports of various types of child maltreatment reported in the United States (American Humane Association, 1987). This represented an increase of over 1.5 million cases reported since 1976. Child abuse or maltreatment is usually categorized as physical abuse, physical neglect, sexual abuse, and emotional abuse.

Physical abuse refers to nonaccidental injury inflicted by a caretaker. There is often a fine line between discipline through physical punishment and physical abuse. In the United States physical punishment is commonplace in many families as a child-rearing practice. Few states have prohibitions against corporal punishment in schools. Some state statutes consider corporal punishment as abusive if bruises are visible after twenty-four hours. Others view an act as abusive if the individual intends to harm the child. Physical indicators include unexplained bruises and welts, unexplained burns, unexplained fractures, and unexplained lacerations and abrasions (Tower, 1992).

Physical neglect involves the deliberate neglect or extraordinary inattentiveness of a child's physical well-being. Parents can be cited for neglect when older siblings are forced into child-care responsibilities. With the lack of extended families nearby, immigrants and single parents are sometimes caught in this dilemma. However, when older siblings too young to provide responsible care are placed in that position, by law, it is considered neglect. Children who suffer from neglect may exhibit poor hygiene, may be inappropriately dressed for weather conditions, or may suffer from hunger. Children who suffer from neglect may have medical or dental needs that have not been attended to. In addition, the religious practices of some religious groups can come into conflict with the law with regard to parental decisions to use the religion's group practices for addressing illness and refusing conventional medical care. The courts have, in some instances, intervened and overturned parental rights when children were considered to be at extreme risk.

Sexual abuse refers to the involvement of children or adolescents in sexual activities which they do not comprehend, or to which they are unable to give informed consent. It also includes practices that violate the social mores of one's culture as they relate to family roles. Sexual abuse is usually found in familial abuse or incest; extra-familial molestation, or rape; exploitation through pornography, prostitution, sex rings or cults; or institutional abuse (e.g., day care centers, etc.).

Children who are sexually abused may become withdrawn or secretive. Some may do poorly in school. However, some abused children may use school as an outlet and may actually excel. They may cry without provocation, may be anorexic or bulimic, and may attempt suicide (Tower, 1992).

Children who are emotionally abused are chronically belittled, humiliated, rejected, or have their self-esteem attacked. Emotional abuse is a pattern of psychologically destructive behavior (Garbarino, Guttman, & Seeley, 1986). Children who are emotionally or psychologically abused may exhibit a low self-esteem by continually demeaning themselves. Some become self-destructive through the use of drugs or may become anorexic or suicidal. While some children exhibit withdrawal behaviors, others may exhibit destructive behaviors. Some, attempting to demonstrate their worth, may become overachievers. These children may also exhibit problems with asthma, hyperactivity, or ulcers (Tower, 1992).

The reasons why individuals become child abusers are numerous and are too extensive to elaborate in this brief section. They do include parents who were themselves abused as children, individuals who suffer from low self-esteem, and individuals who are themselves suffering from psychological disorders (Tower, 1992). Abusive behavior can have a long-lasting effect on a child. The scars may persist into adulthood.

Child abuse is everyone's problem. It is the responsibility of each teacher to report known or suspected cases of child abuse to their school supervisor. The supervisor, in turn, is responsible for reporting these problems or concerns to professionals mandated by state and federal laws to bring the matter to the attention of appropriate protective agencies. These professionals are referred to as "mandated reporters." Every state has mandated laws requiring the reporting of child abuse. State laws differ in that one state has no penalties for failure to report while the others impose fines and even jail terms. Some states stipulate that there must be a report if there is suspicion of abuse; others state that there is to be accountability for failure to report if there is "reasonable cause to believe." Beyond the legal mandates, educators have a professional and ethical obligation to make reports to protect innocent children from abuse.

Adolescent Suicide

One of the most alarming developments in adolescent behavior is the dramatic increase in teenage suicides. Every day, an average of eighteen young Americans kill themselves—5,000 to 6,500 a year. Every hour, fifty-seven children and adolescents try to take their own lives. On an average, one succeeds every 80 minutes. There are well over 1,000 attempts each day. Since 1950, there has been a 300 percent increase in adolescent suicides. Only accidents and homicides exceed suicide as a cause of adolescent deaths, and many of those deaths are suspected suicides (Gelman & Gangelhoff, 1983; Griffin & Felsenthal, 1983; Guetzloe, 1989; Sidel, 1990).

While the United States once had a low rate of suicide among young people, the rate among young males is now among the highest in the world (Hendin, 1985). The statistics we have reported here are considered by researchers as inaccurate and understated (Guetzloe, 1989; Pffeffer, 1986). The number of reported suicides is probably less than half the actual number (Jobes, Berman, & Josselsen, 1986). This underreporting may be in part due to attempts to protect the family from the social and religious stigma associated with suicide. Consequently, many suicides are reported as accidental deaths (Hawton, 1986).

The increase in the adolescent suicide rate is due primarily to the increase in suicides among young males. By 1980, the ratio of male suicides to females was five to one. Most of the male victims are white (89 percent). While the suicide rate for males in other racial groups has also increased, it has remained lower than that of whites (Centers for Disease Control, 1986). The suicide rate for white males fifteen to nineteen years of age has been slightly over twice that of black counterparts. The rate of white females of the same age is higher than that of their black counterparts.

In 1983, a teenager in a Dallas suburb was killed in an accident. Within eight weeks, the accident victim's best friend took his own life, and two others did the same. In an eight-month period, there were sixteen suicide attempts by adolescents and young adults between the ages of thirteen and twenty-four in this community. The following year, four teenagers in a Houston suburb took their lives in a one-week period. Six killed themselves in a two-month period.

Numerous theories have been advanced for the adolescent suicide phenomenon. Among the reasons offered is the decline in religion, the breakup of the nuclear family, and the competitiveness in school (Gelman & Gangelhoff, 1983). The most common emotion felt by suicidal individuals is depression (Miller, 1975). Because of their youth and lack of experience in making accurate judgments, depressed adolescents are more prone to respond to the suggestion of suicide than an adult (Hyde & Forsyth, 1978).

Adolescent depression is a function of a wide range of situations, perhaps involving failure, loss of a love object, or rejection. It can also be a function of biochemical imbalances in the brain (Hipple & Cimbolic, 1979). The loss of a parent through death, divorce, separation, or extended absence has been cited as a possible variable in adolescent suicides (Ray & Johnson, 1983). Less than 38 percent of this country's children live with both natural parents. Strong, stable support systems are unavailable to many children (Gelman & Gangelhoff, 1983). The loss of a parent may be viewed as parental rejection, which may lead to feelings of guilt in the adolescent (Ray & Johnson, 1983). Some mental health professionals attribute adolescent suicide to the widespread availability and use of both legal prescription and illegal drugs. Some believe that the tightening of the job market and the bleak prospects for the future among the less affluent is another contributing variable (Sidel, 1990).

The Dallas suburb where the 1983 suicides took place has all the trappings of an ideal suburban community. Middle- to upper-level management and high-tech professionals occupy the community's many expensive homes, attracted by the community's good schools and low crime rate. Many of the community's teenagers have their own expensive cars. A closer look, however, provides some interesting statistics. Among its 90,000 residents in 1983, there were about 1,000 divorces a year. Of the residents, 82 percent had lived there less than ten years, 59 percent for four years or less. Almost everyone and everything there was new. There were few roots in the community.

Alienation in the family is cited as another major contributor to adolescent suicide. Where family ties are close, suicide rates are low; where families are not close, suicide rates tend to be high (Wenz, 1979). Adolescent suicide victims come from all socioeconomic backgrounds, but many are from middle- and upper-income homes. The parents in these homes are generally high-achieving individuals, and they expect similar behaviors from their children. Failure to conform to parental expectations may lead to alienation. There are, of course, many other causes of family alienation. Guetzloe (1989) lists the following risk factors that may be related to youth suicide: biological factors, psychiatric disorders, family problems, environmental and sociocultural factors, and factors related to learning and cognition.

No single variable or factor can be identified as the cause of adolescent suicide. However, adolescent suicide is an apparent response to the frustrations of life, and in the attempted suicides, it is a possible cry for help or a call to attention to the adolescent's profound problems. As Griffin and Felsenthal (1983) suggest, suicides are cries for help that have backfired, and which others can heed or help.

Substance Abuse

The use of harmful substances, primarily by children and adolescents, has been one of the most problematic areas faced by parents, schools, and law enforcement agencies in the past two decades. It will inevitably continue to be a major problem in the 1990s. The problem is a national phenomenon, and many of the problems of adult substance abuse have their roots in adolescence.

Numerous problems related to substance abuse affect the community. Intravenous drug users are one of the high-risk groups of Acquired Immune Deficiency Syndrome (AIDS). The spread of this virus among adolescents had, by 1990, already exceeded expectations. In many cities, drug-related gang violence has led to the deaths of hundreds of adolescents. To support their drug use, many adolescents and adults have resorted to criminal activities.

Another major result of adolescent substance abuse has been the physical and mental effects on embryos and fetuses carried by pregnant adolescent drug and alcohol abusers. There is also increased risk of accidental deaths among infants when parents are involved in substance abuse. Whereas some infant deaths are reported as accidents rather than being linked to drug use, they are often the result of negligence or violence related to the parents'(often adolescents themselves) substance use and reduced capacity to provide appropriate care (Cormerci, 1986).

In adolescence and early adulthood, over half the motor vehicle fatalities are associated with alcohol abuse. Prom time almost always portends an increase in the number of traffic deaths resulting from drinking. Many deaths are also likely associated with other drug use (Cormerci, 1986).

The use of harmful substances among adolescents has reached alarming proportions. A 1992 University of Michigan study of 50,000 American youths reported that among eighth-graders, the use of drugs had increased from the previous year. Among those thirteen-years-olds, 9.5% (up from 9%) used inhalants such as glue, solvents, etc.; 7.2% (up from 6.2%) smoked marijuana; and 2.1% (up from 1.7%) used LSD. There were, however, some encouraging findings. Drug use had actually decreased that year among high school seniors. For example, marijuana use had decreased from 23.9% to 21.9%. Researchers credited the decrease to the anti-drug messages presented in schools and on television (Time, 1993). Actual usage may be higher or lower in specific communities or schools.

These substances are used to produce altered states of consciousness. The adolescents who use them often seek relief, escape, or comfort from stress related to the prolonged and intense period of their life. The social institutions to which the adolescent must relate, including the family and particularly the educational system, may be perceived as unresponsive or openly hostile. Their inability to focus on long-range goals, their desire for immediate gratification, and their lack of appreciation for the consequences of their behavior may contribute to some adolescents' use of substances (Millman & Khuri, 1981). The use of "psycho-active drugs remains one of the few pleasurable options for many adolescents; it may be a predictable, reliable method to punctuate an otherwise unrewarding life" (p. 740).

The media, particularly television, in both commercials and programming, have tended to glamorize the use of substances such as alcohol. Children and adolescents who see entertainment and sports personalities promoting the use of beer, wine coolers, and so forth, tend to be influenced by what they think is "cool" behavior (Cohen, 1985). Some are obviously influenced by peers, using drugs to gain perceived acceptance. Others are sensation-hungry risk-takers. After trying drugs for the first time, an adolescent may be drawn to repeated use by the dreamy state of altered consciousness, by the excitement, by heightened acuity, or by feelings of power and confidence. For some, the presumed benefits may come from visual hallucinatory experiences or a sexual sensation (Whaley & Wong, 1987).

There are two broad categories of adolescent drug users: the experimenters and the compulsive users. The experimenters make up the majority. A few progress from experimenters to compulsive users. While most experimenters will eventually abandon such use, the fear of progression to compulsive use is a serious concern of parents and authorities. Recreational users fall somewhere in between experimenters and compulsive users. For them, alcohol and marijuana are often the drugs of choice. Their use is primarily to achieve relaxation, and use is typically intermittent. However, for a few, the goal is intoxication, and these recreational users pose a threat to themselves and others (Whaley & Wong, 1987).

Whaley and Wong (1987) suggest that there are four groups of adolescents who are involved in substance abuse:

Social group: These individuals are involved and motivated by social reasons. They are usually members of the same social group, and use tends to be intermittent.

Escapist group: These individuals view the use of substances as a means to escape from feelings of anger and depression. Escape, however, is only temporary, and the problems remain unresolved.

Punitive group: A small group of adolescents see the use of substances as a way of striking back at parents and others. If they are arrested, then others will also experience the suffering that they themselves feel.

Self-destructive group: These individuals are particularly dangerous to themselves. Their behavior flirts with death, which sometimes becomes a reality either deliberately or accidentally.

The use of alcohol and drugs by adolescent males tends to exceed that of females. Gender ratios, however, vary with the type of substance. The use of amphetamines, for example, has been slightly higher among female high school seniors than among males. Gender differences in the use of tobacco has declined in recent years, as evidenced in the increasing rate of lung cancer among females. Racial differences in drug use tends to be small except for heroin use, which is two to three times more prevalent among blacks than among white adolescents. On the other hand, whites tend to be more involved in alcohol use than African Americans. Rates of substance abuse tend to be higher in metropolitan areas (Spiegler & Harford, 1987).

The abuse of legal drugs usually precedes the use of illegal drugs. Three distinct stages of adolescent exposure and experience with drugs have been identified as (1) alcohol and tobacco use, (2) marijuana use, and (3) use of other illicit drugs (Spiegler & Harford, 1987).

The relationships between parents and their adolescents tend to have a bearing on the use of substances. For example, closeness to parents was found to have a positive correlation to moderate teenage drinking compared to heavy drinking. Drinking behavior was found to be less problematic among adolescents who reported similar interests and expectations as their parents. It has consistently been found that adolescents are more likely to drink and use drugs if their parents do (Fawzy, Coombs, & Gerber, 1983). Consequently, children of alcoholics are at high risk of developing alcoholism (Spiegler & Harford, 1987).

While it has been shown consistently that adolescents demonstrate drug use behaviors similar to those of their friends, peer influences are more important for certain substances than others. Use of both marijuana and alcohol is better predicted by the behavior of friends than is the use of other illicit drugs.

The problem of substance abuse is a national crisis and a national tragedy. It is a complex problem that deserves more attention of educators than the brief coverage here. The problem can and must be dealt with through the home, school, and law enforcement authorities, as well as through social agencies and responsible media.

Gang Membership

Juvenile gang activity in the United States can be documented as far back as the mid-1800s. The general public has always known of their existence, but it was only in the 1970s and 1980s that gangs came to the forefront of public awareness. Prior to the 1970s, gang activity and violence tended to impact only those in their immediate communities. Middle-class white Americans had little to concern themselves about with respect to street gangs. However, by the 1970s, and especially by the 1980s, gang organization became more sophisticated and their activities began to impact a wider range of individuals (Drowns & Hess, 1990; Kratcoski & Kratcoski, 1990).

Miller (1983) lists five characteristics that distinguish today's street gangs. First, gang leadership tends to be clearly defined and identifiable. Second, these gangs tend to be better organized. Third, bonds are stronger and more continuous. Fourth, "turf" claims on locations or facilities are made by the gangs. Finally, the gangs are involved in some form of illegal activity.

For many of the gang members, their affiliation with a gang is their means of achieving status in a community. The gangs themselves acquire power in a community by their involvement in violent behavior and the fear such behavior generates (Drowns & Hess, 1990). Today's street gangs are typically well-armed. For many, AK-47 assault rifles are the weapon of choice. With weapons such as these, drive-by shootings have become commonplace among gang members struggling for turf, avenging an insult, or in retaliation for a rival gang's previous assault. These drive-by shootings claim almost as many innocent bystanders as intended victims. In cities such as Los Angeles, the number of innocent bystanders injured or killed each year is in the hundreds. Acts of violence such as these generate public fear and give gangs power in the community.

Gang membership is usually structured by race or nationality. Most visible among these gangs are Hispanic, black, and Asian gangs, and Jamaican posses. Hispanic gangs tend to operate out of barrios, or lower-income neighborhoods, and are some of the older gangs in existence. Some gang members belong to the same gangs that their fathers did before them. Among the best known gangs are the African American gangs, the "Bloods" and the "Crips." The Crips began in the Los Angeles area as high-school-age youth who extorted money from classmates and were involved in other violence. The Bloods are the primary rivals of the Crips. Both gangs have extended well beyond Los Angeles, spreading as far north as Alaska and as far east as Washington, D.C., making inroads in communities across the country.

Some Chinese and Vietnamese communities have Asian gangs. Among the Chinese gangs, the Yu Li, Joe Boys, and Wah Ching are the most prominent. Asian gangs are by their own choice less visible, but are capable of the same levels of violence as the other ethnic gangs. They have also spread across the United States and Canada (Drowns & Hess, 1990; Dannen, 1992).

Gang members are identifiable by their clothing, communication, graffiti, and tattoos. Bloods and Crips often wear bandannas on their heads. The color of the Bloods is red; the Crips, blue. Clothing may identify individuals as a gang member. For some gang members, an identifying piece of clothing may be oversized pants or jackets and sweatshirts with gang names. Tattoos on the hands, arms, and shoulders are common among Hispanic gang members, but are not usually displayed by African American gang members. Hand signs identify an individual with a specific gang.

Graffiti used by gangs can provide a considerable amount of information. African American gang and Hispanic gang graffiti differ. Black gang graffiti often contain profanity and other expressions absent from Hispanic gang graffiti. Hispanic gangs have graffiti with more flair and attention to detail. Gangs use the graffiti to state a claim to territory, or turf. If the graffiti is crossed out and new graffiti written, another gang is challenging the former's claim to the turf. Through careful observation, law enforcement can determine the sphere of influence that a gang has. Graffiti indicate where the gang has unchallenged influence, and where in the community challenges begin and by whom.

In inner-city schools, gang members may be involved with student extortion and teacher intimidation. Violence occasionally erupts on school campuses. The presence of several gang members in the same class may be intimidating to teachers as well as to other students. Discipline in such classes may be a considerable challenge. In addition, many gang members are involved in the sale and distribution of cocaine and crack cocaine. This has spread across the country and the fight for drug turf—the territory on which a gang has exclusive rights to sell drugs—is the cause of much of the violence. The emergence of street gangs over the past two decades has become a major challenge for educators. In some instances, schools have become scenes of violence resulting in the installation of metal detectors and security guards. If law enforcement officers are unable at this time to stem the growth of gang violence, it is unlikely that educators are any better equipped to do so. Somehow society has failed in providing better alternatives than gang membership. Perhaps that is a challenge for education.

Interaction of Class, Ethnicity, and Age

With one-fourth of our nation's children living below the poverty level, the effects of poverty are often manifested in the schools. In some areas of the country (e.g., southern California), the cost of living is so high that even some of those who technically live above the poverty level are not realistically able to develop a standard of living different from those technically living in poverty in many other regions. Many of these children suffer from inadequate housing, supervision, nutrition, and medical care. Many of their homes have inadequate heat or cooling, which affects their sleep and physical well-being. Homes are often old and in neighborhoods where residents live in fear of their personal safety.

Dolan (1989) indicates that many of the nation's poor children are living in homes or areas where they are vulnerable to lead poisoning. Lead is found in the dust and chippings from the leaded paint on walls in older homes, in automobile exhaust fumes, and in emissions from industry. One-fifth of the children examined were affected by lead poisoning, which often leads to irreversible neurological impairment manifested in learning disabilities, mental retardation, and behavioral problems.

See the box "The Example of Los Angeles" that illustrates the result of the interaction of oppressed minority groups, poverty, and oppressed youths.

THE EXAMPLE OF LOS ANGELES

On April 29, 1992, the verdicts for the first Rodney King trial were handed down for four police officers charged with beating Rodney King in Los Angeles. The jury found all defendants innocent on all but one of the charges. On that one charge of assault, the jury reported that they were hopelessly deadlocked on the question of guilt of one of the officers.

Within hours, news of the verdicts unleashed a fury on Los Angeles that no earthquake, flood, or any natural disaster had every accomplished with the City of Los Angeles. When the calm finally came after three days of rioting, burning, and looting, the toll was staggering and unprecedented in United States history. The tally sheet (*The Los Angeles Times*, 1992) read:

Deaths	58
Injuries	2,383
Arrests	17,000
Fire Calls	10,000
Property Damage	$1 billion

The riot following the announcement of the verdicts in the Rodney King trial was a riot waiting to happen. The King incident, the subsequent trials, verdicts, and the riot were all symptoms of deep-seated problems which plague Los Angeles and many of the country's inner cities. An examination of some of the historical events leading up to the L.A. riot may serve to explain the roots of some of this civil unrest.

In the 1950s thousands of people migrated to southern California from around the country. The promise of good weather and jobs brought a constant stream of people. Between the 1940s and 1950s, the African American population had doubled to 461,000 in southern California. By the 1960s, most of the African Americans were living in south-central Los Angeles because of poverty and/or discrimination. Living conditions were generally poor, but better, for the most part, than they were in places from which the people had moved. Discrimination against African Americans was commonplace. There were many hotels and clubs exclusively for whites. Blacks arrested by the Los Angeles Police Department were routinely harassed and brutalized, shouted at, and insulted (*The Los Angeles Times*, 1992).

In schools in Watts, a section of south-central Los Angeles inhabited primarily by African Americans, test scores were extremely low compared to those of the predominantly white schools. Los Angeles prided itself in its excellent freeway system. The mass transit system, which was utilized primarily by poor minorities, was neglected, and is considered woefully inadequate by those who must use it. (*The Los Angeles Times*, 1992). In spite of the many problems faced by African Americans in Los Angeles, there were still jobs available. There was Bethlehem Steel, Firestone Tire Company, Goodyear Tire Company, and General Motors. There were aerospace companies and there was the defense industry. As might be expected, the best jobs often went to whites, but some African Americans were able to obtain good jobs, buy homes, and send their children to college.

In 1964, the unemployment in south-central Los Angeles was ten percent, double the rate of other parts of Los Angeles. In that year riots broke out in New York, Pennsylvania, Illinois, and New Jersey. The following year, 1965, on a hot August evening, a young African American man was arrested in Watts for speeding and reckless driving. A scuffle broke out with the police. The man's mother and brother were arrested, and the Watts riot began. A commission was appointed to determine the causes of the riots. It found high unemployment, poor public schools, police brutality, poor living conditions, and poor public transportation (*The Los Angeles Times*, 1992).

In the 1970s more immigrants began pouring into southern California. They came from Mexico to escape poverty, Central America to escape war, and Southeast Asia to escape the communist takeover. Chinese came from Hong Kong and Taiwan, Koreans and Filipinos came in mass. All of the new immigrants added to the competition for jobs and affordable housing. In 1977 the Goodyear plant closed.

The 1980s were troubled years for many in Los Angeles. While the wealthy became wealthier, the poor seemed to become poorer. In 1980 the Firestone plant closed and it was followed by the closing of Bethlehem Steel in 1982. By the late 1980s the average price of a home in Los Angeles County was approximately $250,000, out of the reach of most, and dashing the hopes of home ownership for many. Rent prices, except for the housing projects and slum-like apartments, were also more than most could afford.

Few of the major supermarket chains elected to maintain businesses in south-central Los Angeles and Korean immigrants began opening convenience stores there. Because of their relatively low volume of business compared to the supermarkets, the Koreans charged more for their goods. They made much of their profit in alcohol sales. Because the crime rate was high and holdups were common, Koreans shop owners began arming themselves. With limited English skills, many of the Koreans had difficulty in communicating with African Americans, so they hired other Koreans, whom they could communicate with, to work for them. Seeing the Koreans leaving each night to go to their homes outside of south-central L.A., the African Americans viewed the store owners with suspicion. The Koreans, they felt, took all of their money out of the community and gave nothing in return.

In March 1991, an amateur cameraman caught the Rodney King beating on videotape. Less than two weeks after the King beating, Latasha Hollins, a fifteen-year-old African American teenager, got into a scuffle with a female Korean store owner, Soon Da Ju. The store surveillance camera caught the store owner shooting the teenager in the back of the head as she started to walk away. In the trial that followed, the judge sentenced Soon Ja Du to five years probation for killing Hollins. The African American community, as well as many people outside of that community, were enraged over the fact that the life of a young black woman was apparently worth only five years probation to the white judge. As it had so many times before, the judicial system had failed Black America once again. In July 1991, General Motors announced the closing of the Van Nuys plant. In that same year, gang-related deaths in Los Angeles approached 800. Half of the victims were innocent bystanders. On April 29, 1992, the King trial verdicts were announced.

The 1992 Los Angeles riot can provide very real lessons for society. The commission findings and recommendations after the 1965 Watts riot could also have provided Los Angeles with a partial blueprint for eliminating seeds of unrest. Ironically, the problems in 1992 were similar to the problems in 1965, and have for the most part gone unchecked. Similar problems exist in cities such as Chicago, Detroit, Washington, D.C., and in many smaller communities that are microcosms of Los Angeles. Most of the individuals arrested for looting during the 1992 Los Angeles riot were poor. Only one-third of those arrested were employed, most in low-paying jobs. Nearly two-thirds were high school dropouts. Nearly all of the arrested looters were nonwhites. Some of the looting may have been prompted by anger over the Rodney King beating verdict. However, most of the participants were caught up in the looting frenzy because it was an opportunity to get what they needed or to get things that their poverty had made impossible to obtain (Lieberman & O'Reilly, 1993).

Los Angeles suffers from high unemployment, inadequate schools, poor housing conditions, and a poor public transportation system. These were problems that were present in 1965 and they are still present today. Changes are being made to improve police and community relations, but a long history of a dual justice system leaves many African American and Hispanics, and others, with serious doubts. Until our government, our communities, and our citizenry are prepared to make the commitment and the financial sacrifices to remediate the problems of poverty, riots will again occur and the destructive cycle will repeat itself. The financial costs to correct the problems will undoubtedly be staggering. However, one billion dollars in property damage resulted from the L.A. riots. There is nothing to show for it except burned building shells, many for which there are no plans for rebuilding. Had a billion dollars been spent toward jobs and the improvement of living conditions in Los Angeles, it is likely that the riots could have been averted.

The Young African American Male

The destiny of many young African American males has become an enigma in American society.

> Miseducated by the educational system, mishandled by the criminal justice system, mislabeled by the mental health system, and mistreated by the social welfare system. . . . They have become—in an unenviable and unconscionable sense—rejects of our affluent society and misfits in their own communities (Gibbs, 1992, p. 6)

Although young African American males live in representative communities throughout the United States, they live primarily in inner-city neighborhoods. Disproportionately represented in the lower end of the socioeconomic continuum, and failing to become an integral part of society due to rejection and continued discrimination, many have become endangered, embittered, and embattled (Gibbs, 1992).

Gibbs (1992) suggests that there are six social indicators or serious problems experienced by black males in our society: lack of sufficient education, unemployment, delinquency, drug abuse, teenage pregnancy, and high mortality rates. Since the beginning of the 1980s, black males have sustained losses in all of these areas.

Dropout rates in inner-city schools remain disproportionately high. Among those who do graduate from high school are many who are functionally illiterate and are lacking in basic skills necessary for entry-level jobs, military service, or postsecondary education. College enrollments for African Americans have been declining in recent years.

The unemployment rate for black males remains disproportionately high, typically at least twice that of the general population. The unemployment rate of black males exceeds that of black females by a ratio of 2 to 1. Those who are employed are frequently in menial, lower-paying jobs (Gibbs, 1992). Even these jobs have become increasingly difficult for blacks to obtain because of increased competition from other minorities, particularly immigrants. Added to this factor is a disposition of some employers to hire from groups other than

African Americans. Unemployment statistics fail to report the problem of disproportionately high numbers of unemployed blacks who become so discouraged that they drop out of the job-seekers market (Auletta, 1982).

While black youths comprise less than 20 percent of the total youth population, they account for nearly a third of the arrests. They are arrested in greater frequency than whites for robbery, rape, homicide, and aggravated assault. They are also more likely than white youth to be arrested for other violent personal crimes (Krisberg et al., 1986). While disproportionately involved as violent and high frequency offenders, research studies suggest few, if any, consistent and substantial differences between the delinquency involvement of the different racial groups (Huizinga & Elliot, 1985; Krisberg, 1986). Yet the arrest and incarceration rates of black males are the highest of all groups. This finding suggests that black youths are treated more harshly in the criminal justice system.

With the exception of inhalants and hallucinogens, nonwhite youths have an equal or higher rate of drug abuse as compared to white youths. The use of heroin and cocaine (including crack) is disproportionately high among African American youths. The related problem of AIDS among intravenous drug users is particularly problematic with those who are sexually active because they run a very high risk of infecting or being infected by their sexual partners or by sharing needles. While both a legal and moral problem, drug use among African American youths is an even greater problem because these individuals are destroying themselves physically, psychologically, and socially (Gibbs, 1992).

Teenage pregnancy in the United States is the highest of all industrialized nations (Gibbs, 1992). The pregnancy rate for African Americans is twice that of white youths (Children's Defense Fund, 1986a). White teenagers are more likely than black teens to terminate their pregnancies (Gibbs, 1992). Studies indicate that many black males have negative attitudes toward the use of contraceptives and discourage their partners from their use (Shapiro, 1980; Children's Defense Fund, 1986b; Gibbs, 1986). Some of these young black males may view the birth of a child as confirmation of their virility (Gibbs, 1992). These attitudes enhance both the likelihood of pregnancy and the spread of AIDS and other diseases.

Teenage mothers are more likely to drop out of school, go on welfare, and experience complications in pregnancy. Teenage mothers are also more likely to have children born at risk with low birth rates. These infants are at greater risk for developing neurological problems and other prenatal and postnatal health problems. As a group, children born to teens are more likely to suffer from abuse, and grow up in single-parent, welfare-supported families. They are less likely to be academically successful (Gibbs, 1992). The young black males who father children are more likely to attain lower levels of academic achievement, and lower occupational status. They tend to have larger families and experience unstable marriages (Chilman, 1983).

Young African American males have had an alarmingly high mortality rate due, primarily, to homicides and suicides. A young black male has about a one in twenty chance of being murdered before the age of 25. Each year thousands of black youths die from gang-related killings, primarily in the inner city. While accidents are the primary cause of deaths among white youths, homicides are more typically the cause of death among young black males. While suicides tend to be lower among black youths than among whites, Gibbs (1992) suggests that the rates would be higher for blacks if the reporting were more reliable. Accidents from single car accidents, drug overdoses, victim precipitated homicides and other violent accidents may actually be suicides. Given their disadvantaged place in society and feelings of hopelessness, Gibbs (1992) suggests that black youths are more vulnerable to suicide.

Gibbs (1992) suggests that there are four variables that have contributed to the deteriorating status of African American males in the United States. Throughout most of the 1960s and in periods of the 1970s liberal federal administrations were committed to increasing opportunities for minorities. However, a conservative attack on these advances began in the 1980s with a federal administration which dismantled or diluted many of the civil rights and social welfare programs. As the economy stopped expanding and as other disadvantaged groups began to compete with blacks for the scarce resources, African Americans saw many of their short-lived gains slip away.

Meanwhile, most of the middle-class African Americans moved out of the inner city into the integrated urban centers or suburbs. This left the inner city with a lack of the strong leadership and role models its residents needed. These sociocultural factors contributed significantly to the demise of many inner-city, young black males. Gibbs (1992) suggests that the isolation from the black middle class and the alienation from the white community left the inner cities' ghettos as "welfare reservations" where black youths lack access to positive role models, quality education, recreation, cultural facilities, job opportunities, and transportation.

The loss of influence of the black church in the inner city has meant that, in many instances, the church is no longer the center of activity in the community and no longer exerts the high level of influence as the monitor of norms and values. There has been a breakdown in traditional black community values such as the importance of family, religion, education, self-improvement, and social cohesion. Many of the inner-city residents no longer have the feelings of concern and responsibility for one another that they once did. The sense of shared community and common purpose has been replaced by a sense of hopelessness, alienation, and despair (Gibbs, 1992).

Among the economic factors contributing to the frustration and alienation of this country's black youths are the structural changes in an economy which had a predominantly manufacturing and industrial base to one with a high technology and service base. With many manufacturing jobs moved out of the country and new jobs moving out to the suburbs, black youths are often at a disadvantage without adequate transportation or skills to adequately compete (Gibbs, 1992).

The fourth factor contributing to the overwhelming problems faced by America's black youths is the political climate of the country. A conservative political backlash gave the conservative administrations of the 1980s through the early 1990s what they believed to be a mandate to dismantle the antipoverty and affirmative action policies of earlier administrations. Gibbs (1992) suggests that the goal of providing all Americans with a decent standard of living through federally subsidized health and welfare programs was placed on hold. At the same time, the poor and disadvantaged were often characterized by their critics as lacking motivation, having dysfunctional family systems dependent on welfare programs. The resulting cutbacks on programs such as CETA, the Job Corps, federally subsidized college student loans, and youth employment programs had a direct negative impact on black youths. These cutbacks resulted in reduced training and employment opportunities and, in many instances, cut off young African Americans' access to the American dream.

While many of the programs instituted in the Johnson and Carter eras were indeed expensive to maintain, their discontinuance or near elimination has been costly in civil unrest and in the deterioration of our cities. Perhaps the greatest cost of all has been in the loss of human spirit and dignity.

The Elderly

In our society, one can often hear individuals speak of looking forward to retirement. It is quite possible that there are many individuals frustrated with day-to-day existence working in jobs that provide little intrinsic rewards, or who would readily give up the stress created by their jobs' demands for a more comfortable, less stressful lifestyle. Sometimes financial security or a comfortable lifestyle may be viewed as synonymous with getting older. It is true that Americans must be, at minimum, sixty-two years of age to draw their usual social security retirement benefits, and that in many instances one must typically reach some specified age level, whether it is 50, 55, 60 or 62, to be eligible for pension benefits. However, while one may look forward to the leisurely lifestyle that some enjoy in retirement, few would look forward to advancing age and the physical changes associated with growing older.

All individuals who live into their mid-sixties become members of the microculture of the aged, along with their membership in other microcultures. As with other minority groups, the aged are often discriminated against. But unlike discrimination against minority groups, the individuals who discriminate will also someday become a part of the aged group, and they themselves may become victims of discrimination. Butler and Lewis (1991) describe ageism as "aversion, hatred, and prejudice toward the aged and their manifestation in the form of discrimination on the basis of age" (p. 557). They further suggest that the elderly are stereotyped as senile, rigid in thought and manner, garrulous, and old-fashioned in morality and skills.

In our society, little value is placed on nonproduction. It is understandable, then, why some individuals who view the aged as nonproductive, may adopt

If they have the financial means, many older people are able to travel and enjoy life far beyond the time that they stop working.

an ageist attitude. American society also places much emphasis on physical beauty. The physical ideal is associated with youth, and the aging process only serves to remove an individual farther from the accepted norms related to physical beauty.

As the body changes because of the aging process, health problems develop. Death is inevitable, and the older an individual becomes, the greater the likelihood of death. Because many of the aged live on a limited income, they often become victims of poverty. These realities of advanced age, coupled with genuine philosophical and value differences with younger generations, may contribute to the attitudes of ageism. If ageists live long enough to become old, their attitudes may turn into self-hatred (Butler & Lewis, 1991).

In 1991, there were an estimated 31.7 million people who were sixty-five years of age or older in the United States (U.S. Bureau of the Census, 1992). With the advent of modern medical technology and improved living conditions, average life expectancy in the United States is now 75.4 years (U.S. Bureau of the Census, 1992). This compares with an average life expectancy of forty-seven years in 1900, when only 4 percent of the population was sixty-five or older. Every day, while approximately 5,600 Americans reach the age of sixty-five, 4,077 individuals over the age of sixty-five die. This, however, provides a net increase of over 1,500 a day into the ranks of the elderly. This translates into an increase of about 550,000 per year (Butler & Lewis, 1991). Today, only 1 percent of the U.S. population is eighty-five years of age or older. By 2050, however, it is estimated that the figure will increase to 5 percent of the total population (Schulz & Ewen, 1993).

The aged constitute slightly more than 10 percent of the American population. As such, they constitute a statistical minority. The aged resemble other oppressed minority groups in that they suffer from prejudice, discrimination, and deprivation. On the other hand, they differ from other minority groups in that they are not born into their age-group.

The aged are discriminated against in many areas that affect their well-being and life-style. For example, many employers discriminate against them in hiring and retention. In addition, many medical personnel admit that they prefer not to treat the elderly (Palmore, 1978).

As a group, the aged make up a potent political force. As the federal and state governments move toward balancing their budgets, social and welfare programs have often been cut. With many of the elderly living on fixed incomes, they are rightfully fearful of cuts that directly impact the quality of their lives. Consequently, as a group, they typically exercise their right to vote to a greater extent than other age-groups. The recognition of their voter influence was evident in recent elections, where presidential candidates openly courted the votes of this group, pledging to support their interests.

The aged are understandably concerned about voter issues related to the maintenance or enhancement of Social Security and health care benefits. They are more likely than other groups to support "taxpayer revolts" and resist any efforts toward revenue enhancement, which will affect their incomes. Since they are typically no longer involved in their education or that of their children, attempts to increase school revenues through taxes are often resisted. Efforts such as California's Proposition 13, which rolled back property taxes but had a negative impact on education, have had wide support. As the ranks of the aged grow, and as they successfully lobby for a greater share of the available resources, they are at greater risk of ageist attacks. The working population is increasingly aware that greater amounts of their paychecks are being deducted to provide for social security benefits and other programs to provide for the elderly. In addition, younger workers may perceive older workers who hold higher paying supervisory positions as obstacles to their own advancement. They want them to retire so that there will be greater opportunity for advancement. Yet, when aged workers do retire, younger workers may resent them because they must pay social security taxes to fund their retired colleagues' pensions.

In the United States, the life expectancy is lower for blacks than for whites. It can be assumed that the lower socioeconomic conditions accorded to African Americans are prominent factors in this phenomenon. African Americans make up nearly 12 percent of the general population but only about 8 percent of the older age-group. Poor health conditions for many of them contribute greatly to the disproportionately high mortality for this group. Butler and Lewis (1991) suggest that institutionalized racism falls most heavily on black men; their average life expectancy in 1986 was 64.9 years of age, compared with 72.3 years of age for white men. With improved opportunities and living conditions for blacks, however, life expectancy of this group was on the rise through the mid-1980s. However in 1988, the life expectancy gap between whites and African Americans increased once again. Butler and Lewis (1991) suggest that killings, accidents, disease, and infant mortality were contributing factors.

Without the resources to provide for a quality retirement, it is understandable why ethnic minorities as a group may tend to perceive old age less favorably than whites. However, within the traditional culture, older Native Americans do have the respect accorded them because of their cultural values, which identify wisdom and old age. Older Asian Americans enjoy the deference paid to them by the young as part of their traditional Asian cultural values. However, individuals from these groups who are highly assimilated may respond to the aged in a manner more typical of the mainstream culture.

Poverty is a very serious problem with the aged. In 1987, there were 19 million families headed by individuals over sixty-five years of age. Fifty percent of these families had incomes in excess of $20,000 a year. Ten percent had incomes in excess of $50,000. However, 20 percent had incomes less than $10,000 a year. While the elderly comprise 12 percent of the nation's population, they represent 28 percent of the nation's poor (Butler & Lewis, 1991).

Socioeconomic status tends to be a major factor in the adjustment to old age. As with the earlier years in life, income influences the longevity, health status, housing, and marital status of the aged. Elderly persons with a high income have a number of advantages associated with their greater financial resources. In earlier years, they were able to maintain better living conditions and better health care, which often translates into better health in the advanced years. Their financial resources enable them to maintain these higher living and health care standards. This advantage, in turn, may result in extended quality leisure activities, such as travel, which makes the retirement years more pleasurable. It is understandable, therefore, why individuals from high socioeconomic backgrounds tend to view old age more favorably than those from low socioeconomic backgrounds.

Educational Implications

As with other microcultures, the various age-groups of the U.S. population contribute greatly to the pluralistic nature of this society. There are some basic educational considerations in the study of age-groups as a function of culture. American society in general has not always been viewed as particularly supportive or positive in its perception of all age-groups. For example, the discussion on adolescence noted that this period is often viewed as a time of storm and stress, whereas in some cultures this period passes with few crises. In American society, the first view tends to prevail. In addition, advancing age is not viewed by the dominant society with the respect or reverence that is found in many other cultures. Ageism does exist and is regretfully as much a part of our social system as is racism and sexism.

For these reasons, it is critically important that students be exposed to age as it relates to culture. Moreover, studying age and its relation to culture is important because students, if they live to full life expectancy, will become members of each age-group. Thus, unlike the study of different ethnic groups, students can learn to understand and appreciate microcultures of which they have been members, are presently members, or will eventually be members. By addressing the issues of various age-groups in the classroom, educators can assist students to better understand their siblings, parents, and other important persons in their lives. Knowledge can eliminate fear of the unknown as students begin to move into different age-groups at different times in their lives. It is important that issues related to age-groups be appropriately introduced into the curriculum.

Students need to understand the concept of ageism. Just as the school assists students in understanding the problem of racism, the school should be responsible for helping students to understand the aged and to dispel the myths related to this group. Field trips to retirement homes or visits to the class by senior citizens may provide useful experiences. As students become aware of the nature and characteristics of each age-group, they will develop perceptions of each individual, regardless of age, as being an important and integral part of society.

It is important for educators to understand age as it relates to both students and their parents. Understanding the particular age-group characteristics and needs of the students can assist the educator to better understand and manage age-related behavior, such as reactions or responses to peer group pressure. Understanding the nature of parents, siblings, and other important individuals (e.g., grandparents) will assist the educator in parent-teacher relationships, as well as in helping students to cope with their interaction with others. For example, as an elderly grandparent moves into the family setting, this event may impact on a child and affect classroom behavior.

The School's Responsibility and Child Abuse

The school is perhaps in the best position of any agency in the community to observe the effects of child abuse. The classroom teacher is an important agent in detecting and reporting abuse and in all states is required by law to do so. To do this, the teacher must be aware of the problem of abuse, the manifestations of abuse, and the proper authorities to whom abuse is reported. If the teacher's immediate supervisor is unresponsive to the reporting of a potential abuse problem, the teacher should then continue to seek help until it is provided by competent and concerned individuals in positions of authority.

The single most important factor in determining possible child abuse is the physical condition of the child. Telltale marks, bruises, and abrasions that cannot be adequately explained may provide reason to suspect abuse. Unusual changes in the child's behavior patterns, such as extreme fatigue, may be reason to suspect problems. The parents' behavior and their ability or lack of ability to explain the child's condition and the social features of the family may be reason to suspect abuse. While physical abuse or neglect may tend to have observable indicators, sexual abuse may occur with few if any obvious indicators. Adults may be unwilling to believe what a child is saying and may be hesitant to report alleged incidents. There is no typical profile of the victim, and the physical signs vary. Behavioral manifestations are usually exhibited by the victims but are often viewed as insignificant or attributed to typical childhood stress. Chronic depression, isolation from peers, apathy, and suicide attempts are some of the more serious behavioral manifestations of the problem (Sarles, 1980).

The majority of suicides are planned and not committed on impulse. The majority of suicide victims mention their intentions to someone. Of adolescents who commit suicide, 80 percent make open threats beforehand (Griffin & Felsenthal, 1983). There are often a number of warning signs that can alert teachers, other professionals, and parents. The following are some of the danger signals (Griffin & Felsenthal, 1983):

- Aggressive, hostile behavior
- Alcohol and drug abuse
- Passive behavior
- Changes in eating habits
- Changes in sleeping habits
- Fear of separation
- Abrupt changes in personality
- Sudden mood swings
- Decreased interest in schoolwork and decline in grades
- Inability to concentrate
- Hopelessness
- Obsession with death
- Giving away valued possessions
- Euphoria or increased activity after depression

If trouble is suspected by teachers or other school personnel, friendly, low-key or casual questions or statements may provide an appropriate opening: "You seem down today"; "It seems like something is bothering you." If an affirmative response is given, a more direct and probing (but supportive) question may be asked. If there is any reason whatsoever to suspect a possible suicide attempt, teachers and other school staff should alert the appropriate school personnel. Teachers should recognize their limitations and avoid making judgments. The matter should be referred to the school psychologist, who should in turn alert a competent medical authority (i.e., a psychiatrist) and the child's parents. Assistance can also be obtained from local mental health clinics and suicide prevention centers. Prompt action may save a life.

Our coverage of adolescent substance abuse has been brief. But the importance of the problem is such that every educator should be aware of the problem and work toward providing children at an early age with appropriate drug education. No agency, group, or individual alone can wage an effective campaign against substance abuse. Only with a united effort can an effective battle be waged.

Hafen and Frandsen (1980) indicate that there are danger signs for drug or alcohol ingestion that may place the individual at life-threatening risk:

1. *Unconsciousness.* [The] individual cannot be awakened or if awakened lapses back into deep sleep.
2. *Breathing difficulties.* Breathing stops altogether, may be weak, or weak and strong in cycles. Skin may become bluish or purple indicating lack of oxygenated blood.
3. *Fever.* Any temperature above 100°F (38°C) is a danger sign when drugs are involved.
4. *Vomiting while not fully conscious.* In a stupor, semiconscious, or unconscious state, vomiting can cause serious breathing problems.
5. *Convulsions.* Twitching of face, trunk, arms or legs; muscle spasms or muscle rigidity may indicate impending convulsions. Violent jerking motions and spasms likely indicate a convulsion.

In the event that these signs are observed in the classroom, the school nurse should be summoned immediately. If none is available, then someone trained in CPR should be summoned. It would be advisable for a list of all personnel with CPR training to be made available for all teachers and staff.

As parents hurry children into adulthood, educators may also contribute to the hurrying process. Teachers, administrators, and support personnel should be cognizant of the fact that the children they teach and work with are children and not miniature adults. Children have but one opportunity to experience the wonders of childhood. In comparison to adulthood, childhood and adolescence are relatively short periods of time, and these young people should have every opportunity to enjoy these stages of their lives to the fullest extent possible.

Summary

The study of age as a microculture is important to educators because it helps them to understand how the child or adolescent struggles to win peer acceptance and balance this effort with the need for parental approval. In some instances, the pressures from peers are not congruent with those that come from the home.

As each child develops into adolescence, we observe a growing need for independence. Adolescence for some is a time of storm and stress, while for others it passes with little or no trauma. Adulthood is one of the most exciting times in life. It is a time for courtship, marriage, children, and career choices. It is a time when individuals reach their physical and their occupational prime. Young adulthood can also be a threatening time, as choices made at this time often have a lifetime impact on the individual. Adulthood is the time when dreams are either fulfilled or become forever elusive. With the latter can come bitterness, resentment, and anger.

With life expectancy increasing each year, those in the aged cohort increase in numbers daily. There is a net increase of over a half million into the ranks of the aged each year. Like the ethnic minorities and those with disabilities, the aged face discrimination and prejudice in the form of ageism. Those who discriminate will someday become aged, perhaps to face the treatment that they themselves imposed on others.

Questions for Review

1. Explain why child abuse is a problem, and cite some of the signs of child abuse.
2. When does ethnic identification begin in children, and how is it manifested?
3. What are some of the variables that contribute to prejudice in children?
4. What are the sources of alienation between adolescents and their families?
5. What is the extent of substance abuse among adolescents, and what are some of the underlying causes of substance use in this age-group?
6. What are the causes of adolescent suicide, and what are the warning signs?
7. What are some of the primary differences between the younger and the older baby boomers?
8. How do the baby busters differ from the baby boomers?
9. What are some of the factors that have contributed to some African American males being considered a risk in our society?
10. How does old age relate to ethnicity and socioeconomic status?
11. What are the roots of ageism?

References

Aboud, F. (1988). *Children and prejudice.* Cambridge, MA: Basil Blackwell.

American Human Association. (1987). *Highlights of Official Child Neglect and Abuse Reporting, 1985.* Denver, CO: American Humane Association.

Auletta, K. (1992). *The Underclass.* New York: Random House.

Bagley, C., Mallick, K., & Verma, G. K. (1979). Pupil self esteem: A study of black and white teenagers in British schools. In G. K. Verma & C. Bagley (Eds.), *Race education and identity.* London: Macmillan.

Bagley, C., Verma, G. K., Mallick, K., & Young, L. (1979). *Personality, self esteem and prejudice.* England: Saxon House.

Bowers, V., & Swanson, D. (1988). *More than meets the eye.* Vancouver, Canada: Pacific Educational Press.

Butler, R. N., & Lewis, M. I. (1991). *Aging and mental health: Positive psychosocial and biomedical approaches (4th ed.).* New York: Macmillan.

Centers for Disease Control (CDC). (1986, November). *Youth suicide in the United States, 1970-1980.* Atlanta, GA: Department of Health and Human Services.

Children's Defense Fund. (1986a). *Welfare and pregnancy: What do we know? What do we do?* Washington, DC: Children's Defense Fund.

Children's Defense Fund. (1986b). *Building health programs for teenagers.* Washington, DC: Children's Defense Fund.

Chilman, C. (1983). *Adolescent sexuality in a changing American society.* New York: John Wiley and Sons.

Cohen, S. (1985). *Substance abuse problems (Vol. 2).* New York: Haworth Press.

Cormerci, G. D. (1986). Foreclosing on life. *The Journal of Pediatrics*, 109(4), 723-725.

Cranston, K. (1992). HIV education for gay, lesbian, and bisexual youth: Personal risk, personal power and the community of conscience. In K. M. Harbeck (Ed.). *Coming out of the closet: Gay and lesbian students, teachers, and curricula.* New York: Harrington Press.

Dannen, F. (1992). Annals of crime—The revenge of the Green Dragons. *The New Yorker*, November 16, 1992, p. 76-99.

Dolan, M. (1989, June 2). Study finds perilous levels of lead in 20% of children. *Los Angeles Times*, pp. 1, 28-29.

Drowns, R. W., & Hess, K. M. (1990). *Juvenile Justice.* St. Paul, MN: West Publishing.

Elmer-Dewitt, P. (May, 1993). Making a case for abstinence. *Time, 141*(21), 64-65.

Fawzy, F.I., Coombs, R.H., & Gerber, B. (1983). Generational continuity in the use of substances: The impact of parental substance use on adolescent use. *Additive Behaviors*, 8, 109-114.

Garbarino, J., Guttman, E., & Seeley, J. W. (1986). *The psychologically battered child.* San Francisco: Jossey-Bass.

Gelman, D., & Gangelhoff, V. K. (1983, August). Teenage suicide in the sunbelt. *Newsweek, 15*, 70-74.

Gibbs, J. T. (1986). Psychosocial correlates of sexual attitudes and behaviors in urban early adolescent females: Implications for intervention. *Journal of Social Work and Human Sexuality, 5*, 81-97.

Gibbs, J. T. (1992). Young black males in America: Endangered, embittered, and embattled. In M. S. Kimmell & M. A. Messner, *Men's lives* (2nd ed.). New York: Macmillan.

Gibbs, N. (May 24, 1993). How should we teach our children about sex? *Time, 141* (21), pp. 60-66.

Gispert, M. (1981, February). Sexual conflicts and concerns of adolescent girls. *Medical Aspects of Human Sexuality, 2*, 32a, 32e.

Griffin, M. E., & Felsenthal, C. (1983). *A cry for help.* Garden City, NY: Doubleday.

Guetzloe, E. C. (1989). *Youth suicide: What the educator should know.* Reston, VA: The Council for Exceptional Children.

Hafen, B. Q., & Frandsen, K. J. (1980). *Drug and alcohol emergencies.* Center City, MN: Hazelden Foundation.

Hawton, K. (1986). *Suicide and attempted suicide among children and adolescents.* Beverly Hills, CA: Sage.
Hendin, H. (1985). Suicide among the young: Psychodynamics and demography. In M. L. Peck, N. L. Farberew, & R. E. Litman (Eds.), *Youth suicide* (pp. 19-38). New York: Springer.
Hipple, J., & Cimbolic, P. (1979). *The counselor and suicidal crisis.* Springfield, IL: Thomas.
Huizinga, D., & Elliot, D. (1985). *Juvenile offenders prevalence, offender incidence, and arrest rates by race.* Boulder, CO: Institute of Behavioral Science.
Hyde, M., & Forsyth, E. (1978). *Suicide.* New York: Franklin Watts.
Jobes, D. A., Berman, A. L., & Josselsen, A. R. (1986). The impact of psychological autopsies on Medical Examiners' Determination of Manner of Death. *Journal of Forensic Science, 31*(2), 177-189.
Johnson, L. D., O'Malley, P. M., & Bachman, J. G. (1986). *Drug use among American high school students and other young adults: National trends through 1985* [Publication No. (ABM) 86-1450]. Rockville, MD: National Institute on Drug Abuse.
Katz, P. A. (1982). Development of children's racial awareness and intergroup attitudes. In L. G. Katz (Ed.), *Current topics in early childhood education* (Vol. 4). Norwood, NJ: Ablex.
Katz, P. A., & Zalk, S. R. (1978). Modification of children's attitudes. *Developmental Psychology, 11,* 135-44.
Kratcoski, P. C., & Kratcoski, L. D. (1990). *Juvenile delinquency* (3rd ed.) Englewood Cliffs, NJ: Prentice-Hall.
Krisberg, B., Schwartz, I., Fishman, G., Eiskovits, Z., & Guttman, E. (1986). *The incarceration of minority youth.* Minneapolis: H. H. Humphrey Institute of Public Affairs, University of Minnesota.
Lieberman, P., & O'Reilly, R. (1993). Most looters endured lives of crime, poverty. *The Los Angeles Times,* May 2, 1993, pp. 1, 34.
The Los Angeles Times. (1992). *Understanding the riots.* Los Angeles: The Los Angeles Times.
Manegold, C. S. (1993, April 8). To Crystal, 12, school serves no purpose. *The New York Times, CSLII*(49,295), A1 & B7.
Miller, J. (1975). Suicide and adolescence. *Adolescence,* 10, 13-23.
Miller, W. B. (1983). Youth gangs and groups. In S. H. Kadish (Ed.), *Encyclopedia of crime and justice V. 4* (pp. 1671-79). New York: The Free Press.
Millman, R. B., & Khuri, E. T. (1981). Adolescence and substance abuse. In J. H. Lowinson & P. Ruiz (Eds.), *Substance abuse: Clinical problems and perspectives.* Baltimore: Williams & Wilkins.
Mitchell, S. (1993). The baby busters. *San Jose Mercury News,* May 23, 1993, p. 1L and 5L.
Morland, J. K. (1972). Racial acceptance and preference of nursery school children in a southern city. In A. R. Brown (Ed.), *Prejudice in children.* Springfield, IL: Thomas.
Newman, B. M., & Newman, P. R. (1986). *Adolescent development.* New York: Merrill/Macmillan.
Palmore, E. (1978). Are the aged a minority group? *Journal of the American Geriatrics Society, 26,* 214-216.
Pffeffer, R. (1986). *Suicidal child.* New York: The Guilford Press.
Piaget, J. (1932). *The moral judgment of the child.* London: Kegan Paul.
Ray, L. Y., & Johnson, N. (1983). Adolescent suicide. *The Personnel and Guidance Journal, 62*(3), 131-135.
Roof, W. C. (1990). Return of the baby boomers to organized religion. In C.H. Jacquet, Jr. (Ed.), *1990 Yearbook of American and Canadian Churches.* Nashville: Abingdon Press.
Sarles, R. M. (1980). Incest. *Pediatric Review, 2*(2), 51-54.
Schulz, R., & Ewen, R. B. (1993). *Adult development and aging* (2nd ed.). New York: Macmillan.
Shapiro, C. (1980). Sexual learning: The short-changed adolescent male. *Social Work, 25,* 489-93.
Sidel, R. (1990). *Own her own: Growing up in the shadow of the American dream.* New York: Viking.
Spiegler, D. L., & Harford, T. C. (1987). Addictive behaviors among youth. In T. D. Nirenberg & S. A. Maistro (Eds.), *Developments in*

the assessment and treatment of addictive behaviors. Norwood, NJ: Ablex.

Time (1993, April 26). Wasted Youth, *Time*, 141, p. 15.

Tower, C. C. (1992). Child abuse and neglect. In N. A. Cohen (Ed.), *Child welfare*. Boston: Allyn & Bacon.

U. S. Bureau of the Census. (1992). Statistical abstract of the United States: 1992 (112th ed.). Washington, DC: Government Printing Office.

Wenz, F. (1979). Self-injury behavior, economic status, and the family anomie syndrome among adolescents. *Adolescence, 14*, 387-397.

Whaley, L. F., & Wong, D. L. (1987). *Nursing care of infants and children* (3rd ed.). St. Louis: Mosby.

Suggested Readings

Butler, R. N., & Lewis, M. I. (1991). *Aging and mental health: Positive psychosocial and biomedical approaches* (4th ed.). New York: Macmillan.

This thorough and detailed treatment of the elderly provides insightful information on this growing and important segment of the population.

Guetzloe, E. D. (1989). *Youth suicide: What the educator should know.* Reston, VA: The Council for Exceptional Children.

A very good monograph written in two parts. Part I, "Toward an Understanding of Youth Suicide," provides information on trends, issues, statistics, risk factors, events precipitating suicide, treatment, and so forth. Part II, "Suicide Prevention in the School," has nine sections and includes school plans for intervention, assessment of suicide potential, working with parents, and counseling suicidal students.

The Los Angeles Times. (1992). *Understanding the riots.* Los Angeles: The Los Angeles Times.

A special publication by the staff of The Los Angeles Times. A fascinating and thought-provoking account of the Los Angeles riot of 1992. Provides insights into the underlying reasons for one of the greatest man-made disasters in the history of this country.

Gibbs, J. T. (1992). Young black males in America: Endangered, embittered, and embattled. In M. S. Kimmell and M. A. Messner, *Men's lives* (2nd ed.) New York: Macmillan.

An excellent discussion of African American males in the United States and the variables that have placed them at risk in our society.

CHAPTER 9

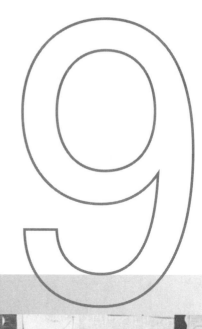

Teaching Chart 108:
Vocabulary
1. ancient
For thousands of years, the ancient village had remained at the edge of the sea.
2. generation
The boy's mother recalled a violent storm that had struck when her generation was young.
3. urgently
Due to the violence of the storm, the children urgently needed protection.
4. falter

Teaching That Is Multicultural

Natisha Loftis had not said a word to any of her teachers since the beginning of school. It is not that she is a "bad" student; she turns in assignments and makes B's. She certainly doesn't cause her teachers trouble. Therefore, the high school counselor, Mr. Williams, was somewhat surprised to hear that she was thinking of dropping out of school. He had been Natisha's advisor for over two years, but he didn't really remember her. Nevertheless, it was his job to conduct an interview with students who were leaving school for one reason or another.

Natisha described her school experiences as coming to school, listening to teachers, and going home. School was boring and not connected at all to her real life, in which she had the responsibility for helping her father raise five brothers and sisters. She might even be able to get a job with the same cleaning firm that her dad worked for. For sure, nothing that she was learning in school could help her get a job. And she knew from more than ten years of listening to teachers and reading textbooks that her chances of becoming a news anchorwoman or even a teacher were about the same as winning the lottery. The last time a teacher had even asked about her family was in the sixth grade, when her mom left the family. The only place that you were paid attention to was in church.

School had helped silence Natisha. Classes provided no meaningful experience for her. The content may have been important to the teachers, but she could find no relationship to her own world. Why has Natisha decided to drop out of school? How can the curriculum be made more meaningful to students who are not white and middle-class? How can teachers make a student like Natisha excited about learning?

Multicultural Education

It is no easy task to incorporate cultural knowledge throughout your teaching. In the beginning you will have to consciously think about it as you interact with students and plan lessons and assignments. You should approach teaching multiculturally as an enthusiastic learner with much to learn from students and community members who have cultural backgrounds different from your own. You may need to remind yourself that your way of looking at the world evolved from the personal experiences you've lived through, which may vary greatly from the experiences of the students in your school. You will need to listen to the histories and experiences of students and their families and integrate them into your teaching. You will need to validate students' values within both school and their out-of-school realities—a process that is not authentic if you have feelings of superiority.

Educators are often at a disadvantage because they do not live, nor have ever lived, in the community in which their students live. Often, the only parents with whom they interact are those few who attend parent-teacher meetings or who have scheduled conferences with them. In many cases, they have not been in their students' homes nor been active participants in community activities. To make our classrooms multicultural we need to learn the cultures of our students, especially when the students are members of oppressed groups.

How do we begin this learning process? Ogbu (1992) suggests that we can learn through

> (a) observing of children's behavior in the classroom and on playgrounds, (b) asking children questions about their cultural practices and preferences, (c) talking with parents about their cultural practices and preferences, (d) doing research on various ethnic groups with children in school, and (e) studying published works on children's ethnic groups. (p. 12)

Participation in community, religious, and ethnic activities can provide another perspective on the way students live.

Our knowledge about our students' cultures should allow us to make the academic content of our teaching more meaningful to students by relating it to their own experiences and building on their prior knowledge. It should help us make them and their histories the center of the education process in the effort to help them reach their academic, vocational, and social potentials. In the process, students should learn to believe in their own abilities and to become active participants in their own learning.

Teaching multiculturally also requires the incorporation of cultural diversity throughout the total learning process. If ethnicity, class, and gender are not interrelated in the curriculum, students will begin to think that they are separate elements of multicultural education. Neither educators nor students can afford to neglect one while trying to overcome the others. Although Chapters 2 through 8 addressed membership in various microcultures separately, topics concerning each microculture should be interwoven whenever possible in one's own teaching. For example, if we develop activities to fight racism, but continue to perpetuate sexism, we are not providing multicultural education. At the same time, we should not forget women of color and poor women when discussing the impact of sexism and other women's issues.

The authors believe that all teaching should be multicultural and all classrooms should be models of democracy and equity. To do this requires that educators

1. place the student at the center of the teaching and learning process
2. promote human rights and respect for cultural differences
3. believe that all students can learn
4. acknowledge and build on the life histories and experiences of students' microcultural memberships
5. critically analyze oppression and power relationships to understand racism, sexism, classism, and discrimination against the disabled, young, and aged
6. critique society in the interest of social justice and equality
7. participate in collective social action to ensure a democratic society.

Finally, the authors believe that the teachers and other school personnel can make a difference. In a study of a New York City high school, Fine (1989) found that "educators who feel most disempowered in their institutions are most likely to believe that 'these kids can't be helped' and that those who feel relatively empowered are likely to believe that they 'can make a difference in the lives of these youths'" (p. 158). Making one's teaching and classroom multicultural is an essential step in empowerment for both teachers and students. We hope that you have the desire and courage to take that step.

Curriculum and Instruction

In some school districts teachers are provided a curriculum guide that outlines the goals, objectives, and activities for their teaching assignments. In other schools, the textbook selected for the course serves as the curriculum guide for teachers. The teacher's guide that accompanies the textbook usually outlines activities and supplementary resources that can be used with the text. Other teachers are given instructions about the concepts to be taught and the level that students are expected to attain by the time they finish the year. These teachers have the opportunity to select activities, supplementary materials, and textbooks that will assist in that process. How, then, does curriculum and instruction become multicultural?

There are a number of components and concepts that should be included in a multicultural curriculum. Components of multicultural education that might be included are

- ethnic, minority, and women's studies
- bilingual education
- cultural awareness
- human relations
- values clarification.

Concepts include racism, sexism, classism, ageism, prejudice, discrimination, oppression, powerlessness, power, inequality, equality, and stereotyping.

Curriculum is more than the composite of courses that students are required to take—the so-called official curriculum. The school setting includes what researchers call a hidden curriculum as well. This hidden curriculum consists of the unstated norms, values, and beliefs about the social relations of school and classroom life that are transmitted to students (Giroux, 1988). Some observers of schools find that "students learn values and norms that would produce 'good' industrial workers. Students internalize values which stress a respect for authority, punctuality, cleanliness, docility, and conformity" (Giroux, 1988, p. 29).

Regardless of the level of formal schooling, multicultural education should permeate both the formal and hidden curriculum. It should be directed toward all students from both dominant and oppressed groups. It is important for students in a multicultural setting, as well as those in a more homogeneous setting, to develop a multicultural perspective.

Although communities are not always rich in ethnic diversity, there is always cultural diversity. Educators need to determine the microcultures that exist in the community. Schools that are on or near Native American reservations will include students from the tribes in the area, as well as non-Native Americans. Urban schools typically include multiethnic populations and students from middle and lower socioeconomic levels; inner-city schools are likely to have a high proportion of poor students. Appalachian schools include poor and middle-class families generally from fundamentalist backgrounds. Teachers who enter schools attended by students from different cultural backgrounds will need to adjust to that setting; otherwise, both students and teachers could suffer. It is important that curriculum and instruction be multicultural in all schools, including those with little and great cultural diversity. Educators should implement the following practices to make their own teaching and classrooms multicultural.

Teaching the Subject Matter

Knowledge about cultural diversity and students' cultures contributes to teaching subject matter effectively. The challenge for educators is to facilitate the learning process for all students. Teaching that is multicultural can increase academic achievement "through the use of teaching approaches and materials that are sensitive and relevant to the students' cultural backgrounds and experiences" (Suzuki, 1980, p. 34).

Researchers at the Institute for Research in Teaching have found that there is a relationship among teachers, learners, and subject matter that can be improved with knowledge and understanding of cultural diversity. McDiarmid (1991) argues that teachers need to:

- know how school knowledge is perceived in their learners' cultures. Resistance to school authority and knowledge among poor, working-class, and minority youngsters is well documented.
- know what kind of knowledge, skills, and commitments are valued in the students' cultures. Such knowledge is critical to developing representations of subject matter that either bridge or confront the knowledge and understandings that students bring with them.
- know about students' prior knowledge of and experience with the subject matter. The frameworks of understanding, based on prior experience, that students use to make sense out of new ideas and information are also critical if teachers are to make their subject matter meaningful to students.
- understand that how a given subject matter is taught and learned determines, in part, the kinds of opportunities teachers create for students to understand.
- have a repertoire of different representations for a given idea, concept, or procedure. Teachers' ability to generate or adapt representations and their capacity to judge the appropriateness of representations for different students depends, probably equally, on their understanding of their subject matter and their knowledge about their students.
- understand the relationship of their subject matter to the world to help students understand these connections. Such connections are critical to students' need to see the relationship between what they are studying in school and the world in which they live. Such connections are critical if teachers are to help oppressed students increase their control over and within their environment.
- understand the role that they and schools play in limiting access to vital subject matter knowledge by addressing what they define as individual differences through organizational arrangements such as individualization, tracking, and ability grouping.

- know that, for students, they are representatives of their subject matter. If teachers represent mathematics as repetitious drill and practice, and if they express negative attitudes toward mathematics, their students are likely to develop similar beliefs and attitudes.
- consider their role in the classroom and how that role shapes the roles students assume. If students are to explore problems and ideas with classmates, teachers need to consider how their behavior facilitates or inhibits such collaboration. (pp. 267-268)

The first step in being able to teach the subject matter effectively is to know it well. However, knowing the subject matter alone does not automatically translate into helping students learn it. If there is no understanding of the students' cultures, it becomes difficult to develop instructional strategies that can be related to students' life experiences.

Examples from and relationships to students' cultural backgrounds should be used to teach academic concepts. Rural students do not relate to riding a subway to school or work, nor do inner-city students easily relate to single-family homes with large yards. If students seldom see representations of themselves, their families, or their communities, it becomes difficult to believe that the academic content has any meaning or usefulness for them. It will appear to them that the subject matter has been written and delivered for a different group of students. At the same time, they can still *learn* about other lifestyles based on different cultural backgrounds and experiences. The teacher's repertoire of instructional strategies must relate the content to the realities of lives of students. An example of how a teacher was able to do this was described by a migrant student:

> I always am a little scared when I try a new school, yes; but I try to remember that I won't be there long, and if it's no good, I'm not stuck there like the kids who live there. . . .To me a good school is one where the teacher is friendly, and she wants to be on your side, and she'll ask you to tell the other kids of the things you can do, and all you've done—you know, about the crops and like that. There was one teacher like that, and I think it was up North, in New York it was. She said that so long as we were there in the class she was going to ask everyone to join us, that's what she said, and we could teach the other kids what we know and they could do the same with us. She showed the class where we traveled, on the map, and I told my daddy that I never before knew how far we went each year, and he said he couldn't understand why I didn't know because I did the traveling all right, with him, and so I should know. But when you look on the map, and hear the other kids say they've never been that far, and wish someday they could, then you think you've done something good, too—and they'll tell you in the recess that they've only seen where they live and we've been all over. (Coles, 1967, pp. 72-73)

The teacher who understands the experiences of students from different cultural backgrounds can use that knowledge to help students learn the subject matter. A teacher's sensitivity to those differences can be used to make students from oppressed groups feel as comfortable in the class as those from the dominant culture.

Incorporating Student Voice

Teaching that is multicultural seeks, listens, and incorporates the student voice. Students are encouraged to speak from their own experiences, to do more than regurgitate answers that we would like to hear. Teaching that incorporates the student voice allows students to make sense of the subject matter within their own realities. Listening to student voices helps us know students' prior knowledge of the subject matter, including any misinformation or the lack of information that should suggest future instructional strategies. Student voices help us learn important information about students' cultures. Teaching must start from the students' life experiences, not the experiences of the teacher, nor the experiences necessary to fit into the dominant school culture (Shor & Freire, 1987).

Most schools today legitimize only the voice of the dominant society—the standard English and world perspective of the white middle-class. Many students, especially those from oppressed groups, learn to be silent, disruptive, and/or drop out because their voices are not accepted as legitimate in the classroom. In an ethnographic study of an urban New York City high school, Fine (1989) discovered that students were

> routinely discouraged from critically examining the conditions of their lives, dissuaded from creating their own curriculum, built of what they know, were often encouraged to disparage the circumstances in which they live, warned by their teachers: "You act like that, and you'll end up on welfare!" (Most were or had been surviving on some form of federal, state, or city assistance). (p. 162)

Teaching multiculturally requires educators to recognize the conflict between the voice of the school and the voices of many students. Success in school should not be dependent on the adoption of the school's voice. O'Connor (1988) states

> The organization of school discourse, in a way that permits all cultural voices to search for skills and concepts to reconstruct their cultural principles in their own terms, must come to serve as the basic formula for equal educational opportunity." (p. 20)

Dialogic Inquiry

Teachers need to position themselves "as less masters of truth and justice and more as creators of a space where those directly involved can act and speak on their behalf" (Lather, 1991, p. 137). One approach is the use of dialogic inquiry in which instruction occurs as a dialogue between teacher and students. It requires that teachers have a thorough knowledge of the subject being taught. Rather than depending on a textbook and lecture format, the teacher listens to students and directs them in the learning of the discipline through dialogue. Dialogic inquiry "is situated in the culture, language, politics, and themes of students" (Shor & Freire, 1987, p. 104). It incorporates content about the students' backgrounds as well as that of the dominant society. It requires discarding the traditional authoritarian classroom to establish a democratic one in which both teacher and students are active participants.

Introducing student voices to the instructional process is not always easy, especially when the teacher and students are from different cultural backgrounds. "Prior experiences may have created feelings of intimidation, resentment, and hurt; an imposition of silence, or the self-imposed habit of silence, may be ingrained in some of the participants. Conversely, prior experiences may also have created feelings of superiority and a tendency to silence others" (Burbules & Rice, 1991, p. 410). The teacher may face both anger and silence, which will be overcome over time with dialogue that develops tolerance, patience, and a willingness to listen (Burbules & Rice).

Although this strategy increases the participation of students in the learning process, some teachers are not comfortable with handling the issues that are likely to be raised. Too often teachers ignore students' attempts to engage in dialogue and, as a result, halt further learning by many students. Fine (1989) observed that:

> Pedagogic and curricular attempts to not name [that is, facilitate discussions about inequitable distributions of power and resources] or to actively avoid such conversation indeed cost teachers control over their classrooms. Efforts to shut down such conversations were usually followed by the counting of money by males, the application of mascara or lipstick by females, and the laying down of heads on desks by students of both genders: the loss of control over the classroom. (p. 159)

In addition to dialogue between students and teacher, student voices can be encouraged through written and artistic expression. Some teachers ask students to keep a journal in which they write their reactions to what is occurring in class. The journal allows the teacher to be aware of learning that is occurring over time. To be effective, students must feel comfortable writing whatever they want without the threat of reprisal from the teacher.

What should be the teacher's role when students express biased beliefs about other groups? Although students have the right to hold biased beliefs, they must be challenged as well. Freire (Shor & Freire, 1987) explains,

> The educator has the right to disagree. It is precisely because the teacher is in disagreement with the young racist men or women that the educator challenges them. This is the question. Because I am a teacher, I am not obliged to give the illusion that I am in agreement with the students. . . .In the liberating perspective, the teacher has the right but also the duty to challenge the status quo, especially in the questions of domination by sex, race, or class. What the dialogical educator does not have is the right to impose on the other his or her position.

HOW WOULD YOU RESPOND?

You observe the following dialogue in a business class:

WHITE TEACHER: What's EOE?
BLACK MALE STUDENT #1: Equal over time.
WHITE TEACHER: Not quite. Anyone else?
BLACK FEMALE STUDENT: Equal Opportunity Employer.
TEACHER: That's right.
BLACK MALE STUDENT #2: What does that mean?
TEACHER: That means that an employer can't discriminate on the basis of sex, age, marital status, or race.
BLACK MALE STUDENT #2: But, wait, sometimes white people only hire white people.
TEACHER: No, they're not supposed to if they say EOE in their ads. Now take out your homework. (Fine, 1989, pp. 161-162)

How has the teacher incorporated student voices in this exchange? What other responses could the teacher have made? What would be the advantages and disadvantages of encouraging student voices in this situation? What issues might have surfaced in the subsequent discussion? How would you have handled this situation?

> But the liberating teacher can never stay silent on social questions, can never wash his or her hands of them. (pp. 174-175)

The dialogues developed through these approaches can help students understand the perspectives brought to the classroom by others from different cultural backgrounds. It helps them relate the subject matter to their real world and perhaps take an interest in really studying and learning it. It also will "help students to begin to consider how they are both created and limited by their particular life circumstances and to consider what alternative ways of working and living could be supported by other possible ways of defining one's work in the world" (Simon, 1989, p. 144).

Promoting Critical Thinking

As the result of being taught multiculturally, students learn to think critically about what they are learning and experiencing. What is critical thinking? Starr (1989) defines it as having "the freedom to ask questions and the tools to reason, liberating [one's] mind from unthinking prejudice, and promoting an appreciation for pluralistic democracy" (p. 107). Students should be supported in questioning the validity of the knowledge presented in textbooks and encouraged to explore other perspectives. "Children [and prospective teachers] who have been provoked to reach beyond themselves, to wonder, to imagine, to pose their own questions are the ones most likely to learn to learn" (Green, 1988, p. 14). However, critical thinking is not currently included in most classrooms. In a study of 1,000 classrooms, Goodlad (1981) found that less than one percent of class time dealt with open-ended critical inquiry.

Developing the skills to think critically about issues helps students make sense of the events and conditions that affect their own lives. In multicultural teaching, students are provided opportunities

> to develop the critical capacity to challenge and transform existing social and political forms, rather than simply adapt to them. It also means providing students with the skills they will need to locate themselves in history, find their own voices, and provide the convictions and compassion necessary for exercising civic courage, taking risks, and furthering the habits, customs, and social relations that are essential to democratic public forms. (Giroux, 1991, p. 47)

Multicultural teaching deals with the social and historical realities of American society and helps students gain a better understanding of the causes of oppression and inequality, including racism and sexism (Suzuki, 1980). Students are encouraged to investigate institutional racism, classism, and sexism and how societal institutions have served different populations in discriminatory ways. Even though we may overcome our own prejudices, and eliminate our own discriminatory practices against members of other cultural groups, the problem is not solved. It goes beyond what we individually control. The problem is societal and is imbedded in historical and contemporary contexts that we must help students understand.

For one, educators can help students examine their own biases and stereotypes related to different cultural groups. "Stereotypes caused by ignorance, hard times, and folk wisdom socialization can be countered by accurate information about the group(s) being stereotyped" (Garcia, 1984, p. 107). These biases often surface during class discussions or incidents outside the classroom. They should not be ignored by the teacher. Instead, they should be confronted and discussed.

Being able to think critically and to teach students to think critically is essential for a democratic society. These skills will help us realize the vision that Starr (1989) describes:

> It's a vision of active cooperation and mutually respectful disagreement, side by side. It's a vision of teachers being free to choose from a diversity of instructional materials and methods of evaluation, if and when they want. It's a vision of all points of view being given a sympathetic hearing, so that all students can have the courage of their own convictions. It's a vision of students feeling free to bring into the classroom issues that concern them in real life. It's a vision of learning together and growing together without being lost in the crowd. (p. 109)

Establishing Cooperative Learning

When students and teachers are mutually involved in learning, trusting relationships are more likely to develop (Oakes, 1985). Cooperative learning is an instructional strategy that assists in developing these trusting relationships and in increasing academic achievement. Students work together in small heterogeneous groups and are rewarded for their group performance. In the traditional classroom, on the other hand, the teacher usually lectures and leads the discussion. Also, competition is more frequent in classrooms based on the values of the dominant culture and correlates more directly with field-independent learning and teaching styles. In some cooperative learning activities, competition is included, but it occurs between groups, rather than between individuals. "The key to cooperative learning is positive interdependence and individual accountability" (Sapon-Shevin & Schniedewind, 1991, p. 166).

The principles which undergird cooperative learning are supportive of multicultural teaching. It is designed to be democratic, to help students take responsibility for both themselves and others, and to value heterogeneity and diversity (Sapon-Shevin & Schniedewind, 1991). It is also supportive of positive intergroup relations. To be effective, students in cooperative learning settings need to learn "social skills [such] as listening, encouraging others, giving constructive feedback, and checking for understanding" (Sapon-Shevin & Schniedewind, p. 172). Learning these social skills are not only helpful in learning the subject matter, but also helpful in working with others in both personal and work settings.

The research on cooperative learning activities indicates that there is often a positive effect on academic achievement. In addition, there is a positive effect on race relations, with students of different races being chosen as friends more often than occurs in traditional classroom settings. Furthermore, "minority students appear to gain academically as a result of participating in cooperative learning more than do white, middle-class students" (Wilkinson, 1988, p. 214). At the same time, white, middle-class students do not achieve less than in other situations; their achievement just does not increase as dramatically as does that of students from oppressed groups.

Understanding Learning and Teaching Styles

In multicultural teaching, the learning styles of students and the teaching style of the teacher are used to develop effective instructional strategies. Knowing the cultural background of students helps the teacher determine how to structure the classroom to take advantage of students' natural learning styles. Learning styles are often correlated with how assimilated students are into the dominant society. Students from oppressed groups are more likely to be field-sensitive than most students from the dominant group. Many Asian American students are an exception in that they are more likely to be field-independent.

Most traditional instruction is provided in a field-independent mode, which favors students from the dominant group. Teachers are likely to become very frustrated when students don't work well independently or don't respond quickly enough to questions asked by the teacher. When students are having difficulty learning, teachers should review their own teaching style; it may be incompatible with the natural learning styles of the students. Teaching style affects the way the teacher presents information and responds to students.

Cognitive, or learning styles refer to the ways in which individuals learn. One example of differences in cognitive style is the *impulsive/reflective dimension*. Impulsive students respond rapidly to tasks; they are the first ones to raise their hands to answer the teacher's question and the first ones to complete a test. Reflective students, on the other hand, respond much slower, even though they usually have fewer errors than the impulsive responder. Knowing whether you tend to encourage more reflective or impulsive behavior can assist you in having a positive effect on student learning. If you tend to promote impulsive behavior, you will need to develop some strategies for fostering reflectiveness in students. At the same time, you should help reflective students learn to respond more impulsively in some situations, such as during timed tests.

One dimension of learning style is that of *field independence* and *field sensitivity*. Field-sensitive individuals have a more global perspective of their surroundings; they are more sensitive to the social field. Field-independent individuals tend to be more analytical and can more comfortably focus on impersonal, abstract aspects of stimuli in the environment. As you probably would expect, field-sensitive persons are more likely to choose careers in teaching or social work, while field-independent persons select mathematics and science. Table 9-1 outlines the learning style characteristics of field-sensitive and field-independent students.

Teaching behaviors reflect the teacher's learning style. The teacher who is aware of his or her own teaching style can learn to organize instruction and classroom activities that are conducive to both cognitive styles. Ramirez and Castañeda (1974) found that these teachers were also able to teach students to become bicognitive. *Bicognitive* students are able to respond appropriately no matter what the situation—whether it is taking a standardized test or working in a group. Instruction that encourages field sensitivity includes group projects, close work with the teacher, and material in tune with the ethnic and social backgrounds of students. Cooperative learning activities are ideal. Field-independent instruction focuses on independent activities, minimal participation of the teacher, curriculum materials, charts and diagrams, and student work that emphasizes individual achievement.

Table 9-1.
Differences in Behavior Between Field-Independent and Field-Sensitive Students

Field-Independent Behaviors of Students	Field-Sensitive Behaviors of Students
Relationship to Peers	
• Prefers to work independently • Likes to compete and gain individual recognition • Is task-oriented; is inattentive to social environment when working	• Likes to work with others to achieve a common goal • Likes to assist others • Is sensitive to feelings and opinions of others
Personal Relationship to Teacher	
• Rarely seeks physical contact with teacher • Is formal; restricts interactions with teacher to tasks at hand	• Openly expresses positive feelings for teacher • Asks questions about teacher's tastes and personal experiences; seeks to become like teacher
Instructional Relationship to Teacher	
• Likes to try new tasks without teacher's help • Impatient to begin tasks; likes to finish first • Seeks nonsocial rewards	• Seeks guidance and demonstration from teacher • Seeks rewards that strengthen relationship with teacher • Is highly motivated when working individually with teacher
Characteristics of Curriculum that Facilitate Learning	
• Details of concepts are emphasized; parts have meaning of their own • Deals with math and science concepts • Based on discovery approach	• Performance objectives and global aspects of curriculum are carefully explained • Concepts are presented in humanized or story format • Concepts are related to personal interests and experiences of children

Adapted from Ramirez, M., and Castañeda, A. (1974). *Cultural democracy, bicognitive development and education*, pp. 169-170. New York: Academic Press.

The individual differences in learning and teaching styles develop from early and continuing socialization patterns. They are not indicative of general learning ability or memory. Members of the dominant cultural group in the United States are more likely to be field-independent, while many oppressed group members are field-sensitive. To serve all students effectively, teachers should be aware of their own styles and be able to identify the learning styles of students in order to develop instructional strategies that are compatible with them. Teachers should begin to function bicognitively in the classroom and teach students to operate bicognitively.

Integrating Cultural Diversity in the Curriculum

Teaching multiculturally requires affirmative steps to ensure that cultural diversity is integrated across the curriculum, no matter what subject matter is being taught. The current traditional curriculum is based on the histories, experiences, and perspectives of the dominant group. The result is the marginalization of the experiences of oppressed groups. Multicultural teaching brings the students' diverse cultures from the margin to the center of the curriculum (Herrington & Curtis, 1990). To accomplish this goal requires continuous monitoring of the instructional materials used and supplementing them with the stories and perspectives of others. This is not an easy task because "we always 'see' from points of view that are invested with our social, political, and personal interests, inescapably 'centric' in one way or another, even in the desire to do justice to heterogeneity" (Bordo, 1989, p. 140).

Today's teacher should be able to locate materials, information, and visual aids about most oppressed groups. These materials should become an integral part of the curriculum in every subject regardless of how culturally diverse the community is. It may be more difficult to find resources on microcultures where the membership is small or somewhat new to the United States, but it is not impossible. Although teachers cannot possibly address each of the hundreds of microcultures in this country, they should attempt to include the groups represented in the school community, whether or not all of them are represented in the school.

For example, in western Pennsylvania, a teacher should include information about and examples from the Amish. This approach will help the Amish students feel like a valued part of the school and will signal to other students that cultural diversity is acceptable and valued. In schools in the southwest United States, teachers should include materials on and by Mexican Americans and Native Americans. In other areas of the country, the curriculum should reflect the perspectives of Mormons, Muslims, Vietnamese Americans, Jamaican Americans, Chinese Americans, and Puerto Ricans. Knowledge and perspectives of these groups should be integrated throughout the curriculum to an even greater degree in geographic regions in which they live. The curriculum should always reflect the perspectives of women and low-income individuals as well as those of males and the middle-class.

Herrington and Curtis (1990) provide an example of bringing students' experiences to the center of the curriculum. After a number of racial incidents had disrupted their campus, they revamped their basic college writing class to focus on readings by minority authors. This approach allowed the incorporation of student voices, the inclusion of multiple perspectives, and the encouragement of critical thinking. They (Herrington & Curtis, 1990) concluded that

> Our aim [is] not to force self-disclosure, but to validate voices from the margin—voices, both heard and unheard, that have for too long and too often been

> excluded from curricula. And we do this by making these voices the center of our readings, in a classroom in which we strive to create an environment that encourages reflection, not confrontation, and encourages us all to listen to and respect one another. We should aim to do no less. (p. 496)

Educators are cautioned against giving superficial attention to microcultures. Multicultural education is not tasting ethnic food and learning ethnic dances. Even celebrating African American history only during February is not multicultural education. It is much more complex and pervasive than setting aside an hour, a unit, or a month. It becomes the lens through which the curriculum is presented.

The amount of specific content about various microcultures will vary according to the course taught, but an awareness and recognition of the culturally pluralistic nature of the nation can be reflected in all classroom experiences. No matter how assimilated students in a classroom are, it is the teacher's responsibility to ensure that they understand cultural diversity, know the contributions of members of oppressed as well as dominant groups, and have heard the voices of individuals and groups who are from a different cultural background than that of the majority of the students.

It is important for students to learn that individuals from other ethnic, religious, and socioeconomic groups may have different perspectives on the same issues and that these perspectives may be as valid as their own. On the other hand, perspectives and behaviors that degrade and harm members of other cultural groups are not considered valid by the authors of this text. The perspectives of the Ku Klux Klan and the Nazi party are examples of such invalid perspectives.

As an educator teaches about different values, lifestyles, religions, and ethnic backgrounds, these differences must not be described as inferior to the educator's own. Students easily perceive superior attitudes. Multiculturalism must not be viewed as a compensatory process. Multicultural teaching recognizes cultural differences as reflected in human relations, motivational incentives, and communication styles. Students should be helped to develop openness, flexibility, and receptivity to cultural differences and alternative lifestyles.

When one first begins to teach multiculturally, extra planning time will be needed to discover ways to make the curriculum and instruction reflective of cultural diversity. With experience, however, this process will be internalized. The teacher will begin to recognize immediately that materials are not multicultural and respond by expanding the standard curriculum to reflect cultural diversity and multiple perspectives.

Teaching multiculturally requires examining sensitive issues and topics. It requires looking at historical and contemporary events from the perspective of white men, African American women, Puerto Ricans, Japanese Americans, Central American refugees, Jewish Americans, and Southern Baptists. Reading books, poems, and articles by authors from various microcultural backgrounds is helpful, as it allows students to begin to understand the perspectives of other microcultural groups and how those perspectives differ from their own. Teachers also should help students understand the relationship of power and knowledge by comparing classical and contemporary writings in the subject being taught. This strategy can help students explore why some works are included in the curriculum while others are not (McLaren, 1988).

There are a number of resources for integrating cultural diversity across the curriculum. See the *Suggested Readings* at the end of this chapter for an annotated listing of selected resources. You may want to add one or more of these resources to a personal library for use in your own classroom.

Cultivating Community Resources

To teach multiculturally requires starting *where students are*. Educators must know the community to understand the lived cultures of families in that community. In a school in which a prayer is said every morning regardless of the Supreme Court's decision forbidding prayer in public schools, one should not teach evolution on the first day of class. In that school setting, one may not be able to teach sex education in the same way that it is taught in many urban and suburban schools. In another school, Islamic parents may be upset with the attire that their daughters are expected to wear in physical education classes, and they would not approve of coed physical education courses. Jewish students might wonder why the school celebrates Christian holidays and never Jewish holidays. Girls in some communities might question why they are restricted from participation in industrial arts courses and some vocational programs. In another part of the country, parents may be adamantly against their daughters enrolling in such courses.

In 1974, parents in Kanawha County, West Virginia, bombed classrooms because they believed that the textbooks selected by the school district did not reflect their own values and, in fact, would corrupt their children. On the other hand, urban families in the same county strongly supported the inclusion of the broad range of perspectives offered in the textbooks. It is essential that educators know their community as they develop curriculum and instruction for the classroom.

Because members of the community may revolt against the content and certain activities in the curriculum does not mean that the educator cannot teach multiculturally. It does suggest that the teacher must know the sentiments of the community before introducing concepts that may be foreign and unacceptable. Only then can the educator develop strategies for effectively introducing such concepts. The introduction of controversial issues may need to be accompanied by education of parents and the presentation of multiple perspectives that places value on the community's mores.

In addition, the community becomes a resource in a multicultural classroom. We can learn much about cultures in the community through participation in activities and by inviting community members into the school. Community speakers and helpers should represent the diversity in the community. Speakers also should be selected from different role and age groups.

In summary, teaching multiculturally means teaching about the real world—a world that includes individuals and groups with cultural backgrounds very different from one's own. As educators, we should understand that students receive cues about cultural differences not only in the classroom, but also from television, movies, advertising, and family discussions. We should be concerned about controlling or mediating many of these cues. Many misconceptions and distortions of individual and group differences are perpetuated through this social curriculum. It is our responsibility to help students understand the historical and contemporary experiences of their own and other groups. We live in an increasingly interdependent world and nation—a fact that requires us to learn to respect cultural differences and understand the differential power relationships that currently exist.

Student and Teacher Interactions

> The heart of the educational process is in the interaction between teacher and student. It is through this action that the school system makes its major impact upon the child. The way the teacher interacts with the student is a major determinant of the quality of education the child receives. (U.S. Commission on Civil Rights, 1973, p. 3)

The development and use of multicultural materials and curricula are important and necessary steps toward providing multicultural education. Alone, however, these steps are not enough. A teacher's behavior in the classroom is a key factor in helping all students reach their potential, regardless of gender, ethnicity, age, religion, language, or exceptionality.

In addition, the teacher who is enthusiastic about multicultural education will be more likely to use multicultural materials and encourage students to develop more egalitarian views. In a project designed to promote gender equality in kindergarten and fifth- and ninth-grade classrooms, researchers found that teacher enthusiasm was a key factor in affecting attitudinal change of both boys and girls at all levels (Guttentag & Bray, 1976).

Other research studies have found that warmer and more enthusiastic teachers produce students with greater achievement gains. These teachers solicit better affective responses from their students, which leads to classrooms with a more positive atmosphere. Warmth of the teacher seems to be especially important with students from low-income families and students who are targets of prejudice and discrimination (Brophy, 1983). However, teachers need to carefully assess the needs of individual students in the classroom in order to develop effective teaching strategies. They should not generalize the research findings to all students.

"Recent teacher-effectiveness research has provided clear evidence that individual teachers do make a difference in student learning" (Good, 1983, p. 57). They can make students feel either very special or incompetent and worthless. In a year-long study of schools, researchers found that "students, over and over again, raised the issue of care. What they liked best about school was when people, particularly teachers, cared about them or did special things for them" (Institute for Education in Transformation, 1992, p. 22). Teachers can make the subject come alive, or they can make students almost hate the subject. What are the qualities of teachers who make positive differences in the lives of their students? "When students are asked to describe successful teachers, one quality that comes up again and again is fairness—the ability to establish a democratic classroom where all students are treated equitably" (Sadker & Sadker, 1982, p. 97).

Impacting the Hidden Curriculum

Because the hidden curriculum includes the norms and values that undergird the formal curriculum, it must also reflect cultural diversity if teaching is to become multicultural. Although the hidden curriculum is not taught directly nor included in the objectives for the formal curriculum, it has a great impact on students and teachers alike. It includes the organizational structures of the classroom and school as well as the interactions of students and teachers.

Elements of the hidden curriculum are shaped by crowds, praise, and power (Jackson, 1990). As a member of a crowd, students must take turns, stand in line, wait to speak, wait for the teacher to provide individual help, face interruptions from others, and be distracted constantly by the needs of others. They must develop patience in order to be successful in the school setting. They must also learn to work alone within the crowd. Even though they share the classroom with many other students, they usually are not allowed to interact with classmates unless the teacher permits it. These same characteristics will be encountered in the work situations for which students are being prepared. They are not part of the formal curriculum, but central to the operation of most classrooms.

Praise can be equated with evaluation. Teachers usually evaluate students' academic performances through tests and written and oral work. However, much more than academic performance is evaluated by teachers. Student behavior probably receives the most punishment, usually when classroom rules are not adequately obeyed. In a study of elementary classrooms, Jackson (1990) found that the hidden curriculum is reflected more in student difficulties than successes:

> Why do teachers scold students? Because, try as he [she] might, he [she] fails to grasp the intricacies of long division? Not usually. Rather, students are commonly scolded for coming into the room late or for making too much noise or for not lis-

> tening to the teacher's directions or for pushing while in line. The teacher's wrath, in other words, is more frequently triggered by violations of institutional regulations and routines than by signs of his [her] students' intellectual deficiencies. (pp. 34-35)

Classroom research also has found that teachers provide boys more negative attention than girls because boys tend to be more aggressive in the classroom. Girls are more often praised for being quiet, not interrupting, and writing neatly. Similarly, students who have been assigned a low-ability status often receive negative attention from the teacher because of not following the rules, rather than because they are not performing adequately on academic tasks.

In addition to evaluations based on academic performance and institutional rules, teachers often make evaluations based on personal qualities (Jackson, 1990). Teachers sometimes group students according to their clothes, family income, cleanliness, and personality rather than potential academic abilities. This practice is particularly dangerous since most tracking perpetuates inequities rather than improves students' academic achievement.

Another aspect of the hidden curriculum is that of unequal power. In many ways this is a dilemma of childhood. By the time students enter kindergarten, they have been taught that power is in the hands of adults. The teacher and other school officials require that their rules be followed. In addition to the institutional rules, teachers may require that students give up their home languages or dialects in order to be successful academically or at least to receive the teacher's approval. Most often, students are required to adopt middle-class, white values to be successful.

How can the hidden curriculum reflect multicultural education? A first step is to recognize that it exists and that it provides lessons that are probably more important than the academic curriculum. Establishing a democratic classroom helps in overcoming the power inequities that exist. Students' curiosity must be valued and encouraged. Too often the requirements of the classroom place more value on following the rules (e.g., being quiet and handing in all assignments) than on learning. Trying hard is sometimes more important than being able to think and perform. Our interactions with students should be evaluated to ensure that we are actually supporting learning rather than preventing it.

PAUSE TO REFLECT

Think about your own college classes. What rules are you expected to follow? How much time is spent by the instructor in enforcing the rules? What classes operate in a democratic fashion? What have you learned from other students or sources about being successful in your classes? How do your college experiences compare to your high school experiences?

Improving Cross-Cultural Communications

In multicultural teaching, oral and nonverbal communication patterns between students and teachers are analyzed to increase the involvement of students in the learning process. Lack of skill in cross-cultural communications between students and teachers can prevent learning from occurring in the classroom. This problem is usually the result of misunderstanding cultural cues when students are from different cultural backgrounds than the teacher.

Just as cultures differ in the structure of their language, they also differ in the structure of oral discourse. Moves made in teaching-learning discourse, who is to make them, and the sequence they should take vary from culture to culture. These rules are not absolute laws governing behavior; in fact, they are closer to expectations and norms by which participants make sense out of "the messiness of naturally occurring conversation" (Erickson, 1980). But when these patterns differ from culture-of-teacher to culture-of-child, serious misunderstandings will occur as the two participants try to play out different patterns and assign different social meanings to the same utterance or gesture (Ainsworth, 1984, p. 134).

These differences are likely to prevail in schools with large numbers of students from oppressed groups. The "silent Native American child" described by a number of writers provides such an example. Philips (1983) identified four types of classroom interaction used by teachers from the dominant culture in schools on the Warm Springs Indian Reservation:

1. The teacher interacts with all students by addressing them as a group or as a single student in the presence of the class; the students respond as a group or individually.
2. The teacher interacts with a subgroup of students rather than with the entire class.
3. A student interacts with the teacher while working independently, and there is no audience for the interaction.
4. Students interact in small groups that they run themselves.

Philips found that the students were reluctant to participate in the first two types of interaction, which are most commonly used in schools. In the last two types of interaction, the students were actively involved.

Miscommunications occur when the same things "look and feel quite different to members of different cultural groups" (Burbules & Rice, 1991, p. 405). When students, especially those from oppressed groups, are not responding appropriately in the classroom, teachers should consider the possibility of communication cues being read differently based on culture. Burbules and Rice suggest that the success of dialogue across differences depends on what they call *communicative virtues* that include:

- tolerance, patience, and respect for differences
- the willingness to listen
- the inclination to admit that one may be mistaken
- the ability to reinterpret or translate one's own concerns in a way that makes them comprehensible to others
- self-imposition of restraint in order that others may "have a turn" to speak
- a disposition to express one's self honestly and sincerely.

Direct and continuous participation in cultures that are different from our own can improve our competency in their communication systems and should help us be more sensitive to differences in cultures with which we are not familiar. Teachers who are aware of these differences can redirect their instruction to use primarily the communications that work most effectively with the student. At the same time, the teacher can begin to teach students how to interact effectively in the situations with which they are most uncomfortable. This approach will assist all students in responding appropriately in future classroom situations that are dominated by interactions with which they are not familiar. Further, Ainsworth

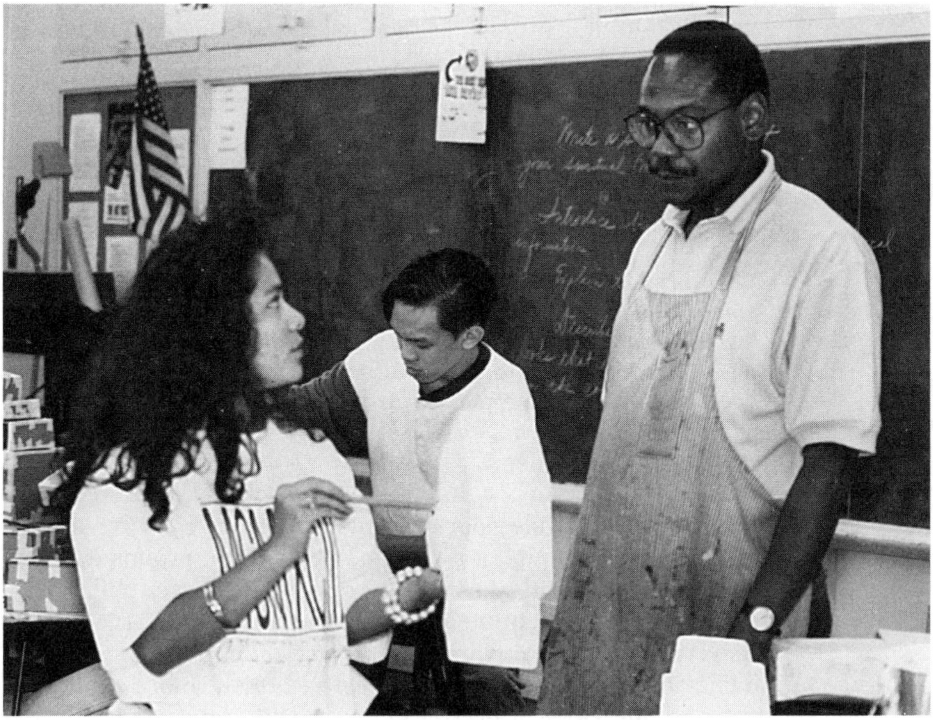

Effective cross-cultural communications between students and teachers promote student learning. When the cultural cues between students and teacher are not understood, communications and learning often are affected adversely.

(1984) suggests that "if teachers and students of many different cultural backgrounds in this multicultural nation are to avoid the embarrassment and anger caused by unwitting violation of sociolinguistic rules, both teachers and students must discover and make explicit these implicit rules" (p. 137).

Raising Teacher Expectations

Unfortunately, some teachers respond differently to students because of their microcultural memberships. Researchers have found different expectations and treatment of students based on their race, gender, and class. Some educators expect less academic achievement from minority and poor students than they expect from students from the dominant cultural group. Teachers' expectations are often based on generalizations that lower-class students and students from oppressed groups do not perform as well in school (Baron, Tom, & Cooper, 1985). When these generalizations are applied to all or most of the students from those groups, grave damage can be done, because students tend to meet the expectations of the teacher, no matter what their actual abilities are. Self-fulfilling prophecies about how well a student will perform in the classroom are often established early in the school year, and both students and the teacher unconsciously fulfill those prophecies. Educators need to develop strategies to overcome any negative expectations they may have for certain students and plan classroom instruction and activities to ensure success for all students. At the same time, Garcia (1984) warns that teachers should not overcompensate for minority students:

> Too often in the attempt to win over minorities, teachers have acquiesced to demands to "make it easy for the downtrodden." Or, teachers have recoiled with guilt when accused of being prejudiced because they gave low grades to minorities. Minorities need to be encouraged to excel in all areas of academic pursuits lest a self-fulfilling prophecy perpetuate lower academic expectations and outcomes for minorities. (p. 107)

Students from the upper middle-class are placed disproportionately in higher academic tracks while poor students are placed in lower tracks. "One critical aspect of ability grouping is that membership in groups tends to remain quite stable over time, with the work of upper- and lower-ability groups becoming more sharply differentiated as time passes" (Good, 1987, p. 175). Teaching behavior for high-quality groups is much different than for low-ability groups; middle-ability groups usually receive treatment more similar to that of high-ability groups. Good (1987) describes the differences:

> The assignments extended to lows often are practice/review-oriented and, in a word, dull. Those extended to high-ability groups involve more abstraction and

> conceptualization and are more likely to involve students actively in constructing knowledge meaningfully. Students in low-ability groups are more likely encouraged to endure; students in high-ability groups, to think and to understand. (p. 175)

To a large degree, students learn to behave in a manner expected of the group in which they are placed. Through tracking, educators have a great influence not only on directing a student's potential, but also on determining it by their initial expectations for that student. The sad reality is that tracking does not appear to work anyway. Researchers are finding that heterogeneous grouping is more helpful in improving academic achievement for students from poor and oppressed groups. Contrary to popular belief, such grouping does not limit the academic achievement of the most academically talented students, especially when the instruction is geared to challenging them. All students in the class benefit.

Many educators think that grouping students makes the classroom more manageable. They also think that it is better for students because it meets their individual needs. In a study of twenty-five schools and hundreds of research studies, Oakes (1985) found that these assumptions are wrong. She concludes that

> Tracking seems to retard the academic progress of many students—those in average and low groups. Tracking seems to foster low self-esteem among these same students and promotes school misbehavior and dropping out. Tracking also appears to lower the aspirations of students who are not in the top groups. And perhaps most important, in view of all the above, is that tracking separates students along socioeconomic lines, separating rich from poor, whites from nonwhites. The end result is that poor and minority children are found far more often than others in the bottom tracks. And once there, they are likely to suffer far more negative consequences of schooling than are their more fortunate peers. (p. 40)

The students who suffer the most from tracking practices are those from oppressed groups who are disproportionately placed in the low-ability groups. Compared to students in other tracks, these students develop more negative feelings about their academic potential and future aspirations. Educational equality demands a different strategy. It should mean "that all students are provided with the same kinds of experience in schools—a common set of learnings, equally effective instruction, and equally encouraging educational settings" (Oakes, 1985, p. 135).

Eliminating Biases

Unknowingly, educators often transmit biased messages to students. For example, lining up students by gender to go to lunch reinforces the notion that boys and girls are distinct groups. Why not line them up by shoe colors or birth dates instead? What messages do students receive when girls are always asked to take attendance and boys are asked to move chairs; or when upper-middle-class students are almost always asked to lead small-group work; or when retired people are never asked to speak to the class? Most educators do not consciously or intentionally stereotype students or discriminate against them; they usually try to treat all students fairly and equitably. However, we have learned our attitudes and behaviors in a society that has been ageist, handicappist, racist, sexist, and ethnocentric. Some biases have been internalized to such a degree that we do not realize that we have them. When educators are able to recognize the subtle and unintentional biases in their behavior, positive changes can be made in the classroom (Sadker & Sadker, 1982).

Classroom research has also found that teachers often treat boys and girls differently in the classroom. Boys receive more teacher disapproval and criticism than do girls. Boys tend to be more aggressive than girls, but these behavioral differences are not based on biological factors; instead, they are based on socialization patterns from birth. Traditionally, teachers have been part of the socialization process that teaches different male and female behavior based on gender. Although boys are often more aggressive, many of the differences observed in the way teachers treat the two are based on their own beliefs about male and female behavior. Thus, boys are criticized in more harsh and angry tones, girls in more conversational tones (Brophy & Good, 1974). Teachers have more interaction with boys through discipline and instruction. They ask boys more direct and open-ended questions and are more likely to give boys extended directions so that they can learn to do things for themselves. In contrast, teachers are more likely to do things for girls, as shown by the following example:

> In one classroom, the children were making party baskets. When the time came to staple the paper handles in place, the teacher worked with each child individually. She showed the boys how to use the stapler by holding the handle in place while the child stapled it. On the girls' turns, however, if the child didn't spontaneously staple the handle herself, the teacher took the basket, stapled it, and handed it back. (Serbin & O'Leary, 1975, p. 102)

Educational research also shows that students from oppressed groups often are treated significantly differently from white students. Because many white students share the same European and/or middle-class culture with the teacher, they also share the same cultural cues that foster success in the classroom. Students who ask appropriate questions at appropriate times or who smile and seek attention from the teacher at times when the teacher is open to such gestures are likely to receive encouragement and reinforcement from the teacher.

On the other hand, students who interrupt the class or who seek attention from the teacher when the teacher is not open to providing the necessary attention do not receive the necessary reinforcement. When students are from the same cultural background as the teacher, many of these verbal and nonverbal cues are natural to both students and teacher. When the students and teacher are from different backgrounds, the verbal and nonverbal cues may be incongruent, to the detriment of the students (Brophy & Good, 1974).

Miscommunications with teachers are more likely to be initiated by students from oppressed groups. As a result of the teacher's misreading of the cultural cues, students begin to establish ethnic boundaries within the classroom. This situation is exacerbated when students from the dominant group receive more opportunities to participate in instructional interactions and receive more praise and encouragement. Minority students receive fewer opportunities to participate, and the opportunities usually are of a less substantive nature. They also may be criticized or disciplined more frequently for breaking the rules than white students.

Teachers tend to be more directive and authoritarian toward students of color and more open and democratic with white students (Gay, 1977). Unless teachers can critically examine their treatment of students in the classroom, they will not know whether they treat them inequitably because of cultural differences. Once that step has been taken, changes can be initiated to ensure that cultural background is not a factor for automatically relating differently to students. Teachers may need to become more proactive in initiating interactions and providing encouragement, praise, and reinforcement to students from cultural backgrounds different from their own.

How can teachers analyze their own classroom interactions and teaching styles? There are at least two types of data that should be collected: (1) how much talking is done by the teacher and individual students and (2) the nature of the interactions (e.g., giving praise, criticizing, asking questions, or initiating discussion). A number of instruments have been developed by researchers to assist in this process, and there are several methods for collecting the data. If equipment is available, teachers can videotape or audiotape a class and then systematically record the interactions as they view or listen to the tape later. An outside observer could be asked to record the interaction on an instrument while sitting in the classroom. An analysis of the data will show teachers how much of the class time they spend interacting with students and the nature of the interaction. These data will show whether there are differences in interactions based on gender, ethnicity, or other characteristics of students. Such an analysis would be an excellent starting point for teachers who would like to ensure that they do not discriminate against students from different ethnic groups.

Every effort must be made to ensure that prejudices are not reflected in these interactions. Teachers must continually assess their interactions with boys and girls and students from dominant and oppressed groups to determine whether they provide different types of praise, criticism, encouragement, and reinforcement based on the cultural background of the student. Only then can steps be taken to equalize treatment.

Recognizing Positive Teacher Attributes

Although there are many positive teaching attributes, the purpose here is to identify some of those that are essential to multicultural teaching. Good (1987) outlines six attributes of good teachers:

1. They view their main responsibility as teaching.
2. They know that diagnosis, remediation, and enrichment are key aspects of teaching.
3. They expect some difficulties in helping all students learn, but are prepared to provide the appropriate follow-up instruction that will be more successful.
4. They expect all students to meet at least the minimum specified objectives.
5. They expect to deal with individuals, not groups or stereotypes.
6. They build a stimulating classroom environment that makes learning enjoyable for all students, not just those in the high-ability group.

These six characteristics are essential in multicultural teaching. To provide the greatest assistance to all students, teachers cannot provide the same treatment to each student, since they should be working toward meeting individual needs and differences. However, teachers must be sure that they are not treating students differently based solely on the students' membership in certain microcultures.

The preceding suggestions were designed to help teachers become more aware of the importance of their behavior in providing equitable education. With the elimination of bias from the teaching process and the emergence of proactive teachers who seek to best meet the needs of individual students, the classroom can become a stimulating experience for most students, regardless of their cultural background and experiences.

Textbooks and Instructional Materials

One can easily be overwhelmed by the total number of instructional materials available for use in the classroom. There are over 500,000 different materials available for classroom use. A recent edition of *Elementary/High School Textbooks in Print* listed over 20,000 titles of textbooks alone, and the National Center for Educational Media listed more than 500,000 unpublished titles. The textbook industry is big business. Over $1 billion a year is spent on elementary and high school books—more than is spent on all other hardcover and paperback books sold in the United States (Starr, 1989).

How important are instructional materials in the classroom? "Ninety percent of all classroom activity is regulated by textbooks" (Starr, 1989, p. 106).

Much of the student's classroom time also is structured around printed material. How much control an educator has over the instructional materials to be used in the classroom often depends on the school district or state in which one teaches. There are now twenty-four states, including the two largest—Texas and California—where textbooks must be adopted by the state before they can be used in the classroom (Starr, 1989). In some other states, the teacher may have a role in selecting the textbook to be used in the classroom. Most often, however, texts are assigned to teachers. Although a few teachers serve on a school district committee or state committee to select textbooks for the area, most teachers have no role in the selection process.

Although it may seem that the teacher often does not have much control over the textbooks to be used in the classroom, it is an area in which the teacher can make many important decisions. In most cases, there is a great deal of latitude about the kind of supplementary materials to be used. In most cases, there is a choice about how dependent the curriculum is on the textbooks and materials that are assigned to the classroom. In many schools, students are expected to be at a certain level of academic competency by the time the school year ends. How the teacher ensures that students learn the necessary concepts depends on the teacher. As instructional decision makers, educators are in influential positions (Gollnick, Sadker, & Sadker, 1982).

Many teachers have come to rely heavily on the textbook. A textbook has often been used to determine the curriculum and subsequent instructional strategies. Remember the teacher who announced on the first day of school how far in the textbook students had to be by the last day of school? Even for teachers who do not rely heavily on the textbook to teach, it probably remains the most important educational tool in the classroom. Other than the teacher and the chalkboard, the textbook is probably the most standard item in all classrooms. How textbooks and other instructional materials are used is extremely important in providing multicultural education.

One of the problems in depending on the textbook for classroom instruction is that many educators never question the validity of its contents. "Knowledge is often accepted as truth, legitimizing a specific view of the world that is either questionable or patently false" (Giroux, 1988, p. 31). Too often, we read the information as if it were unquestionably accurate. Consequently, it is difficult to begin reading critically for multicultural content and sensitivity. A first step is to recognize the biases that often exist in such materials and develop instructional strategies to counteract those biases. Sadker and Sadker (1978) have identified six forms of bias in classroom materials. They are invisibility, stereotyping, selectivity and imbalance, unreality, fragmentation and isolation of nondominant cultures, and linguistic bias.

Invisibility

The first bias, invisibility, is the underrepresentation of specific microcultures in materials. This omission implies that these groups have less value, impor-

The textbook remains a standard item in the classroom. However, most do not yet effectively integrate cultural diversity in the content, pictures, and perspectives presented.

tance, and significance in our society (Sadker & Sadker, 1978). Invisibility in instructional materials occurs most frequently for women, minority groups, disabled individuals, and older persons. In an examination of forty-seven textbooks used for grades 1 through 8 in social studies, reading and language arts, science, and mathematics, Sleeter and Grant (1991) found that "Asian Americans and Hispanic Americans appear mainly as figures on the landscape with virtually no history or contemporary ethnic experience, and no sense of the ethnic diversity within each group is presented. Native Americans appear mainly as historical figures" (p. 97). Females do appear in textbooks, but not as often as males. The poor and disabled are usually invisible (Sleeter & Grant, 1991).

In part because children need strong positive role models for the development of their self-esteem, the omission of members of their own microcultures is serious. It often teaches members of those groups that they are less important and less significant in our society than are majority males.

Stereotyping

A second bias, stereotyping, assigns traditional and rigid roles or attributes to a group. It denies the diversity, complexity, and variety of individuals (Sadker & Sadker, 1978). Stereotyping occurs across cultural groups. Probably the most common occurrence is in the area of vocational and career choices, especially for men, women, minority, and disabled individuals. For example, when Mexican Americans are shown working only in fields as migrant workers and never in professional jobs, stereotyping is occurring. Such bias denies the reality of individual differences and prevents readers from understanding the complexity and diversity that occurs within groups.

Selectivity and Imbalance

Selectivity and imbalance occur when issues and situations are interpreted from only one perspective, almost always the perspective of the dominant group. The authors of textbooks collect hundreds of pages of notes from which they write the book. They must decide what is most important and should be included. The authors determine whether the emphasis in a history book will be on wars and political decisions or on families and the arts. As the authors select content, the contributions of one group of people may be highlighted, and those of another group may be partially or totally omitted. In a study of the portrayal of the labor movement in secondary school history textbooks, Anyon (1979) concludes that the textbook

> Suggests a great deal about the society that produces and uses it. It reveals which groups have power and demonstrates that the views of these groups are expressed and legitimized in the school curriculum. It can also identify social groups that are not empowered by the economic and social patterns in our society and do not have their views, activities, and priorities represented in the school curriculum. The present analysis suggests that the United States working class is one such group; the poor may be another. Omissions, stereotypes, and distortions that remain in "updated" social studies textbook accounts of Native Americans, Blacks, and women reflect the relative powerlessness of these groups. (p. 382)

Generally textbooks present only one perspective. For example, the relationships between the U.S. government and the Native Americans are usually examined only from the government's perspective in terms of treaties and protection. A Native American perspective would also examine broken treaties and the appropriation of native lands. This is an example of bias through selectivity and imbalance.

Unreality

A fourth bias is unreality. Textbooks frequently present an unrealistic portrayal of our history and contemporary life experiences. Sleeter and Grant (1991) report that the forty-seven textbooks that they reviewed conveyed "the image that there are no real issues involving sexism today, that any battles for equality have been won . . .that the United States is not stratified on the basis of social class, that almost everyone is middle-class, that there is no poverty and no great wealth" (p. 98). Controversial topics are glossed over, and discussions of social movements, dissent, homosexuality, sex education, divorce, and death are avoided. "A recent survey of social studies textbooks found that the coverage of contemporary problems faced by the U.S. is so scant or disconnected that students find it difficult to understand the depth of passion these issues produced or their relevance to society today" (Woodward, Elliott, & Nagel, 1986, p. 52). This unrealistic coverage denies students the information needed to recognize, understand, and perhaps someday conquer the problems that plague our society. When sensitive or unpleasant issues, such as racism, sexism, prejudice, discrimination, intergroup conflict, and classism, are not included in instructional materials, students are not provided the facts and information they need in order to handle them in their daily lives.

Contemporary problems faced by persons with disabilities or those who are aged are often disguised or simply not included. Native Americans in discussions or illustrations, are often pictured in an historical context rather than in a contemporary context. Most materials do not consider gender, race, and class biases that exist in employment practices and in salaries. Many issues that are avoided or omitted from teaching materials are the very ones that students will have to face in the future. Obviously, the achievements and successes of the United States should be presented in textbooks. However, the problems and difficulties should be analyzed as well. No wonder students find that what they study does not relate to their lives. "As a result, young Americans today display little interest and even less knowledge of social and political affairs" (Starr, 1989, p. 107).

Fragmentation and Isolation

Some textbooks and instructional materials address nondominant groups and related issues in a fragmented and isolated manner. Issues, contributions, and information about various groups are separated from the regular text and discussed in a section or chapter of their own. This additive approach is easier to accomplish than trying to integrate the information throughout the text. However, the isolation of this information often has negative connotations or messages for students. This approach suggests that the experiences and contributions of these groups are merely an interesting diversion and not an integral part of historical and contemporary developments. There is nothing wrong with having some information separate from the regular text if it is not the *only* place students read about members of a specific microculture. The same phenomenon occurs when members of a specific microcultural group are illustrated interacting only among themselves, and not among members of the dominant culture, and having little or no influence on society as a whole. Society is multicultural, and it is important that instructional materials and textbooks reflect this diversity as a part of the total text rather than discussing microcultures in a separate section.

Linguistic Bias

Finally, linguistic bias is often seen in classroom materials, especially in the older editions that are sometimes used. Examples include the use of masculine pronouns or only Anglo names throughout a textbook. The lack of Spanish, Polish, Filipino, African, and other non-Anglo names in materials, as well as the lack of feminine pronouns or names will be evident to the sensitive teacher. When teachers are aware that linguistic bias blatantly omits female and many ethnic group references, they can develop strategies to correct the biases and to ensure that these groups are an integral part of the curriculum.

How do educators overcome the biases that exist in instructional materials, especially if they have been assigned a set of classroom materials that may be old and may not even include the positive changes of the past decade? They must become aware of the biases that often exist and then begin to critically examine the materials used in the classroom. Textbook analysis is neither a quick nor an easy task. However, there are evaluation instruments and studies that are helpful for examining classroom materials.

One does not have to depend totally on the text for instruction; teachers can supplement the textbook instruction with discussions. When using the text, it is appropriate to point out omissions. Students can examine the author's perspective with the understanding that there may be other perspectives, and discussions can focus on some of these. For example, an examination of how several Native American groups look at science would provide a perspective that contrasts with a traditional Western view of science. As a result, students would begin to understand that environmentalism is not a new phenomenon.

If the textbook includes few or no women, older persons, or persons of color, students can talk about these omissions. Students should be assigned to read other materials about the particular subject being studied that focus on the contributions of some of the omitted groups. Most schools have a library from which students can find materials to supplement classroom materials. Another valuable resource for exploring cultural diversity is the critical examination of television shows and movies that students are likely to know about or see. Through these resources the educator can ensure that students are presented a multicultural perspective.

CHECK YOUR TEXTBOOK BIASES

Select a textbook from one of your other courses (preferably one of which you have already read a large portion). Which of the following examples of bias do you find?

1. Invisibility of diverse cultures
2. Stereotyping of cultural groups
3. Selectivity and imbalance, including the lack of multiple perspectives
4. Unreal portrayal of contemporary society
5. Fragmentation and isolation of non-dominant microcultures
6. Linguistic bias

On a scale of 1–10 with 10 = excellent, how multicultural is the textbook? Why do you think the book was reflective or not reflective of multiculturalism? How would you integrate cultural diversity into this course?

This emphasis on the selection of multicultural materials is extremely important. It means exposing students to the multicultural nature of this country. All students—regardless of where they live or their religious or ethnic background—should know that other individuals come from different cultural backgrounds. Unless they help students understand the multicultural nature of American society, educators are not being honest about the world in which their students live.

School Climate

Another area in which commitment to multicultural education can be evaluated is the general school climate. Visitors entering a school can usually feel the tension that exists when cross-cultural communications are poor. They can observe whether cultural diversity is a positive and appreciated factor at the school. If only minority students or only males are waiting to be seen by the assistant principal in charge of discipline, the visitors will wonder whether the school is providing effectively for the needs of all its students. If bulletin boards in classrooms show only white characters, visitors will question the appreciation of cultural diversity in the school. If the football team is made up primarily of minority players and the chess club of white players, they will wonder about the inclusion of students from a variety of cultural backgrounds in extracurricular activities. If school administrators are primarily men and most teachers are women, or if the teachers are white and the teacher aides are Hispanic, the visitors will envision discriminatory practices in hiring and promotion procedures. These are examples of a school climate that does not reflect a commitment to multicultural education.

Although all schools are multicultural, the cultural diversity that exists is not always positively reflected. A school that affirms multiculturalism will integrate the community in its total program. Not only will the educators know and understand the community, but the parents and community will know and participate in the school activities. As long as members of the community feel unwelcome in the school, they are not likely to initiate any involvement. The first step in multiculturalizing the school is developing positive and supportive relations between the school and the community. Teachers can assist by asking parents and other community members to participate in class activities by talking about their jobs, hobbies, or experiences in a certain area. Teachers can initiate contacts with families of students. They can participate in community events. A sincere interest in the community, rather than disgust or patronage, will help to bridge the gap that often exists between the school and the community.

Staffing composition and patterns should reflect the cultural diversity of the country. At a minimum, they should reflect the diversity of the geographical area. Women, as well as men, will be school administrators; men, as well as women, will teach at preschool and primary levels. Minorities will be found in the administration and teaching ranks, not primarily in custodial and clerical positions.

When cultural diversity is valued within a school, student government and extracurricular activities will include students from various microcultural groups. There should be no segregation of students based on their membership in a certain microculture. In a school where multiculturalism is valued, students from various cultural backgrounds hold leadership positions. Those roles are not automatically delegated to students from the dominant cultural group of the school.

If the school climate is multicultural, it is reflected in every aspect of the educational program. In addition to those areas already mentioned, assembly programs reflect multiculturalism in their content, as well as in the choice of speakers. Bulletin boards and displays reflect the cultural diversity of the nation, even if the community is not rich in cultural diversity. Cross-cultural communications among students and between students and teachers are positive. Different languages and dialects used by students are respected. Both girls and boys are found in industrial arts, home economics, calculus, bookkeeping or accounting, and vocational classes. Minority students, as well as white students, comprise the college preparatory classes.

The school climate must be supportive of multicultural education. When respect for cultural differences is reflected in all aspects of the students' educational program, the goals of multicultural education are being attained. Educators hold the key to attaining this climate.

Preparation for Providing Multicultural Education

"A teacher in search of his/her own freedom may be the only kind of teacher who can arouse young persons to go in search of their own" (Green, 1988, p. 14). There are a number of actions that educators should undertake to prepare for the provision of multicultural education in the classroom. First, they should know their own cultural identity and the degree to which they identify with the various microcultures of which they are members. The degree of identification will probably change over time. Second, they should be able to accept the fact that they have prejudices that may affect the way they react to students in the classroom. When they recognize these biases, they can develop strategies to overcome or compensate for them in the classroom.

Educators need to learn about cultural groups other than their own. They might read about different cultural groups, attend ethnic movies or plays, participate in ethnic celebrations, visit different churches and ethnic communities, and interact with members of different groups. Teachers who enjoy reading novels should select authors from different cultural backgrounds. The perspective presented may be much different from their own. Novels may help the reader to understand that other people's experiences may lead them to react to situations differently than the reader would. It is often an advantage to discuss one's reactions to such new experiences with someone else in order to clarify one's own feelings of prejudices or stereotypes.

Educators should make an effort to interact with persons who are culturally different from themselves. Long-term cultural experiences are probably the most effective means for overcoming fear and misconceptions about a group. One must remember, however, that there is much diversity within a group. One cannot generalize about an entire group based on the characteristics of a few persons. In direct cross-cultural contacts, one must learn to be open to the traditions and perspectives of the other culture in order to learn from the experience. Otherwise, one's own traditions, habits, and perspectives are likely to be projected as better rather than just different.

If individuals can learn to understand, empathize with, and participate in a second culture, they will have had a valuable experience. If they learn to live multiculturally, they are indeed fortunate. Welch (1991) describes one way in which teachers from the dominant group can earn respect from members of other groups:

> For those with more areas of commonality, a different sort of work enables genuine conversation to occur. A genuine conversation between those who are privileged by way of class, gender, or race and those who have experienced oppression or discrimination on the basis of those characteristics is possible when those who are privileged work to end the oppression or discrimination they denounce. As we do more than vote for those opposed to racism, challenging racism directly in our workplaces, in our families, in our own lives, we can be trusted in a way that enables those oppressed because of race to speak with us more honestly. In our

> work, we see more clearly the costs of racism and the intransigence of structures of oppression. Men who work against rape or domestic violence, who are involved in challenging the value systems that lead to such violence, are able to hear the voices of women, and women are able to trust them in a way impossible if the only form of relation is a dialogue. (pp. 98-99)

Teachers who have made their teaching multicultural confront and fight against incidents of racism, sexism, and other discrimination in schools and society. They develop strategies to recognize their own biases and overcome them. Finally, they use their knowledge and skills to support a democratic and equitable society.

Summary

Multicultural education is a means for positively using cultural diversity in the total learning process. In the process, classrooms should become models of democracy and equity. To do this requires that educators (1) place the student at the center of the teaching and learning process; (2) promote human rights and respect for cultural differences; (3) believe that all students can learn; (4) acknowledge and build on the life histories and experiences of students' microcultural memberships; (5) critically analyze oppression and power relationships to understand racism, sexism, classism, and discrimination against the disabled, young, and aged; (6) critique society in the interest of social justice and equality; and (7) participate in collective social action to ensure a democratic society.

Multicultural education can help students increase their academic achievement levels in all areas, including basic skills, through the use of teaching approaches and materials that are sensitive and relevant to the students' cultural backgrounds and experiences. The voices of students and the community must be heard in order to deliver multicultural education. Educators should develop skills for individualizing instruction based on the needs of students. No longer can we afford to teach all students the same knowledge and skills in the same way. Individualizing the instruction is one way to help all students reach their potential and develop their unique talents. Teachers must make an effort to know all of their students and to build on their strengths and help them overcome their weaknesses.

Multicultural education must be integrated throughout the curriculum at all levels. It can help students to think critically, to deal with the social and historical realities of American society, and to gain a better understanding of the causes of oppression and inequality, including racism and sexism. Multicultural education must start *where people are* and incorporate multicultural resources from the local community.

Positive student and teacher interactions can support academic achievement, regardless of gender, ethnicity, age, religion, language, or exceptionality.

Oral and nonverbal communication patterns between students and teachers are analyzed and changed to increase the involvement of students in the learning process. The learning styles of students and the teaching style of the teacher are understood and used to develop effective instructional strategies. However, teachers must be sure that they are not treating students differently based solely on the students' membership in certain microcultures. We need to evaluate our own academic expectations of students, our practices of ability grouping, our own biases, and our attributes to ensure that we are helping all students have access to knowledge.

Educators should be aware of the biases that exist in most classroom materials and be able to draw on supplementary materials to reflect cultural diversity more accurately. In addition, the recognition of biases can lead to discussions about the inclusion of different ethnic, religious, gender, socioeconomic, disabled, and age groups.

Educators will face a tremendous challenge in the next decade to effectively use the cultural diversity that students bring to the classroom. Every subject area can be taught in ways that reflect the reality of cultural differences in this nation and the world. Skills to function effectively in different cultural settings can also be taught. For students to function effectively in a democratic society, they must learn about the inequities that currently exist. Otherwise, our society will never be able to overcome such inequities.

As educators, we must teach all children. The ultimate goal of multicultural education is to meet the individual learning needs of each student so that all students can progress to their fullest capacity. This goal has not been reached in the past, partly because educators have been unable to effectively use the cultural backgrounds of students in providing classroom instruction. As multicultural education reaches into all levels of schooling, the maximum development of all students, regardless of their cultural background, will be supported. Acceptance of the challenge to multiculturalize our schools is vital to the well-being of all citizens.

Questions for Review

1. What is multicultural teaching?
2. How is membership in microcultures related to multicultural education?
3. How can a student's culture be used to teach academic content? Give examples that apply to the subject area that you plan to teach.
4. If the textbook that you have been assigned to use includes no information or examples pertaining to nondominant groups, what can you do to provide a balanced and realistic view of society to students?
5. How can you incorporate student's voices into the subject that you plan to teach?

6. Why have tracking systems developed in many schools? What are the characteristics used to track students? What is the danger in tracking students?
7. Identify teacher behaviors and attributes that should positively support the delivery of multicultural education.
8. In what situations would it be appropriate to use cooperative learning strategies?
9. What is your teaching style, and what strategies should you develop to work more effectively with students whose learning style is not compatible with your own?
10. What characteristics would you look for to determine if a school is committed to multicultural education?

References

Ainsworth, N. (1984). The cultural shaping of oral discourse. *Theory into Practice*, 23, 132-137.

Anyon, J. (1979). Ideology and United States history textbooks. *Harvard Educational Review, 49*(3), 361-386.

Baron, R. M., Tom, D. Y. H., & Cooper, H. M. (1985). Social class, race and teacher expectations. In J. B. Dusek, V. C. Hall, & W. J. Meyer (Eds.), *Teacher expectancies* (pp. 251-270). Hillsdale, NJ: Lawrence Erlbaum Associates.

Bordo, S. (1989). Feminism, postmodernism and gender-skepticism. In L. Nicholson (Ed.), *Feminism/postmodernism*, 133-156. New York: Routledge.

Brophy, J. E. (1983). Classroom organization and management. In D. C. Smith (Ed.), *Essential knowledge for beginning educators* (pp. 23-37). Washington, DC: American Association of Colleges for Teacher Education.

Brophy, J. E., & Good, T. L. (1974). *Teacher-student relationships: Causes and consequences.* New York: Holt, Rinehart & Winston.

Burbules, N.C. & Rice, S. (1991). Dialogue across differences: Continuing the conversation. *Harvard Educational Review, 61*(4), 393-416.

Coles, R. (1967). *Migrants, sharecroppers, mountaineers. Vol. 2 of Children in Crisis.* Boston: Little, Brown.

Erickson, F. (1980). Timing and context in everyday discourse: Implications for the study of referential and social meaning. In R. Bauman & J. Sherzer (Eds.), *Language and speech in American society*. Austin, TX: Southwest Educational Development Laboratory.

Fine, M. (1989). Silencing and nurturing voice in an improbable context: Urban adolescents in public school. In H.A. Giroux & P. McLaren (Eds.), *Critical pedagogy, the state, and cultural struggle*, 152-173. Albany, NY: State University of New York Press.

Freire, P. (1970). *Pedagogy of the oppressed.* New York: Seabury.

Garcia, R. L. (1984). Countering classroom discrimination. *Theory into Practice, 23*, 104-109.

Gay, G. (1977). Curriculum design for multicultural education. In C. Grant (Ed.), *Multicultural education: Commitments, issues, and applications* (pp. 94-104). Washington, DC: Association for Supervision and Curriculum Development.

Giroux, H. A. (1991). Postmodernism as border pedagogy: Redefining the boundaries of race and ethnicity. In H.A. Giroux (Ed.), *Postmodernism, feminism, and cultural politics: Redrawing educational boundaries*, 217-256. Albany, NY: State University of New York Press.

Giroux, H. A. (1988). *Teachers as intellectuals*. Granby, MA: Bergin & Garvey.

Gollnick, D. M., Sadker, M. P., & Sadker, D. M. (1982). Beyond the Dick and Jane syndrome: Confronting sex bias in instructional materials. In M. P. Sadker & D. M. Sadker (Eds.), *Sex equity handbook for schools* (pp. 60-95). New York: Longman.

Good, T. L. (1983). Recent classroom research: Implications for teacher education. In D. C. Smith (Ed.), *Essential knowledge for beginning educators* (pp. 55-64). Washington, DC: American Association of Colleges for Teacher Education.

Good, T. L. (1987). Teacher expectations. In D. C. Berliner & B. V. Rosenshine (Eds.), *Talks to teachers* (pp. 159-200). New York: Random House.

Goodlad, J. I. (1981). *A place called school*. New York: McGraw-Hill.

Green, M. (1988). *The dialectic of freedom*. New York: Teachers College Press.

Guttentag, M., & Bray, H. (1976). *Undoing sex stereotypes: Research and resources for educators*. New York: McGraw-Hill.

Herrington, A.J. & Curtis, M. (1990). Basic writing: Moving the voices on the margin to the center. *Harvard Educational Review, 60*(4), 489-496.

Institute for Education in Transformation. (1992). *Voices from the inside: A report on schooling from inside the classroom*. Claremont, CA: Author.

Jackson, P.W. (1990). *Life in classrooms*. New York: Teachers College Press.

Lather, P. (1991). *Getting smart: Feminist research and pedagogy with/in the postmodern*. New York: Routledge.

McDiarmid, G.W. (1991). What teachers need to know about cultural diversity: Restoring subject matter to the picture. In M.M. Kennedy (Ed.), *Teaching academic subjects to diverse learners*, 257-269.

McLaren, P. L. (1988). Culture or canon? Critical pedagogy and the politics of literacy. *Harvard Educational Review, 58*(2), 213-234.

Oakes, J. (1985). *Keeping track: How schools structure inequality*. New Haven, CT: Yale University Press.

O'Connor, T. (1988, November). *Cultural voice and strategies for multicultural education*. Paper presented at the annual meeting of the American Educational Studies Association, Montreal, Canada.

Ogbu, J.U. (1992). Understanding cultural diversity and learning. *Educational Researcher, 21*(8), 5-14.

Philips, S. U. (1983). *The invisible culture: Communication in classroom and community on the Warm Springs Indian reservation*. New York: Longman.

Ramirez, M., & Castañeda, A. (1974). *Cultural democracy, bicognitive development and education*. New York: Academic Press.

Sadker, M., & Sadker, D. (1978). The teacher educator's role. In S. McCune & M. Matthews (Eds.), *Implementing Title IX and attaining sex equality: A workshop package for postsecondary educators*. Washington, DC: U.S. Government Printing Office.

Sadker, M. P., & Sadker, D. M. (1982). Between teacher and student: Overcoming sex bias in classroom interaction. In M. P. Sadker & D. M. Sadker (Eds.), *Sex equity handbook for schools* (pp. 96-132). New York: Longman.

Sapon-Shevin, M. & Schniedewind, N. (1991). Cooperative learning as empowering pedagogy. In C.E. Sleeter (Ed.), *Empowerment through multicultural education*, 159-178. Albany, NY: State University of New York Press.

Serbin, L. A., & O'Leary, K. D. (1975, December). How nursery schools teach girls to shut up. *Psychology Today*, 9(7), 56-57, 102-103.

Shor, I., & Freire, P. (1987). *A pedagogy for liberation: Dialogues on transforming education*. South Hadley, MA: Bergin & Garvey.

Simon, R. I. (1989). Empowerment as a pedagogy of possibility. In H. Holtz, I. Marcus, J. Dougherty, J. Michaels, & R. Peduzzi (Eds.), *Education and the American dream: Conservatives, liberals and radicals debate the future of education* (pp. 134-149). Granby, MA: Bergin & Garvey.

Sleeter, C. E. & Grant, C. A. (1991). Race, class, gender, and disability in current textbooks. In M. W. Apple & L. K. Christian-Smith, *The politics of the textbook*, 78-110. New York: Routledge.

Starr, J. (1989). The great textbook war. In H. Holtz, I. Marcus, J. Dougherty, J. Michaels, & R. Peduzzi (Eds.), *Education and the American dream: Conservatives, liberals and radicals debate the future of education* (pp. 96-109). Granby, MA: Bergin & Garvey.

Suzuki, B. H. (1980, April 23-25). *An Asian-American perspective on multicultural education: Implications for practice and policy.* Paper presented at the meeting of the National Association for Asian and Pacific American Education, Washington, DC. (ERIC Document Reproduction Service No. ED 205 633)

U.S. Commission on Civil Rights. (1973). *Teachers and students, Report 5, Mexican American education study: Differences in teacher interaction with Mexican American and Anglo students*. Washington, DC: Government Printing Office.

Welch, S. (1991). An ethic of solidarity and difference. In H.A. Giroux (Ed.), *Postmodernism, feminism, and cultural politics: Redrawing educational boundaries*, 83-99. Albany, NY: State University of New York Press.

Wilkinson, L. C. (1988). Grouping children for learning: Implications for kindergarten education. *Review of Research in Education*, 15, 203-223.

Woodward, A., Elliott, D. L., & Nagel, K. C. (1986, January). Beyond textbooks in elementary social studies. *Social Education, 50*(1), 50-53.

Suggested Readings

Appleton, N. (1983). *Cultural pluralism in education.* New York: Longman.

This examination of multicultural education includes goals and a conflict-sensitive curriculum. The teaching resources includes a comprehensive annotated list of helpful simulations.

Bulletin. New York: Council on Interracial Books for Children.

This periodical is published eight times a year. It includes thought-provoking, issue-oriented analyses of storybooks, textbooks, audiovisuals, and other learning materials. Includes surveys, teaching strategies, lesson plans and bibliographies, as well as regular departments that suggest useful resources and review children's books.

Derman-Sparks, L. & the A.B.C. Task Force. (1989). *Anti-bias curriculum: Tools for empowering young children.* Washington, DC: National Association for the Education of Young Children.

These recommendations for creating an anti-bias curriculum and environment include how to deal with children's stereotyping and discriminatory behaviors. This handbook provides guidelines and activities to help children learn about cultural differences, including race, disabilities, and gender identity.

Elliott, R. (1992). *We: Lessons on equal worth and dignity*. Minneapolis: United Nations Association of Minnesota. (1929 S. 5th St., Minneapolis, MN 55454)

This curriculum module provides opportunities for students to develop knowledge about issues and events of intergroup relations, increase student awareness of the dynamics of intolerance, and help students build a framework for developing their thinking about these issues. It also includes selected resources, with special attention to materials related to the United Nations.

Equity and Choice. (Published in cooperation with the Institute for Responsive Education and the Center on Families, Communities, Schools and Children's Learning by Corwin Press)

This magazine is a forum for the exchange of ideas, insights, and practices among those working to increase educational equity. Contributors include teachers, parents, administrators, students, researchers, policymakers, and educational activists.

Good, T. L. (1987). Teacher expectations. In D. C. Berliner & B. V. Rosenshine (Eds.), *Talks to teachers*. New York: Random House.

This presentation of research on teacher expectations provides practical skills for working with students who are failing and suggestions for improving performance of low achievers.

Grant, G. (Ed.). (1977). *In praise of diversity: Multicultural classroom applications.* Omaha: The University of Nebraska at Omaha, Teacher Corps, Center for Urban Education.

This reference includes fifty-one classroom activities for social studies, language arts, science, math, and art.

Guidelines for selecting bias-free textbooks and storybooks. (1984). New York: Council on Interracial Books for Children.

This document is a collection of criteria and checklists to identify stereotypes and other forms of bias against women, people of color, persons with disabilities, and the elderly.

Guttentag, M., & Bray, H. (1976). *Undoing sex stereotypes: Research and resources for educators.* New York: McGraw-Hill.

This excellent resource provides suggestions for making the curriculum nonsexist at all levels. It includes a description of the research by the Nonsexist Intervention Project, on which the suggestions are based, bibliographies and a list of resource organizations.

Hansen-Krening, N. (1979). *Competency and creativity in language arts: A multiethnic focus.* Reading, MA: Addison-Wesley.

This multiethnic approach to language arts at the primary and intermediate levels includes lesson plans that address sensory awareness, music, art, listening, speaking, writing, movement and nonverbal communications, creative dramatics, myths, legends, and folktales.

Hernandez, H. (1989). *Multicultural education: A teacher's guide to content and process.* New York: Merrill/Macmillan.

This practical guide makes recommendations for incorporating multicultural education in different aspects of classroom instruction and what teachers should know about students' homes, neighborhoods, and communities. Areas covered include the hidden curriculum, bilingualism, special/gifted education, instructional materials, and multicultural curriculum.

Horne, G. (1988). *Thinking and rethinking U.S. history.* New York: Council on Interracial Books for Children.

The analysis of twelve history textbooks provides the context for helping students develop critical thinking and problem-solving skills. This handbook includes lesson plans and handouts to encourage probing of four lines of inquiry for each historical period from precolonial America to post-Civil-War.

Institute for Education in Transformation. (1992). *Voices from the inside: A report on schooling from inside the classroom.* Claremont, CA: Author.

This report sets forth the perceptions, complaints, satisfactions, fears and hopes of students, teachers, parents, administrators and staff inside four schools. It includes recommendations for improving schools.

Kendall, F. E. (1983). *Diversity in the Classroom.* New York: Teachers College.

This resource book for preschool, primary-grade, and day-care teachers includes a resource unit and activities on affirming cultural diversity, as well as recommendations for working with children and parents.

Multicultural Education. (Published from the National Association for Multicultural Education by Caddo Gap Press, 3145 Geary Blvd., Suite 275, San Francisco, CA 94118)

This quarterly magazine features articles by major scholars and practitioners in the field of multicultural education. It also includes promising practices, multicultural resources, and book and film reviews.

Olsen, L. & Mullen, N.A. (1990). *Embracing diversity: Teachers' voices from California's classrooms.* San Francisco: California Tomorrow.

California teachers talk about the arduous and creative task of reshaping their teaching approaches and redefining schooling to make it appropriate to the multicultural, multinational, and multilingual realities. These stories portray the complexities of validating each child's culture and simultaneously knitting a strong sense of community across ethnic, cultural, and language groups.

Perl, T. (1978). *Math equals: Biographies of women mathematicians and related activities.* Reading, MA: Addison-Wesley.

These classroom activities are based on the work of nine female mathematicians for all grade levels.

Ramirez, M., & Castañeda, A. (1974). *Cultural democracy, bicognitive development and education.* New York: Academic Press.

This helpful research report of the learning styles of Mexican American children and teaching styles of their teachers describes an intervention strategy for training teachers to teach students to be bicognitive.

Sadker, M. P., & Sadker, D. M. (Eds.). (1982). *Sex equity handbook for schools.* New York: Longman.

This handbook provides an overview of the critical areas of sex equity in schools and practical strategies for the elimination of sex bias in education. It includes lesson plans and units with a synopsis of relevant research and a narrative on the nature of sex bias in today's classrooms.

Shor, I., & Freire, P. (1987). *A pedagogy for liberation: Dialogues on transforming education.* South Hadley, MA: Bergin & Garvey.

These conversations about teaching for liberation by two practitioners include recommendations for dialogical teaching and developing critical thinking skills of students. It also addresses some of the problems teachers may face when using this approach, as well as giving recommendations for handling unruly behavior, silence, and discontent.

Simms, R. L., & Contreras, G. (1980). *Racism and sexism: Responding to the challenge.* Washington, DC: National Council for the Social Studies.

This exploration of the responses of the social studies to racism and sexism also includes a helpful resource list, including alternative publishers and projects that address these topics.

Sleeter, C.E. (1991). *Empowerment through multicultural education.* Albany, NY: State University of New York Press.

Ethnographic studies illustrate how students from oppressed groups view their world, their power to affect it in their own interests, and their response to their growing sense of powerlessness. Educators describe the strategies they have used to empower these students, including the analysis of the popular media and cooperative learning.

Sleeter, C. E., & Grant, C. A. (1988). *Making choices for multicultural education: Five approaches to race, class, and gender.* New York: Merrill/Macmillan.

This examination of five approaches to teaching multicultural education focuses on the integration of race, class, and gender issues. It includes research activities and lesson plans that assist the reader in changing curriculum to implement the different approaches.

Strike, K. A., & Soltis, J. F. (1985). *The ethics of teaching.* New York: Teachers College, Columbia University.

These case studies and discussions examine ethical situations that teachers may face in the nation's classrooms. It addresses a number of multicultural issues: the equal treatment of students, censorship, equality, grading policies, the Pledge of Allegiance, values clarification, social reproduction, equality of opportunity, separation of church and state, sex education, and teaching values.

Teaching Tolerance. (Published by the Southern Poverty Law Center, 400 Washington Ave., Montgomery, AL 36104)

This semi-annual magazine provides teachers with ready-to-use ideas and strategies to help promote harmony in the classroom. Contributions address politics, race, economics, abilities, culture, and language.

Critical Incidents in Teaching

The critical incidents described in this section reflect real-life situations that have occurred in schools or classrooms or are parts of different incidents that have been combined to provide you with a problematic situation that could very well take place in your school. The purpose of this section is to provide you with an opportunity to examine your feelings, attitudes, and possible actions or reactions. In some respects, these exercises are not realistic for you as a potential problem solver because in reality, decisions must be made quickly, and you may not have even five minutes to ponder your options and decide on an appropriate action. However, these exercises in problem solving may facilitate and sharpen your skills to think critically, which may enhance your functioning in various school situations and help you to better meet the diverse needs of your students.

Sex/Gender Role Identification

Jane Irwin is the director of the Model Learning Center at a regional university located in the Southwest. The center is a kindergarten laboratory school located on the university campus to provide observation and practicum opportunities for students in the teacher education program. Ms. Irwin is affectionately referred to as Miss Janie by the children at the center. At the end of a lesson on health, the children are dismissed by Miss Janie for thirty minutes of free play in the classroom. Each child is free to select his or her activity of choice. The Model Learning Center is well equipped with a wide variety of play materials, and the children quickly move to their chosen activities. In the classroom, there are two undergraduate students in early childhood education who are in the center as part of their required practicum.

Some of the children choose puzzles, some a large playhouse, others an indoor slide, airplanes, dolls, and various other activities. One of the boys, Tim, moves over to an area where two of the girls are playing with dolls. Tim gently picks up a doll and begins combing its long blonde hair. Shocked by this behavior, one of the practicum students rushes over to Tim, helps him to his feet, takes the doll and comb out of his hands, places them on the floor and says, "Come with me" as she leads him by the hand to an area where two boys are playing with a model airplane and a helicopter. Picking up an airplane, she hands it to Tim and says, "Here, you play with this. Boys like airplanes, not dolls."

Miss Janie has observed the entire sequence of events as she sits at her desk watching her students and the university teacher education student.

Questions for Discussion

1. What should Miss Janie do with regard to the child who is now obediently playing with the airplane?
2. What should she do with regard to the class, since several children observed the incident?
3. What should she do with regard to the university student?

Religious Discrimination

Janice Ferguson is a five-year-old Jewish girl living in a conservative Protestant community where there are few non-Christian families. She is the only Jewish child in her kindergarten class. She is an outgoing child, well liked by her classmates. While playing out in the playground with two of her classmates, one of them asks Janice what she expects to receive for Christmas. Janice answers by stating that her family does not observe Christmas. "Why not?" the other girls ask. "Because we're Jewish and we have Hanukkah instead," Janice explains.

The next day, Janice, visibly upset, seeks out Mrs. Jenkins, her teacher, on the playground. "Mary Ellen said that her daddy told her that Jews were bad people because they killed Jesus. I don't think she wants to be my friend anymore," she says.

Questions for Discussion

1. What can Mrs. Jenkins do for Janice to provide her with some immediate comfort?
2. What can or should Mrs. Jenkins do with regard to Mary Ellen?
3. Should Mrs. Jenkins do anything with regard to the class to stop a potential problem in bigotry from spreading? If so, what are some activities she can plan for her class?

Acceptance of Hearing-Impaired Student

Jeb Benson is a first-grade student in Ms. Storey's class. Unbeknownst to his classmates, Jeb, in the past two months, has been examined by an otologist, tested by an audiologist, and found to have a bilateral hearing loss of forty decibels. He has been fitted for a behind-the-ear hearing aid, and without either warning (except for Ms. Storey) or fanfare, has shown up in class with an unobtrusive but noticeable hearing aid in his right ear.

By the time Jeb sits down in his seat, several of his classmates have noticed his new hearing aid and are beginning to gossip about it. None know exactly what it is, and Jeb is acutely aware of the fact that his classmates are talking about him. He suddenly feels embarrassed and removes the hearing aid from his ear and places it in his pocket. From her desk, Ms. Storey observes all that is going on. She is determined to help Jeb feel comfortable wearing his hearing aid in her class.

Questions for Discussion

1. How can Ms. Storey facilitate Jeb's adjustment to his new hearing aid in the class?
2. What should she say to Jeb?
3. What, if anything, should she say to the class?
4. What activities could she devise to enhance acceptance and understanding of Jeb's problem?

Placement of a Child with Epilepsy

Mr. Potts is a sixth-grade teacher in a middle-class suburban school. After school, Mr. Potts finds a note in his box indicating that the principal and the special education resource room teacher would like to meet with him the next day before the students arrive.

At the meeting the next day, his principal, Dr. Levy, explains to him that a new student, Chris Erickson, will be placed in his class the following Monday morning. He is informed that Chris is slightly above average in academics and a personable young man. However, Dr. Levy wants Mr. Potts to know that Chris is a student with epilepsy who occasionally has grand mal seizures. While the seizures are generally under control through medication, there is a good possibility that sometime during the school year Chris will have a seizure in the classroom.

At this time, Ms. Kim, the resource room teacher, describes the grand mal seizures. She explains that they are the most evident and serious type of epileptic seizure. They can be disturbing and frightening to anyone who has never seen one. Chris would have little or no warning that a seizure was about to occur. During a seizure, his muscles will stiffen and he will lose consciousness and fall to the floor. His whole body will shake violently, as his muscles alternately contract and relax. Saliva may be forced from his mouth, his legs and arms may jerk, and his bladder and bowels may empty. After a few minutes, the contractions will diminish, and Chris will either go to sleep or regain consciousness in a confused and drowsy state (Heward & Orlansky, 1992).

Stunned at this information, Mr. Potts sits in silence as Ms. Kim briefs him about what procedures to take if and when a seizure occurs in the classroom. She also explains to him that he should inform the other students that the seizure is painless to Chris and that it is not contagious.

Mr. Potts is aware that he has no option as to whether or not Chris will be in his class. Determined to make Chris' transition into his class as smooth as possible, and also determined that he will help his class adjust and prepare for the likely seizure, Mr. Potts begins to map out a plan of action.

Questions for Discussion

1. What can Mr. Potts do with regard to his class?
2. Should he talk to his class about Chris?
3. Should he explain what epilepsy is?
4. What should he say to Chris? What other actions can he take?

Student with a Health Problem

Michelle Adams is a third-grade teacher in a cattle and farming community of 40,000 in Colorado. Some of the residents in the community and students in the school come from lower socioeconomic backgrounds; others come from middle- and upper-class backgrounds. The students are primarily white, and several are descendants of early German settlers in the region. A few students are Hispanic, and some are children of migrant workers who work in the sugar beet fields. There are a handful of Asian students, mostly third- and fourth-generation Japanese Americans.

On the day after Christmas vacation, Ms. Adams notes that one of her students, Terry, is constantly touching his teeth with his index finger. Walking over to his desk, she asks him what his problem is. "My teeth hurt," he replies.

Asking him to open his mouth, she is shocked to see one of his teeth visibly eaten away with decay.

"Do your parents know about this?" she asks the student.

"Sure they do," he responds.

"Then why don't you go to a dentist to have it taken care of?" she asks.

"'Cause we ain't got no money," he replies.

Questions for Discussion

1. Should Ms. Adams have pursued the questioning in front of the class?
2. What could she have done to minimize any embarrassment to Terry in front of his classmates?

3. Is the health and dental needs of a child the responsibility or concern of the teacher?
4. Should she contact Terry's parents? The principal? The school nurse?

Attempts to Censor

Mitchell Aoki is a second-year English teacher in a midwestern community of 80,000. He teaches sophomore and junior English classes. A fourth-generation Japanese American, Aoki majored in English and religion and received his teaching credential from a private southern Baptist university. His evaluations from his principal for his first year were considered excellent for a first-year teacher.

When his principal asks him to come to his office, Aoki is surprised when he is handed a letter from a parent. The letter reads:

> *Suzanne came home crying in the heart. I don't know who this Mr. Aoki is, but he needs to know that it is important to respect the religious values of others even if he does not believe in our God. There will be retribution, for one cannot take the name of God in vain and not expect punishment for such blasphemy.*

Stunned, Aoki asks the principal what the letter is all about.

"That's what I was about to ask you," the principal replies.

"I never use profanity in front of the students. In fact, I don't use profanity at all," Aoki responds. "I don't know what this is all about. The letter implies that I'm a nonbeliever, a non-Christian. Maybe an atheist? I'm an active member of a Baptist church. I even majored in religion."

"I know, Mitchell. That's why I'm trying to get to the bottom of this," the principal says.

Suddenly, it strikes Aoki. "It was the series of poems I read to the class last week. They were examples of poetry by some contemporary writers, and there was a passage in one where the author referred to someone as a 'God damned weasel.' I read that as a direct quote to a class of high school juniors and now I'm branded as a blasphemer! He's assuming that because of my ethnic background I'm a buddhist or an atheist."

Questions for Discussion

1. Did Mitchell Aoki exercise poor judgment in reading a poem to the class that contained words offensive to the student and her father?
2. If he did nothing wrong, should he take precautions in the future to avoid similar reactions?
3. Should the student and father be contacted by Aoki? By the principal? By both? If so, what form should the contact take? A letter? A conference? An apology? An explanation? What type of explanation?
4. Are minority group teachers at greater risk of being perceived as nonmainstreamed in values, morals, and so on?

Differences in Socioeconomic Status

The middle school in a rural community of 9,000 residents has four school-sponsored dances a year. At the Valentine's Day dance, a coat and tie affair, six of the eighth-grade boys showed up in rented tuxedos. They had planned this together, and their parents, among the more affluent in the community, thought it would be "cute" and paid for the rentals. The final dance of the year is scheduled for May, and it, too, is a coat and tie dance. This time, rumors are circulating around the school that "everyone" is renting a tux and the girls are getting new formal dresses. Three boys' parents are, according to the grapevine, renting a limousine for their sons and their dates. These self-imposed behaviors and dress standards are far in excess of anything previously observed at the middle school.

Several of the students, particularly those from lower socioeconomic backgrounds, have said that they will boycott the dance. They cannot afford the expensive attire, and they claim that the ones behind the dress-up movement have said that only the nerds or geeks would show up in anything less than a tux or a formal gown.

Questions for Discussion

1. Should the school administration intervene?
2. Should the parents be contacted?
3. Should the matter be discussed in the homerooms? In a school assembly?
4. Should the dance be canceled?
5. Should there be limits on how dressed up students can be? Could the school legally enforce limits?
6. Can and should there be any issue made on the hiring of limousine services for middle school students?

Religious Dietary Attitudes

Allison Beller is a fourth-grade teacher in a suburban school district. The community is primarily middle class. The children come from diverse ethnic and religious backgrounds. Part of her curriculum includes some basic lessons in cooking. Today's lesson involves the preparation of hamburgers. Beller is aware that one of the children is a vegetarian and that two others do not eat red meat. She has prepared burgers with ground turkey for two students and substituted what she felt was an appropriate alternative for the vegetarian child.

Beller is stunned, therefore, when the vegetarian child states before the class that eating hamburger is wrong and sinful. "My daddy says that hamburgers come from cows that are killed and it is wrong to kill cows or anything else. He says that if you eat the hamburgers, you are as bad as the people who killed the cow."

The other children in the class are also shocked at the accusation and sit in their places speechless.

Questions for Discussion

1. How should Ms. Beller respond to the accusation?
2. What should she say to the class?
3. Should she go on with the lesson?
4. Should she contact the child's parent? If so, what should she say and/or do?
5. Should she consult with the principal?
6. Should she discontinue the cooking lessons?

Student's Conflict Between Family and Peer Values

Wing Tek Lau is a sixth-grade student in a predominantly white and African American southern community. He and his parents emigrated from Hong Kong four years ago. His uncle, an engineer at a locally based high-tech company, had encouraged Wing Tek's father to immigrate to this country and open a Chinese restaurant. The restaurant is the only Chinese restaurant in the community, and it was an instant success. Mr. Lau and his family have enjoyed considerable acceptance in both his business and in his neighborhood. Wing Tek and his younger sister have also enjoyed academic success at school and appear to be well-liked by the other students.

One day when Mrs. Baca, Wing Tek's teacher, calls him by name, he announces before the class, "My American name is Kevin. Please, everybody call me Kevin from now on." Mrs. Baca and his classmates honor this request, and Wing Tek is "Kevin" from then on.

Three weeks later, Mr. and Mrs. Lau make an appointment to see Mrs. Baca. When the teacher makes reference to "Kevin," Mrs. Lau says, "Who are you talking about? Who is Kevin? We came here to talk about our son, Wing Tek."

"But I thought his American name was Kevin. That's what he asked us to call him from now on," Mrs. Baca replies.

"That child," Mrs. Lau says in disgust, "is a disgrace to our family."

"We have heard his sister call him by that name, but she said it was just a joke," Mr. Lau adds. "We came to see you because we are having problems with him in our home," Mr. Lau states. "Wing Tek refuses to speak Chinese to us. He argues with us about going to his Chinese lessons on Saturday with the other Chinese students in the community. He says he does not want to eat Chinese food anymore. He says that he is an American now and wants pizza, hamburgers, and tacos. What are you people teaching these children in school? Is there no respect for family, no respect for our culture?"

Mrs. Baca, an acculturated Mexican American who was raised in east Los Angeles, begins to put things together. Wing Tek, in his attempt to ensure his acceptance by his classmates, has chosen to acculturate to an extreme, to the point of rejecting his family heritage. He wants to be as "American" as anyone else in the class, perhaps more so. Like Wing Tek, Mrs. Baca had acculturated linguistically and in other ways, but had never given up her Hispanic values. She knows the internal turmoil Wing Tek is experiencing.

Questions for Discussion

1. Is Wing Tek wrong in his desire to acculturate?
2. Are Mr. and Mrs. Lau wrong in wanting their son to maintain traditional family values?
3. What can Mrs. Baca do to bring about a compromise?
4. Is there anything Mrs. Baca can do in the classroom to resolve the problem or to at least lessen the problem?

Placement of a Child with a Contagious Disease

At a special education student placement meeting, one case involves a three-year-old male with a history of medical problems. The child is developmentally delayed and is not ambulatory. Further, the child is not toilet trained. He also lacks oral muscle control and drools constantly.

The medical report indicates that the student tests positive for cytomegalovirus (CMV). This is a herpes-like virus that is excreted in urine and saliva. CMV may result in mental retardation, severe hearing loss, microcephaly, and chronic liver disease when transmitted to newborns. Women who may have contracted CMV several years previously and who have been asymptomatic may transmit the virus in utero, during delivery, or via breast-feeding. Eighty percent of all persons over age thirty-five show serologic evidence of previous infection. The majority of these infections are asymptomatic.

The school district's special education policy concerning CMV is checked by the placement committee, and it is discovered that there is no justification for excluding children who are known shedders of this virus. According to the *least restrictive environment clause* of PL 94-142, a special day class in a special school is the most appropriate placement.

Since the child is only three years old, he qualifies for only one of the seven preschool classes. The preschool program is run by an innovative instructional team consisting of five young female instructors (of childbearing age), one older female, one male teacher, and fourteen female assistants (of childbearing age). Three of the teachers are pregnant. The preschool staff members are a very strong, informal group. Further, four of the teachers have leadership roles on the school's steering committee.

The student placement meeting is concluded, and the parent is told that the child will be placed in one of the preschool classes and that transportation will begin in two weeks. Word leaks out that a child with CMV is about to enter the preschool program. A panic begins in the preschool department, and two teachers threaten to transfer if the child is put into their classroom.

Questions for Discussion

1. How should the administrator proceed?
2. How would you, as a teacher, react?
3. Where should the child be placed?
4. What would you do if the child was put in your class?

Racial Identification

Roosevelt High School annually celebrates Black History Month in February. The month-long study includes a convocation to celebrate African American heritage. For ten years, students have organized and conducted this convocation in which the whole student body participates.

The students who have organized the event this year begin the convocation with the black national anthem. The African American students, a few of the other students, and some of the faculty members stand for the singing of the anthem. Many of the African American students become very angry at what they perceive to be a lack of respect by the students and faculty who refuse to stand.

In discussions that follow the convocation, some of the students and faculty who did not stand for the anthem argue that the only national anthem to which they should be expected to respond is their own national anthem. They say that it is unfair to be required to attend a convocation celebrating the heritage of one racial group when there is no convocation to celebrate their own racial or ethnic heritage.

Questions for Discussion

1. What may have been happening in the school that led to the tensions that surfaced during this convocation?
2. How may the African American students perceive the refusal to stand by some of the students and faculty?
3. Do you think that the reasons for not standing during the anthem are valid? Why or why not?
4. If you are meeting with a class immediately after the convocation, how will you handle the tension between students?
5. What activities might be initiated within the school to reduce the interracial tensions that have developed?

Religious Discrimination

Nadar Hoseini is a third-grader in a suburban community in northern Virginia. Nadar's parents immigrated to the United States from Iran in the mid-1970s and are now naturalized citizens. Nadar was born in Virginia where his father is a chemist for a large manufacturer. During recess Ms. Nash notices that Nadar is sitting alone and is visibly upset. After some probing into an apparent problem, she learns that Nadar's friends have shunned him. Michael, he tells Ms. Nash, told the group that Michael's father says that the World Trade Center was bombed by Moslems who are all fanatics trying to blow up America and kill innocent Americans.

"Your friend Nadar is one of them Moslems and you had better not let me catching you playing with him again. We ought to ship all of them Moslems back where they came from," Michael quotes his father as saying.

Protesting, Nadar insists that he was born in America and that he and his family are Americans. The protests fall on deaf ears as Nadar's classmates join Michael in shunning him. Ms. Nash is determined to help Nadar's situation, but at the moment is at a loss as to how she will approach the problem.

Questions for Discussion

1. What should Ms. Nash say to Nadar?
2. Should Ms. Nash go directly to Michael and the other boys involved?
3. How can she change the perceptions of the boys without seeming to attack Michael's father?
4. What sensitivity activities can she conduct in the class?

Cultural Attitudes Toward the Aged

"That is really stupid!" exclaims Keith to Michael Wong. "You have the neatest room of anyone in the class with your own stereo, TV, and computer. Now you have to share it with your grandfather! Why? Why do you have to share your bedroom with an old man? It isn't fair."

"Because he's too old to care for himself and he can't share my sister's room. She's a girl," Michael explains to his best friend, Keith.

"Why don't your parents put him in an old people's home like my parents did with my grandmother?" Keith protests. "When they get old, they're useless. They just get in your way. Old people just don't have the right to interfere with other people's lives. When I get too old, I want someone like Dr. Death, that guy in Michigan, to just help me to go away—peaceful-like. Old people are a pain in the butt to everyone. I'm not going to be a bother like that to anyone. Besides, it'll be a zillion years before I'm ever old. Ha!"

Trying to explain, Michael says to Keith, "My grandfather really isn't a bother. He's a neat guy. He may be old, but he's very wise, you know. Real smart. Besides, we Chinese don't like to put our parents and grandparents in nursing homes. It's kinda a disgrace to the family. Sure, I'd rather have my room to myself, but it's okay. I really don't mind." Hearing the discussion, Mr. Fitzpatrick, Michael and Keith's sixth-grade teacher, is trying to decide if he should intervene.

Questions for Discussion

1. Should Mr. Fitzpatrick intervene in the discussion or let the boys work it out themselves?
2. Should the teacher discuss attitudes toward the aged? If so, what should be discussed?
3. Should the teacher discuss how different cultures perceive old age differently?
4. Should the teacher address the ageist attitudes of Keith? If so, how?

Cultural Attitudes Toward the Mentally Disabled

Larry Gladden is a junior high school social studies teacher and the head football coach for the eighth-grade team. With a poor turnout for his initial recruitment effort, Gladden has received permission from principal W. O. Smith to make another recruitment pitch over the school public address system. Making a strong appeal for all interested able-bodied boys to come out, Coach Gladden sets a meeting time immediately after school. As the new prospects arrive, the coach is shocked to see Massey Brunson walk into the room. Recognizing Massey from the special education classroom adjacent to his own, the coach knows that Massey is a student with mild mental retardation. The others in the room know this too.

"Hi coach," says Massey. "You said you need strong healthy players. That's me! I work out every day at the Nautilus Fitness Center and I'm in great shape."

Massey is indeed a great physical specimen. He is among the tallest of the new recruits and very muscular. When he saw the other team prospects shaking their heads as Massey entered, the coach had serious doubts as to how Massey might fit on the team. Would he be accepted by his teammates? Could he learn the plays and follow instructions?

Questions for Discussion

1. Is the coach obligated to allow Massey to try out?
2. Should he discourage Massey from trying to play?
3. Should he treat him differently from other players?
4. Should he make special allowances for Massey?
5. If Massey is good enough to play, how should the coach foster his acceptance by other team members?

Religious-Based Criticism in the Classroom

Charlotte Silva is a fifth-grade teacher in a suburban school near a major city in Texas. "Ms. Silva," Deborah Smith blurts out, "Cindy Segal's sister is getting an abortion next week. That's a sin."

"It's not," protests Cindy. "My parents said it is a woman's right to do as she pleases with her body."

"She's going to have an unborn child killed. She's only seventeen and she's pregnant. She's not even married. That's a sin, too. My mother and daddy told me that those things are sins. They are aren't they? Our preacher says that you can rot in hell for sins like that, and he doesn't lie. That's true isn't it Ms. Silva? Will you please tell Cindy?"

The entire class has heard this outburst and they are all staring at the teacher, waiting for her response.

Questions for Discussion

1. While the teacher must provide some response, should she allow a discussion on religious ethics in the classroom?
2. If she decides not to discuss the issue, how should she acknowledge the question and avoid a judgmental response to the ethics question?
3. If the teacher decides to allow a discussion of the issues, how should she proceed? What can she allow in the discussion? What must be avoided?

Name Index

Subject Index

ISBN 0-02-344491-6
90000>
9 780023 444913